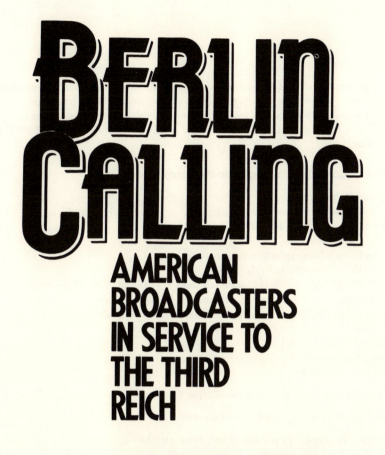

BERLIN CALLING

AMERICAN BROADCASTERS IN SERVICE TO THE THIRD REICH

JOHN CARVER EDWARDS

PRAEGER

New York
Westport, Connecticut
London

Every reasonable effort has been made to trace the owners of copyright materials in this book, but in some instances this has proven impossible. The publisher will be glad to receive information leading to more complete acknowledgments in subsequent printings of the book and in the meantime extends its apologies for any omissions.

Library of Congress Cataloging-in-Publication Data

Edwards, John Carver.
    Berlin calling : American broadcasters in service to the Third
  Reich / John Carver Edwards.
       p.   cm.
    Includes bibliographical references and index.
    ISBN 0–275–93905–7 (alk. paper)
    1. World War, 1939–1945—Propaganda.   2. World War, 1939–1945—
Biography.   3. Propaganda, German.   4. Radio broadcasters—Germany—
Biography.   5. Radio broadcasters—United States—Biography.
I. Title.
D810.P7E38   1991
940.54′88743—dc20
 [B]   90–20841

British Library Cataloguing in Publication Data is available.

Library of Congress Catalog Card Number: 90–20841
ISBN: 0–275–93905–7

First published in 1991

Praeger Publishers, One Madison Avenue, New York, NY 10010
An imprint of Greenwood Publishing Group, Inc.

Printed in the United States of America

The paper used in this book complies with the
Permanent Paper Standard issued by the National
Information Standards Organization (Z39.48–1984).

10 9 8 7 6 5 4 3 2 1

Contents

Photographs follow page 114

Preface

As a teenager living in the late 1950s in Spartanburg, South Carolina, I was intrigued by community whispers concerning a prominent local banker whose brother had been convicted as a Nazi radio traitor. The lifelong fascination of how this son of a respected Methodist minister and fellow graduate of Wofford College could assume the treasonous role of Radio Berlin's notorious "Mr. Guess Who" led to this review of Germany's World War II radio propaganda effort and the Americans who served it. Predictably, the completion of one biographical profile suggested another, and another, until I had chronicled the careers of five major U.S.A. Zone commentators and three minor ones. For over a decade this study of the North American Service's more interesting representatives has been an absorbing preoccupation.

The lives of these figures have been somewhat difficult to follow. United States expatriates and naturalized German-Americans all, my subjects either assumed residency in Europe early in life or pursued nomadic, trans-Atlantic lifestyles that left little in the way of personal histories in this country. Moving within the Continent's demiworld, they afforded too few glimpses into their private lives and thoughts. They did, however, cast longer shadows in their occupational pursuits as they moved about the great writers, journalists, and political figures of Europe as moths about a flame. Surprisingly enough, as conditions developed during the interwar years, the most insightful and rewarding commentaries on these obscure people came from those celebrities and dignitaries who piqued their interest for whatever personal or professional reasons. Happily, too, several of my protagonists possessed the sagacity to author one or more autobiographies in later life; several more appear in novels as fictional surrogates—this linkage established by the author through the subjects' close association with the writers, geographical locations, and primary source materials; and one left his academic tracks on both sides of the Atlantic Ocean. A few random letters mined from the files of family, friends, and professional colleagues were highly prized, as were assorted trial transcripts, the contents of the wartime monitoring service of the British Broadcasting Corporation, and the case files of my subjects from the Federal Bureau of Investigation, as well as other federal agencies.

This book is from the perspective of those Americans involved. It is not meant as an organizational history of the Ministry for Public Enlightenment and Propaganda, or of any of its subordinate units; nor is it a definitive consideration of the strategy of Nazi Germany's propaganda campaign. German sources were proven to be surprisingly infertile in relation to its U.S. broadcasters, suggesting that management, outside immediate supervisors, knew little about these people. Rather, the U.S.A. Zone of the Reichrundfunk has served as a convenient historical pinnacle from which to survey the lives of those who did its bidding.

As in most studies of human motivation, the questions come to mind more readily than the answers. Were these subjects influenced to broadcast for the Nazis by subjective or political considerations? There were those observers who insisted that their Yankee roots had withered in Europe's soil during a long expatriation. As transplanted Americans abroad did they suffer from a sense of historical displacement in regard to their homeland? When most of them emigrated from the United States following the Great War, they left behind a country awash in patriotic fervor, its people totally convinced of the ultimate goodness of government and the morality of the West. The Great Depression of 1929 brought changes on the American scene these expatriates neither completely understood nor liked. The collapse of international markets and the greed of marginal traders on Wall Street had demanded strong remedial action in the way of big government, huge bureaucracies, and intrusive federal regulatory legislation that they could not appreciate from afar. Had America's economic disaster brought in its wake an even greater threat from the establishment of an alien form of government on American shores supported by a growing immigrant constituency and committed to the betrayal of a value system grafted upon the New World by the Founding Fathers? Those future radio traitors who came to Europe during the 1930s felt even more strongly about the Depression, the New Deal and its architects, and the effects of its regulatory policies upon their own lives. One wonders whether or not the Nazis paid these commentators for a service they would have performed from personal prejudices, given the availability of a microphone.

Perhaps the notions of conspiracy and betrayal came too easily to those Americans having lived on the Continent for over a decade. The ubiquitous armed street-gang representative of the political right or left, the instability of both Clerical Fascist and Republican forms of government, and the almost commonplace occurrence of political assassinations left behind strong impressions that may have taken their toll over time. Could this Europeanized perspective have given them a false impression of America's benign revolution? Then, too, what of the Soviet Union and its designs on the West? Did they think it was within Hitler's power to checkmate potential Soviet expansionism, bring social, political, and economic order to Europe, and, through example, show the United States the way to renewed prosperity and international prominence?

Still, other friends and colleagues of these turncoats have suggested that job dissatisfaction may have prompted the majority of them to work for Germany. Did their bosses back home in the United States fairly mirror for them in reprimands their own professional shortcomings, or were they the victims of unscrupulous superiors who fed upon their modest field successes? Did some of them prostitute the trust placed in their hands, or were they in search of occupational integrity within the bounds of flawed professions? With all points of social and occupational reference gone on the eve of the war, did the North American Service provide them with the satisfying camaraderie of fellow travelers who had also made the leap of faith into treason, or merely with 30 pieces of silver for their trouble? In the rarified atmosphere of the Reichrundfunk's broadcasting studios and conference rooms, did they discover ideological dedication or moral complacency and personal betrayal?

Were these broadcasters dedicated Nazis, the self-styled vanguard of America's isolationist movement a long way from home, or simply hucksters in search of a payroll check? One irreverent historian has suggested that they lacked the stature to be evil. Did they believe what they said, or believe for the sake of belief? Were they solitary individuals obscure in character and origin who craved to belong to a historical force greater than themselves, or frustrated romantics enraptured by the pomp and circumstance of Hitler's staged theatrics?

In the end, as Nazi Germany lay prostrate, did these people come to admit their intellectual inconsistencies in denouncing the proclaimed despotism of Franklin Roosevelt's New Deal policies while in service to national socialism? Could they not make the distinction between the governance of a citizenry— be it ever so disgruntled—by its democratically elected representatives on the one hand and the master-slave principle of *Fuhrerprinzip* on the other, or did they consider this distinction a semantical nicety? More importantly, how could these individuals not have known of the misanthropic kernel of nazism?

The staffs of numerous manuscript repositories and archival facilities merit special recognition in connection with the completion of this work. The personnel of the special collections divisions of the University of Illinois at Urbana-Champaign; the McKeldin Library, University of Maryland, College Park; Marquette University; the George Arent Research Library, Syracuse

University; the South Caroliniana Library, University of South Carolina; the Glendale (California) Public Library; the Hoover Institution, Stanford University; the Wofford College Archives; and the Waltham (Massachusetts) and Suitland (Maryland) regional centers of the National Archives and Records Service were unstinting in their support of my project. Correspondents William L. Shirer, George Seldes, Joseph C. Harsch, Walter Trohan, Francis Cunningham, and Joseph W. Grigg provided contemporary perspectives on my broadcasters that were available nowhere else. I salute the patience and generous spirit of the late Dame Rebecca West, who tolerated my letters during the last months of her life. Academicians Joan Givner and Louis J. Halle offered fresh insight from their respective areas of interest. Professor John Haag has been most helpful with his extensive knowledge of Nazi Germany. I am indebted to the declassifiers associated with the Freedom of Information–Privacy Act reference branch of the Department of Justice. Without their assistance, this study would have been much the poorer. I also thank the Atlanta *Historical Journal* and the *North Dakota Quarterly* for their kind permission to reprint some of this material, which appeared in article format. I owe the University of Georgia Research Foundation for its moral support and unrestricted financial assistance. Last, but certainly not least, I appreciate the professional guidance and enthusiastic support of literary agents Aleta M. Daley and Maximilian Becker.

1

The Beginnings of the U.S.A. Zone and Its Pioneer American Broadcasters

Radio had become a commonplace aspect of life for many Germans during the interwar years. A creature of the Weimar government, its transmitters, radio stations, programming, and bureaucracy were controlled by the Reichpostministerium (Office of the Postmaster General of Germany) and the Ministry of the Interior. This network was financed by the government and by a user fee of two reichsmarks monthly, which was about 90 cents for every radio receiving set. Income from advertisements covered only a fraction of the total costs.

After Hitler came into power on January 30, 1933, the German radio policy changed dramatically. Newly appointed propaganda minister Paul Josef Goebbels transferred control of radio from the Reichpostministerium to his own Ministry for Public Enlightenment and Propaganda. The executive decree of Reichschancellor Adolf Hitler, of June 30, became the legal basis for this change. The Reich Chamber of Culture was established in September to control (under the supervision of the Propaganda Ministry and within the framework of policy decreed by its management) personnel engaged in all propaganda endeavors. The Reichkulturkammer was a so-called *Nachgeordnete Dienststelle* (junior office) of the parent organization. Together with its subordinate chambers, it was charged with the oversight of all employees active in any field under the jurisdiction of Goebbels' leviathan, or Promi, as the ministry came to be called. All individuals engaged in the performing arts or other cultural professions were obligated to register with one of the subordinate chambers. The chambers, in turn, were responsible for investigating the work and political reliability of their members. Power was granted to the chambers to prosecute members in defiance of Nazi standards or persons pursuing their careers without being duly registered. The corrective measures included expulsion from membership, which was tantamount to the loss of livelihood. The chambers could also issue directives, which had the force of law, regulating the cultural activities under their control.[1]

The president of the Chamber of Culture was Goebbels, who nominated the vice-presidents. In 1937, the latter included Walter Funk, Max Amann (Reich leader of the Press Chamber), and Leopold Gutterer (secretary of state in the Propaganda Ministry). The Chamber of Culture was divided into seven distinct chambers:

1. the Reich Press Chamber
2. the Reich Chamber of Fine Arts
3. the Reich Music Chamber
4. the Reich Theater Chamber
5. the Reich Film Chamber
6. the Reich Chamber of Literature
7. the Reich Radio Chamber[2]

Goebbels placed the Radio Chamber under the direction of an assistant, Eugen Hadamowsky. As the central headquarters of all Reich broadcasting, the Radio Chamber governed state radio partly directly and partly through sub-agencies created for certain functions or regions. One such administrative section was the Reich Radio Corporation, the Reichrundfunkgesellschaft, which was the comprehensive agency embracing all German broadcasting stations. Under this system every broadcasting station and transmitter in Germany was owned by the Reich. All personnel were governmental employees, and all persons working directly or indirectly for the German radio were licensed by the National Radio Administration. These licenses for employment were issued only to individuals politically reliable from the Nazi perspective and racially desirable. On August 16, 1933, Hadamowsky issued a report outlining his early accomplishments and plans for the total transformation of the Reichrundfunk into a political instrument. Existing personnel who could not show a strong Party record immediately fell to Hadamowsky's administrative axe. From then on German radio was controlled down to the smallest detail by Goebbels' lieutenants and their corps of Party ideologues. As one might imagine, the precise relations of operation between the different administrative units within this bureaucratic labyrinth proved impossible for the outsider to decipher. Coordination turned on day-to-day contacts, with departmental and functional boundaries subject to dominant rather than recessive personalities.[3]

Throughout the day and evening the German public heard broadcasts portraying the Fuhrer as the nation's messiah; describing the Nazi lifestyle as desirable; and stressing patriotism, rationalism, and the great mission of Aryan Germany. Meanwhile, Goebbels insisted that only radio could successfully consolidate national socialism's political gains while spreading its message. "What the press has been in the nineteenth century," he predicted, "radio will be for the twentieth century." Hitler, too, championed the persuasive powers of radio. He had convinced himself that the German army had never been defeated in an honest fight; that the Kaiser lost the Great War on the home front; and that the national resolve for victory had been undermined by Allied propaganda campaigns. His studies on the psychology of the masses persuaded him of the irrationality, emotionalism, and extremism of the crowd. In order to manipulate the people, topics and slogans should be limited and constantly repeated. Of course, he himself had experienced this lesson on numerous soapboxes across Germany. How incredible it seemed that radio could transform an entire nation into a monster rally hanging on his every word![4]

The genius of Nazi propaganda, however, had been in the direct action appeal of the street speaker to his audience. It bespoke the grassroots directness of a people's crusade during the twilight of the Weimar period. Ironically, Hitler's message seemed its strongest when there were rival political parties on the left and right to play against. With most of his old enemies either dead or in concentration camps, the Fuhrer's tiresome *Kampfzeit* themes began to bore most Germans. As political analyst Charles H. Wilson observed in 1939:

What the Propaganda Ministry and its satellite organizations illustrate is the total inadequacy of the simple, categorical, and repetitive type of propaganda under monopoly conditions. Contrary to the general impression, monopoly propaganda is over a long period much more difficult to handle than competitive propaganda. It requires not monotonous repetition, but variation, both of address and of content. It requires to be circumscribed in physical mass to avoid overwhelming the attention of the average consumer. It requires considerable psychological subtlety.[5]

A recent author has noted that Goebbels simply had to adjust to the difference between a mass rally in a closed hall and the reality of an audience endowed with the freedom of turning a knob.[6]

The heads of the Radio Chamber included the ministerial counselor Horst Dressler-Andress, Alfred Ingemar Berndt, Eugen Hadamowsky, Hans Gottfried Kriegler, and Wolfgang Diewerge until November 3, 1942, and then Hans Fritzsche through the end of the war. With the exception of Fritzsche, Goebbels discovered each of his preceding appointees to be long on Party loyalty and short on managerial competence. When Goebbels dubbed Fritzsche to head the Radio Division, he demonstrated his preference for ability and not political fanaticism from the *Kampfzeit* period. True, Fritzsche joined the Party's ranks late (May 1, 1933), but he brought to the job a technical expertise of which his predecessors were ignorant. Both attributes, however, made him suspect among the Promi's rank and file. Still, he had made a name for himself as chief of the ministry's Press Division (1938–42) and as a political correspondent (1942) on the eastern front.[7]

As commissioner for the political structuring of the Greater German Radio, Fritzsche's authority was unparalleled. Reporting directly to Goebbels, Fritzsche's power was limited only by the Fuhrer's directives and by decisions of the radio political division of the Reich Foreign Office, which controlled all foreign language transmissions. Fritzsche not only was in charge of planning and organizing the entire German radio and television system but also issued decrees to subordinate sections and offered recommendations to other agencies of the Reich cabinet. Under Fritzsche's command, the Rundfunk-kommandostelle (or "Radio Command") received and transmitted orders to the various radio sections. This unit acted autonomously in matters of transmission and program difficulties. Fritzsche's Reconnaissance Service was responsible for monitoring and transcribing foreign broadcasts, which were summarized and distributed to Goebbels. Since many of these enemy transmissions were heard clandestinely by Germans, the transcriptions permitted the Nazis to discredit enemy broadcasts before rumors developed. The Reconnaissance Service also provided Goebbels with military, economic, and political information about the Allies. This work complemented the Foreign Office's archival division, which supplied material to Promi to structure its radio programs. Also under Fritzsche's supervision were the Radio Economy Section, which constructed and distributed radio receivers, and the Foreign Radio Section (Runkfunk Ausland). The latter was limited in scope, as most decisions were made by Fritzsche in daily conferences with the chief of the Foreign Division of the Reich Radio Corporation.[8]

Fritzsche served not only as the Radio Chamber's chief executive but in the capacity of one of its ace broadcasters as well. His program, "Hans Fritzsche Speaks," enjoyed an impressive following in the United States. In the beginning his commentaries possessed a measure of entertainment value with their light, supercilious air; but after the military fiasco at Stalingrad, the soft nuances of his wit disappeared. He praised Axis defeats as "heroic struggles" and belittled enemy victories while denying the possibility of a second front. The words "tough resistance," "adversity," and "faith" would creep into his dialogues, and "miracle weapons" were touted as the Fatherland's avenue to salvation.[9]

As the war progressed, Goebbels was faced with a serious radio problem. The average German, bored with shopworn propaganda and leery of biased reporting, tuned in the British Broadcasting Corporation (BBC) for a balanced perspective. Although such actions were regarded as treasonable, most such listeners were never caught. During the first year of the war, however, 1,500 Germans were sent to concentration camps or local jails for dialing London.[10]

Goebbels also utilized the Reichrundfunk as a long-range propaganda weapon. He was eager to project an impression of benign neighborliness to the world community, even as stormtroopers swept away any remaining vestiges of opposition to Hitler's authority. In 1933 he established a five-year plan for foreign broadcasting, directing his shortwave stations to bolster their number of frequencies from 3 to 18 and their broadcasting hours from 2 to 119, a project completed before the invasion of Poland. Initially, he ordered the shortwave system to feature operatic performances from Berlin, Dresden, and Munich and symphonic concerts from Leipzig. From this beginning he gradually introduced subtle messages favorable to nazism. Countries outside the Reich were inundated with special broadcasts: Alsace-Lorraine was served by the Frankfurt am Main station; Denmark, by programs from Hamburg and Bremen; Belgium, by Cologne commentators; Czechoslovakia, by stations from Breslau and Gleiwitz; and Austria, by airways from Munich. The world audience was reached by a huge broadcasting studio operating on 100,000 kilowatts from Zeesen, a suburb of Berlin. Transmissions began to the United States in 1933; to South Africa, South America, and East Asia in 1934; and to Central America and South Asia in 1938. By this time shortwave messages were being transmitted from Germany in 12 languages at every minute of the day and night.

Appeals to pan-German sentiment were beamed internationally. In 1933 Nazi broadcasts were used to incite revolution in Austria; and several years later the Saar inhabitants, separated from Germany by the Versailles Treaty, were coaxed to vote their conscience and rejoin the Reich. Thereafter, Goebbels employed his ministry to prepare the stage for each succeeding Nazi adventure. The Reichrundfunk's broadcasts to France emanated from transmitters along the Rhine and in other sectors of western Germany: Radio Stuttgart, Frankfurt, Cologne, and Saarbrücken. These messages were presented by Goebbels' pioneer radio traitors, Frenchmen Paul Ferdonnet and André Obrecht, whom their loyal countrymen denounced as the "traitors of Stuttgart." These broadcasts to France were anti-Semitic, anti-plutocratic, anti-British, and even anti-French. Government leaders were singled out as Jews or "tools of British diplomacy" in the first phase of a campaign to paralyze mobilization and divide national sentiment. As the crisis over the Free City of Danzig and the Polish Corridor came to the forefront of world attention in the summer of 1939, Ferdonnet and Obrecht entreated their countrymen to forget these issues. When war erupted with France, the Stuttgart traitors claimed that Hitler killed its soldiers only because they served as Churchill's proxies. "The British will provide the machines; the French will provide the breasts," concluded Obrecht.[11]

The Reichrundfunk began its campaign against Britain in English in 1938, followed by Lord Haw-Haw's debut on April 10, 1939. Prefacing his broadcasts with the words "To some, I may seem a traitor—but hear me out," he offered a full repertoire of news, commentaries, plays and skits, and off-color music hall jokes with topical twists. He relished attacking England's gentry

class, accusing its members of everything from the rise of commodity prices
to falling church attendance. There were comic dialogues between a fictitious
German named Schmidt and a fictitious Englishman named Smith, played
by Haw-Haw himself. Having accidentally met in a Swiss hotel, Smith
acquainted his new German friend with a roster of his (also fictitious) associates in England: Sir Izzy Ungeheimer, who advised Smith on how to
evade tax laws; "good old Bumbleby Mannering," a pious minister sustained
by munitions profits; and Sir Jasper Murgatroyd, an insufferable British
Foreign Office official who helped engineer Britain's war against the Reich.
Lord Haw-Haw's laundry list of reforms included appeasement, with the
savings realized from British weapons production rerouted to a spate of social
programs for the poor. Following the Nazi invasion of Norway and Denmark,
he spread panic and defeatism with commentaries on the awesome power of
the Wehrmacht. When France fell, he demanded the removal of England's
war party as a first step in a negotiated settlement with that country.

There were two Lord Haw-Haws, and in late 1939 William Joyce assumed
the role. Haw-Haw's popularity dropped, as Joyce could not match his
namesake's entertaining wit. Moreover, the conflict had become too serious
for a loyal Britisher to listen to an enemy agent. The popularity of Churchill's
government also tended to dilute Joyce's indictments.[12]

Radio Berlin gained popularity in the United States soon after 1933, with
the estimated number of listeners as high as 500,000. Mounting tensions
associated with weekly reports of Nazi excesses and the undeclared German-
American naval blockade of 1939–41, however, reduced this audience to one-
third its original size. A month after the outbreak of war in 1939, a Gallup
poll showed that nearly three-fourths of the American people wanted the
Allies to win; less than 2 percent favored a German victory. A more realistic
worry for Goebbels had to do with the possibility of extending additional
aid to the Allies. It was this concern that prompted the Nazis to launch a
propaganda campaign to circumvent increased U.S. involvement in the struggle. The Promi thus responded with programming gimmickry and a "most
favored correspondent" policy directed toward those few news reporters who
consistently portrayed the "New Order" in a flattering light. Conversely,
Goebbels' retribution proved swift and sometimes professionally damaging
to those recalcitrant journalists who criticized the Fatherland.[13]

In February, 1941, the U.S.A. Zone of the Overseas Service urged its
faithful in North America to forward broadcast requests through the use of
cost-free telegrams to Berlin. As one might expect, a cynical U.S. press and
broadcast industry greeted the plan with derision. There were calculated
attempts to clog the German end of the telegram pipeline. Newsroom wags
joked that the program should continue, as its cost ($200,000) would oth-
erwise permit Hitler to deploy five additional Messerschmitt fighter aircraft.
The U.S. intelligence community warned that the large number of telegrams
forwarded to Germany could contain data helpful to a potential enemy. The

conclusion of this promotional antic precipitated a flurry of 10,241 telegrams to Berlin during the last week of February. In March, the ministry began a question-and-answer program entitled "America Asks—Germany Answers" as a sequel to its earlier venture. This feature lasted for 30 minutes and was preceded by the musical lyric "The cables are coming, oha!" Listener reaction appeared receptive to such "write-in" segments, thus sparking an interest in the American broadcast personality.[14]

Among the great world powers, Germany was the first to employ foreign nationals as propagandists to their respective countries. A roster of the Runkfunk Ausland's "foreign correspondents" (as they liked to be called) would include representatives from Britain, the United States, France, Italy, Egypt, Mexico, South Africa, and an assortment of other nations. Although the North American Service had been operational for six years, not until the eve of World War II did Goebbels really attempt to staff his U.S.A. Zone. Those expatriates hired were charged with one mission—to raise the credibility of Germany in the United States at Great Britain's expense. As broadcasters they would assume the role of semi-detached yet patriotic Americans who were motivated solely by their country's best interests and a general sense of fair play. They would present folksy, idiomatic patterns of speech in order to highlight their roots deep within America's geographical and ideological heartland. Despite the seriousness of their appeals, Goebbels also tolerated the use of absurd exaggerations and fantastic assertions, for they meshed with his overall propaganda strategy. A measure of ballyhoo erased the stigma of the canned message, affording it the semblance of burlesque. Likewise, if these American commentators chose to play the comedian or display personality aberrations over the air from time to time, it was no reflection on their employer; indeed, these indulgences only served to demonstrate the Reich's devotion to freedom of thought and expression.[15]

Life inside the North American Service demanded a personal commitment to the work measured only by one's tolerance for its daily liabilities. Goebbels often exhibited a violent temper and a sadistic streak to those limited junior executives who could not comprehend or appreciate his vision for the ministry or for Germany. These tantrums would, in turn, be followed by long periods of cold detachment that everyone in the bureaucracy found uncomfortable. Predictably, a number of subordinates aped their chief's behavior, thus perpetuating a constant state of low morale. Relatively low pay and withheld ration coupons were also constant sources of frustration. Gestapo surveillance kept those Americans in check who might otherwise seek to resurrect certain constitutional guarantees from their homeland. The Reich Foreign Office and the Propaganda Ministry always tried to outdo each other in the recruitment of foreign broadcasters. Because this competition was so intense, and because von Ribbentrop and Goebbels despised each other, the spurned agency was not above taking reprisals against an indifferent candidate. Censorship proved to be another thorny issue. The U.S.A. Zone personnel were free to rework scripts so that they were presentable in broadcasting form, but they were not permitted to advance perspectives of their own or transmit banned information without Goebbels' approval. The minister dominated his broadcasters and news editors by requiring their attendance at his ministerial conferences.

Despite few benefits and unpleasant working conditions, most of these Americans remained at their posts, even following the intervention of the United States into World War II. What ruling ambition, ideology, or prejudice compelled them to put their very being at risk, either from wartime conditions in Berlin, Nazi prisons, or an Allied court of justice? Perhaps a brief consideration of the lives of an arbitrary selection of these shadowy individuals will suggest an answer.

Frederick Wilhelm Kaltenbach, the dean of the U.S.A. Zone's stable of radio traitors, might well have become a professor of history instead of a Nazi propagandist. Born in Dubuque, Iowa, on March 29, 1895, the son of a German immigrant butcher, he attended public schools there. In 1914, young Fred and one of his brothers took a summer vacation in Germany. On the outbreak of World War I, both were arrested by the police on suspicion of being spies. However, they were released and returned to the United States in December of that year.[16] Over a quarter of a century later Kaltenbach recalled that happy time for the benefit of his Nazi employers:

I was swept by a powerful emotion and something inside me said "I am going home." That was back in 1914 when I visited the land of my forefathers as a young high school student. Ever since then I have done what I could to further the relations between the land of my fathers, Germany, and my native land, America. I love them both.[17]

Kaltenbach entered Grinnell College in Ames, Iowa, in 1915. In the summer of 1918 he secured a commission as a second lieutenant in the Coast Artillery. He was en route to France with his unit when the Armistice was signed, and he subsequently returned to the United States. The following year he entered Iowa State Teachers College, receiving his B.A. degree in 1920. In the succeeding ten years he held a variety of jobs; taught in the public schools at Manchester and Dubuque, Iowa; and spent a year at the University of Chicago, where he earned a master's degree in history. A chance trip to Germany in 1932 convinced Kaltenbach that America's opposition to the National Socialist groundswell there was based on personal envy and political chicanery.

There was unemployment everywhere and in the industrial areas every one of them [workers] were Communists, while the Jews were living in luxury. Then Hitler came who gave the German people a new lease on life. At once the wise boys in Washington and London started on their anti-German campaign.

Roosevelt knew he could not tackle the social ills the way the Americans thought he could and should, and the only way out was to blame Hitler for his [Roosevelt's] failure and to detract public criticism by focusing attention on an imaginary threat from the other side of the ocean.[18]

Kaltenbach's tenure on the faculty of the Dubuque High School ended abruptly and dramatically in 1933. He had organized a group of high school boys into a "hiking club" known as the Militant Order of Spartan Knights and modeled on the pattern of the Hitler Youth. The members wore brown-shirt uniforms, carried canes, and engaged in secret initiation rituals. The school authorities ordered the disbanding of this group because of its obvious Nazi orientation and fired Kaltenbach. At an American Legion meeting to which he was invited to state his side of the controversy, Kaltenbach so offended certain of the members with his pro-Fascist rhetoric that he was engaged in a fistfight from which he emerged second best.[19]

Kaltenbach went to Germany in June 1933, ostensibly to study for his Ph.D. at the University of Berlin (a goal he achieved in 1936). In his spare time, he worked as translator and freelance writer and, ultimately, for the government-controlled radio system.

While in Berlin Kaltenbach penned a monograph entitled *Self-Determination, 1919* (London: Jarrolds Publishers, 1938), giving his permanent address in the preface as Waterloo, Iowa. He offered himself as an impartial student of the concept of self-determination as set forth in the treaties of Versailles and St. Germain; but as his narrative unfolded, so did his bias. The Entente-controlled territorial commissions, wrote Kaltenbach, presumed to dictate the fate of German minorities outside the Reich. Measurements used by these deliberative bodies to gauge the national sentiment of provinces on Germany's eastern and southern borders—the application of language tests, ethnological statistics, and election returns—earned his scorn. "Nationality is . . . a state of mind," he insisted, "a subjective psychological feeling that transcends race, and is largely sentimental. It is not something that can be arbitrarily created by diplomacy . . . Blood is thicker than water and those who lightly choose to disregard this do so at their peril." It was Kaltenbach's contention that the German enclaves in Poland and Czechoslovakia had been sacrificed by the Paris Peace Conference to further French strategic consid-erations.[20] This expatriate's only return to the United States was for a brief period in May 1939, when the Reichrundfunk paid his way back home to see his dying father. Accompanying him was his wife, a German national who served as a secretary on one of Luftwaffe chief Herman Goering's aviation magazines. Kaltenbach earned $25 by addressing Waterloo Rotarians on the virtues of national socialism. The Rotarians suggested, "If you like it so much, why don't you go back there?" He took their advice with alacrity. When the State Department urged U.S. citizens to leave Germany in 1940, Kaltenbach refused to do so, giving as his reason his intention to write a

book about the war. His strong Nazi sympathies were well known to many
in the American colony in Berlin, to whom he voiced arrogant disdain for
democracy, rabid anti-Semitism, and pride in his affiliation with the Party
and the Reich Ministry of Propaganda. He began his regular broadcasts to
the United States in 1939, addressing his remarks usually to "Dear Harry"
and to other Iowa friends. The "Dear Harry" to whom Kaltenbach com-
municated was Harry Hagemann, a former schoolmate and attorney in Wav-
erly, Iowa, who grew quite uneasy about this one-sided relationship.[21]

On January 2, 1940, Kaltenbach portrayed his Fuhrer to Harry as the
symbol of a resurrected Europe.

England's battle-cry "Down with Hitlerism" was most ridiculous. Why should Germans start a revolution? And a revolution against whom? Against a German government who have carried out the mandate of the German people, wiped out the disgrace
of 1919, liberated Danzig and the Corridor, refused foreign interference in their
affairs, resolved to end England's role as international policeman and master, and
successfully fought inhuman and illegal blockades of German women and children?
Would Germans be likely to rebel against such a government? British people do not
know the present temper of the German people: if they did, they would be looking
around for some neutral to initiate peace negotiations.

[The] American people should not be astonished at the enormous popularity enjoyed by Hitler in Germany. Hitler gives life and time for his people: his selflessness
has earned him popularity. Christmas holidays given up to be with his soldiers at
the front. Where did Chamberlain, Daladier spend Christmas? Hitler was the first
soldier of the Reich among soldiers, not Commander-in-Chief.

The commentator admitted that he was moved by a ditty drifting around
Berlin, "We're sailing against England, Yo-Ho, Yo-Ho."[22]

Lord Hee-Haw, as Kaltenbach was known in the precincts of the Rundfunk
and among his audience, received his title from the English, who sometimes
dialed his programs. Previously the British public had bestowed the title of
Lord Haw-Haw on William Joyce, a former Mosleyite Fascist, who had
become internationally famous. This same audience subsequently decided
that Kaltenbach, too, deserved to be included in the peerage. Kaltenbach
seized on this undeserved anointment to enhance his own radio presence,
and from the beginning it seemed to work. On February 13, 1940, he poked
fun at English pretentions in characteristic banter.

Lord Haw-Haw has joined the distinguished ranks of soldiers, statesmen and American heiresses who have achieved British titles. And now the "Daily Telegraph" of
27th January calls me the American Lord Haw-Haw. I'll try to live up to that honor.
Perhaps later I may get the C.B. but never quite a K.G. as even the Lord High
Pretender to the throne of Neptune, Winston Churchill, hasn't got that yet. The
"Daily Telegraph" wants to give me a cap and bells, but what's to stop a jester telling
the truth? Anyhow, I'll do my best to make Americans give English pretensions in
this war, the big Hee-Haw.

England is fighting for the freedom of the seas—Hee-Haw. England is fighting for the rights of small nations, including India and Ireland—Hee-Haw. English methods, including the hunger blockade and incitement of Russia against Germany are humane—Hee-Haw. England thought the Germans would revolt—Hee-Haw. England thought Germany would attack the Maginot Line—Hee-Haw. Churchill thought he could tackle submarines and magnetic mines—Hee-Haw. England thinks she can starve Germany and hang up her washing on the Siegfried Line—Hee-Haw.[23]

Evidence that Lord Hee-Haw commanded a following in the United States was provided by the fan mail he acknowledged at the end of his "Letter to Iowa." This pioneer radio traitor gave his business address as "Iowa, In Care of His Short-Wave Station, Berlin." As in the case of his colleagues, Kaltenbach played a variety of roles. He served as Mr. Reader, who announced many of the evening topical talks. He was Jim, the smart-alecky Canadian in the series "Jim and Johnny," and Honest American Fred in the dialogues "Fritz and Fred." Kaltenbach was also the author of the Saturday night (8:45 P.M.) "Military Review" and of the series "British Disregard for American Rights." The American Revolution entitled American listeners to charter membership in Kaltenbach's "British Lion Tamers' Club," to which he also admitted East Indians, Irishmen, Japanese, and others who had opposed British hegemony. Unlike some of his associates, he avoided emotional tangents and vituperative outbursts, adopting instead a simple, direct and "reasonable" approach. His broadcasts, however, patterned the familiar Nazi propaganda line that involved anti-Roosevelt, anti-British, and isolationist arguments designed to sap morale in the United States by attacking the government and its leaders. In November 1937, when the Soviet Union's ruling oligarchy was still "blood-stained criminals" to Nazi ideologues, Kaltenbach wrote a countryman: "We German-Americans with our traditional conservatism cannot stand by and see our American spiritual heritage threatened by Bolsheviks." In 1940, following the Russo-German Non-Aggression Pact and the partition of Poland, it was not bolshevism but U.S. "predatory capitalism" that Kaltenbach attacked.[24]

Kaltenbach had a weakness for jingles, name-calling, and gag lines. He mocked Roly-poly Windsey Churchill's statements. The prime minister he called "Umbrella Man." The BBC he dubbed the "Bullitt—Biddle Corporation—Atrocity Manufacturers Unlimited." The nation of Monrovia—in his imagination— became a mythical republic that behaved just as the Fuhrer would have the United States behave. For example, "News flash: Monrovia seizes British gold deposited in Monrovian banks as security for debt payments . . . The government of Monrovia sends cruisers to protect Monrovian mails to Europe." From his grab bag of propaganda ideas, Kaltenbach peddled his opposition to money as a medium of exchange, a third term for Franklin Roosevelt, and the possibility of the have-not nations of Europe and Asia forming a powerful economic cartel under Axis supervision.[25]

In his *Berlin Diary*, newsman William L. Shirer acknowledged Kaltenbach's ability as an announcer but added that his unalloyed devotion to national socialism frequently got him into spats with less doctrinaire members of Rundfunk management. Journalist Joseph C. Harsch concurred:

Fred Kaltenbach . . . is the most effective [American radio traitor] from the German point of view because he, like [William] Joyce, is also sincere in his Nazism. I know because he preached it to me and argued it with me most of the way from Berlin to Paris on a three-day bus trip. He never made any attempt to conceal his position or his relationship with the Germans. He is engaging in personality and has courage— even when it comes to differences of opinion with his employers, who show far less cordiality toward those openly on their payroll than toward the independents. Such people have burned their bridges behind them and are at the mercy of German whim.

At the Compiègne Forest during the signing of the Franco-German Armistice, Kaltenbach gave the air of an ideological lapdog in service to an ungrateful master. Due to an earlier squabble, his supervisors ordered that he not be allowed to witness France's humiliation. Undaunted, Lord Hee-Haw hitched a ride with some army officers and "gate-crashed" the proceedings. Over and over Kaltenbach was ejected from the grounds, but each time he came back.[26]

When this pariah returned to his microphone on July 1, he swallowed his pride and portrayed those present at the tiny railway coach as gallant and generous victors. Between attempts by the security police to remove him from the premises, he glimpsed a touching scene: "A French officer came out of the car in which the negotiations were taking place, walked up to a German for some bit of information . . . and the German officer, a very large man by the way, put his arms affectionately around the smaller Frenchman. This little gesture," postulated Kaltenbach, "was characteristic of the spirit in which the negotiations took place."[27]

Everywhere in France, but especially in Paris, Kaltenbach witnessed manifestations of Hitler's magnanimity directed toward a conquered people.

In the shops on the Boulevard Italian fashionable women were making their purchases as unconcernedly as though no German soldier was within miles of Paris. . . . It was apparent that Parisians were agreeably surprised by the manners of the German soldiers. . . . German authorities in France are doing what they can to help the refugees. . . . German soldiers salute the memorial to the Unknown Soldier. A proprietor who lived in Paris for 40 years said the French collapse came as no surprise to him. The breakdown of the French people was evident before the war. The French had taken their liberty too lightly. A streetwoman blamed the British for letting their ally down.[28]

In a broadcast from a U.S. war cemetery on the outskirts of Paris, Kaltenbach recalled the memories of several school chums who had become victims of their government's adventurism during the Great War. Standing there, amidst rows of impersonal markers, he pondered rhetorically who now would suggest that these same young lives be wasted in a similarly unworthy cause. "I left . . . that afternoon thanking God that the cup of sorrow had passed the lips of American mothers this time," he concluded.[29]

Life in wartime Berlin changed dramatically as Great Britain began to repay the Reich for its earlier aggression. Ration queues and daily Royal Air Force (RAF) bombing raids became unpleasant aspects of everyday life, much to Kaltenbach's chagrin. On January 23, 1940, he remarked:

Well, Harry, I really set out to pay my respects to Winston Churchill, First Lord of the Admiralty, Lord High Pretender. I hear that he is going to intensify the blockade in the near future. . . . I don't know whether it's German air, German food, or the English hunger blockade that's adding to my waistline. If the blockade intensifies much more I'll look more like Humpty Dumpty Sea Lard than myself.[30]

As the enemy capitals came to death grips during the height of the Battle of Britain, nightly aerial bombardment brought the real possibility of death and dislocation to those in the U.S.A. Zone. In his broadcast of August 27, 1940, Kaltenbach tried to make light of the bombings:

I don't mind admitting that the fireworks on the outskirts of Berlin last night robbed me of some hours of sleep. The fireworks were great while they lasted. The English must have been restless last night to wander so far from home. Maybe there was method in their madness. Perhaps after hearing that the Goering air armada yesterday rained something like 1,500 bombs on England's harbours, munitions plants and airfields, some members of the R.A.F. decided that the air over Germany was healthier than that close to the ground in England.

During this high tide of Nazi conquests, the effects of such Allied air strikes were more psychological than destructive, as suggested in the words of Kaltenbach's fellow announcer Edward L. Delaney on August 27, 1940:

Berlin was a doomed city yesterday. . . . The raid lasted from 12:20 A.M. until 3:00 A.M. and was the first over this part of Germany. It was annoying to keep awake for three hours and listen to the noise. First the small guns started. Then larger ones took up the tune in an enormous crescendo, added to which was the din of explosions. It was not a good night.[31]

Three years of maximum military effort, German reversals on many fronts, and civilian deprivation stripped Kaltenbach's scripts of their old levity. The crowning indignity came with his indictment for treason by a federal grand jury (in absentia) on July 26, 1943.

Technically, I suppose, I am guilty of treason to Roosevelt and his warmongers, but not to the American people. If I took service with the German radio as a free lance commentator in the autumn of 1939, two years before the U.S. officially entered the war, it was done out of a genuine desire to promote good relations between Germany, the land of my fathers, and America, the land of my birth. It was clear to me from the start that the war in Europe was not an ideological war, but a fight for the future of the German people. Since that time, it has become a fight for the existence of the German people. . . . If I am engaged in treasonable activity against my native land, I am doing so under the conviction that this war has never for a moment been America's war. This war began on the European continent, in settlement of primarily European problems and affairs. Germany never had the slightest intention of carrying the war across the ocean. . . . If Germany declared war on the U.S.A. on 8 December 1941, it was only a formality, because Roosevelt had for more than a year before that date been making undeclared war against Germany. I am not an enemy of the American people, but I shall remain the implacable enemy of those forces in America who wish to deny Germany her rightful place in the European sun. If that be treason, make the most of it.[32]

On September 30, 1943, Lord Hee-Haw talked about America's eighteenth-century minuteman mystique and how his boyhood conceptualization of those brave patriots thrilled him as a youth. Since his native land's entry into the war, however, his countrymen had become little more than skybound assassins who dropped death on defenseless German civilians. Kaltenbach challenged Roosevelt's GIs to come and meet the Wehrmacht and its panzer divisions on the French Atlantic coast—toe to toe, bayonet to bayonet—until the issue was settled. Clearly, Kaltenbach no longer thought of himself as a U.S. citizen or, for that matter, a viable propagandist when on November 30 of that year he warned:

The German people will continue to shout defiance if every city is covered with dust. They will never say quit—never, never, never. The people who went through the Thirty Years War can stand anything except defeat. . . . To their tormentors from the air the people of Berlin cry, in the words of the immortal Goetz von Berlichingen: "You can go to hell, God damn you!" Let the British not forget there will be a day of reckoning. . . . If the Germans hate the English, they have only supreme contempt for the Americans. What a cowardly thing it is to bomb and destroy German property and kill German civilians in the firm knowledge that the American people in American cities are safe from reprisals. Why don't Americans come out and fight like men?[33]

Perhaps a few of those Americans who followed Kaltenbach's programs—for whatever reasons—empathized with his plight as the Allies brought the war to his doorstep.

So far I have missed but one raid. . . . After every raid I urge my wife to leave Berlin, but she won't hear of it. "Where you stay, I stay," she says. Can there be greater courage than this which suffers in silence, receives no reward, is given no publicity in the Press? I see other German women about me on those fearful nights when it seems that the very heavens are going to break over our heads. Grim, sometimes weeping, but resolved to stick with it to the end. On at least six occasions we have had to put out fires in our own or adjoining buildings.

Kaltenbach confessed in an April 8, 1944, broadcast that frequently he and his wife returned home from an air-raid alert to discover broken window panes strewn across every room, cracked walls, and gale-force winds blowing through their apartment.[34] The prospect of a second front in Europe cast a pall over Kaltenbach's life and preoccupied his talks. He denied that the Anglo-American invasion of Italy would compromise French coastal defenses, concluding in late fall of 1943: "American mothers with sons in the fighting line may take fresh comfort from experiments recently made in the Soviet Union on seriously wounded and disfigured men. . . . Such treatment," said Kaltenbach, "was now available to American soldiers and would undoubtedly benefit those mutilated on the Italian front."[35] According to Kaltenbach, the example at Monte Casino, where U.S. aerial bombardment utterly failed to dislodge a battalion of German paratroopers, convinced General Dwight Eisenhower to postpone a continental invasion in 1944. As he lamented on April 18, 1944: "What a pity that Western Europeans—and most Americans are related to them by blood—should be pitted against each other in Italy, mutually destroying each other, while hordes from the Soviet Union are knocking at the gates of Western Europe."[36]

The Normandy Invasion (June 6, 1944) sealed Germany's fate, and Kaltenbach sensed it. The Soviets mounted an offensive in the east several weeks later along a 450-mile front, resulting in the loss of an entire German army group. As the Allies closed in on Berlin, the tenor of Lord Hee-Haw's broadcasts alternated between shrill defiance and abject self-pity. Talk of Nazi secret weapons and Nazi determination left his audience unconvinced. Paris and Bucharest fell in August, and by mid-November the Wehrmacht abandoned Greece. Germany's ill-starred December offensive in the Ardennes crushed Kaltenbach's fading hopes for a negotiated peace. Soviet troops reached the Oder in early February of 1945, and an advance U.S. column crossed the Rhine on March 7. Hitler committed suicide on April 29.

Kaltenbach was captured by Russian soldiers on July 14, 1945, after the fall of Berlin. In August, U.S. military intelligence learned of his incarceration at a detention camp known as "xyz" near Frankfurt on the Oder. At first, U.S. negotiators offered to trade a pair of SS guards for the Iowan, but the Soviet secret police demurred, disclaiming custody of the former radio traitor. Finally, the Soviets ceased communications altogether. Kaltenbach died in October, reputedly of natural causes. In June 1946, Moscow informed Washington that the prisoner was indeed in custody and that he would be turned over to U.S. authorities soon. This final Soviet response— or the motives behind it—was never explained.[37]

Constance Drexel was born in Darnstadt, Germany, on November 28, 1894. She was brought to the United States by her father the following year and obtained derivative citizenship when he was naturalized in Boston, Massachusetts, in 1898. Theodore Drexel, scion of a wealthy family of Frankfurt, Germany, and her mother, Zela Audeman Drexel, daughter of a prominent Swiss watch manufacturer, tended to spoil young Constance. The child grew up in the town of Roslindale, Massachusetts, and attended the public school there. As an adolescent she divided her time between the United States and the Continent, attending school in four different countries and honing her skills as a writer. She completed her education at the Sorbonne in Paris.[38]

When World War I erupted, Constance was living in France with her mother and sister. One of the first American women to volunteer as a Red Cross nurse, she served in a French hospital at Domville in the summer of 1914.

In the Casino at Domville, its gaming tables removed to make room for the cots of an emergency hospital, I saw the men paying their share of the hideous price. To me, who had never seen blood and must now watch shot-torn peasant boys die in the twisted tortures of tetanus, dress the revolting, neglected wounds, feed living men in ghastly bandages concealing what had once been a face, it seemed as though no one could pay more than those poor, shattered wrecks of human beings had paid. And then, after a week or two, I lost the horror of it. I began to realize that this was only part of the price, that all the horrors I saw and heard were far, far easier to bear than the slow, cruel, killing price that war demands of women. When I came back to Paris late in December of that year . . . I held a firm conviction—I still hold it [1926]—that women were even heavier sufferers from war than men. I put this feeling into some magazine articles—I had begun to write for publication.[39]

When a group of American women led by social worker Jane Addams decided to accept the call of the women of Holland for an International Woman's Congress at The Hague in April 1915, Drexel offered to send cable dispatches to the New York *Tribune*. Addams consented, and Drexel debuted as a professional journalist. Back home she appeared at the Democratic National Committee headquarters on August 4, 1916, to endorse Woodrow Wilson's reelection to the presidency. She warned those in attendance that Charles Evans Hughes would never back the suffrage amendment.[40] Her writings suggested an enthusiasm for Germany's preparedness campaign, and especially women's role in that effort.

All German women became painstakingly saving. When the Government needed brass and tin and gold the women were appealed to. I saw homes dismantled of chandeliers. I saw women wearing iron wedding rings and iron pins in place of the gold ones gladly given to the common cause . . . the women tilled the fields with renewed ardor, and every inch of ground was cultivated. Women of "Kinder, Küche und Kirche" fame have shown surprising capacity in handling all sorts of relief work.[41]

Federal Bureau of Investigation (FBI) records show that this reporter-activist was denied another passport to the Continent in 1918 because of her pro-Hohenzollern sympathies.[42]

During the Paris Peace Conference, Drexel wrote daily signed articles cabled to the United States and also published in the European edition of the Chicago *Tribune*. She collaborated with the leaders of the International Women's Suffrage Alliance and the International Council of Women, who succeeded in obtaining the women's equality clause, Paragraph 3 of Article 7 in the Covenant of the League of Nations. When the peace treaty was signed she made a trip to Czechoslovakia and Poland as a guest of these two governments to study the role of women there. Returning to the United States in 1920, Drexel joined the staff of the *Public Ledger* to follow the suffrage campaign.[43]

Her next assignment was Washington, D.C. Having won the vote, what would women do with it? In January 1921, the paper dispatched its young reporter to uncover the answer to this question. She appeared on Capitol Hill as the first woman political correspondent, remaining—with the exception of summers in Europe and Septembers at the Assembly of the League of Nations in Geneva—until 1923. Drexel covered the more notable achievements of women during this period, the campaign for and final passage of the Sheppard-Towner Bill (the maternity and infancy act), and women's participation in the Washington Conference for the Limitation of Armaments. On the whole, however, Drexel remained disappointed in the accomplishments of the movement. In 1926 she set her frustrations to paper:

I should have preferred to continue my journalistic work covering the interests of women in politics, but frankly, they were not doing enough to make it worthwhile. So I have enlarged my scope of writing, spending at least half of each year in Europe, where I am particularly interested in following the League of Nations.[44]

America's reform impulse had been particularly deflected by the inability of the Women's Joint Congressional Committee to force through the legislative process needed social and political bills, fretted Drexel, who extolled her sisters to eschew factionalism and manipulation by male politicos:

Both the movement for peace and the movement to change the status of women are clearly visible in the United States and in Europe. But they are more apparent in Europe—especially the movement for peace. This is because the United States is drugged with prosperity. Women are flocking to the beauty parlor instead of to the ballot box. No one is thinking about anything.[45]

Indeed, according to Drexel, the banality of American culture was beginning to infect many of her European friends.

"Yes, we have no bananas!" has taken Europe by storm. . . . Senseless, foolish ditty? But, having proved to be the main contribution of the United States to international relations for many years past, it has more than passing interest. . . . I remember most distinctly one evening at the restaurant Des Eaux Vives where it was quite the thing to give dinner parties. . . . Hardly had we finished our coffee and liqueurs when the jazz orchestra struck up: "Yes, we have no bananas." There must have been twenty nationalities among those who got up to dance to that tune, everybody laughing and humming the words. Even Lord Robert Cecil, who does not dance, left the table to watch the dancing, highly amused. We may be absent from the [League] conference table, but we are present in the cabaret and the dance hall.[46]

During the next 20 years Drexel embraced the career of a newspaper woman, freelance writer, campaigner for various causes, and world traveler. She worked at one time or another for the Philadelphia *Public Ledger*, the Chicago *Tribune*, the McClure Syndicate, and others. A fanatical supporter of the League of Nations, world peace, and many international reform movements, she blamed the limited success of these ventures on U.S. isolationism fostered by an unholy alliance of reactionary politicians and unprincipled journalists.

Several of the best-known American correspondents whom I met in Europe this summer [1924] were wearing in their buttonholes the little red ribbon of the French Legion of Honor. This is given for services to France; it is not only thanks for past assistance, but by the subtlest psychological ties binds one for the future. . . . The editor of one of the largest eastern newspapers told my syndicate manager and myself over a festive luncheon table that he would not be interested in my series from the Ruhr if I were to talk to the German population. He stated frankly that his paper wanted to uphold the French side.[47]

The ravages of the international opium traffic threatened the moral fiber and the productive vitality of the American people, while the United States' frenetic manufacture of arms and munitions compromised its national integrity in the world community and courted war. Concerning the arms traffic convention signed at St. Germain-en-Laye on September 10, 1919, Drexel wrote:

The Convention of St. Germain was ignored. Yet, the United States having proved itself an apparently inexhaustible source for the production of war supplies, this matter concerned that country more than any other and its adherence was a *sine qua non*. . . . When delegates to the first sessions of the League of Nations met at Geneva in 1920 and 1921, they were greatly disturbed by the non-ratification of this St. Germain Convention, especially by the United States. . . . But as this was the period when the United States was not only not represented at Geneva but when even communications from the League were ignored and left unanswered by the State Department, no reply was vouchsafed until July 29, 1922. . . . Under the guise of patriotism, defense and other catch words, they [U.S. merchants of death and their allied political lobby] have succeeded in the United States alone in forcing an increase of 197 per cent in Government appropriations for military expenditures, from 1914 to 1931.[48]

Columbia University president Nicholas Murray Butler and Idaho senator James P. Pope hailed Drexel, who had covered the Geneva Arms Conference of 1932, as an authority on international arms control and as a champion of world peace. In the spring of 1935 Senator Pope placed before Congress Drexel's blueprint for disarmament based upon the Kellogg Pact. But despite her perseverance and her growing stature among the press corps and certain political circles, Drexel's efforts went unrewarded.[49]

Even at this early date, Drexel was known among her colleagues to cast an approving eye toward Germany. As a social critic, she offered no apology; after all, Adolf Hitler advocated a reform agenda comparable to her own. Issues such as the greater role of German women in the new Reich, the eradication of a parasitic social elite, welfare legislation for minors, and social hygiene regulatory laws all impressed her. Drexel eagerly anticipated visits to the new Reich, and on several of these working holidays the Propaganda Ministry awarded her writing assignments.[50]

Back in the United States in 1937, Drexel attempted to establish herself as a columnist, writing on foreign affairs. The following year she was employed in Philadelphia on the Works Progress Administration (WPA) Writers' Project and, later, as an instructor of French on the WPA Education Project. During this brief period, Drexel's writing came to the attention of journalist George Seldes, who claimed that she had already become a Nazi propagandist when publisher Richard H. Waldo hired her in 1939 to pen numerous articles for his newspaper chain. According to Seldes, "The Constance Drexel pro-Nazi stuff was even worse than what appeared in [Waldo] McClure Syndicate's papers because one of Waldo's secretaries insisted that as written the items were too raw and would get Waldo into trouble. Waldo referred to Miss Drexel as his favorite contributor."[51] Drexel left suddenly for Berlin in 1939, explaining that her passage was being paid by the German government. Her official explanation for this surprise departure was the need to care for her ailing mother in Wiesbaden. Her broadcasts over the Reichrundfunk commenced in 1940. The Propaganda Ministry introduced her as "a famous American journalist" and a member of "a socially prominent and wealthy Philadelphia family," which she was not. Goebbels' new society and cultural affairs commentator was well known among Berlin's American colony, where she was regarded as something of a pest and a crackpot. She escaped internment with other U.S. citizens when war was declared.[52]

Drexel confined her broadcasting for the Nazis largely to social and cultural items, describing the pleasures of life in wartime Germany, the concerts and exhibitions, and the abundance of food, clothing, and entertainment. Her apparent intention—if, indeed, she had one—was to convince her listeners of Germany's stability under the pressures of war and to contrast these conditions with life in the United States.[53]

It appears that what remained of Constance Drexel's once-promising career disintegrated under Nazi supervision. She aired each Sunday at 8:45 P.M.

(EST), covering the trite calendar of Berlin's American community and all cultural activities in the greater Reich. Pompous masters of ceremony grandiloquently introduced her as "a Philadelphia socialite heiress," but beyond earshot they mockingly denounced her as "*wirklich dumm*" (just plain stupid) and her work as "*schrecklich*" (terrible).[54] This pathetic figure confided to correspondent Joseph C. Harsch in 1940 that Runkfunk officialdom drafted her scripts and that she simply mouthed the words. According to Harsch, Drexel failed to comprehend that she was working for a potential enemy.[55]

During a ministry banquet, reporter Harry W. Flannery was introduced to Goebbels' diminutive blueblood from Philadelphia:

She was an ebullient character and often dressed in a bizarre fashion. On this occasion she wore a loose-hanging red and brown dress that looked as if it had been made of burlap. I asked her about it. She posed, with one hand adjusting her hair at the back, and said it was her own creation.[56]

Well-known newsman and journalist William L. Shirer avoided Drexel's company in Berlin whenever possible, considering her "a sort of forlorn person and a rather shabby journalist."

Constance Drexel, an insignificant, mixed-up, and ailing woman of forty-six who always had a bad cold, used to tell me during the first winter of the war in Berlin that she needed money—and wouldn't I hire her as a broadcaster? But she went over to the service of Dr. Goebbels mainly because she had always been pro-German and Pan-German and since 1933 had been bitten by the Nazi bug. The money the Germans paid her no doubt was welcome, but she would have taken mine (which had an anti-Nazi taint) had I been fool enough to hire her.[57]

Historian Charles J. Rolo observed in 1942 that on occasion Drexel shed her mantle as *Kultur* critic for that of a political propagandist. When the German government published documents that allegedly proved that with promises of U.S. aid U.S. diplomats had "encouraged" London to declare war, Drexel assured her faithful: "I was among those who saw the documents and had no doubt that they were the genuine article." In a talk on August 25, 1940, she discussed German speculation to the effect that Franklin Roosevelt "deliberately sent the ship *American Legion* through the war zone [ostensibly to repatriate stranded Americans in those areas] in the hope that it might create an international incident which would arouse American opinion to the point of entering the war."[58]

Following V-E Day, Drexel was arrested by American GIs on August 16, 1945. Reports indicated that this unlikely fugitive had approached a *Stars and Stripes* reporter, Fred Wackernagel, and naively divulged her identity and her pending criminal indictment in the United States.[59] Taken into custody, she spent a year in jail and internment camps before her release. Through all of this, Drexel denied any wrongdoing: "I was only interested in culture, in Beethoven and music and things like that. . . . They said I was giving aid and comfort to the enemy. I was always against war. I thought that I was following President Roosevelt's line—you know, harmonizing things."[60] A special board of inquiry decided that Drexel had not forfeited her citizenship due to her long absence from the United States. Still uncertain as to her future, she arrived in New York City on October 2, 1946, aboard the transport *Ernie Pyle* and was whisked away immediately to Ellis Island. Justice Department officials, however, professed no intention to prosecute her, since their lawyers in Germany were unable to uncover evidence that would warrant prosecution. On April 14, 1948, federal judge David A. Pine dismissed the treason indictment.[61]

In retirement, Drexel continued to write, even authoring a piece on the childhood of her old nemesis, Franklin Roosevelt.[62] In the last year of her life, this 62-year-old spinster relished her appointment to the Woodrow Wilson Centennial Committee. On the morning of August 28, 1956, Constance Drexel suddenly collapsed and died at the home of a cousin in Waterbury, Connecticut. She had planned to leave the United States that very afternoon to take up residence with her mother's family in Geneva, Switzerland.

Reichrundfunk management considered Edward Leopold Delaney's induction into the U.S.A. Zone as a coup, never doubting his latent ability to convince the home folks of John Bull's perfidy. After all, this American world traveler had spent the majority of his 45 years as an advance man for vagabond theater groups, an actor, a salesman, a commodities broker, an author of pulp fiction, a public relations representative, and a Hollywood press agent. For a mere $200 a month, the Nazi bureaucrats expected to parlay this unknown ballyhoo artist into a U.S. version of the British Zone's celebrated Lord Haw-Haw. In time, an irreverent wing of Delaney's radio audience would take his measure by awarding him the title of Lord Ho-Hum.

Born of a poor Irish family in Olney, Illinois, on December 12, 1885, young Delaney grew up in Glenview, a suburb of Chicago. He started his stage career around 1910 in San Francisco. Haunting Harry Corbett's bar, Delaney met and befriended a wide circle of sportsmen and thespians. Several promoters of the silver screen persuaded him to accompany them to New York City, and for the next five months he studied under an acting coach. Subsequently, armed with a bogus "previous experience" dossier, he signed a contract to play a leading role in a road company's production of *Under Southern Skies*, which opened in Jacksonville, Florida.

For the next several years Delaney appeared in numerous road companies, interspersed with stock engagements from coast to coast. There were even one-night stands in the maritime provinces of Canada. For two seasons Delaney played the part of Blackie Daw in one of Cohan and Harris' productions of *Get-Rich-Quick Wallingford*. Starring opposite actress Olive Artelle, the handsome leading man came to the attention of J. C. Williamson, Ltd., theater owners and producers in Australia. Traveling with Josephine Cohan (sister of George) and troupe, Delaney's first port of call was Wellington, New Zealand, where he appeared as the killer in *Seven Keys to Baldpate*. It was there he learned that Austria's Archduke Francis Ferdinand had been assassinated, and that World War I had commenced.

Once back in California, Delaney was cast by Cecil de Mille, Jesse Lasky, and James Young opposite star Blanche Sweet in *The Thousand Dollar Husband*. The ungrateful actor fell into an argument with Lasky over wages. He threatened a walkout before the end of shooting, so the studio relented. In reprisal, Delaney suffered the effects of a temporary blacklisting. Without work, he pooled his money to bankroll a partner who toured Central and South America showing American films with Spanish subtitles. Before the end of 1916, the disillusioned entrepreneur was back in the United States.

The following year Delaney assisted the director Charles Miller, then involved in a motion picture starring Norma Talmadge. America's entry into World War I found Delaney back in San Francisco preparing to embark for Australia again via the Orient. There he represented several Melbourne exporters in Southeast Asia. Delaney found these promotional jaunts too exhausting, so in 1920 he repaired to South Africa, where he aided a Johannesburg film mogul in the restriction of British and U.S. competition. Still dissatisfied with his station in life, this Flying Dutchman left for Paris and London the next year, becoming involved in several disastrous road company ventures.

In 1924, Metro-Goldwyn-Mayer (MGM) offered the World War I epic *The Big Parade*, as well as the screen version of *The Merry Widow* featuring John Gilbert and Mae Murray. MGM's public relations department sent Delaney to Detroit, Michigan, to promote these silent films. Concomitantly, he was asked to manage a tour of the popular "Our Gang" kids. There followed years of association with the corporation's promotion department. Delaney established Chicago as his headquarters, and in 1926 he was made advertising and publicity director for Loew's, Inc., the owner of MGM and a national chain of theaters. The stock market crash of 1929 crippled him financially. Then, in 1930, Loew's relieved him of his position. Without family or funds, Delaney again returned to Europe.[63]

In and out of the United States frequently during this period, Delaney, always mum about his personal life, was something of a mystery man even to his close friends. In 1934 this lifelong bachelor published his first book, *The Lady by Degrees*, following it the next year with *The Charm Girl*, advertised as the "screamline correspondence of a radio charmer and his girlfriend." A typical sentence read, "Remember darling, you can't always judge a man by *how* he *looks* as by *where* he glances, which sometimes makes me long for the good old days when Fanny was a girl's name." A New York *Times* review of Delaney's early work concluded, "Readers with a partiality for action and romance, regardless of the quality, should be entertained by the story." Despite its mixed reception, *The Lady by Degrees* ran serially in the New York *Mirror* and several other newspapers in the country.[64]

Franklin Roosevelt's reelection to the presidency of the United States distressed Delaney and rekindled an old hatred that stemmed from FDR's campaign to afford the Soviet Union diplomatic recognition. In three years' time, the expatriate would applaud from Berlin the work of Congressman Martin Dies, Democrat of Texas, who sought to expose Communists inside Roosevelt's New Deal administration. Moreover, Chicago *Tribune* publisher Robert McCormick had suffered from a White House campaign of disinformation, fumed Delaney, and the Reverend Charles E. Coughlin lost U.S. radio affiliates weekly due to political pressure. In retrospect, Delaney would feel a certain kinship with the Catholic priest:

A few radio broadcasters, including myself, who had the temerity to present their "views in the news" soon found that such views did not agree with those of the station or network owners. The popularity of the broadcaster was assured if he reflected the editorial policies of the New York *Times*, the Washington *Post*, the Des Moines *Register*, or others of the emerging liberal persuasion.

Widespread American support for the Republican cause in the Spanish Civil War he likewise attributed to left-wing propaganda.[65]

Constant criticisms of the Roosevelt administration paid dividends in July 1939 when Delaney received word that the Reichrundfunk might have need of his services. Going to the broadcasting station, he met Dr. Harry Eisenbrown, an American educated at Heidelberg and a former professor at Princeton. Eisenbrown introduced him to Dr. Hans Schirmer, head of the Reich Foreign Office's Radio Department. It seemed that Herr Schirmer had an opening for someone proficient in writing and broadcasting human interest material. He desired "word pictures" to counter anti-German commentary abroad. His office would permit complete editorial freedom—an inducement most attractive to Delaney—and no travel restrictions to locales of civilian or military significance. Flattered by his host's attentions, Delaney agreed to ponder the offer.

Only days after Hitler's September 1, 1939, invasion of Poland, Delaney traveled to England to observe conditions. He found that most Englishmen and women were willing to accept an ally's absorption in order to "get on with their lives." In late autumn of 1939, Delaney boarded a U.S. vessel bound for New York City. Several hundred miles west of Ireland, the ship came across a U-boat about to sink a British freighter. Perhaps Delaney experienced déjà vu, having been aboard a passenger liner months earlier, on September 3, whose captain rescued survivors from the *Athena* following a similar torpedoing. In this instance the submarine commander permitted the enemy crew time to man the lifeboats. Suddenly, the U-boat came under

attack from an RAF bomber. Holding the aircraft at bay, the sub finished
the freighter before its crash dive. With the British vessel gone, Delaney
interviewed the chief officer. According to Berlin's unofficial reporter, this
seaman insisted that the chivalrous German captain had escaped unscathed.
The BBC congratulated the bomber crew on its "kill" and, added Delaney,
the New York City press refused to print the British officer's version of the
contest. Months later, during a broadcast over Radio Berlin, Delaney derived
great satisfaction in reading from the freighter's papers confiscated by the
submarine captain, thereby proving that the U-boat had survived.[66]

In December 1939 Delaney sailed for several Mediterranean ports aboard
a U.S. liner, the SS *Excalibur*. The first stop was Genoa, Italy. A British
warship intercepted the ship at the Straits of Gibraltar. The vessel's company
endured search parties, and its mails and cargo were confiscated. Months
later Delaney would blast this action as rank piracy. The *Excalibur*'s captain
filed a protest with William Chapman, U.S. consul in Gibraltar. Chapman
confided to Delaney that this protest—like all the others—would be pigeon-
holed in Washington. The consul's Irish-American guest exploded when he
learned that all detained ships at Gibraltar would be required to pay port
fees: "That right of might which they [Great Britain] deplore in other powers
they exercise against the United States and other ships, and order unarmed
merchantmen to Gibraltar just as Jesse James and other U.S.A. bandits held
up mail years ago."[67]

During the winter of 1939–40, Delaney agreed to work for Radio Berlin
as a roving correspondent and broadcaster. He rationalized that such a course
of action would permit him to neutralize Allied propaganda back home by
giving an objective slant to central European affairs. Foreign Office Radio
Department supervisors presented him with a new microphone identity:
E. D. Ward. Unfortunately, this partnership began to deteriorate almost
immediately. Delaney informed his bosses that he did not subscribe to national socialism, and that he would assert his independence whenever he
deemed it best. Dr. Schirmer agreed to Delaney's bold demands in all par-
ticulars, except in matters relevant to military intelligence. The Reich Foreign
Office even acceded to the newcomer's demand of payment in U.S. dollars.[68]

On April 9, 1940, Berlin radio announced that German troops had occupied Denmark and Norway. The following day, Delaney's plane touched
down in Copenhagen. Everywhere he discovered German troops doing everything possible to mollify their Danish cousins. The populace told him that
King Christian had acted in the best interests of his country when he refused
to allow Denmark the status of a belligerent.

This evening I want to talk to you about the "visitation" of German armed forces to
Denmark for the purpose of maintaining Danish neutrality. . . . German forces are in
possession of vital strategic positions in Denmark at which it might be expected that
Britain and France might want to make an effort to insert a wedge which would open

up the whole country as a field for military operations. Had German forces not arrived when they did the whole country might have been turned into a battlefield. . . . The Danish communiques announcing the death of certain Danish soldiers killed when the German forces entered the country, expressed regret, but no recriminations are heard. The press publishes an official statement of the War Minister eulogising those who fell but stating that they can only be regarded as extremely unfortunate.[69]

The only discordant note reported by Delaney involved the brief stay of *Christian Science Monitor* correspondent Joseph C. Harsch. Soon after the appearance of E. D. Ward, the American journalist arrived in the city with Horst Cleinow, director of Goebbels' shortwave station, in tow. Several days later Harsch's copy appeared in the *Monitor* observing that he, a U.S. citizen, had been forced to remain in Copenhagen for three days. Although he did not say that the occupation army had detained him there, Delaney denounced his countryman's deliberate attempt to convey a false impression. On April 24, E. D. Ward answered Harsch's innuendo on the air. For one entire day, bad weather had grounded the newsman's plane from Norway to Copenhagen to Berlin, explained Delaney. Conditions persisted the second day. The Harsch party left on the third day, minus several members of the entourage who were kept behind for dubious reasons. Delaney concluded that these men were held because they desired to leave the Reich (formerly Denmark) for England, a belligerent.[70]

In his 1941 book, *Pattern of Conquest*, Harsch remembered a dispirited citizenry in Copenhagen, and that Delaney's behavior added a bit of levity to an otherwise gloomy environment. While on assignment there, Harsch stated, he met this mysterious American who identified himself as a "lecturer." It was not until his return to the United States that Harsch learned of Delaney's true function and status when a friend sent him a publication from the German Library of Information in New York City. In this particular issue, "Mr. Ward" devoted two pages to a refutation of what Harsch had written about Denmark's national demise. "He . . . ignored in his attempted rebuttal every single fact and every single general statement I made," mused Harsch, "limiting himself to drawing a false implication from my concluding sentence and then attacking his own implication." Furthermore, he continued:

The last sentence of my story about the occupation of Copenhagen had stated that I "was held up three days in getting away." Mr. Ward purported to see in this an attempt to make it appear that the Germans had deliberately held me "incommunicado" for that length of time. Actually I was trying unsuccessfully to let my editor know that for those three days I had sat at the Copenhagen airport, watching every kind of airplane the Germans could lay their hands on head for Norway. Their invasion had run into difficulties. Their transports were being sunk. For three entire days not a single plane of any kind went south to Germany from Copenhagen. If the English had only known how desperate the plight of the German invading force was during those crucial days, they might have taken a chance with their fleet and would almost certainly have succeeded in driving Germany back out of the Scandinavian peninsula. As it was, the British fleet tarried while the Germans made good by air what they lost on water.[71]

On May 10, 1940, the Wehrmacht crossed into Belgium and Holland. Within 48 hours Delaney arrived on the Dutch border to obtain firsthand information. He denied that German parachutists had worn Dutch uniforms, adding that there were some half dozen different types of Nazi military garb that might have been mistaken for Dutch. Pronouncement after pronouncement lauded the work of the Luftwaffe and ridiculed the Allied naval blockade. Yes, African troops were being used by these countries against Germany's Nordic fighters. E. D. Ward himself had seen these black colonials in makeshift prisoner-of-war compounds on the Holland frontier. King Leopold of Belgium commanded his army to surrender on May 28, while the British expeditionary forces beat a hasty retreat. The Belgians were used as cannon fodder, trumpeted Delaney, to cover this ignominious flight. The British press and several MPs—in a show of proper respect for this sacrifice— branded their old comrades as cowards. Going further, E. D. Ward reported that Belgian authorities had damned the fleeing British for wrecking their telephone exchanges when the British expeditionary forces decamped. This action virtually ensured that rearguard Belgian units would hold their positions against the Germans until a bloody end.[72]

That same month, Delaney was hailed before U.S. consul A. Dana Hodgson in Berlin. Ostensibly there on a routine matter, he quickly found himself being pressed about his work. The consul expressed consternation about E. D. Ward's incessant attacks on his own government. Delaney defended his constitutional right to question the motives of any politician in the United States, especially those of Franklin Roosevelt. This heated exchange got nowhere.

The German army entered Paris on June 14, 1940. Five days later Delaney, seemingly intoxicated by this display of Nazi power, smirked that England's turn would be next, "that tight little isle whose leaders last September declared war to save the ideals of Christianity and Western Civilization." His tone darkened as he warned his fellow countrymen:

America's entry into the last war was a horrible mistake. Had the U.S. minded its own business over a million British and French lives might well have been saved. If America had stayed out of the war and minded her own business, none of the "isms" would today be sweeping the Continent of Europe and breaking down Parliamentary Government.

In the wake of the Franco-German Armistice, Delaney again tried to "reason" with his audience.

The British Press has devoted much attention to the entry into the Cabinet of Mr. [Henry] Stimson who advocated the waiving of the so-called Neutrality Bill and America's entry into the war on the side of the Allies. If America is involved in war by those who want it, it will not be as the result of German provocation, but of America's self-made invitation. Campaign speeches at the Republican Convention this year will probably be more concerned with Europe's warfare than America's welfare. The war in Europe provides admirable distraction from domestic problems. . . . America may, however, make her greatest contribution to European peace with ballots instead of bullets.[73]

His Majesty, intoned Delaney, strove for nothing less than the recolonization of North America. In his "scoop" of the war, he confided:

Why was the Duke of Windsor sent to the Bahamas? The Duke is to be the First Viceroy of Britain in Washington when the two nations are melted into one. It's not so fantastic as it sounds. Having an American born wife he would be well received into the post of Governor General—sort of assistant to the President. Or would the President be subordinated to him? Who knows? Not I, least of all the people of America. They'll be told about it when the details are all worked out, and only then. Just now you're being informed in advance by E. D. Ward in Berlin. Good night.[74]

On July 3, a fortnight after the signing of the armistice between Germany and France, the British fleet cornered a number of French capital ships in the harbor of Oran, Algeria, and, railed Delaney, massacred 1,200 French seamen. Four days later he and four other Berlin radio commentators visited the scene. Horst Cleinow, director of the shortwave station, orchestrated the tour. Instructions were issued to Delaney to interview the surviving sailors. According to their testimony, the cruisers *Dunkirk*, *Province*, *Bretagne*, and *Strassburg*; the aircraft carrier *Teste*; and the destroyers *Magador*, *Valta*, *Lynx*, *Terrible*, *Tiger*, and *Kersaint* were anchored in Oran's harbor when they were encircled by a hostile British fleet. Admiral Sir James Sommerfield then issued his French counterpart (Jousel) an ultimatum to be convoyed to a British port or be destroyed. The Vichy fleet had orders to remain in a French national or colonial port in compliance with the Franco-German Armistice.

Delaney understood that Admiral Sommerfield opened fire before the allotted time for reflection expired. The subsequent bombardment immediately disabled the carrier; heavy damage was inflicted upon the cruisers, with one completely sunk and only the *Strassburg* remaining unscathed. The destroyer *Magador* alone failed to escape to the open sea. Comparing the British naval officers to "assassins" and their handiwork to Japan's subsequent sneak attack on Pearl Harbor, Delaney concluded in a later autobiography that the Nazis never meant to redeploy the interned French men-of-war. He likened John Bull's actions to those of King Herod who, "in his mad rage at his inability to lay hands on the Christ Child, ordered the slaying of the innocents."[75]

July 27 found Delaney in the rearguard of a panzer division advancing through northern France and the Low Countries. Throngs of displaced people made the roads virtually impassable.

We were in a long motor convoy composed of about 40 cars and ambulances of the German Red Cross. On recognizing the flag of the Red Cross the refugees crowded round, expressing intense gratitude at the good treatment they received. They said they had expected the Germans to be barbarians, but in fact it was their own friends, their former ally, who had deserted them and left them to their hopeless plight. One old woman in a wheeled chair, apparently unable to move, thought she was going to be left behind as the cars moved off. There had been some misunderstanding about where she wanted to get to. She cried out to us not to leave her there to fall again into the hands of her "friends." Her friends of yesterday had become the enemies of today—the enemies of yesterday had befriended her. . . . Going through Flanders the people stood in the streets and waved to us. At each place we dropped groups of refugees at their homes. In many places the people lined up to watch the ambulance cars arrive and greeted us with the raised arm salute.[76]

Back in Berlin, Delaney again received a summons to the U.S. consulate. This time Hodgson demanded his travel papers on instructions from Washington. Anticipating this eventuality, the expatriate suggested that the reasons for this "request" be put in writing. The consul balked, and Delaney retained his passport.[77]

When several U.S. correspondents commented in print on the depressing atmosphere of wartime Berlin, Delaney set out to discover this gloom in the spirit of Diogenes. As one might expect, he found among Berliners "smiles as would rival Jim Farley's face on the occasion of a national convention." Seven months later, on September 26, 1940, he revealed over the air that he had just returned from a rest cure in Vienna. With surprising candor, Delaney attributed his recent case of nerves to nightly RAF bombing raids. In the autumn of 1941, a U.S.A. Zone commentator observed that his American friend had been readmitted to a nearby hospital as a "wartime casualty."

Delaney put the necessity for commodities rationing in its best light. He castigated an American newsman for suggesting that the German people suffered from deprivation. Why, fruit was always on his breakfast table, huffed Delaney, and he never missed a hot shower in the morning; and while there were few Beau Brummells in Berlin, still most wardrobes were adequate. "Naturally things are not the same as in peace time," added E. D. Ward indignantly, "but the surprising thing is that they are not worse." "That they are not is due to the amazing organization of economic genius," he concluded. Managing to introduce a measure of humor into his script, Delaney confided that as a non-smoker he had put his allowance of cigarettes to good use among a circle of addicted fräuleins.[78]

Delaney genuinely regarded himself and his colleagues as the vanguard of America's isolationist sentiment. He noted that the New York *Daily Mirror* compared Colonel Charles Lindbergh's rhetoric with his own. In regard to the use of U.S. naval convoys, E. D. Ward warned that it was only a matter of time until an aggressive U-boat captain fell into Roosevelt's trap and sank a U.S. ship. Fortunately, however, there were supporters of the America First movement who still emphasized the perils Delaney repeatedly stressed. At the time of the Republican Convention in June 1940, ex-President Herbert Hoover was commended for his opinion that the United States should remain neutral. After Henry Ford refused to manufacture airplane engines for Britain, E. D. Ward exclaimed, "Would that there were more Fords in America."[79]

Delaney liked to discuss war hysteria and its sinister influence on his countrymen, and he especially enjoyed ridiculing rumors of an anticipated Axis invasion of North America:

I present my newly discovered plan for the invasion of America.... The new air bases which Germany will use for this invasion will be on submarines. The newest U-boats have quarter-decks, after-decks, shelter-decks; all filled with planes which will take off and land at speed. These semi-porpoises can deliver their bombers as far inland as St. Louis or Pittsburgh.... Smaller airplane carriers, submarines of course, then go up other rivers as far as Minnesota. All are designed to take diesel engines and fuel will be made from the by-products of corn. German chemists will see that two crops of corn are raised each year, which will give us more fuel than planes. Other airplane carriers will go up the St. Lawrence and it is said they can navigate the Niagara Falls, so that they can reach Chicago. This airplane-and-submarine carrier is secretly known as the Sixth Column. I could tell you more of this stupendous scheme but it might be censored.

Staged interviews with Europeans recently back from the United States confirmed Delaney's prognosis of a national paranoia there.[80] On October 18, 1940, E. D. Ward sharply attacked the U.S. defense program as a "palpable subterfuge for goading a nation into a fever of hysteria." "Let no one mislead you as to the purpose back of all this disguised defense," he purported. "Change the names, the dates, the serial numbers and you have the same story that was written 22 years ago.... It happened before, didn't it?" On November 6, German news broadcasts explained that the election was a "purely American affair" and that the breaking of the third-term tradition seemed quite "in line ... with such political changes as the remaking of the Supreme Court." To Delaney, the election was "no surprise," and the reason was simple: Roosevelt had been reelected through the efforts of the "Administration machine" and the profit-hungry munitions makers.[81]

While ardently protesting their devotion to the Fatherland, hundreds of thousands of National Socialists, once they escaped from Germany—with all its restrictions and regulations—never looked back. Small wonder that

Delaney relished his Balkan assignments. There were commodities to be purchased, food in abundance, and plenty of tobacco without bother of coupons or ration tickets or black market swindlers. Several weeks prior to the invasion of the Soviet Union, E. D. Ward paused in Bucharest on his way to Athens to cover the Wehrmacht's subjugation of that country. He subsequently observed in one of his three autobiographies (*Five Decades before Dawn*, 1969) that Rumanian streets were alive with rumors of the impending Operation Barbarossa.

Delaney's itinerary next took him to Bulgaria, where he obtained audiences with many state officials through the efforts of Luben Zonew, director of commerce. In both countries Delaney regaled his hosts on the evils of the Roosevelt administration. FDR had beguiled the Yugoslavian government into defying Berlin's overtures of limited economic and political control. The United States, of course, never meant to assist Yugoslavia in keeping its freedom, and promises of U.S. support evaporated on April 18, 1941, when Germany, Bulgaria, and Hungary crossed Yugoslavia's borders and drove King Peter from the throne.[82]

Yugoslavia's absorption into the Reich prompted an official visit by Delaney. The Reich Foreign Office's roving correspondent discovered many sections of Belgrade in ruins. He attributed this widespread damage to the Bolshevik cadres that used the city as a bastion, thereby inviting useless Axis bombardment. These nefarious elements comprised only 10 percent of the country's population, announced E. D. Ward, while the vast majority of Yugoslavians eventually saw the wisdom of supporting the pro-German government of Prince Paul and Premier Swetkovitch. Perhaps, he mused, Yugoslavia's ordeal would signal a message to others who conspired to oppose Europe's New Order.

The [Belgrade] agitation followed the visit of Col. William Donovan, Roosevelt's representative, and was whipped up by a coterie of financial buccaneers and American meddlers. Undersecretary of State Sumner Welles had been in Belgrade a short while before. The Washington message he gave the people was—"defy Hitler and we're behind you." Just how far behind—he failed to state. . . . From a disillusioned Belgrade resident I learned of the show that was staged in the city on the day of the coup d'etat. Monitored by agitators, the people crowded around the American Legation, that being the symbol of the might in which they had put their trust. Arthur Bliss Lane [U.S. minister] appeared with the Stars and Stripes. There were cheers— huzzahs and demonstrations of enthusiasm. That American flag was their guarantee against the hordes of the Swastika. . . . Lane knew that his superiors in Washington were playing power politics and playing to lose. They had virtually signed the death warrant for thousands of Serbians.[83]

American correspondent Harry W. Flannery had the unenviable task of accompanying Delaney part way on this particular Balkan jaunt.

We picked up Delaney, the former American, in Sofia. From the moment we set out, this old maid complained unceasingly about the wind, the sun, the occasional rain, the food, and the roads. For my edification, he compared everything disagreeable in the Balkans with what he considered "the heaven" of Germany. His Nazi sojourn, however, had not improved his disposition.

At dinner [in Belgrade] Delaney handed a script to [Erich] Kunsti [a Rundfunk official]. "Have you made your broadcast?" Kunsti asked. "Yes, just finished," he said. "That's the copy."

Then he turned to me.

"You saw what happened," he said. "Well, you fellows are always saying I have to submit my scripts to Nazi censorship. Now you see for yourself that I've already made the talk before the censors have even seen it."

Delaney's logic was becoming Nazified. It was obvious that the Nazis did not even have to censor his scripts; they knew they could trust him as one of themselves. And, what was more, he did not make a direct broadcast, but a recording that would not go on the air if it was not just what the Nazis ordered.

We were in Vienna only overnight. As we prepared to leave the hotel, the clerk returned our passports. Delaney and I were at the desk at the time. I took mine and noticed that Delaney grabbed furtively for his, but not fast enough to prevent my seeing he no longer had a United States passport. Appropriately, he had a German *Fremdenpass*—that given to the friends of the Nazis.[84]

Hitler's invasion of the Soviet Union thrilled Delaney as the opening barrage in a global assault on bolshevism; the Fuhrer's subsequent persecution of Soviet minorities soured his enthusiasm for nazism considerably.

The Russian people and even more so the Ukrainians welcomed the invaders as their saviors. Had the masterminds of the Nazi cultists not been so warped with their "herrenvolk" ideas, considering themselves masters of western Europe as well as eastern Asia, they could in all probability have changed the course of history.... The millions who would have united with the Germans to throw off the Communist yoke of Moscow, turned into an underground force and began waging guerrilla warfare against both the Soviets and the Germans.[85]

In late July of 1941 Delaney paid Copenhagen a second call. Fifteen months of occupation had agreed with the city, announced E. D. Ward, who proclaimed that its economy was superior to any other metropolis in Europe. This excess wealth had stimulated the growth of amusement centers while retarding political censorship. Belgium, too, was well on the road to recovery. In Brussels, Delaney lunched with the former world's heavyweight boxing champion Max Schmeling and Admiral Felix von Luckner, who had commanded a World War I surface raider that sank over 300,000 tons of Allied shipping without the loss of a single life. After the meal a stocky tour guide approached their table. This man had been the heavyweight boxing champion of Belgium. Seizing the moment, Delaney pirated the substance of their conversation for his propaganda mill that evening.

In sport, he [the Belgian boxer] said, "There are no lasting hates or grudges. I am a Belgian, you Max are German. Both of us have been champions in our day." He went on to say that he admired Schmeling as a boxer. The fact that he was German had nothing to do with their friendship. Yes, there was a feeling in Belgium against the Germans, but why couldn't they look at things as boxers do? When the fight is over they buried whatever differences they had—because they were not personal.

The Belgian pugilist, Delaney crowed, concluded by asking, "Why can't the rest of the world be like we fellows of the ring?"[86]

At this juncture the celebrated English humorist P. G. Wodehouse was causing British and U.S. publishers some embarrassment while providing E. D. Ward with good copy. Wodehouse had been an internee of the German government. His capture in France on May 22, 1940, as Wodehouse later phrased it over the air, was due entirely to the misinformation released by the BBC. These bulletins aired by the BBC stated that the Germans were being pushed out of France, so naturally Wodehouse remained at his chateau. As a result, he was taken prisoner. The author spent a year passing through internment camps in France, Belgium, and Germany. On his sixtieth birthday he was released. While incarcerated, the writer completed a novel, which the Germans allowed to be sent to his publishers in the United States. There followed an article submitted to the *Saturday Evening Post* in which Wodehouse good-naturedly poked fun at his German hosts. The Allies took his writings as pro-Nazi propaganda.

Eventually Wodehouse agreed to make five broadcasts between June 28 and August 6, 1941. This action was in response to a flood of supportive mail from his fans in the United States. These chats dealt with his arrest at the Touquet and his imprisonment at Loos Prison, Liège Barracks, the Citadel at Huy, and Tost Lunatic Asylum. His actions created a firestorm of protest in England and the United States. It was ironic that Delaney attributed Wodehouse's bad press in the West to the work of paid British agents:

That sort of thing shouldn't be tolerated; it wasn't cricket, you know, said some in England. Others took the stand that he [Wodehouse] had betrayed the Empire. He should have stayed in his internment camp as a martyr . . . telling stories of cruelty and hardship instead of making the world laugh. . . . Those people with preconceived ideas about Germany may not have believed him, but the sensible ones are sure to have understood his talks and to have enjoyed them.[87]

Delaney's broadcasts lambasted Roosevelt's policies of armed neutrality and undeclared warfare against Germany during the spring and summer of 1941. Roosevelt, said E. D. Ward, prepared to let slip the dogs of war at the expense of the American people:

The declaration of war will be catastrophic for the United States. Not only in men and materials, in blood and tears, but in the loss of our priceless heritage of independence and principles. The meaningless and deceptive slogans about salvaging democracy and upholding the principles of Christian civilization will prove to be but shibboleths that lead but to the shambles. This war is for control of European politics and the economic life of Europe's many nations—regardless of the phrases used to camouflage it.

Twenty-eight years later Delaney would remind his countrymen that FDR had invited the Japanese attack on Pearl Harbor in hopes of seizing a leadership role in World War II. Unwilling to accept the consequences of his sinister scheme, Delaney then stated, Roosevelt denied commanding officers Admiral Husband E. Kimmel and General Walter Short all avenues for self-vindication in connection with this military debacle.[88]

On the day of America's entry into the war, Schirmer informed Delaney that there would be arrangements made for his internment in Bad Nauheim prior to his repatriation. He could either proceed to the detention center or remain in Europe for the war's duration. The Foreign Office dangled before Delaney the extra inducement of free movement inside the Reich. "The situation was rather unusual," pondered Delaney. "Millions of Americans would be fighting to get to Berlin. I am there. Moreover, I am told I may remain there, or elsewhere in the Axis area, if I choose to do so. I could record and experience much there behind the front. Undoubtedly I might be able to refute much fiction which other writers would produce about Central Europe from their vantage points—at great distances. I decided to remain." There was a financial consideration involved in Delaney's election to remain in Europe, as well: "I had sufficient funds in German currency to cover my expenses for two or three years, if necessary. That currency could not be exchanged for coin of other countries except at a ruinous discount."[89]

Unexpected editorial criticism from the United States took Delaney by surprise, and on December 18, 1941, his temper flared before a Reichrundfunk microphone:

Some people hold that believers in Democracy cannot live among a people who believe in a totally different form of Government. . . . It must be a matter for each individual not called upon for active service to decide what course to take. If therefore one acts according to one's lights, and if that act is regarded by certain people as treason, then, in the words of Patrick Henry, "Let them make the most of it."[90]

Delaney persuaded himself to become a transnational correspondent on assignment in the Balkans. His affiliation with the Foreign Office seemed to him a minor technicality. From a personal perspective, Slovakia represented an Eden in comparison with Germany; its new moderate president, Josef Tiso, and its enviable standard of living beckoned to Delaney. True, he learned that many Czechs were deposed from government, but they were not deported or otherwise persecuted. President Tiso had expressed pride in his limited autonomy, which permitted him to curb the pogroms against

the Jews, Poles, and Hungarians. The monsignor admitted to Delaney that
the Nazis were robbing his country through a rigged balance of trade, but
that the Wehrmacht's presence served to forestall a greater evil—Bolshevik
uprisings.[91]

How Delaney loved to attend Rundfunk social functions when in Berlin!
Correspondent Harry W. Flannery recalled a chance meeting with him early
in the war.

A slender, greying, spectacled man with a tolerant smile was introduced to me as
Delaney. We talked affably at first. I was glad to meet a man who seemed to be an
American, a business executive, I presumed. Delaney chatted on. Finally, proud of
his ability to talk dialect, he told a story that compared the Irish to monkeys. I laughed
politely, but wondered about this man with the Irish name. "Oh, he's Edward Leopold
Delaney, who goes on the air for the Germans as 'E. D. Ward,' " I was told. Delaney
formerly had been a lecturer and newspaperman in the United States and considered
himself a world traveler and, I gathered from talking with him, a world authority.
He was a man without principles, an opportunist typical of the so-called British and
Americans who spoke for the German radio.[92]

Edwin Hartrich with the Columbia Broadcasting System (CBS) said of Delaney: "After a while he became a rather tragic figure (his social networking
notwithstanding). He couldn't find an audience to listen to his line of preach-
ing. Even the Nazis avoided him." William L. Shirer did not consider him
too dangerous. This noted journalist recalled that in Delaney's latter days
in Berlin he was simply bored and boring.[93]

In April 1943, Delaney ended his tenuous connection with the Reich
Foreign Office and assumed residency in Slovakia. On the day of his departure from Berlin there came to his attention a U.S. magazine article listing
him—along with other radio traitors—as one who was "currently haranguing
listeners" over Radio Berlin. Dispatching a message to the Swiss legation
protesting his absence from a German microphone for 18 months, he vowed
to sue the publication's owner for "maliciously intended slander."[94]

Branded as a turncoat, Delaney saw plots and conspiracies aimed at his
discreditation everywhere. These machinations were, of course, masterminded by the Bolshevik International, of which FDR and his minions were
a part. In one such incident a bogus letter was routed to the U.S. Department
of Justice over Delaney's forged signature. The document portrayed him as
the head of a Hungarian diamond-smuggling scheme.[95]

Delaney made his new home in Bratislava's Carlton Hotel. Scarcely had
he arrived when the local secret police dropped by to evaluate his intentions.
Unnerved, Delaney sought and received assurances from Slovakian officials
that he would not be returned to Germany. As a precaution, the American
decided to move to the village of Piestany, 60 miles away. There he hoped
to escape the prying eyes of the Gestapo. Unfortunately, the town became

the unlikely haven for Italian political and military exiles sympathetic to the Marshal Pietro Bodoglio government. Forced to live with these anti-Fascists under the Grand Royal Hotel's roof, Delaney grew edgy as Berlin's attention focused on these traitors. President Tiso continued to resist the repatriation of these people to German-occupied northern Italy, but he ultimately agreed to have them sent to Vienna, and then to Silesia for the war's duration.

Life for Delaney became a nightmarish combination of boredom and mental apprehension. To pass the time he collaborated with an Austrian playwright, Siegfried Geyer, on a manuscript. Following the Nazi occupation of Slovakia, Geyer disappeared on the night of September 8, 1944. Tales of Soviet advances to the West, seemingly corroborated by long convoys of bedraggled refugees clogging the roads, haunted Delaney. To add to his misery, the Germans turned Piestany into a formidable redout amidst growing partisan activity, and the SS interrogated him periodically.[96]

He fled to Prague, only to witness its bloody uprising on May 4, 1945. At first anti-German feeling manifested itself in isolated attacks on collaborators and shops catering to German tastes, and in the alteration of street signs. Conditions worsened as unruly mobs halted traffic and electric street trams. In an attempt to reverse this mounting unrest, German soldiers and armored cars converged on Wenzelsplatz, the city's hub. Delaney saw civilians beaten to death, even as German observation planes dropped explosives among their attackers. Czech nationalists seized Prague's radio station as its occupiers began the evacuation of the capital. Hourly appeals were beamed to General George Patton's Third Army to rescue the city, but to no avail: "It is an undeniable truth that General George Patton was not stopped by the Germans, but by the pro-Soviet coterie in Washington who had surrendered to Stalin." Red Army units reached Prague's outskirts on May 9, 1945. For years afterward Delaney would revile President Tiso's successor, Eduard Beneš, as Stalin's stooge and the enemy of the Czechoslovakian people.[97]

On May 18 two correspondents for the U.S. armed forces *Stars and Stripes*, Klaus Mann (son of German philosopher Thomas Mann) and Howard Byrne, made Delaney's acquaintance. In the course of their conversation, Delaney proudly showed them correspondence linking him with the Reichrundfunk. The reporters immediately turned their talkative host in to the Prague authorities, who charged him with writing anti-Soviet articles. Dispatched to Bartholomegasse Prison, Delaney spent the next six weeks in a common cell with 16 political prisoners. Always a resourceful man, he arranged to have a large quantity of dried fruits and vegetables taken from his hotel room and smuggled into the prison's mess. A bribe to the cook provided both him and a pugilist-bodyguard with an adequate diet until his release. Eventually he smuggled a note to the Swiss legation on toilet tissue, after which Czech authorities placed him under house arrest in Prague's Sroubek Hotel. Next,

U.S. military police carted Delaney off to Freising, a small Bavarian town near Munich. There he met Boyd V. Sheets and associates, representatives of the Department of Justice.[98]

Delaney complained bitterly about his living conditions. The United States Army Counter-Intelligence Corps (CIC) ran the detention centers, an outfit he branded as the American Gestapo. His jailers, according to Delaney, pocketed $800 of his money. Threats of a congressional investigation restored his cash, he subsequently recalled in his autobiography. The former president of Slovakia, Josef Tiso, and his cabinet shared their American friend's lodgings and his spartan treatment. Delaney reported that these men were severely beaten by the CIC guards before being turned over to Moscow for execution. This act of perceived treachery he traced to the U.S. Department of State.[99]

Soon thereafter Delaney was released from confinement and allowed to live in a small hotel. Still smarting from his treatment from the occupation forces, he claimed to have nearly starved in the winter of 1945–46. In mid-March of 1946, Delaney was again taken into custody and transported to Oberusel, near Frankfurt am Main. There he was locked away a second time. During this period the prisoner somehow obtained a letter from FBI Director J. Edgar Hoover to Frederich Ayer, Jr., U.S. Department of Justice representative in Germany, stating that there was no legal basis for holding him. Over the ensuing several months Delaney proudly displayed this document to every guard in the detention center.[100]

On August 6, 1946, the CIC released Delaney from custody. This time he immediately applied for a new passport. Delay followed delay. Finally, he complained to Carmel Offie, aide to Ambassador Robert Murphy, that the White House and State Department were denying him the right of clearing his name before the American people. Offie sent Delaney home on his own authority.[101]

Traveling aboard the United States Army transport *George W. Goethals*, Delaney was taken into custody by FBI agents just outside New York harbor. Assistants to the U.S. attorney general Raymond Whearty and Victor C. Woerheide arraigned their prisoner before U.S. commissioner Garrett W. Cotter. From federal detention headquarters Delaney insisted to the press that he was being persecuted for writing anti-Soviet literature. The grand jury must have partially agreed, for it dismissed the indictment on August 28, 1947. Delaney later contended that Commissioner Cotter told him in private: "I would like you to know that when you were brought in here, the day of your return to New York, I believed your story and not that of the Attorney General's assistants. I thought perhaps you'd like to know it."[102] Following his release Delaney appeared on the lecture circuit as an ardent anti-Communist spokesman. His poster captions read "Delaney Was Behind the Iron Curtain When It Fell: He Tells All!!" Modestly billed as an internationally known novelist, speaker, publicist, foreign correspondent, news commentator, and world traveler, he acknowledged his decision to remain in Nazi-dominated Europe as one based on intellectual curiosity. Rapt audiences listened as he described the Soviet occupation of Prague with all its sordid aspects.[103]

On August 15, 1949, Congressman John Phillips of the 22d California District contacted the FBI about Delaney. It seemed that a "hot argument" raged in his bailiwick over whether or not Riverside County should permit the construction of a cement plant near Palm Springs. During the fight, which ultimately went to a countywide vote, the radio station in Riverside (KPRO) employed Delaney. Representative Phillips recounted how businesspeople of Palm Springs and the Coachella Valley area opposed the plant. Their pressure ultimately forced the County Board of Supervisors to deny a construction permit.[104]

On January 1, 1949, however, two new members of the board took their seats and, along with a third plant supervisor, decided to lift the building restriction. As a result, the Desert Associates retaliated with a referendum. The election, set for July 26, only divided the electorate even more. From his KPRO broadcasting studio, Delaney blasted both the Desert Associates and the Truman administration, despite the fact that his boss was one of the most powerful Democrats in southern California.

On the night of July 21, a debate was held between the Desert Associates and the County Board of Supervisors of Riverside. During this contest, attorneys for the Desert Associates asked Delaney if he had in fact worked for the Nazis and had been indicted by the Justice Department. Chagrined by this unexpected turn of events, the accused took the podium in his own defense.

I have been trying since 1942 for this opportunity to refute lies, tyranny, and character assassinations, put out by some people—I'm sure Mr. Harper [district attorney] had no difficulty in finding those books in the libraries of some people in Palm Springs— books that are filled with libelous statements. . . . I appreciate the fact that Mr. Harper is saying that I have been heard throughout the whole country. That I have been so effectively heard is quite an honor, in a sense, isn't it.

Delaney rambled on at the meeting about his treatment in Europe after the war at the hands of "those" in the State Department who groveled before the Soviets.[105]

The outcome of this local dispute is not relevant to Delaney's story. Apparently, this surprise disclosure soured his relationship with KPRO management. What is germane to this chronicle is that he resurfaced in Arizona in the summer of 1951 in an even more controversial setting. Tucson's Good Government Ltd. constituted a Republican action group with Delaney's KCNA talk show "Speak Your Piece" as its mouthpiece. It appeared that station manager Wayne Sanders knew of his 66-year-old employee's former association with the Reichrundfunk but kept him on the payroll because of his entertaining anti-Communist rhetoric. Unfortunately, the affluent GOP backers of this group had no inkling of their leader's past. When an anonymous source exposed his Nazi connection, Delaney's sunshine patriots beat a hasty retreat. An outraged Pima County Republican Women's Club was forced to withhold a thousand copies of his booklet *America at the Crossroads*. He informed an impertinent press corps that his last Berlin broadcast had been on the evening of the Pearl Harbor attack. No, President Tiso of Slovakia had not been a Nazi puppet, argued Delaney, but rather his pupil with regard to U.S. geopolitical and cultural considerations. Yes, his delayed return to the United States he attributed to conspirators back home who had tried to keep him in perpetual exile.[106]

The Arizona *Daily Star* countered Delaney's entreaties with a pointed rebuke by its editor, William R. Matthews:

If Mr. Delaney was considered an able exponent of such matters [state of U.S. government and society], and if Mr. Delaney considered that nearly all American writers "slanted" their stories on Nazi Germany, how can he expect to be accepted today as an authority on "good government" or the proper way for a democracy to function? . . . It is high time that the public begins to ask a single question regarding the individual who takes it upon himself to speak or write on public affairs as an interpreter or adviser, the question should be, who's talking?

On July 20, 1954, FBI headquarters learned that station KCNA had removed Delaney's program from the air. By that time its former host had already switched to publishing *The Guardian*, a right-wing tabloid in Tucson.[107]

Delaney believed that the State Department and the Justice Department had been responsible for all the damaging public disclosures concerning his 1943 indictment for treason. On August 24, he threatened to sue the latter agency. Simultaneously, a letter of denial to FBI "smears" was sent by Delaney to all newspapers in the area. The Arizona *Daily Star* ran an unflattering background study and interview of Delaney. Its rival, the *Daily Register*, accused *Daily Star* reporter Roger O'Mara of character assassination. An appeal by the aggrieved to the White House for presidential exoneration went unanswered.[108] Embattled and alone, Delaney moved to Glendale, California, in 1952. There he lived modestly in a tiny apartment, drove a decrepit automobile, and gave the appearance of a slightly seedy grandfather. A devout Roman Catholic, Delaney lived a half block from his parish. At 76 he won a minor position as political columnist for the Santa Ana (California) *Register*.[109]

At home and abroad, Delaney conducted a vigorous anti-Bolshevik campaign. He cultivated close ties with the Anti-Bolshevik Bloc of Nations, usually called the ABN. Headquartered in Munich, Germany, the ABN was composed of anti-Bolshevik Ukrainians, Slovaks, Hungarians, Croats, and anti-Beneš Czechs. The last prime minister of a free Ukraine, Jaroslaw Stetzko, served as its president. From Glendale, Delaney maintained a constant correspondence with these people and visited their home office on several occasions.[110]

International communism struck Delaney as a deadly contagion that moved relentlessly forward on a global front. This aged Red-baiter visited West Germany just before the erection of the Berlin Wall on August 13, 1961. He wrote home that in the days prior to the erection of the Wall, escapees numbered 3,000 every 24 hours. Returning there the next year, he witnessed the shooting of several East Berlin citizens trying to cross the lethal zone. In one incident, Delaney saw West Berlin guards kill a Vopo sentry who had in turn shot an escapee. It was Delaney's contention that a pro-Soviet coterie in Washington labored to push the German Federal Republic into the Soviet orbit. These were the leftist politicos and bureaucrats who, according to Delaney, spread the "Germanophobic myth" among the gullible:

They like to conjure an image of goose-stepping legions, responding to the tense commands of an Erich von Stroheim sort of Prussian officer: U-boats sinking passenger vessels without warning and dive bombers strafing civilians. The sinister element in the United States, so zealously seeking to undermine confidence in the present German Federal Republic, is using all manner of propaganda to further the aims of the Soviet Union.[111]

Delaney had branded the Morganthau Plan, devised by Secretary of the Treasury Henry Morganthau and his assistant, "the Communist Harry Dexter White," as a plan of genocide. This scheme, initiated by FDR and Churchill on October 15, 1944, in Quebec, was designed to close down the industries of the Saar and Ruhr and to convert Germany into basically an agricultural nation. Had it succeeded, pontificated Delaney, this Red stratagem would have eliminated 30 million Germans through starvation and brought the survivors to bolshevism. To further Morganthau's scheme, Secretary of State Dean Acheson had established a Department of Public Affairs in West Germany to infect Germans with pro-Communist ideology. Its literature assailed "McCarthyism" and "all those people who believed that the House Un-American Activities Committee is rendering a service to our country." Delaney praised the Wisconsin senator and publicly criticized the de-Nazification "kangaroo courts" in Europe, egged on by "vindicative minorities" in the United States.[112]

Radio Free Europe, wrote Delaney, continually spread Communist ideology drafted by State Department operatives and subsidized by U.S. taxpayers. It was Delaney's contention that the Korean War had not been directed by the Commander-in-Chief and the Pentagon, but rather a Kremlin-controlled United Nations. Because General Douglas MacArthur stubbornly refused to be deceived by the Acheson-Marshall-Truman faction then seeking to placate Communist China, he had been dismissed from his command. Not only had Dwight Eisenhower refused to recompense all those despoiled by "Bolshevik bandits" in Europe, but the president blocked every effort by McCarthy to investigate Soviet influence in the Washington bureaucracy.[113]

The recurring themes of appeasement and betrayal of national interests continued in Delaney's writings when applied to the administrations of John F. Kennedy and Lyndon Johnson. Soviet apologists Secretary of State Dean Rusk and Walt Rostow, chairman of the State Department Policy Planning Board, had undermined the resolve of Kennedy and Johnson to face the enemy. Johnson's refusal to blockade or mine Haiphong Harbor in North Vietnam infuriated Delaney.[114]

On the evening of July 1, 1972, this 86-year-old gadfly was fatally struck by an automobile in downtown Glendale, California. Even at his advanced age, Delaney had been serving both as a reporter for the Montrose *Ledger*, the weekly of a Glendale suburb, and moderator for radio station KWKW in Pasadena. His death certificate listed him as "DOA" at the city hospital. The same document also showed this lifelong bachelor to have been without surviving kin. It is ironic that Delaney's old nemesis, the FBI, overlooked his passing in its files, and that only his brief association with Hitler's Propaganda Ministry rescued an otherwise checkered career from obscurity.[115]

2

Jane Anderson, Alias the Georgia Peach

Four American women emerged from World War II charged with treason. Two of these women, Mildred Gillars (Axis Sally) and Iva Toguri (Tokyo Rose), were convicted of collaboration with the Axis powers. The indictment against a third defendant, Constance Drexel, was dropped because of insufficient evidence, and the presumption of Atlanta-born Jane Anderson's wartime death negated the fourth's trial.

For nearly four decades journalists and historians have searched for common traits that compelled a few Americans to denounce their homeland in broadcasts over Hitler's shortwave network. Their interpretations have ranged from character weaknesses to the wayward expatriates' inability to reintegrate themselves into a more complex American society. The unique case of Jane Anderson afforded these commentators a different perspective, for her drive for international recognition and social respectability brought her to the brink of treason.

For a quarter of a century Jane Anderson enjoyed a measure of success unfamiliar to many of her fellow broadcasters in the Reichrundfunk's U.S.A. Zone. Anderson had overcome a difficult youth and the prejudices of a male-dominated professional world to become an accomplished feature writer, a foreign correspondent, and the *persona grata* of many distinguished literary and political figures internationally. Who could have guessed that this beautiful redhead from Atlanta would end her career in the spring of 1941 as a Nazi propagandist?

The only child of Robert M. and Ellen Luckie Anderson, Jane was born as Foster Anderson on January 6, 1893. She inherited the Christian name

This Chapter has been adapted with permission from John Carver Edwards, "Atlanta's Prodigal Daughter: The Turbulent Life of Jane Anderson as Expatriate and Nazi Propagandist," *The Atlanta Historical Journal* 28, no. 2 (Summer 1984): 23–42.

of her wealthy and socially correct maternal grandfather, Foster Luckie. Jane's mother, Ellen Luckie, enjoyed access to many of Atlanta's most exclusive circles. The clan's community standing is traced to patriarch Alexander F. Luckie, a pioneer in the city's development. Luckie had moved to Atlanta from Newton County in 1847, having already served his state in the General Assembly. A successful farmer and landowner, the elder Luckie was also a prominent lay worker in the Presbyterian Church. Today, Luckie Street, which meanders down past the Georgia Tech campus and terminates in the heart of the city, memorializes this family's contribution to the area.[1]

For unknown reasons, Robert M. "Red" Anderson departed for the Southwest soon after his daughter's birth. In time, Red Anderson became an Arizona marshal during territorial days. He briefly acted as chief of police under General George W. Goethels during the construction of the Panama Canal, and eventually he returned to his adopted state as sheriff of Yuma. Fragmentary documentation of Anderson's life for this period is replete with brawls—official and personal—and bloody confrontations with outlaws and unruly Apaches. This remarkable frontier lawman made a lasting impression on one of his daughter's suitors:

The most unforgettable character I know was Red Anderson. When I first met him he was seventy-eight. His breakfast consisted of a bottle of whiskey and a 2 lb. steak. Anderson had been an associate of Buffalo Bill [Cody]. . . . He once showed me his revolver, which had twenty-eight notches, and told me they represented the criminals he had killed, not including the Mexicans. At seventy-eight he had a mistress, a woman of not more than thirty-five, who was in love with him.[2]

When Red left Atlanta, Ellen Luckie Anderson chose to stay behind with her relatives. Apparently, the couple never reunited. When Jane was only ten years old, her mother died and the family decided that she would live with her grandmother in Demorest, Georgia, where she spent her remaining childhood. She attended nearby Piedmont College with fellow student Meiling Soong, later to become Madame Chiang Kai-shek. One suspects that Georgia's hill country held little charm for the teenager, who then elected to join her father in Yuma, Arizona.[3]

Lonely and isolated, Jane found herself in the care of a Mexican housekeeper while waiting for "Daddy Bob's" boisterous homecomings to dispel temporarily the tedium of her life. The solitude helped young Anderson to develop a promising new talent as a writer in Arizona. Soon she dropped the name of Foster for the byline "By Jane Anderson." Red Anderson sent his daughter to Kidd-Key College in Sherman, Texas, for a period; and although Jane accrued too few credits to graduate, the coed posted good grades in French, music, and English literature.[4]

After college, Jane surprised her Luckie kin by returning to Georgia to visit her mother's grave in Atlanta's Rock Springs Cemetery. She refused all invitations to stay longer. Jane was headed to New York to find a publisher for her western fiction. She soon lost hope of ever publishing her work. While in New York she married the world-famous musicologist Deems Taylor and found artistic expression through short stories and a limited newspaper career.[5]

Apparently Anderson's marriage quickly soured, because in the spring of 1915 the Georgian fled New York City for London. There she joined the staff of Lord Northcliffe's London *Daily Mail* and soon won her stripes as a daring war correspondent. In a time when the public regarded flight as a novelty, Anderson broke convention by flying the English Channel and looping-the-loop over Hyde Park, then reporting on the experience:

I was up in some new world, where blue immensity had substance, where men in machines of their own making set themselves in defiance of all laws of space, and time, and proportion. . . . I do not under-estimate this privilege; I do not under-value it. I am the first woman to make a flight across London, in one of His Majesty's war machines.[6]

When a Zeppelin raid over London killed scores of wartime citizens, Anderson was first on the scene in a taxi. Later, as news reached her that one of the raiders had been downed with its dead and dying crew strewn over a suburban pasture, she sped to the crash site, disguised herself as a nurse, and cleverly penetrated a military cordon for the story. Novelist and critic Rebecca West recalled her first encounter with Jane Anderson:

I was friendly with her as one was friendly with journalists one comes across. I was once sent over on some assignment with her to an ammunitions factory that worked all night and occasionally the night bombers would find it. It was frightfully unsafe and I complained because we were taken round by an official who was obviously drunk.[7]

In France, Anderson relayed back coverage of the campaigns on the western front for both the *Daily Mail* and the *Daily Express*, and she shunned advice that she remain behind in the staging areas. Living in the lice-infested bunkers, she risked her life to German and Allied bombardment and interviewed desperate soldiers on both sides.[8]

As soon as time permitted, Anderson cajoled Northcliffe into providing her with letters of introduction to two of England's most celebrated literary figures, H. G. Wells and Joseph Conrad. After Wells rebuffed her initial overture, she begged him to reconsider: "Somehow everything seems to work out in a very contrary sort of way for me in this country. Nothing is as I expected it to be. And I do all of the small things backward. I have not mastered the minor courtesies and learn with horror the enormity of my [social] omissions."[9] The Georgian eventually got her audience and gained admittance into the noted author's elite circle as an entertaining, if somewhat

undistinguished, member. Sixty-eight years after Anderson's arrival in England, Dame Rebecca West spoke for the Wells coterie, when she summarized
her impression of the woman: "We [Wells and West] rather liked her, and I
do not think she knew one belligerent side from another. . . . I may be prejudiced . . . but I really think she was far too simple-minded to be taken as a
serious interviewer in the war."[10]

Although Jane Anderson's initial attempts to meet Conrad also failed, she
did gain entrance to the Conrad household through a friendship with a
doughboy who had generously carried a message to the elder Conrad son in
France. In return for the favor, the soldier was invited to lunch at Capel
House. From then on, Anderson was a constant guest,[11] and in August 1916
Conrad wrote a friend:

We made the acquaintance of a new young woman. She comes from Arizona and
(strange to say!) she has a European mind. She is seeking to get herself adopted as
our big daughter and is succeeding fairly. To put it shortly, she's quite yum-yum.
But those matters can't interest a man of your austere character. So I hasten away
from these petty frivolities.[12]

Certainly the frivolities at Capel House were many. Mrs. Conrad (Jessie)
caught their spirit in her *Memoirs*:

One Sunday Miss Anderson was staying with us and a French Red Cross Officer
and his wife came down to lunch. Our American friend was at once aware of the
Frenchman's interest—and incidentally so was his wife. Miss Anderson seated herself
before the fire like an idol. M. Paul Vance immediately seized a pair of tall vases full
of flowers and solemnly placed them before the figure on the rug, making at the same
time a deep obeisance. There was a sniff of disgust on the part of the wife and a
rather vexed laugh from Joseph Conrad, who at once held out his hand to assist his
guest to rise, and upset both the vases in the process.[13]

Robin Douglas, son of Norman Douglas, writer-friend of Conrad, recalled
how Anderson captivated him and the Conrad children when he was a youth:

It may have been her exploits in the air that thrilled our imagination; it may have
been her American accent that intrigued us; it may have been that we fell in love
with her even. . . . After tea we went into the drawing-room, where the "American
flying girl" played and sang Negro songs of the cotton fields and plantations. Conrad
listened, spellbound by the plaintive melodies of the South. . . . She arrived, she was
enchanting, she went away.[14]

Twelve-year-old John Conrad did not conceal his boyish fascination for the
Georgia beauty. During a casual bicycle outing with Jane, an unexpected
gust of wind gave him the opportunity to compliment his companion on her
attractive legs. When Anderson laughingly reported John's remark to her
host, Conrad expressed satisfaction in his son's powers of observation.[15]

Anderson's role in the Conrad household proved perplexing to guests. In one instance correspondent George Seldes came to interview Conrad about submarine warfare and was unsure of Jane's position:

I do remember being stunned by that glorious person Jane Anderson, and I remember Conrad introducing her either as his "ward" or his "protegee." I did not suspect that Jane was Conrad's mistress—if she was it was certainly a menage à trois, because I was also introduced to Mrs. Conrad at the time.[16]

Anderson returned to France on assignment, and the 58-year-old Conrad was ordered to the English east coast to inspect naval stations. The British War Office was in hopes that the author's tour of duty would result in effective Allied propaganda. In September of 1916, Jane Anderson returned from France to Capel House as an invalid—her health undermined by the western front. Jessie referred to her new charge as an "interesting invalid." Despite Jane's transparent designs, Jessie appreciated the younger woman's seeming concern for her elder son, Borys, and even grew to enjoy the American's presence while Conrad was on duty.[17] For his part, Conrad expected the two women to maintain an amiable relationship. During this period Conrad wrote his wife concerning Anderson's deteriorating relationship with Lord Northcliffe:

I fancy she feels her position to be not without danger (of a shake up) and would be perhaps glad to know (or to feel) that you, I mean *you* personally as a woman (as distinct from *us*) would be likely to stand by her. I was very reserved on these matters generally.[18]

Two weeks later Conrad informed his spouse that the threat to Jane had evaporated:

Had a letter from your pair-mate about N'cliffe. N. had obviously cooled down a lot. Letter curiously indefinite but I seem to see that N. has found some new American wonder. Just what I expected. . . . The dear Chestnut filly is obviously putout. Am trusting to the dearest dark brown mare to steady that youngster in her traces. See?[19]

In late September Anderson suddenly announced to Jessie that Conrad loved her alone and that he had sent her a passionate note to that effect. Perhaps Jessie believed her rude guest, since she had not received the accustomed stream of notes and telegrams from her husband. She was unaware that Anderson had been intercepting Conrad's correspondence. On assignment, Conrad had undertaken a risky aerial patrol over the North Sea after which Jessie met him for a holiday. She was greeted with the question, "Where is your stable companion?" meaning, of course, Jane. By this time Jessie had pieced together Anderson's malicious designs:

The seriousness of that deliberate attempt to spoil our long understanding affection had probably never struck her and more than likely would not have troubled her if it had. Something of this I made Joseph Conrad understand before we reached the hotel. I was not present when the first interview took place, but I gathered that it had been more than a little stormy. We stayed two days longer at Folkestone and when we left our lady friend elected to return to town.[20]

Back in town, the redhead collected another gentleman friend, Joseph Hieronymous Retinger, and departed for France where, "deprived of the father, she sought the son." Borys Conrad subsequently recorded an account of this interlude in a book on his father:

I took her to dine at one of the fashionable restaurants and quickly discovered that she appeared to be upon friendly terms with most of the clientele, the majority of whom seemed to be high ranking British and French officers. Moreover, she was clearly a valued patron of the establishment and somewhat to my embarrassment, we were escorted with great ceremony right across the room by the maitre d' hotel to what proved to be her favorite table.[21]

The remainder of the evening was spent nursing a jealous Retinger, who had conveniently taken ill.[22] This noble deed prompted Borys' arrest for unexcused leave by an unsympathetic provost marshal. After arranging Borys' release, Jane treated her guest to a full day of sightseeing in Paris. Back with his unit, Borys wrote his father about the episode. In a letter to his agent, Joseph Conrad confided, "If he [Borys] must meet a 'Jane,' it's better he should meet her at nineteen than at twenty-four. Or, one might add, at fifty-nine."[23] Many contemporary scholars agree that Jane Anderson became part heroine as Rita de Lastaola in one of Conrad's last novels, *The Arrow of Gold*.[24]

Doubtless, Jane Anderson's affairs came to the notice of the Allies. It was rumored that the Georgian had been the mistress of powerful diplomats in the British Foreign Office and the Quai d'Orsay. Because of her flamboyance and personal indiscretions, she had become a potential liability to those in high places. An FBI background study would reveal in 1942:

In 1917 Anderson had a suite at the Hotel Crillon in Paris. Close relations with both Japanese and Italian ambassadors. Lunched with people like Mandel, Phipps—then Counselor of the British Embassy—Atholston Johnson, First Secretary of the British Embassy, generals and other officials in high places. During a long and violent "battle" in Paris for the Unified Allied Command, Jane Anderson was immersed in the intrigues which developed from the rivalries of certain British generals and the War Office. . . . In Paris, Jane Anderson had no reputation of promiscuity, but was not a woman of entirely rigid virtue.

Whether or not Northcliffe's "bon vivant" left for the United States in the spring of 1918 of her own volition or whether she was encouraged to leave is still a mystery. Gilbert Seldes, the brother of correspondent George Seldes, was working for Great Britain's Ledger Syndicate when he met Anderson on board a liner bound for the United States. During a whirlwind romance, Seldes proposed marriage, but she still was not available, since her divorce from Deems Taylor was not final.[25]

Soon after the ship docked, Anderson visited an old classmate from Kidd-Key College, Kitty Barry Crawford, who was about to enter a tubercular hospital in Denver, Colorado. Anderson enjoyed her return to the West. She needed tranquil surroundings in which to complete several writing assignments, so she convinced Crawford to share expenses for a cabin called Watson Lodge on Cheyenne Mountain near Colorado Springs. Scarcely had they occupied the place than Anderson sent for Gilbert Seldes. When this arrangement became awkward, Anderson invited Crawford's friend, Katherine Anne Porter, to balance out the group.[26] Crawford's letters to Porter had frequently touched on Anderson's European exploits, so Porter seized this opportunity to meet her. Porter's arrival at the lodge was a supreme disappointment to her, however, for neither Anderson nor Seldes preferred her companionship, their superciliousness stemming from Porter's limited travel and inexperience as a writer.

In turn, both Crawford and Porter were alarmed by Jane Anderson's outlandish behavior. The Georgian's hyperactivity grated on the nerves of those around her. She seemed to be forever on the road to Denver and dashing off to such distant points as Los Angeles and San Francisco. (She had resolved to become an actress.) The mailman and special messengers flooded the retreat with an avalanche of communications, and Anderson—far too nervous to work—monopolized the telephone, Seldes' attention, and the sanctuary's stock of liquor. The barbiturates she took each night to escape this frenetic state usually kept her sedated well into the following day. Porter tolerated the name-dropping and the incessant commentary about Hollywood, but she grew to dislike Anderson's belittlement of everything American. When Anderson refused to pay her share of the household expenses, the relationship snapped, and Kitty Crawford fled to a nearby hotel for several weeks. The hapless Porter, with nowhere to go, remained behind until Anderson and company departed and her friend Kitty returned to complete the vacation. Neither woman ever met Anderson again, although both were destined to become contenders for the affection of Joseph Retinger. Porter's authorized biographer insists that despite this bitter rivalry, the writer's lifelong fascination for Jane Anderson would ultimately evoke the character of La Condesa in *Ship of Fools*.[27]

Little documentary information has survived on Anderson's life during the 1920s. It is known that she took an apartment in New York City and that she continued to toy with the emotions of her many suitors. Her flat became a place of political and social ferment. Retinger infected her with his hatred of the Bolsheviks during America's Red Scare hysteria, and for months the two plotted the assassination of Lenin, a fantastic scheme that Anderson defended as both "simple and workable." The couple's spirits were temporarily buoyed by the Baroness Souiny, an acquaintance of Retinger, who presented the conspirators with correspondence reputedly from the hand of Princess Anastasia.[28] In the end Retinger's association with Anderson cost him a marriage, his friendship with Joseph Conrad, and eventually his health. His letters hinted at suicide as early as 1917, and Gilbert Seldes was even clearer about the Pole's intentions: "Retinger was ill—dark and gaunt—carried amyl nitrate capsules for a heart condition. . . . At one time during his stay in New York he took an overdose of sleeping pills, but we saved him." Retinger dogged Anderson's life until she summoned her 78-year-old father to the rescue. The confrontation occurred at the LaFayette Hotel in Washington, D.C., where "Daddy Bob" discouraged his daughter's pursuer by drawing his revolver and threatening to cool Retinger's ardor permanently. Seldes also found himself no longer a viable contestant for the redhead's affection. "By the time Jane got involved in American politics, we were both aware of having drifted apart," he noted in an unpublished memoir. Anderson's momentary political and personal interests were directed toward the Democratic National Convention of 1920 and a former campaign manager for Woodrow Wilson, William F. McCombs. In due course she abandoned politics and returned to Texas for an affair with a favorite son. "I had met Austin—a lineal descendant of the Texas hero [Stephen] Austin—with Jane sometime before," Seldes recorded. "He had been in love with her and was tragically unhappy."[29]

During the remainder of the U.S. stay, Jane Anderson slipped into relative obscurity. Her work for *Harper's*, *Collier's*, *Century*, and other publications eventually took her to some 20 European countries, and in 1922 she covered the Washington Naval Conference. In the spring of 1923 Anderson was in Warsaw claiming to represent the U.S. firm of Wilson and Colby and requesting the aid of the legation there in negotiating with the Polish government. She stated that if the Poles would grant oil concessions in Eastern Galicia to a group allegedly represented by Colby, it would be possible to stop the ongoing Ukrainian agitation. Polish intransigence, however, would result in increased tensions in the area, she warned. Anderson alternately cajoled and threatened staff officers unless her demands were met. She said that she was preparing an extensive publicity campaign for the Hearst Newspaper Service, and that her findings could adversely affect the careers of certain foreign service personnel. When contacted by the U.S. government, the firm of Wilson and Colby denied any knowledge of Anderson's scheme; nor did the partners know her personally. As she criss-crossed the Atlantic during the hectic period, she abruptly surfaced in a nostalgic letter to H. G. Wells in the fall of 1932:

Yes, I'm back here again. Like Lazarus. Do you remember the day in my flat on Duchess Street, when you turned over an aeroplane for me? It's only a few centuries ago. I've never forgotten. . . . I would be so happy if you would write to me, H. G. It's all the more important because Northcliffe and Conrad are not here with us any more. They were for me, the two others whose opinion mattered.

Anderson confided that she had been living in the French underground for three years gathering information for a book on the Parisian street people to be entitled *Courtisane*, and she coyly requested Wells' criticisms.[30] On April 8, 1933, Anderson thanked her adopted mentor for his benign review, which had "worked magic for her fingers," and reported that she already had 30,000 words in the hands of a publishing house despite reservations about her own worth as a writer. As with so many other projects in her life, the book was never completed.

About this time Jane became engaged to a Spanish nobleman, the Marquis Alvarez de Cienfuegos, whom she had recently met at a U.S. embassy reception in Paris. She described her new love to Wells:

Maybe, H. G. you'll like the Marquis. He has an infallible perception of the beauty of the written word and stands in awe of your work. Not that he will bother you with his interpretations. He smokes his cigars, makes millions of francs, and doesn't trouble much about abstractions. Nevertheless, his handsome surfaces match up very well with his soul, and he's anchored me down to reality with about as much finality as if he'd pinned a mountain onto the sailing string of a kite.[31]

The marquis returned with his new fiancée to Spain, to the Cienfuegos dynasty, and to a royal wedding in the ancient Cathedral of Seville. When her name was entered on the church records that day, she had become Juana de la Santísima Trinidad. It seemed that the marquesa would live out her days on a grand scale far from personal danger, but events proved otherwise.

When Francisco Franco's Nationalist forces poured into the Iberian Peninsula from Moroccan bases on July 18, 1936, driving north toward Madrid, Fascist and Communist proxies intervened to foster and repel, respectively, the Generalissimo's adventure. Spain's upheaval seized Anderson's imagination. She argued that the Spanish House of Parliament was packed with Reds bent on establishing their own dictatorship and resolved to draw world attention to the country's trial. A cable to the *Daily Mail* brought an appreciative response; and the marquesa immediately set aside her titled responsibilities to return to the life of a war correspondent, filing dispatches once again for Northcliffe's paper.[32]

As in the Great War, Anderson headed for the battlefront and took her stories under fire. To the amazement of all, this middle-aged woman endured the hardships of Franco's soldiers and kept pace with the march. She adroitly publicized the atrocities of the anti-Franco Loyalist troops—of seeing defenseless prisoners brutally slaughtered, of rapes and crucifixions, and of unspeakable excesses against the church.[33]

Government forces captured Jane Anderson in September, dispatching her to Madrid for trial on a charge of espionage. The "Midnight Tribunal of Twelve" grilled Anderson for hours before rendering a guilty verdict. The members fell into disagreement, however, over her execution date. During the next six weeks the Georgian resided in three of Madrid's most notorious political prisons awaiting death. Her final stop was Madrid's Plaza Torena, where the cloistered courtyard served as a firing squad and where she was made to witness mass executions. The period that she spent in captivity crippled her both mentally and emotionally. The guards subjected the marquesa to blinding lights around the clock, a daily meal of stale rice, and exposure to voracious rats. Packed into a former convent with 1,000 other women where only 28 nuns had lived before, Anderson once witnessed birth and death side by side in unimaginable squalor. "I met more ladies of Spanish royalty there than I ever did outside the prison," Jane reported in later months.

I was horrified to see a weak old woman on her hands and knees trying to scrub the floor. . . . Later I discovered she was a very dear friend of mine, the Duchess of Victoria—but their tortures had so changed and aged her that I had not known her. She was in captivity with her fifteen-year-old daughter and both of them spent days wearing torture bracelets—great bands of steel, three feet long, that were locked over the arms and thighs, and that had sharp steel points inside the extremities.[34]

Finally, Anderson's ordeal ended as abruptly as it began. A secret message sent via a released prisoner to the U.S. consular staff had its effect, and on October 10, 1936, the State Department announced that the Loyalists would free Anderson on condition that she leave Spain immediately. Nearly three decades after her release, correspondent/historian William G. Schofield wrote about the awful change in Jane Anderson's psyche: "She had entered prison as one of the beautiful women of Spain. When she came out she was haggard from scurvy and badly scarred by rat-bite. Her face was deeply lined. Her eyes carried a gleam that was near insanity and near terror, and that stayed with her for weeks."[35] Back in France and reunited with her husband, who bided his time in Cuba during her imprisonment, Franco's champion initiated a full-scale propaganda campaign against her former jailers. Anderson warned of the menace of communism in global terms, and eager publishers on both sides of the Channel paid well for the marquesa's wartime experiences.[36]

Accompanied by the marquis, Jane came to Washington, D.C., in late September 1937 at the behest of Monsignor Fulton J. Sheen to address an important Catholic convention. "I bring you," she told the delegates, "a message from your sisters in Spain, from more than 1,000 women I left behind prison walls, that you might arm yourselves, that you might be vigilant, for war is being waged against you. I hope I am in time to warn you. I hope I shall not see Catholic dead in the streets of Washington."[37] She informed a meeting of Catholic businesswomen that radicals in the

United States kept a blacklist on religious and political leaders active against subversives at home and abroad. According to Anderson, Monsignor Sheen topped the list as "the world's authority on the technics of communism." The speaker begged her audience to oppose worldwide bolshevism and added, "If communism is not stopped in Spain, it will sweep the world." Without mentioning fascism, the marquesa decried the emphasis upon danger of a Fascist America, saying, "There should be less talk about hypothetical dictatorial sabers; we must drive out the real enemy—the enemy from within." In Berlin, Propaganda Minister Josef Goebbels noted in his diary, "Anderson's statements in New York are still the big sensation."[38]

Anderson apparently succeeded in beguiling a few powerful Catholic spokesmen. *Catholic Digest* proclaimed her "the world's greatest woman orator in the fight against communism." *Time* magazine quoted American University's Monsignor Sheen as calling her "one of the living martyrs."[39] But what about those who knew her best? A classmate crossed the marquesa's path in New York City on her 1938 U.S. tour and reported to Kitty Crawford. Crawford subsequently wrote Katherine Anne Porter of her friend's dismal impressions:

One of the old Kidd-Key girls saw her [Anderson] in New York . . . said that Jane was big and fat and pop-eyed like Elsa Maxwell . . . that she had degenerated into a cold, soulless creature completely without feeling or consideration for others. It was very evident that she used drugs. How supremely awful![40]

Jane's pro-Franco ministry brought her into contact with an ultra-conservative New Yorker, Merwin K. Hart, founder of the New York State Economic Council, an anti–New Deal fraternity opposed to all Rooseveltian social legislation. Hart's anger over the administration's coolness toward Franco's military fortunes, likewise, prompted him to create the American Union for Nationalist Spain, a political action group attractive to Anderson and many other Clerical Fascists. Following a well-publicized tour of the Spanish front, Hart returned home to defend the Caudillo's revolution at heroic lengths, even denying that the bombing of Guernica and the massacre at Badajoz had ever happened. As part of this campaign, he offered Anderson's services to the Falangist propaganda office after her declaration before an Economic Council meeting that "America is morally and mentally ripe for a revolution." On November 15, 1938, the chief of the Spanish Ministry of Propaganda, José de la Opincina, eagerly agreed to show the Georgian around his department in appreciation for Hart's good offices. After three years in exile, the marquesa had returned to a more congenial Spain.[41]

Two years passed before Anderson's propaganda work for Franco caught Berlin's eye; but in the winter of 1940–41, the Reichrundfunk invited her to join its U.S.A. Zone. Radio Berlin first aired the "Georgia Peach" on April

14, 1941. She was billed as a world-famous Catholic lecturer whose martyrdom in the cause of Fascist Spain had been trumpeted by the Archbishop of Washington, D.C. Goebbels discussed policy with Anderson on May 10 and resolved, "We must grab America by the horns now. There is no point in treading gently any more." Jane strove hard to merit the Propaganda Ministry's image. She ridiculed the RAF's empty claim of having pulverized the broadcasting station where she debuted. Following her maiden transmission, Anderson dramatically prayed at a nearby cathedral for the Fatherland "and a world freed of Mammon." In the next week's show Anderson described to her American audience the "dynamic life of the Reich" that she experienced in Berlin's streets. She noted the city's astonishing lack of air-raid damage and her splendid hotel with its banqueting halls and orchestra. The Georgian praised Hitler as Germany's great unifying agent and compared him to Moses, declaring that he would "go forth from triumph to triumph, from strength to strength." "He had reached to the stars," she trilled, "and the Lord's will would prevail."[42]

The need for a distinctive radio identity persuaded Anderson to draw upon her role as a nurse to Franco's army. Customarily, the marquesa came to the shortwave station in her Spanish Red Cross uniform with its heavy navy blue cape and basque beret. On special days, however, she appeared in a black tailormade suit from Fifth Avenue, wearing some of her high Falange decorations "for saving thousands of lives from Bolshevik terrors." The Georgia Peach's program began and ended with a ridiculous slogan for Kellogg's Corn Flakes, "Always remember progressive Americans eat Kellogg's Corn Flakes and listen to both sides of the story." The tune of "Scatterbrain" provided background music for the segment.[43]

With Hitler's military and diplomatic adventures at high tide in the fall of 1941, and with German-American relations at their lowest ebb, Anderson embarrassed her government by continuing to espouse the Reichrundfunk's already shopworn themes. From the ministry's repertoire of approved topics Jane stressed several categories: Germany's moral and financial support of Roman Catholicism, the country's ability to wage an international war while sufficiently providing for its citizenry, and the Fuhrer's crusade against world communism. In her first broadcast she compared Germany's commitment to the faith with that of the United States: "Germany gives the Church the strength of her sword, the weight of her wealth, and the protection of her law. In America the church is maintained by fortuitous collections."[44] On October 24, 1941, Anderson motored to the Rhineland for the inauguration of the Archbishop of Paderbern. At the end of his interview with the marquesa, the archbishop added, "I have come from the battlefield to serve the will of the Lord. I speak to you of our soldiers and I am proud to have been on the battlefield. I pay my tribute as a servant of God to the soldiers for they are the soldiers of the Cross." Anderson signed off with the observation that the archbishop "wore the Iron Cross under his robes."[45] She insisted that U.S. troops in Britain had been stationed throughout Northern Ireland at Stalin's direction to crush the Catholic faith: "Though it was the smallest of the Catholic citadels, Eire was called upon to withstand the might of the united Anglo-Saxon world, which would never break its spirit."[46] Time and again she resurrected painful memories of Loyalist prisons as evidence of her opposition to communism:

I left a prison in Madrid to enter the world of liberty. I vowed to dedicate my life to the consecration of the New Order—the gateway by which poverty and suffering would be obliterated. That concept was to dominate not only my thoughts but also my deeds. Men should no longer be permitted to perish under capitalism and communism but come into their heritage.[47]

From her Zeesen broadcasting studio on the outskirts of Berlin, she blasted the U.S. press: "In a communist prison, I was told that U.S. citizens are prisoners of their Press, and I had not been 24 hours on American soil before I verified the truth of this statement. Behind every editor was a key man to kill the story of Spain. . . . America was a ship of rats."[48]

Interviews became a specialty with Jane Anderson, and no doubt she hosted more talk shows than any of her fellow commentators. On August 8, 1941, she profiled a Spanish general of the Blue Division, who grieved over the inability of Hispanics in the Western Hemisphere to participate in Hitler's anti-Communist crusade.[49] Next came the outraged wife of the former German consul-general to Iceland, who suffered imprisonment in British jails before repatriation.[50] When a delegation of Latvian women dramatized Soviet atrocities in their homeland prior to German reoccupation, Anderson petitioned Roosevelt to curb the savage instincts of his Soviet ally.[51] Her most prestigious interview occurred on November 21, 1941, when William Joyce, alias Lord Haw-Haw, agreed to sit for questions. Perhaps Anderson's undisguised awe of the Englishman and the pomposity of their dialogue afforded an amusing interlude for her audience: "Lord Haw-Haw's words carry more weight than those of many an obsolete statesman hastening the doom of the British Empire, to say naught of the pallid proclamations of phantom kings and queens languishing in the glacial shades of Westminister." She asked Joyce why he had always shunned publicity, to which Haw-Haw replied, "I believe in the German proverb, the strongest man is strongest alone." The two pictured the horrors of democracy and reminisced about their respective "narrow escapes" in the cause of national socialism. Said Anderson, "Every time I took the platform in the U.S.A. I thought it would be the last. So many death threats rained on one." Joyce answered:

I lived for months with friends who loved England and could not get enough to eat from her. These men hoped that out of their sacrifice a greater England would be born. Their misery was indescribable when it seemed that all their efforts would be

wiped out by the war. They were benumbed at the thought that there was to be a
conflict between their country and all the beliefs that they had held dear.[52]

The psychological strain from wartime rationing, universal condemnation
of Nazi atrocities, and R.A.F. bombing soon crept into Anderson's broadcasts. British Broadcasting Corporation monitors noticed that her presentations had become wildly denunciatory in tone and far less structured. By
the summer of 1941 their marginal comments frequently contained such
words as "hysterical" and "incoherent." In answer to charges of mass killings
in the Soviet Union she stormed:

The British Press has been full of these lies; of little children having their clothes
torn from their bodies . . . of women being mishandled, and the whole countryside
being devastated. Actually, it was Stalin himself, who started the scorched earth
policy. . . . Soviet infants do not have any clothes, except perhaps a little belly band,
while regarding the virtues of the Soviet ladies—I prefer not to dwell on this subject.[53]

One could hardly believe her claims of "the good life" on the home front
with the Wehrmacht engaged on so many battlefields. "Throughout National
Socialist Germany," she said, "no one, whatever his station of life, had an
empty hearthstone, and no child went hungry this Christmas tide, or was
robbed of the treasures of Santa Claus. This could not be in Russia where
Stalin has killed the Christ in the hearts of the people, nor in . . . the Anglo-
Saxon countries, where, in black tenements that rear their ugly heads to the
stars little children die of hunger because there is no bread."[54]

Anderson became particularly sensitive to personal criticisms that appeared
in the British and U.S. media. The marquesa described English commentators as "marionettes who murmur on with monotonous regularity advancing
fantastic arguments. Pharisees of the airways who regaled the world with
miracles of moralism, but who could not disguise Hitler's amazing victories."
Georgetown University, the National Catholic Welfare Conference, and the
National Convention of Protestants, Catholics, and Jews, Anderson groused,
had warned against the "contaminations contained in the broadcasts which
I am privileged to offer to the American people." The architects of this smear
campaign, she contended, were FDR, "who had chained the Christian forces
in America to the godless hordes of Stalin," and the Archbishop of Canterbury, who secretly prayed for Soviet victory in the East.[55]

Anderson's career as radio traitor ended on the evening of March 6, 1942.
She was the victim of an ill-advised broadcast that infuriated her employers.
The program began innocuously enough with a rehash of her trip to a posh
Berlin theater, where she witnessed newsreels of the torpedoing of U.S.
vessels just outside New York City's harbor. Toward the conclusion of her
program, however, Anderson made a grievous error in judgment. In the
belief that she could embitter her American listeners with news concerning

the delicacies to be found in Germany's fine restaurants and cocktail bars, she reported:

We went into a teashop on the Unter den Linden and found a table. Waitresses went from table to table with silver platters laden with sweets and pastries, and we were served with Turkish cakes with marzipan, of which I am very fond.... My friend ordered great goblets of champagne... and he put in liberal shots of cognac to make it more lively. Sweets and cookies and champagne, not bad![56]

The U.S. Office of War Information turned the tables by rebroadcasting the Georgia Peach's descriptions of lavish Berlin night life back into the Reich in order to anger the average ration-conscious German. The Rundfunk dismissed Anderson's news editors, and she was taken off the air. Its officials expunged every trace of the Georgian from the U.S.A. Zone without explanation, as though they had never known this enigmatic woman.[57] Speculation as to the fate of Jane Anderson covered the spectrum from summary execution to an obscure death during the fall of Berlin, to a Spanish repatriation long before war's end.

Actually, Anderson's indiscretion prompted neither her execution nor her exile, but it did force her "retirement" until June 12, 1944, when she broke her silence with a talk on "America in the hands of the Jews and Bolshevism." On June 19, she announced that she had returned to Germany in the hour of invasion to add the weight of her valor and her international prestige to the world conflict. Anderson summarized the war as a battle between a new world order of social justice and a condemned civilization doomed to death through its own decadence. As the Reich collapsed about them, the Cienfuegoses took flight to Austria, remaining at large for two years before their apprehension at Innsbruck on April 2, 1947. During this time the pair, in the company of a notorious Gestapo agent, tried repeatedly to cross into Switzerland. The marquesa attempted to elude capture by wearing her Spanish Red Cross uniform. Placed under town arrest in Salzburg, the fugitives bided time while the Franco regime engineered their release. On October 27, 1947, the Justice Department publicly declined to prosecute Jane Anderson on the basis of her short-lived involvement with the Nazis, the contents of her broadcasts for that period, and—though not mentioned openly—her Spanish citizenship by way of marriage. Armed with a new passport from Madrid, the marquesa and her playboy husband quietly departed for Spain.[58]

The circumstances that molded Anderson's destiny are evident when one retraces her disjointed life. Bitter memories of her parents' separation in Atlanta, her mother's untimely death, and her lingering sense of childhood displacement and loneliness severed any emotional ties with her native region. Ironically, her southern antecedents awarded the Georgia Peach membership in Europe's smart set, and her cracker provincialism so charmed Joseph Conrad that he captured it in his fiction.

Professionally, Anderson established a satisfactory record as field correspondent for several U.S. and British newspapers, but she was never able to sustain a career or to penetrate the fourth estate's inner circle. When not involved in journalistic endeavors or assorted love affairs, Anderson compensated by attaching herself to the fringes of Europe's world of letters. Unfortunately, once again she lacked the creative genius for success.

Anderson's commitment to nazism came during her marriage into Spanish nobility. Membership in the Cienfuegos dynasty offered her a sense of social position and self-worth she had known second hand from her Luckie forebears. The Georgian's loss of station and inhumane imprisonment at the hands of Spain's leftist government drove her into the employ of Franco and Hitler. In the end, Jane Anderson failed national socialism as she had failed herself in a moment of foolish bravado, nearly at the cost of her own life.

3

Max Otto Koischwitz, Alias Mr. O.K.

Months after the guns of World War II went silent and the transmissions of
Radio Berlin had ceased, charged memories remained in the United States
of those turncoat Americans who carried Hitler's argument over the airways.
To be sure, the U.S.A. Zone's audience was always small and those who
tuned in did so mainly for the purpose of amusement rather than inspiration;
the broadcasts of Max Otto Koischwitz, alias Dr. Anders, alias "Mr. O.K.,"
discoursed with professional authority on such topics as literature, music,
drama, philosophy, and geopolitics. His appeal was directed to America's
college youth and the highly literate German-Americans who, his superiors
believed, might be susceptible to the views of national socialism.

Born on February 19, 1902, in the small Silesian hamlet of Jauer, this
son of a prominent physician spent much of his time in the nearby moun-
tains he grew to love so much. Books were the boy's passion as well, and
this combination of dedicated study and solitary retreats into the nearby
hills inculcated in young Otto a penchant for mysticism and metaphysical
thought rare for his tender years. Patriotism and hero worship were also
key ingredients in Otto's character. How he admired those renowned war-
riors and philosophers who had borne the Fatherland's arms and had de-
fined the German psyche. His grandfather fought against France in the
Franco-Prussian War; his great-grandfather, against Napoleon; his own father and brothers would serve the Kaiser and the Third Reich respectively.[1]

Koischwitz's intellectual precocity saw him through the College de Royal
Française in 1920 and the University of Berlin four years later at the ripe

age of 22. The student's competent performance before the state board of examiners, coupled with his excellent dissertation entitled "Der Theaterherald Im Schauspiel Des Millelalters" (published in 1926), won for Koischwitz the admiration of his mentors. Regrettably, as an inexperienced pedagogue in inflation-ravaged Germany, Koischwitz failed in his every attempt to command subsistence wages. For a year he served as an itinerant lecturer at the Ottilienhaus (Girls College) in Berlin for irregular gratuities. Then, in late 1924, Koischwitz immigrated to the United States in pursuit of improved teaching opportunities.[2]

Upon his arrival in New York City, Koischwitz took lodgings at the newly constructed International House on Riverside Drive. Built by John D. Rockefeller, Jr., admission was limited to students—half of whom were foreigners—taking at least eight college credits or devoting equal time to academic research. Perhaps Koischwitz noticed the murals in the main reception room of International House, painted by Arthur B. Davies, depicting the artist's conception of the unity of all peoples. If so, one wonders what thoughts crossed the young German's mind as he paused to study this tribute to America's mass society. In March 1925, when Field Marshal von Hindenburg was running for president in Germany, Koischwitz cabled the candidate—signing it "in the name of all German-Americans"—urging him to withdraw from the race. The election of a military figure and Prussian aristocrat, according to Koischwitz, would cost the German people the sympathy and support of the world.[3]

During the next several years Koischwitz held minor instructorships and substitute posts at Columbia, New York University, and Hunter College. Fortunately, opportunity called on him at International House in late 1926 in the person of Fräulein Margaret Holz, who comprised the entire German Department of Columbia University's experimental Lincoln School. Professor Holz required immediate assistance, and since Koischwitz's obvious erudition and reserved manner belied his 25 years, she hired him on a provisional basis. For the next year Fräulein Holz followed her understudy's work closely, slipping into his classes to monitor his performance, offering advice, and taking a detached pride in his progress.[4]

The Lincoln School was founded in 1917 by Columbia University's General Education Board with Rockefeller funds. A subsidiary of Teachers College's Institute of School Experimentation, its innovative faculty pursued all avenues of pedagogical research. Under the leadership of Dean James Earl Russell, Teachers College sought to adjust outmoded secondary school curricula to the twentieth century. Faculty findings were applied in the Lincoln School. There began an orgy of studies and measurement analyses designed to overturn the timeworn approaches to kindergarten instruction, manual preparation, and textbook selection still in vogue. At intervals these whirligig activities seemed to lack coherence and direction. Readers with burdensome documentation were discarded, while bibliographical aids might carry astronomical numbers of titles. John Dewey's educational precepts dominated the Lincoln School, and its staff soon formulated a new lexicon to properly capture the classroom spontaneity and the myriad acts of instructional improvisation exhibited daily.[5]

Such a provocative environment gave full rein to Koischwitz's creative talents. In his first major publication, "Our Textbooks and Kulturkunde" (1928), he insisted that the pupil must comprehend both the language and literature of a nation, as well as the temper of its people.

It has always been emphasized that Germany is the typically romantic and irrationalistic country. The rationalistic period between 1871 and 1914 particularly is considered less German than the present time or that of the "Goethezeit" (1770–1830). ... Since we now observe a strong reaction against positivism and naturalism in Germany, the naturalistic writers alone do not give the American student the right information about Germany. If more attention were paid to the Neuromantik, the second goal of language teaching would also be much better attained—a Kulturkundliche Kenntnis des Fremdvolkes.

Koischwitz complained that nearly 50 percent of the German textbooks used in the United States were worthless from the standpoint of literary criticism. He wanted obsolete works stricken from publishers' catalogues. Books with historical orientations should be dropped, he insisted; besides, "psychologists of adolescence have come to the conclusion that youth is generally little interested in history at all." Finally, he demanded that texts reflect the true atmosphere of his country, and that the depiction of German fairy tales and legends should be severely limited.[6]

The field of student testing and concomitant modes of evaluation intrigued Koischwitz. As a member of the Institute of School Experimentation, he devised an ingenious examination for a drama course offered by the German Department of Hunter College. Koischwitz's aim was to allow 35 students the broadest exposure to contemporary plays possible, while exploring each participant's background in contemporary literature. He accomplished this feat with the combination and the partial coordination of two different standard questionnaires, one short answer and one essay in nature, that would be applicable to any individual selection of a stated number of plays.[7]

Teaching was Koischwitz's forte, despite his reputation as an indefatigable researcher. According to noted author and educator Louis J. Halle, of the Graduate Institute of International Studies (Geneva), Koischwitz's gemlike lectures refracted the brilliance of the Lincoln School. Hovering about the lectern, Koischwitz must have put young Halle in mind of an absent-minded English schoolmaster. Recalled Halle, "He was of a light and bony build, with dark hair that was long for that day, and a face in which the nose was excessively prominent. He was a man whose mind dwelt always in the empyrean, in a world of epic visions from which the petty practical affairs of our day-to-day world were excluded." The boy soon learned, however, that his mentor scarcely resembled the bumbling pedant so effectively satirized in the works of Charles Dickens. It seemed that Koischwitz's intellectual interests were so catholic and rarified that the instruction of German could not contain them all. In the end, his lectures—interesting as they were—frequently digressed into chaotic musings quite unrelated to the subject at hand. Halle fondly remembered Koischwitz's instruction:

I recall the day when he opened his class by drawing a railway train on the blackboard. On top of one of the cars in the middle was the figure of a man, and exactly opposite him, on the ground beside the tracks, another. He then drew two jagged lines to represent flashes of lightning, one in front of the train and one behind, taking care to make them equidistant from the two men. That done, he explained how, although the flashes appeared to be simultaneous to the man on the ground, the man on the passing railway car saw the one in front first, since he was moving toward it, and the one behind later, since he was moving away from it. So, Miss Holz being out of the room, he introduced us to Einstein's Theory of Relativity. On that day there was born in me a lifelong interest in the structure of the universe that has been one of the forces by which my mind has been shaped.

As for his mastery of Koischwitz's discipline, it was the German examination that he flunked on his College Boards the following summer. Placed a full year behind in his admission to Harvard, Professor Halle steadfastly refused to condemn his old teacher. Half a century later he would write of his setback: "This was the price I paid for what Dr. Koischwitz did teach me, and in the perspective of the years I count it cheap."[8]

As a university student Koischwitz had specialized in medieval German literature. It was from one of his discursive lectures that Halle first heard the names of Walter von der Vogelweide, the prince of minnesingers, and Wolfram von Eschenbach, the author of *Parsifal*. Koischwitz once confided sadly to his charge how, as a student, he had been so smitten with a certain damsel that he had spent a year or more making, with his own hands, an illuminated book of medieval German love poetry—a token of affection to which the lady displayed monumental indifference.[9]

There were other topics to stir impressionable minds. Koischwitz would stand before his students and regale them on such subjects as German mythology and Oswald Spengler's theory that civilizations underwent the same life-histories as organisms. "The tragic Spenglerian vision of human history [*Decline of the West*]," he said, "kept me enthralled throughout my undergraduate years. So it was that I continued to neglect my assignments in order to devote myself to a course of reading that represented the interest in Spengler's vision aroused by Dr. Koischwitz, who may therefore be held to have been responsible for the poor grades I received in college."[10] Decadence could be seen all about the astute observer, suggested Koischwitz, giving life to Spengler's thesis that Western culture, like empires before it, had entered the twilight of its existence. "This impression," observed Professor Halle, "would have had a special poignancy for one whose mind, inhabiting the heroic world of Wolfram's 'Parsifal' or Wagner's 'Gotterdämmerung,' could not altogether exclude an awareness of how different the world immediately about him was." His writings and lectures reflected a romantic's aversion to the rationalistic and skeptical tradition that had held the West too long in its iron grip. As early as the mid–1920s, long before Adolf Hitler's promises to rid the Atlantic democracies of this sickness and return humankind to the heroic days of the *Nibelungenlied*, Koischwitz would refer to the bonds of blood, to that summons from abroad that could not be denied. In so doing, Koischwitz cast his lot against the purveyors of the Victorian era's cold rationalism, whose code of social and intellectual taboos had stymied Western man's creativity for too long.[11]

To be sure, Koischwitz's mind and energies were not always absorbed in metaphysical abstractions. Asked to his teacher's Sunnyside, Long Island, home for Sunday dinner, young Halle saw his academic idol in a domestic setting for the first time. He was introduced to Erna (Bea Keller) Koischwitz, who had been a German governess in New York City before her marriage to the professor, and their three girls, Stella, Helene, and Renate. Frau Koischwitz, a stately woman with prematurely white hair that haloed the face of a girl, made a lasting impression on her guest. It struck Halle that aside from her role as surrogate mother to Koischwitz, "she was the one who attended to such mundane matters as paying the rent." Recalled Halle:

I see ourselves around the dining table in a small room in a suburban box of a house, the three of us plus three small children, one in a high chair. Mrs. Koischwitz was repeatedly going into the kitchen to return and set before us the glory of her cooking. She had constantly to feed the infant in the high chair . . . and to see to it that the rest of us were satisfied. All happy families are alike, according to Tolstoy, and since this was a happy family I need say no more.

Otto's future wife had emigrated to the United States in 1920 after completing commercial courses in Zurich and Florence. From 1920 to 1923, Erna served as a governess to the daughter of a wealthy New York City family. This impressionable young woman met Koischwitz at International House during his residency there, fell in love, and agreed to marry him at a future date. While so employed, she studied accounting at Columbia University. For the next two years Erna was assistant treasurer of the Hartridge School in Plainfield, New Jersey.

After receiving her M.S. degree in 1925, Erna was engaged by the American College for Women at Constantinople, Turkey, to install an accounting system. On completion of this project, she returned to the United States in September of 1926 and wed Otto that winter. In 1929 her husband was diagnosed as having incipient tuberculosis. The father of Erna's former charge as governess agreed to fund Koischwitz's treatment at a nearby sanitorium. This same benefactor would eventually break with his ward over Koischwitz's political conversion.[12]

For the period 1926–28 Koischwitz made ends meet by alternating between his Hunter College instructorship and the Lincoln School. Then, in 1928, he won an assistant professorship on Hunter College's German faculty at $4,000 per annum. Koischwitz elected to retain contact with Columbia's Institute of School Experimental Research, devoting his evenings to work there. Otto Koischwitz quickly earned the respect and affection of his classes. He lectured on the contemporary novel and drama, German literature, and a host of like subjects. These courses were so popular that many outside students filed into the rear of his classes occasionally to listen, and in 1938 he was voted Hunter's most popular instructor. Paradoxically, in regard to his subsequent career, Koischwitz's most celebrated course dealt with the life and works of Thomas Mann, the international literary giant who had been exiled from his homeland by the Nazis.[13]

As far as his students and colleagues could see, this fragile academician, with the hands of a concert pianist and the gentle manner of a parish vicar, showed neither racial prejudice nor hatred for his adopted country. Even after Hitler's takeover in Germany he continued to favor his Jewish students, once unsuccessfully attempting to send abroad a promising Jewish under-study for whom he had obtained a Berlin scholarship. Failure in his mission apparently distressed him far more than it did the young lady. In 1933 he openly denounced national socialism, particularly before his Jewish students. Once he received a circular from a fraternity at the University of Berlin notifying him that its Jewish members were being purged. The entire affair infuriated Koischwitz, particularly when his letter of resignation brought a reply that, as an Aryan, he could not resign. He privately confessed to students and faculty that his father had been a Social Democrat in Germany, and that he therefore feared for his family's well-being.[14] In retrospect, Pro-fessor Halle agrees that Koischwitz could not have been anti-Semitic, for he revered Einstein, nor would he have endorsed Hitler's monstrous blueprints for genocide, which were being drafted at that time. "In any case, his ideal-ism," Halle sadly concludes, "tended to exclude realism. Well before the end . . . the reality must have at last imposed itself on his consciousness. One can only imagine what the terror of it must then have been."[15]

Koischwitz's academic productivity in the areas of instruction, service, and research bore quiet testimony to his industry and dedication. He customarily taught 20 hours each week in both day and evening sessions, and his classes ranged anywhere from 20 to 37 students. When asked by Hunter's admin-istrative bureaucracy for an accounting of his time, Koischwitz scribbled:

I never look at my watch when in conference with students. I never in my life counted the hours that I spent in libraries or at my desk, preparing my lectures, correcting essays, reading books, etc. I may say, however, that practically every hour of the week is devoted to some activity related to my work in college.[16]

The professor's professional membership roster included the Modern Language Association, the American Association of Teachers of German, and the Alumni Association of International House. On campus he spoke for the National Relief Administration, the National Youth Administration, on assorted radio station programs, and frequently before chapel exercises. In addition, he guest lectured before 21 learned societies over a six-year period. During the summer terms of 1929 and 1930, Koischwitz was visiting scholar at the University of Berlin and West Virginia University, respectively. Caught up in committee work, he staged several comedies and a tragedy for the Deutscher Verein. Not content with a director's chair, he even authored a play for his thespian friends. What's more, he served as advisor to the College's textbook committee, to a German student club (Deutsche Warte), and to puzzled students during Hunter's registration process. Koischwitz took special pride in his editorship of Lippincott's German Series and the private publication of his own textbooks, ventures from which he derived modest subsidies.[17]

Koischwitz's imposing publication record did not suggest his junior rank of assistant professor. By age 35 he had published 15 articles in the German Encyclopedia *Sachwoerterbuch der Deutschkunde*, (Leipzig, 1931); five book reviews in academic journals; four articles on the methodology of teaching and one on problems of historiography; a monograph, *Selection and Application of Illustrative Material in Foreign Language Classes* (New York, Columbia University); a pamphlet, *Preparing a German Workbook* (Madison, University of Wisconsin); and a *History of German Literature* (Chicago, Lippincott). His creative writing efforts included the German language readers *Deutsche Fibel* (New York, 1932), *Bilderlesebuch* (New York, 1933), and *Goetter und Riesen* (Middlebury, 1934). Koischwitz's novels included *Ellilenti* (Berlin, 1933) and *Farmer Hildebrand* (Berlin, 1936). The professor's most ambitious efforts included *A German-American Interprets Germany* (Milwaukee, 1935) and *O'Neill* (Berlin, 1938).[18]

Enthusiastic reviews greeted these early contributions, and soon Koischwitz became known in his field. A colleague at Hunter College wrote of his primers:

Anyone that has used Professor Otto Koischwitz' *Fibel* would expect that his new *Bilderlesebuch* would be "O.K." and would not be at all disappointed. . . . Everything that a person visiting Germany for the first time might find interesting or amusing is reproduced for the young student . . . drawn by the author himself with a delightfully modern and humorous touch. . . . The psychology of the German people is made understandable to American students. . . . For example, the hiking trips of the German youth are contrasted with our own predilection for seeing the country from an automobile. . . . Everything is done to give the student the impression that it is fun and not drudgery to read German.[19]

The *German Quarterly* reviewed his *Introduction to Scientific German* in a 1936 issue: "We think the author is on the right path when he develops in a methodical way the understanding of technical material, which has been difficult to teach. His clever pen drawings make the use of the book a pleasure."[20] The following year this same journal acclaimed Koischwitz's *Reise in die Literatur* as "a text startlingly new in conception and brilliant in execution. . . . As the author is one of the most original personalities among the German teachers in our country, this book (a basic history of German literature) will be especially stimulating for Junior Colleges."[21] By 1934 Otto Koischwitz's scholarship had earned for him an international reputation, and still there was no talk of promotion.

The year 1934 marked a tragic watershed in Koischwitz's *Weltanschuuing*. With random exceptions, his vaulted intellectualism had ignored the state-orchestrated paganism that passed as culture in Hitlerite Germany. Following the New Year, however, he lectured less about contemporary German literature and drama and more about Western decadence and the glorious wellsprings of Teutonic civilization. Almost imperceptibly, this rhetoric began to dilute his once balanced lectures. Hunter's master showman intimated that the democracies were corrupt, a condition artistically depicted by George Grosz and exemplified by the "bloodless" rationalism of Bertrand Russell. All this contrasted, of course, with the heroism of Siegfried and the genius of Wagner's operas—a spirit that some Americans professed to see in the Third Reich's new chancellor. It is difficult at this point to determine whether or not Koischwitz had become a Nazi. Without question the romantic trappings of the movement fascinated him. One suspects that the frustration associated with his stagnant career may have driven him to provocative measures. Taking his cue from Spengler, perhaps he came to see himself as the victim of a failed system even as his own country stood on the threshold of greatness.[22]

The Hunter trustees avoided a confrontation with Koischwitz, a decision partially based on the college's devotion to academic freedom and partially in deference to the reputation of German Department chairman Adolf Busse, who some considered a friend of the new Germany. Subsequent investigations revealed that while Koischwitz and the board members were prepared to coexist despite their growing ideological differences, nonetheless both parties were highly suspicious of each other. An undated note in the professor's personnel folder reads:

Question of whether his [Koischwitz's] letter claiming membership in Modern Language Assn. was false as he didn't send in check for years' dues till next day. Had for years been a dues paying member, presented papers. Owing to financial stringency had not sent in check for membership. *Is said to be very distinguished scholar, recommended by Dept. committee for promotion.*[23]

For Koischwitz's part, he maintained that his academic posts in the United States were challenging at best. During several wartime broadcasts from Berlin, he reminisced about those 16 years—memories possibly colored by time and circumstances:

Two years before Hitler came to power I was told that I wouldn't have a chance of a full promotion, because my name sounded Jewish. The faculty included some Jews, but the percentage was kept low by suggesting that they would not be very happy. . . . You talk about equality, but in Lincoln School the quota for Jewish children is strict. . . . The leaders of a nation behave in the way they have been educated. The Universities share the responsibility.[24]

Again he appeared over the airways following a 1943 air bombardment of Cologne:

In 1925, after completing my course at Berlin University, and imbued with ideals of international understanding and brotherly love, I visited the U.S.A. I saw over the main entrance of the Columbia University School of Mining the symbol of the miners chiselled in stone—two crossed hammers and over them a big white blob. A professor told me that the greeting of the German miners, "Gluck auf," meaning "Good luck," was inscribed there, but in 1917 these two words had been erased. This revelation shook my faith in international goodwill . . . If that stone on Columbia's Mining School poisoned my mind seven years after the end of the last conflict, how much hurt will the damage done by the Cologne Cathedral inflict upon those who caused it, and upon their children and children's children.[25]

Although Koischwitz was showing himself to be a likely spokesperson of pan-German sentiment, his position in the classroom went either unnoticed or unchallenged. It was believed generally that he was experiencing an internal struggle involving his intellectuality versus his Germanic origins, and that in the end the baser instinct won.

During the winter of 1933–34 Koischwitz took it upon himself to place the Third Reich within its proper historical and cultural context. He felt that such a scholarly work, written by a hyphenated American, would help to allay misconceptions and distrust engendered on both sides of the Atlantic. College records show that the trustees granted him a year's leave of absence to commence on September 1, 1934, and then abruptly rescinded their position during a May 10 meeting.[26] This reversal did not deter the professor, however, who completed *A German-American Interprets Germany* and had it published by the Gutenberg Publishing Company of Milwaukee, Wisconsin. The author's second disappointment came with the book's poor reception. One of Koischwitz's colleagues in the department, who was of German extraction, branded the work as "one of the most viciously clever pieces of Nazi propaganda circulated in the American classroom."[27] In his forward Koischwitz quotes from the Norwegian writer Knut Hamsun (1934): "Germany is now facing the head wind of the world's criticism, but she is cruising boldly ahead and will reach port. . . . The day will come when nations great and small will change the tone they adopt with regard to this Reich in the heart of Europe. There is no night without dawn."[28] The history of German literature, art, and intellectual trends comprised this controversial effort. No blatant work of propaganda, its author did not offer national socialism as the centerpiece of German history. When nazism was discussed, it was portrayed as one of many cultural movements, with few references to Hitler and his praetorian guard. This treatment carefully interwove Party dogma within the fabric of Germany's religious and political developments over a 200-year span. Nazism constituted a people's movement only recently mobilized to combat longstanding world prejudice and to help realize Germany's world mission.

Since the Germans as well as the Jews are conscious of their outsiderdom, they conceal or deny more readily than others their national origin—to escape the curse of their name. On the other hand, the realization of their fateful and inescapable isolation may be the psychological cause of a fanatical faith in their great historical mission and the eternal stimulus to fight for full and sincere "recognition" and lasting "equal rights" in the community of nations.[29]

In a section on religion Koischwitz cited both Jewish and other German writers as proof of growing anti-Christian sentiment in the Fatherland. The reader was reassured that although the Fuhrer might be indifferent to the Church in principle, nevertheless he would bow to the popular will and institute a state religion bordering on paganism:

In order to understand the religious attitude of National Socialism, it must be borne in mind, that it is determined by a youthful moral fanaticism which rejects the "hypocrisy" of "so-called" Christianity and wants to replace it by a sincerely practicable religion. . . . Good cannot exist without evil as life cannot exist without death, light without darkness. Jesus is unthinkable without Judas, for conflict is the fundamental fact of life. This is the essential doctrine of German mythology; it is the core of Nietzsche's ethics; it is the philosophy of Goethe.[30]

His treatment of the Jewish question was an intellectualized restatement of Nazi ideology. Jewish influence in Germany diminished, began Koischwitz, after attaining "its great climax" during the uncertain period of the German Republic. Up to that unfortunate hiatus the Jews had maintained an inconsequential, if not parasitic, role within the nation. For Koischwitz, Germany's Jewish population was more the victim of history than SA street thugs:

But this Jewish age in Germany came to a rapid end in the anti-Semitic tide of the national-socialist movement—as the Latin age, one hundred fifty years ago, ended in the revolutionary movement of the Storm and Stress. In both cases, a powerful emotional nationalism revolted against foreign elements. In both cases, German mysticism, irrationalism and romanticism waged war against rationalism, and intellectualism, heart against brain, blood against ink. In both cases, an enthusiastic youth movement fought for moral regeneration, against a decadent and morally corrupt, literature-ridden civilization. In the time of the Storm and Stress, French civilization, as personified in Voltaire, was the target. In the national-socialist revolution, the "relativistic intellectualism" of Jewish civilization was attacked.... The Jews with their long cultural past and their total lack of both political and agricultural contact with the soil are the prototypes of intellectualists.[31]

At best Koischwitz had isolated his native country's Jewish community; at worst he had robbed its members of their very nationality. To him they were the denizens of a foreign land. One might ask how he avoided the presence of Germany's Jewish intelligentsia. He could not skirt the historical reality of this collective genius. But in no instance did Koischwitz present them as Germans: The term he employed for such Germans as Heine, Einstein, Mendelssohn, and Sigmund Freud was "Jewish," a designation suggestive to the reader of the appropriateness of two such categories in Germany.

In his final chapter Koischwitz discussed foreign commentary that charged that Hitler's 1933 ascendancy to power had "put the clock back" and returned Germany into "medievalism." His impression was that most devout Nazis were proud of this accomplishment.

The national-socialist revolution is a reoccurrence of the Reformation. What we read in autobiographical documents of the 16th century about social and economic conditions in Germany, reminds us uncannily of what we see and hear today ... Then as today, a man from the lower class became the leader of a popular movement the emotional strength of which is unequalled in the entire history of Germany. It should be noted that Luther and Hitler are the only two men in Germany, who were ascended from the obscurity of the lower class to national leadership ... Both Luther and Hitler were determined [not only] to reform but to save the existing system (Luther never dreamed of destroying the Catholic church), and consequently they turned against their own radical followers and crushed them with the support of the old ruling class.

Koischwitz optimistically pronounced this medievalism to be the new religion of Germany's young generation. To survive its infancy, however, he insisted the government's reform impulse must overcome the "chaos of relativity" and bind the national will to "a new dominating central idea." "Every form of present-day radicalism," concluded Koischwitz, "is part of the most elemental and the most powerful instinct of all life: Fight against Death."[32] Following the book, the professor's inner struggle appeared almost over and his conversion nearly complete.

Disenchantment with his country of residence did not deter the 33-year-old Koischwitz from becoming a U.S. citizen on March 29, 1935. Would naturalization at last guarantee him the esteem of a full professorship, or would the gatekeepers at Hunter College continue to withhold what was rightfully his due? Whatever his reasons for seeking citizenship, Otto Koischwitz could no longer be deported as an undesirable alien.[33]

This historian is indebted to one of Koischwitz's later pupils who, unlike Louis J. Halle, despised her German instructor. Lillian Ross, who would spend much of her professional career with New York City's *P.M.* newspaper, has handed down a disturbing glimpse of Koischwitz's darker side. Both student and teacher crossed swords repeatedly over Koischwitz's pro-German lectures and his disallowance of any classroom rebuttal. Nazi military and diplomatic victories abroad only seemed to fuel his enthusiasm and inflame his rhetoric. "In 1938, before Munich," Ross recalled, "this thin, dark, Mephistophelian-looking professor could and did put me on the spot for disagreeing with the idea that 'people think with their blood.' " According to Ross, when her peers defended her objections, Koischwitz would throw back his long hair, pound melodramatically at his temples, rub his emaciated face, and glare silently out the window. Then, suddenly, he would whirl about, confront the argumentative undergraduates and shout: "You're hounding me, always, always hounding me! I am the most persecuted man in this school!"

Emotional outbursts such as these did not lessen Koischwitz's popularity among the student body. Indeed, these antics appeared to inflate his reputation as a charismatic educator—one who had progressed beyond the petty concerns of formalized pedagogy. In 1938 he won Hunter's "Outstanding Teacher" award, and his classes were always filled to overflowing. The fact that he was indifferent about attendance, seldom administered written examinations, and reportedly passed out A's to undistinguished students no doubt had some bearing on Koischwitz's popularity. It was his rebellious spirit and fulminations against rationalism, however, that titillated the young ladies under his sway. As Ross recalled:

Koischwitz was different and unconventional. He hated the common people, and had contempt for scholars. In his own field, literature, he was a phoney, and he clothed his phoniness in fantastic and subtle prejudices. He was dramatic and colorful, bombastic and unafraid. He was a good actor and an effective demagogue. He gave the impression of being highly emotional and sensitive, but actually he was cold and hard in the job he was trying to do at Hunter, namely, to get across his Fascist reality.[34]

During her senior year, Ross enrolled in two courses with Koischwitz, one entitled "The Contemporary Novel" and the other "Masterpieces of German Literature." Time and again her old nemesis strayed from the text and his prepared notes. In the midst of one rambling session on degenerate Western literature, Koischwitz examined the works of Thomas Mann as an example of this genre: "Mann's style is crude, very peculiar to those of us who read pure German. Mann's style is involved; he likes to use as much French as possible in his writing. His German is overloaded with foreign words which he uses, though no one else in Germany does." "Once he [Koischwitz] spent an entire period giving us some inside information on the 'real names' of Jewish writers," Ross reflected. "He told us with great delight that Emil Ludwig's real name was Cohen. His dark blue eyes darted quickly around the room as he divulged the information that George Brondes was also a 'Cohen' and that Max Reinhardt was a 'Ginsberg.' "[35]

The monograph *O'Neill* (1938) at once increased Koischwitz's reputation overseas, particularly in Germany, while making him even more controversial at home. In his introduction, Koischwitz examined at length the lamentable state of the American theater, for which he blamed "those greedy sponsors" who rejected artistic creativity through the establishment of a permanent actors' ensemble, preferring instead bloated box-office receipts, Hollywood's loathsome star system, and mindless scripts. Against this backdrop of Philistinism, Eugene O'Neill stood as a literary giant—an unAmerican playwright. In Koischwitz's opinion, O'Neill's significance lay in the fact that he preserved the traditions of classical and Western drama in the United States, extending this heritage to a nation where it would otherwise have been neglected. The author expressed satisfaction that O'Neill's name had never been linked with any anti-German sentiment, nor had his works been cited to reflect such attitudes.

Koischwitz observed that as Friedrich Nietzsche had descended into madness and death, O'Neill had been born prophetically into the New World. Both writers, touted Koischwitz, shared an antipathy to Christianity and the Church, a sense of commitment to the search for a new God, and the recognition of beauty in humanity's tragic and hopeless struggle with fate. As Nietzsche had been in the field of philosophy, O'Neill in drama was the great reassessor of values: "O'Neill Werk ist der starkste Ausdruck Nietzschescher Problematik in Amerika."

Koischwitz insisted that O'Neill was the only truly American author in the United States, arguing that Jews were not Americans and that other authors shared European ancestry that disqualified them. He refused to admit that the playwright himself was the son of an Irish immigrant father. As for his subject's darker side, Koischwitz observed that certain aspects of O'Neill's misdirected life were symbolic of America's lack of national purpose. Both the writer and his homeland squandered energy in a spiritual search for the heights and depths of existence, a compulsion for extremes unknown to Germans.[36]

The University of Wisconsin's Professor Friedrich Bruns reviewed his fellow countryman's brilliance and prejudice in *Books Abroad*:

His analysis of O'Neill's creative work is deserving of high praise. I regret only one thing. Why must it be repeated *ad nauseam* that we Americans have only one God:

the Almighty Dollar. On page 16 we are told that European prejudice is not entirely wrong in assuming that artistic genius is almost an impossibility in "der amerikanischen zivilisation." And creative ability such as O'Neill's is a rare exception (page 17). How about Poe, Emerson, Hawthorne, Whitman, Melville? Or if our "Golden Day" is too far distant, how about E. A. Robinson, Robert Frost, Edna St. Vincent Millay? . . . On page 20 we are told that everybody connected with the theater in America sells his talent for "schweres gold." Does Herr Koischwitz know only the movie? Does he know neither actors nor artists whose one aim is the cause of art? Does bias blind him to the Little Theater Movement? It is greatly to be regretted that in this keen and penetrating analysis of O'Neill a half dozen pages ought to be rewritten—for the enlightenment of the German reading public.[37]

If American letters and the theater were hostages of Babbittry and commercialism, concluded Koischwitz, then Germany's magnificent strides in these areas were the result of the Fatherland's cultural exchange programs and governmental subvention. He had visited a research and propaganda institute in Stuttgart where data were being gathered and assimilated about German settlements and life beyond the Reich's borders. Publishing firms specializing in books by and about Germans abroad enjoyed similar encouragement under Hitler. Germany's men of letters praised the contributions of many American authors, including the works of Thomas Wolfe, despite the North Carolinian's bitter opposition to national socialism. How was it possible, Koischwitz asked rhetorically, for the arts to flourish in a nation so consumed with nationalistic fervor?

The seemingly paradoxical situation of simultaneously existing nationalism and internationalism in the literary life of present-day Germany may be interpreted as a modern symptom of the typically German tradition of Romanticism and Storm and Stress. . . . Despite obvious and basic differences between Romanticism and recent literary trends, some traditional elements of romantic origin cannot be overlooked in the present situation of German literature, and it seems that the strange combination of nationalism and internationalism forms part of Germany's literary tradition since Herder.[38]

For Koischwitz, the unkindest cut of all came on September 1, 1938, when Hunter College tenured him at the level of assistant professor. Despite his recently acquired U.S. citizenship and his enviable record of instruction and research, he had been denied access to a premier academic career. Introspection persuaded him that he had been wronged for his controversial lectures on Europe's New Order—a man damned for his conscience and nationality. This action dissolved Koischwitz's last tie with his adopted country. Hunter's 1938 yearbook captured the depth of the professor's disillusionment: "First thought: The message well I hear, my faith alone is weak. Second thought: I hope that we will not only get a new building [German Department], but also a new spirit of 'higher' education, Lernfreiheit and Lehrfreiheit."[39]

Hunter's rumored Nazi-on-campus remained uncompromised and gave critics no quarter during his final year in the United States. By 1939 Koischwitz was openly disdainful of his fellow instructors in the German Department. They, in turn, usually dismissed his tantrums as the unavoidable byproduct of a brilliant mind. Few doubted that he suffered from delusions of persecution. Koischwitz railed against academic censorship, going so far as to claim that certain of his books had been removed from the college library when, in fact, they had simply been misshelved. The few instructors who challenged Koischwitz's assertions were reprimanded by Chairman Busse. Both men were opposed by the Hunter *Bulletin*, an undergraduate newspaper. When the paper devoted an issue to the condemnation of fascism and asked members of the German Department to declare themselves on the subject, Busse was outraged. He charged its editors with conducting a witch-hunt. Cooler heads prevailed, however, and a disclosure of Koischwitz's activities, together with commentaries of his pro-Nazi publications, was killed by the authorities.[40]

Further controversy greeted Koischwitz following the publication of his essay "Echo from Abroad" in a 1939 issue of *Literatur*, a bimonthly German magazine. The Munich Agreement had frightened the American people into converting their arts and letters into vehicles for Allied propaganda, wrote Koischwitz, while academia funded new "democratic" instructorships to indoctrinate the youth. Superb German performances such as *Heimat* (*Homeland*) had been relegated to obscure ethnic cinemas, while mediocre Soviet films played at prominent theaters. Koischwitz fumed that live anti-German productions were considered "the patriotic fashion" and that the "kitsch" operettas (*Waltz in Goosestep*) distorted the Reich's image.

Koischwitz blamed Jewish censors and a growing number of women authors for the decline of literary excellence in the United States. America's misinterpretation of Europe's New Order he attributed to the psychological tension between a purely feminine culture and a masculine view of the world. In his review of praiseworthy exceptions, Koischwitz wrote of William Faulkner's novel *The Wild Palms*:

The book is unequivocally American, a mixture of barbaric primitivism and technical civilization, and it is gloriously swept by the fresh winds of the continent without horizons. The closing of the one story, "Between death and the agony of life I choose the agony," is reminiscent of Nietzschean feelings.

John Steinbeck's virile *Grapes of Wrath* depicted his country's penchant for violence and lawlessness, noted Koischwitz, much to the chagrin of America's sponsored literati. The national addiction to historical novels Koischwitz believed to be symptomatic of a world power in decline.[41]

Local patriotic societies watched Koischwitz closely. On August 10, New York City's Non-Sectarian Anti-Nazi League notified the Department of

Education that Koischwitz had been under surveillance for six years. Its executive secretary, G. Egerton Harriman, carefully outlined the professor's past indiscretions that preceded the infamous *Literatur* article and concluded:

In the past Dr. Koischwitz has been known to consort with known Nazi propagandists and has appeared as a guest of honor at German-American Bund meetings. Whether under the circumstances . . . he is a fit person to remain a teacher of youth in the city of New York is, we believe, of major importance, particularly at this time when Nazi-inspired incitements to racial hatred and fratricidal strife are so much to the fore.[42]

Unfamiliar with the Koischwitz case, Chairman Ordway Tead consulted respectively with his administrative assistant, Pearl Bernstein, and Hunter president George N. Shuster concerning Harriman's petition. Both parties were surprisingly indifferent to the alleged threat. Bernstein was forgiving:

I waded through the better part of this and found only a skillful account of the current literary scene, conveying but not actually stating a critical attitude toward us Americans and our works. Someone who came in and read it confirmed that impression. He admires—solely on artistic grounds of course—books, etc. sympathetic to Germany or written by those so inclined; similarly he criticizes Van Loon and others unsympathetic to the new German *Weltanschauung*. But I suspect that that is his privilege!
P.S. There was one thing I liked particularly—a quotation to the effect that America was dominated by the female of the species and that this was the reason, perhaps, for our antagonism to the virile, male-worshipping German culture! And this from a male professor in a female institution of learning! It serves us right for allowing you villains in.[43]

Shuster's response, on the other hand, was less generous toward Koischwitz but still considered Harriman's charges unworthy of pursuit:

The article reflects strong pro-German sentiment, and a disposition to deplore those forces in America—Jews, women—which have been eliminated from the Nazi social order. Here as elsewhere Koischwitz does display marked Hitlerite sympathies. But there is nothing here to prove more—i.e. "subversive activities." It seems to me, therefore, that there is no ground for action. . . . After all he cannot write an article for *Die Literatur* unless he attempted to placate the tempers of the reigning German official.[44]

Expressions of public and private dissatisfaction, however, crossed Chairman Tead's desk from as far away as California.[45] On August 30, 1939, the American Council Against Nazi Propaganda chronicled Koischwitz's subversive career in its magazine, *The Hour*, with this final paragraph:

The Hour hereby calls the attention of the Dies Committee to the case of Koischwitz as supplementary to the testimony given on August 21 before the Committee by Dr.

John Harvey Sherman, president of Tampa University, on the extent of Nazi attempts at propaganda in the colleges of Florida, Louisiana and other states.[46]

The Board of Higher Education granted Koischwitz a leave of absence from September 1, 1939, through January 31, 1940, without pay and without increment in 1940. At a farewell luncheon awarded him by the Hunter faculty, Koischwitz kept to himself, rambling on about "the dark hordes trying to snuff out and obliterate the light of learning and culture." A young woman to whom he bared his soul believed, at the time, that he was referring to the Nazis. Only with the benefit of hindsight did she realize that Koischwitz was alluding to democracy. Meanwhile, Chairman Busse retired and departed for Germany to live with his daughter—the wife of a high-ranking Nazi official.[47] This course of events troubled the Board of Higher Education and, in late December, Chairman Tead contacted the State Department as to Koischwitz's activities. In a masterpiece of understatement, Tead concluded:

Apparently he has recently acquired some notoriety in the faculty as a sympathiser with the German cause. He was in Germany this summer but failed to obtain passage to return for his class work in September. . . . But we learn now that with his family he is living in a small town [Nykbling] just over the border in Denmark and we have been led to raise the question as to whether his continued stay there has not been somewhat deliberate. . . . The purpose of this confidential letter is to ask whether it would be possible in any way to find out whether this man is engaged in some type of activity which would have a bearing upon the desirability of his return to a teaching position in our college.[48]

The American Council Against Nazi Propaganda entertained few doubts. Its leaders promised to take draconian measures against Koischwitz should he return to his post. According to its information, the professor began his return trip home after the outbreak of war and for a time resided in the Scandinavian countries, awaiting his family's arrival from Germany. During this hiatus he somehow learned of his impending prosecution in the United States. With little room to maneuver, Koischwitz finally answered "the call of the blood" and returned to Berlin. On January 22, 1940, New York City's Board of Higher Education accepted his resignation without regret.[49]

Three days prior to the official consummation of his resignation, Hunter's fugitive scholar aired at the Reichrundfunk. Curious Columbia Broadcasting System tuners-in debated the identity of a "Dr. Anders" whose metallic voice invaded their living rooms from Berlin. Later "Mr. O.K." was unveiled—with the same voice. Finally, there was "Fritz," of "Fritz and Fred, the Friendly Quarrelers." The German Library of Information, Hitler's cultural exchange in the United States, ended the mystery. On July 1, 1940, during the announcement of Koischwitz's debut in his new "College Hour" program, it incidentally tied him to the other three radio personalities.[50]

As Dr. Anders, Koischwitz acted the role of straight man to a child. The child was "Little Margaret," an American girl who had gone to Germany because her grandmother lived there and her uncle served in the Wehrmacht. Little Margaret responded to her new friend with effusive praise for the Reich. Their skits were virtually identical. After reading letters from Margaret's school chums back home, Dr. Anders (or "Dr. Otherwise") would suggest that she respond to her little friends over the Reichsender. In their initial segment Koischwitz coaxed his guest to describe a day in her life. What followed was an account of Margaret's early morning routine and sumptuous breakfast of sweet breads still warm from a neighborhood bakery. Her favorite song in school was "Wir fahren gegen England," which she sang in German and Dr. Anders then translated into English. Margaret informed her host that while this was a sailor's song, it was also popular among German fliers. The show concluded with the child's luncheon menu, afternoon recreational activities, dinner fare, and bedtime ritual.[51] By early spring Dr. Anders had jettisoned Little Margaret and replaced her with his own observations on American society drawn from stories in the New York *Times*. On March 19, he departed from his commentaries to discount the paper's mention of a BBC claim that a German U-boat had sunk a British freighter and had itself been overtaken and destroyed. "The submarine came back to its base," he reported, "and conveyed the ship's papers of the *Almiristan* to the German Admiralty. These papers were read over the German short-wave station as an illustration of how fact and fiction are combined in the British news service."[52]

Speaking as Fritz, Koischwitz coined the word "Britality" to describe England's "self-righteous conviction that no one else is well-behaved." As an example of Britality, he pointed out to Fred (Frederick W. Kaltenbach) that the British "even despise the American language," which the man in the street referred to as "slanguage." Encouraged by the occasional success of a synthetic political catch phrase in the United States, these clever vaudevillians cloaked their propaganda efforts with good-natured ballyhoo.

Fred: Here's what would happen after the war . . .

Fritz: Powarp! Powarp!

Fred: Now listen, my dear fellow. If you are too dumb to understand, I can't help it. But if you keep calling me names . . .

Fritz: I'm not calling you names. A Powarp is a member of a new British-American fraternity, the "Post-War Planners."

Fred: Ha, ha! That sure sounds mean.

As the Luftwaffe and the Royal Air Force battled over England, the German radio's criticism of the United States grew more outspoken and more strident. On August 10, "the friendly quarrelers" made this exchange:

Fred: DD.

Fritz: What do you mean, DD?

Fred: Well, dynamic democracy. Of course, DD might also mean damned dumb, or daily dozen, or Dorothy Dix.[53]

Beginning June 27, 1940, Koischwitz was put in charge of the "educational" programs "1,000 Years of German History" and "The College Hour," which were specially designed for college students. Sometimes he envisioned the war as the product of "inscrutable" historical forces, with whose providential evolution the United States should not presume to interfere.

There are certain things you cannot escape. For instance, you cannot escape symptoms of old age, even if you dye your hair. Suddenly you look much older than you would look without those experiments. Likewise, mankind cannot escape a new age when it has matured. . . . England went to war to destroy what is called Dictatorship. Now, the British are forced by circumstances . . . to establish the most rigid Dictatorship imaginable in their own country. . . . The establishment in Germany of an authoritarian government on the basis of leadership was the result of slow and natural evolution, and an expression of the will of the people. Churchill, on the other hand, lacks the support of the masses. England, which wanted to escape dictatorship at any price, ran into it.

At other times, Koischwitz retreated to the "injured nation" argument—that Germany was betrayed and humiliated at Versailles and now sought a living space to grow without interference. When he assumed the personae of Mr. O.K., the intellectual became a professional muckraker. Koischwitz began every paragraph with "confidentially," posed as "The Man Who Knows," and claimed a mystical insight into the ways in which the American people were being duped by a bankrupt government.[54]

The U.S.A. Zone's campaign fell broadly into two phases. The first, from the invasion of Poland until the German Blitzkrieg in the West, was to acquire a constituency and to consolidate its support. Selected excerpts from Nazi broadcasts were reprinted in sympathetic German language newspapers across the United States and in literature issued by Berlin's Library of Information. Block parties in German districts gathered about loudspeakers to hear Koischwitz's reassuring words. He defended their exhibitions of pan-Germanism as aroused alarm over pro-British lobbying efforts in the United States. During the period of military stalemate in western Europe, vilification of Britain took priority on Radio Berlin. The Propaganda Ministry seized as its second theme Anglo-American friction in history. While reviewing current American movie-making, Koischwitz focused on *Ruggles of Red Gap*, a film about an English butler who migrated to the United States.

Attention is drawn to the "wonderful" scene where Ruggles is invited to sit down at the same table with his new American master and he says, "It won't do, sir. . . . "

How is it that Americans who made this film with such a keen observation of the British class system still adhere to this system which is in such fundamental opposition to what used to be called Americanism? In Germany the Fuehrer is shown returning from the Western Front and being greeted in Berlin in triumph. He is dressed simply in the uniform of a soldier and he means it. Can you imagine anyone in Germany acting as Ruggles did if the Fuehrer asked him to sit at the same table? No![55]

Throughout the summer of 1940, Mr. O.K. returned again and again to this inflammatory theme.

These Englishmen who now claim to shed their blood for the welfare of the lower classes of all countries, have they not always despised the Americans? Have they not always avoided associating with those whom they consider below themselves?[56]
    I personally always pointed to the British intention of drawing the United States into the British orbit. British statesmen have deliberately mentioned the U.S. as a kind of British dominion. They always used the formula: Great Britain, the dominions and the United States. But yesterday [August 21], the British government for the first time admitted officially that they were anticipating a union between America and England.[57]

By comparison, Koischwitz offered Germany as the centerpiece of a new world order, a Reich friendly to the United States and all U.S. interests.
    Following Hitler's invasion of the Low Countries and Roosevelt's accelerated Lend-Lease aid to the Allies, Goebbels mounted a new campaign to unsettle the American public's faith in its leadership and democratic institutions. Such petitions were somewhat muted, however, delivered as well-intentioned brotherly advice. Appeals to "Yankee horse sense" and economic self-interest were heard repeatedly. While calling for U.S. economic cooperation with the New Order, the Reichrundfunk insisted upon a political Monroe Doctrine for Europe. Koischwitz pretended to comprehend U.S. machinations. Rooseveltian interventionists had maneuvered British statesmen into war with false promises of support in order to usurp John Bull's world position. Now, he warned, the United States must not allow itself to become isolated in a hostile community of nations. Following Britain's complete rout at Dunkerque and the Franco-German Armistice on June 22, Koischwitz toured the ravaged countryside.

Everywhere I found disappointment over the U.S. In Boulogne and in the devastated villages around Amiens the French people simply refuse to believe that America has not declared war on Germany. They had been told for months that America had promised help, in fact was helping in every conceivable way. They grossly overrated the amount of material that had actually been shipped from the States. . . . The British have felt betrayed by the Norwegians, the Dutch, the Belgians and the French. . . . It is most likely that soon the British will feel . . . betrayed by the Americans. And that estrangement will not be the fault of the British people or of other American people, but solely of a short-sighted propaganda policy.[58]

Radio Berlin blasted the anti-Nazi "distortions" of America's "Jewish-plutocratic" media, which catered to the British perspective. Its coverage of one of Germany's greatest naval fiascos still rankled Koischwitz after six months:

Perhaps you will remember the case of the Graf Spee? The Fuehrer gave orders to abandon the ship when he realised the hopelessness of the situation. . . . Next morning the "New York Times" carried an editorial to the effect that the Germans were degenerate and that German sailors of today were cowards. In the meantime this accusation was proved false by the Scandinavian campaign and the Battle of Narvik in particular.[59]

Roosevelt's hireling press, scoffed Koischwitz, had returned to its old game in the wake of the Franco-German Armistice.

Those who want to see Germany defeated and, if possible, wiped off the map, never fail to misunderstand, misquote, misinterpret whatever is said or done by Germany. Germany is called brutal and bestial if she insists on her rights; if she yields in an understanding spirit, she is ridiculed. . . . To the German public they [peace terms presented to France] appear surprisingly mild; viewed objectively they are thoroughly justifiable, just and fair, and they guarantee that degree of security at the back of the German armies.[60]

Exaggerated reports of the death and destruction wrought by Luftwaffe bombers over Britain provided effective grist for Koischwitz's propaganda mill. Germans needed not to have felt remorse for these deadly raids, trumpeted Koischwitz; after all, the Fuhrer had attempted a peaceful accommodation with the British.

Britain is lying awake in long sleepless nights, and is thinking of nothing but the one thing, how to get rid of that growing pain—air raids. The British patient asks: "How is it, doctor; have I a chance?" The answer inevitably is: "You are in the hands of God." "Oh, is it as bad as that?" But the patient, as long as he retains his consciousness, has but one thought—how to get rid of the pain.[61]

The unparalleled success of the RAF belied Koischwitz's dark predictions about the British Empire's fate at the hands of historical evolution. By mid-December of 1940, he asked only for retribution against a mocking enemy.

I had a strange experience the other day. I went to the movies to see the great new picture about Mary Stuart, which is having its first showing in Berlin. It is a remarkable picture . . . but it was not Mary of Scotland nor Queen Elizabeth who provided the thrill, but the newsreel. It was a newsreel of the bombing of London. . . . It was well known to us that London had had a terrible licking, but the pictures in that newsreel came as a surprise even to the German Army. . . . Last Saturday

night the BBC described how cheerful and bright London looks. That must be because
it is on fire![62]

In his world of cosmic determinism Koischwitz could not accept the survival of Britain, the bravery of the Reich Air Ministry's young pilots notwithstanding. The Western democracies, he insisted, were cultural and
political anachronisms on the verge of collapse. The United States stood at
the crossroads of the twentieth century, warned the speaker, too young and
too vital to ally itself with "the forces of yesterday."

The fertility of the American language on the one hand, and the sterility of the
English language on the other hand, reflect a political condition, namely, the old age,
the impotence of Britain, and the youthfulness and vigor of America. The American
language has been exporting words for the last few decades. . . . From the philological
angle, therefore, the Anglo-American Union, the political and military cooperation
of England and the U.S.A. is an abnormality. It is a policy which contradicts natural
evolution.[63]

By October 17, 1941, Koischwitz had determined that this "abnormal" alliance—with the detestable Anglophile Roosevelt in the White House—had
taken its toll on the American public. In one of his rambling "College Hour"
presentations, he concluded:

Life in the U.S.A. becomes more and more abnormal. The standard of living is going
down; the cost of living is going up; the "land of the free" has become a one-man
dictatorship. In time these conditions may appear so usual that they will be regarded
as normal. It is doubtful whether a "return to normal" is desirable, for every "normal"
period in history has been marred by a succession of wars (late 18th and early 19th
centuries instanced). Since life is growing steadily more abnormal, we may be pro-
gressing to a period of "abnormal" peace.[64]

As a wartime partner of "the forces of yesterday," the United States had
consigned itself to the process of national degeneration. During an interesting
broadcast on September 11, 1942, Koischwitz capsulated his views on the
American tragedy.

Less than two years ago American writers ridiculed my interpretation of the war. I
have always been of the opinion that this war was part of the process of historical
evolution. The original British and American war aim—to perpetuate the world of
yesterday—therefore was unreasonable. This evolution could have been accomplished
peacefully if the leaders in the U.S.A. and Britain had recalled that fundamental
changes were necessary. However, they decided to destroy the new movements and
to save what they called "the British way of life"—the perpetuation of a system that
divided people into have and have-nots. I always said that this war would accelerate
this system's fall, that those who went to war against the force of the future would
involuntarily become their allies in their struggle against the past. . . . Roosevelt went

to war to prevent the U.S.A. from being affected by this process, but, by going in, undermined the position he intended to defend. From a historical angle Roosevelt, against his will, indirectly works for the ideas of his enemies.[65]

Americans listened in disbelief on July 6, 1943, when Mr. O.K. took solace in the RAF's destruction of the Cologne Cathedral:

Oscar Wilde had written that men killed the things they loved. . . . They [his countrymen] wanted to save the old world, the only one in which the life of an Englishman is worth living. . . . Yet the wholesale destruction of cathedrals and monuments stood for the destruction of spiritual and cultural values, the very traditions upon which England rested. One day the British would awake: too late.[66]

Koischwitz portrayed his adopted homeland as one in the throes of a war hysteria, counseled by geriatric statesmen and interventionists and led by a madman. On January 16, 1941, he read from a letter sent to him by a Mary M. Foster, who declared that "the idea of wiping all Germans from the face of the earth intrigued her." Such madness had even affected Eugene O'Neill, sighed the American playwright's biographer, whose recent play *The Long Voyage Home* was a "slap" at the Nazis. *Life* reported that in Hollywood "the girlies receive wages in patriotic wrappers," he continued, "and that red, white, and blue liqueurs are served. I doubt whether Goebbels is likely to infuse a little of this democratic spirit by having swastika doughnuts baked in Germany." Other O.K. commentaries further revealed his Nazi bias:

In the U.S.A. the churches support the armaments drive; in Germany the Nazis see to it that the churches don't mix in politics. . . . Our school children draw pictures of Hansel and Gretel and Snow White—terribly old-fashioned compared to New York schools where according to *Life*, youngsters are taught to draw Nazis killing women and children. In South Dakota children torture dachshunds, whilst German children do not even realise that Bulldogs are British. . . . All this in the name of democracy, mankind, and Jesus Christ! (January 22, 1941)[67]

This is no real 4th July; it is a memorial service of death, not the anniversary of a young nation. The U.S.A. was always proud to be a young nation filled with the enthusiasm of youth, confident and vigorous; but today there is a feeling of fear, anxiety, and suspicion. The young nation is ruled by a clique of old men—Knox and Stimson are between the ages of 67 and 83. Unable to appreciate the desires and aspirations of the young generation, they have tied the American people up with capitalist exploitation and communist agitation. If these men really represented the younger generation, America would have no future. (July 5, 1941)[68]

Will Rogers said: "Can't we be friends with Britain without marrying her?," but if he were alive he would be forbidden to broadcast. U.S. public opinion has lost its sanity. A very different type of American enjoys free speech now. "Joiman" Americans they call themselves, these refugees who are willing to spend good American money on foreign wars. They have leanings toward Bolshevism, and taking other people's money is a good old Bolshevik trick. Why is America trying to fight? Because Roosevelt wants the commercial domination of Europe; but how can America get it? After she has spent millions, a broken, war-ravaged Europe won't produce many markets for her. (July 19, 1941)[69]

On June 4, 1941, Mr. O.K. announced that the United States was no longer a democracy. Without public sanction Roosevelt had dispatched secret emissaries to European capitals, had impounded Axis vessels in U.S. harbors, and had negotiated an unpopular "destroyer deal" with Churchill. Worse still, he extended the defense of the United States "to the Maginot Line, the Danube, and Dakar." Under these circumstances the invasion of the United States had commenced, and the unlimited expansion of its frontier meant eventual death for American boys on foreign soil.[70] Throughout the summer and fall Koischwitz observed the mental disintegration of FDR. His cry "Hitler must be stopped" betrayed a complex similar to that of mental patients who shout "I am Napoleon." The U.S. president also shrieked "We are attacked," which was a plain symptom of a persecution complex. Koischwitz announced that Roosevelt believed himself God and suffered from hallucinations, and that his handwriting was that of a lunatic. The professor concluded, "It is surely a calamity that in one of the gravest hours in the history of mankind one of the greatest nations of the earth is ruled by a man with a fevered mind."[71]

There was no doubt in Koischwitz's mind that international bolshevism and world Jewry marched hand-in-hand. Whether he arrived at his anti-Semitism through misguided conviction or political expediency one cannot determine. There is no evidence, however, that he held such beliefs prior to his return to Germany. Professor Louis Halle insisted that Koischwitz's temperament, erudition, and working environment would have militated against his surrender to so irrational an emotion as prejudice. "Anti-Semitism in New York at that time," posited Halle, "would have been about as popular as a denunciation of Judaism at the University of Tel Aviv."[72] Whatever his motives, Koischwitz dutifully mouthed the Party's line on July 12, 1941:

Confidentially, I want to talk about the Jews. This is always an awkward subject, especially in America. The average American does not like Jews. Political observers who are now wondering at the Soviet-Washington alliance should study the Jewish nation. In Soviet Russia the overwhelming majority of the government officials are Jews, and that Roosevelt is surrounded by Jews at the White House is well known. The preponderance of this Jewish element is the only explanation for the Soviet alliance. . . . The President does not talk about the aid he is giving to the Bolsheviks; he calls it aid to Britain, but Britain is only a stooge. If the Dies Committee want something to investigate, let them investigate this.[73]

By the fall of 1943 Koischwitz had adopted a strategy of divide and conquer. In a November 13, 1943, broadcast, he painted Jewish-Americans as the victims of an insensitive majority, latent revolutionaries filled with righteous indignation:

Though Americans do not use the term "ghetto" owing to their deeply rooted anti-Semitism, they have effected such a complete social ostracism of the Jews that the latter are obliged to form themselves into communities of their own. The Jews know how much they are resented by the Gentile Americans and are biding their time and storing up a hatred which demands the destruction of the U.S.A. and its way of life.[74]

On the eve of Hitler's invasion of the Soviet Union, Koischwitz raised the specter of Communist subversion in the United States. The leaders of FDR's New Deal alphabet agencies—even the president's wife—were parties to this nefarious business. America's advanced stage of industrialization would only quicken the process of national disintegration. As German troops slowly encountered stalemate, and with their defeat inside the Soviet Union, Koischwitz redefined the enemy. He confided on September 29, 1942, that there existed a cabal of influential "big money-makers" within the Anglo-American alliance, who were prepared to sacrifice millions of lives in defense of an overaged capitalistic system. Tragedy on such a global scale seized Koischwitz's imagination, and in so doing persuaded him of the reality of his own propaganda.[75]

How Koischwitz enjoyed badgering American correspondents from the comfort of his broadcasting studio! Frequently adopting a tone of professional tolerance, he would entertain his listeners by skillfully rebutting the anti-Nazi commentaries of these well-known personalities. As the United States persisted in making Britain's cause its own, however, O.K.'s words took on an edge, especially when it came to Dorothy Thompson.

Dorothy Thompson . . . was quoted as having said that the majority of the American people is still opposed to war. No, this is in no way a great revelation—we have known it for a long time, but such a statement from Dorothy Thompson carries more weight than a Gallup survey or a leading article from one of the London papers. Miss Thompson has devoted her life to fomenting hatred. She has said she would be willing to sacrifice a million Americans to destroy Hitlerism. . . . In February, this year, a member of the American Embassy in Rome told me that the President would force the German Government to declare war on America in less than 60 days. In Germany I saw private letters from the U.S.A. saying that the outbreak of hostilities . . . was merely a matter of hours. . . . "We have a President who usually gets his own way," says Miss Thompson, and this she knows better than anyone else. Maybe he will get his own way in America, but will he get it in Europe, Africa, and the Far East? That is a very different question. (July 29, 1941)[76]

On April 24, 1941, the New York Board of Education voted to drop two of Koischwitz's publications from the approved list of textbooks for the city high schools. This action was taken at the request of the publisher, J. B. Lippincott & Company, as a result of Koischwitz's questionable activities in Germany. After alluding to the banning of his books *Paul und Purifax* and *Reise in Die Literatur* during an August 1, 1941, broadcast, the professor went on to discuss the problems of censorship there and abroad.

You must say to yourselves that American correspondents over here do not understand the situation, or, if they do, they don't dare to say what is wrong. Mr. [William] Shirer, who lived over here for several years belongs to the first category of reporters. Have you read his book [*Berlin Diary*] published after his return to the United States? In it he states he would never understand the Germans, even if he lived there another ten years. Well, how can anyone who doesn't understand a foreign country write about it?

Koischwitz proceeded to discuss the second category of correspondents, those who were fearful of writing anything of a concrete nature about Nazi Germany. He referred to a series of *Saturday Evening Post* articles that stated that Western correspondents who accurately portrayed Germany's vitality and strength would be lampooned in the United States, while those who characterized the Reich on the brink of collapse would be castigated for false predictions. Alas, concluded Koischwitz, appointment to a German post could be ruinous to an aspiring reporter's career.[77]

In a world of predatory nations the United States had become feminized, continued Koischwitz on August 12, largely through the subtle influences of Eleanor Roosevelt and Dorothy Thompson. These women, he charged, were the real "powers" behind the throne in Washington, D.C. Thompson had boasted over the BBC that "wars were won, not by men, but rather by women." Thompson apologized to the British soldiers for this apparent slight, but said she could not stay to win the war, as she had greater tasks: "I must help the President and the Press of the U.S.A." "Helping the President" is a rather mild term, smirked Koischwitz. As for Eleanor Roosevelt, Harry Hopkins had scheduled a meeting between Mrs. Roosevelt and the wife of Soviet foreign minister Maxim Litvinov. The object of this meeting was to plan cooperative efforts between the women of the U.S.A. and the U.S.S.R. According to Koischwitz, the Dies Committee uncovered evidence showing that the Soviet-backed American Youth Organization had the financial support of the president's spouse. On August 12, 1941, he stated, "There is one American man not influenced by his wife. Perhaps you have forgotten that Miss Dorothy Thompson is Mrs. Sinclair Lewis? He isn't ruled by his wife, like the President. But how many others are there?"[78]

In the August 1941 issue of *Harper's*, author Thompson responded to her Nazi critics in kind. Her article entitled "Who Goes Nazi" afforded five unflattering profiles of individuals who would succumb to the "disease of the so-called lost generation."

The frustrated and humiliated intellectual, the rich and scared speculator, the spoiled son, the labor tyrant, the fellow who has achieved success by smelling out the wind of success—they would all go Nazi in a crisis. Believe me, nice people don't go Nazi. Their race, color, creed, or social condition is not the condition. It is something in them. Those who haven't anything in them to tell them what they like and what they don't—whether it is breeding, or happiness, or wisdom, or a code, however old-fashioned or however modern, go Nazi.[79]

The Reichrundfunk hailed Koischwitz's reply to Thompson as a media event. It was billed weeks in advance and, just before airtime, the announcer importuned the correspondent's associates to ensure her attendance in the radio audience.

Good evening, Dorothy Thompson. The other day I came across an article of yours called, "Who Goes Nazi?" This, though apparently written in a hurry is from the angle of psychological analysis, the most revealing article of yours I have ever seen. You have done better things than this but you yourself will know that superficial remarks are more revealing than carefully worded pronouncements. Historians might study it as the key to war hysteria in U.S.A. . . .

Let us analyse this in my own case. All Americans who have listened to my broadcasts call me a Nazi and unless the American Press lies, I am a Nazi. Let us see where your description fits in.

During a rambling disquisition Koischwitz explained why he was not a frustrated intellectual, a scared speculator, a spoiled son, or a labor tyrant. On September 19, 1941, he concluded:

Am I a fellow who achieves success by smelling out the wind of success? I went to America not to make money but because I wanted to see it. For six months I earned practically nothing and if I was successful later on it was not because of the wind but because of hard work. If a success I should have stayed there and published books against Germans. Publishers in New York were waiting for such copy by someone non-Jewish from Germany. But I gave up everything not for success, but for any kind of job in the country to which I belonged—in the land of my fathers. Since I have told you so many personal things I may say I earned less than $75 monthly in [pre–W.W. I] Germany. Having earned many times that in America, studying in Germany during the war could hardly be called "smelling out the wind of success." So you see, I am none of those things you say. . . .

My mind is somewhat confused. You tell the American people who is Nazi and who is not, and they take your word for it, but you certainly do not know what a real Nazi is. Since you speak for the President your error is the official error.[80]

Koischwitz milked facets of his private life for purposes of propaganda. He carried the microphone everywhere, sharing his vacations, reunions, family, living conditions, and occasionally dietary habits with the faithful. This tactic worked in that it both humanized his broadcasts and masked the

underlying appeal. As the Reichrundfunk's technical consultant to Radio
Rome during the winter of 1941, he implied to Americans on February 6
that the unpleasantness in Europe had been exaggerated.

I am taking a vacation, and am speaking from Italy. Since I left Berlin I have not
seen a single paper, or listened to a broadcast. I do not know whether [Wendell]
Willkie has had lunch with the King, or gone to see what he could do about changing
[Eamon] DeValera's mind about the war. I do not even know whether Britain has
given away any more possessions to the U.S.A. in exchange for some old ships; all
I know is that Italy at this time of year is glorious. . . . A walk around Rome makes
you forget the war completely.[81]

The Greek campaign persuaded Koischwitz of Axis solidarity and German
invincibility. Mussolini anticipated a short struggle following Italy's invasion
of Greece on October 28, 1940. Four months of stubborn Greek resistance
slowed the Duce's advances, however, before his offensive could be resumed.
British troops intervened on March 5, 1941, and German panzers poured
into Greece the following month. The contest was one-sided and, on April
17, the British expeditionary force began its evacuation of the mainland. By
month's end Hitler owned Greece. On May 15, Koischwitz arrived in Athens
on a working holiday to celebrate Greece's induction into the New Order.
"Athens is now normal again," he said. "In one cafe a tattered Greek soldier
was begging, unheeded by the patrons; the proprietor of another had been
very busy but said that he was much impressed by the Germans. He said
the British had no fighting spirit and little discipline. The Greeks were looking
forward to German reconstruction of the Balkans." The fact that the German
consulate and the U.S. legation shared the same building, the speaker reassured his listeners, constituted a sign from Providence. Air-raid damage
had rendered Piraeus useless to the fleeing British. "Everywhere British
influence has given place to German," bragged Koischwitz, "and as Churchill
said, the Balkan campaign marks the turn of the war."[82]

Pearl Harbor drew the United States into global war and overnight trans-
formed the status of its citizens in Axis countries to that of enemy alien.
Those correspondents and diplomats stranded in Germany would spend the
ensuing six months in internment camps before repatriation. Perhaps disturbed by the failure of his early propaganda efforts, Koischwitz arrived in
Lisbon to warn his former countrymen about the costliness of military preparedness. On May 29, 1942, he said:

I heard a lady saying in Portugal the other day, "A thousand dollars will buy only
a cake of chocolate or 20 cigarettes." If you don't believe that's all the dollar is worth,
ask the homecoming Americans when they arrive on the *Drottningholm*. The U.S.
dollar used to be the best money in the world and its rate has always indicated the
economic and political strength of the U.S.A.[83]

Trips to his boyhood house invariably resulted in family discussions concerning the course of the war. Koischwitz placed great store in his mother's wisdom, and occasionally he shared her views with the audience. On August 19, 1942, O.K. reported that Frau Koischwitz initially disbelieved his report that Churchill and Premier Stalin had recently concluded a friendly meeting in Moscow, later commenting: "Well, how embarrassing for the English." She interpreted this rendezvous as a sign of England's desperation. The fact that her two sons served in the army distressed her, but news of the enemy's precarious state lightened her spirits considerably. By late July of the following year most Germans shared his mother's enthusiasm for the war effort, claimed Koischwitz.

In the subway this morning, I heard an elderly woman say: "Now the British and Americans are walking into our trap [Allied invasion of Sicily]." The remark revealed the deep attention with which the German people watch military developments. When I had my haircut, I said to the barber: "You know, there are people in the U.S.A. who firmly believe that they'll have won the war by next October. Everybody in the shop burst out laughing. It revealed the general trend of sentiment in the Reich. (July 20, 1943)[84]

A gourmand, the professor calibrated Germany's wartime success on the availability of foodstuffs. When Herman Goering announced that bread and meat rations would be increased on September 16, 1942, Koischwitz hailed the news as a military victory. The Reichmarshal's proclamation was "visible and tangible proof of Britain's failure to starve the German nation into submission." Hitler's control of the Ukraine, he vowed, would alter the course of the war. The following month his superiors dispatched him to a submarine base on the Atlantic coast to interview a U-boat crew. He used this opportunity to sample Parisienne cuisine, subsequently praising the chef's artistry but complaining about the poor selection of meats.[85]

Egotism was a character trait Koischwitz never bothered to conceal. As his reputation grew among Propaganda Ministry and Reich Foreign Office personnel, he came to fancy himself as an authority on the United States. Koischwitz never missed an opportunity to reinforce this perception in his broadcasts.

I am just back from a reunion, a meeting of alumni of the University of Berlin. . . . Our reunion tonight included a well-known physician, an x-ray specialist, a leading figure in Germany's motion picture industry, a big-shot in the Luftwaffe, lawyers, chemists, engineers and so on. This group is fairly representative of Germany's intellectual class and under prevailing conditions almost everyone in this group has his secrets which he cannot discuss. They asked me time and time again about America. . . . I am supposed to know because I have lived in the U.S.A. (November 7, 1942)[86]

By the summer of 1943 the resumption of food rationing and intensified
Allied bombing plagued Koischwitz's daily life. These conditions took the
spring from his commentaries, and betrayed the gravity of Germany's military position. While awaiting airtime in his Zeesen broadcasting studio on
the evening of August 10, Koischwitz tuned into a BBC station and heard
part of a vaudeville program. Two comedians began a supposedly humorous
dialogue. One said to the other: "You know, I like to sleep during the day
but at night I like to be thrilled. Say, where can I go tonight?" whereupon
the other fellow answered, "Go to Hamburg." Roars of applause and shrill
laughter greeted this remark. Infuriated by what he had heard, Koischwitz
responded several evenings later, on August 12, 1943:

I personally couldn't help feeling that the warmakers of Britain and the U.S.A. had
degraded the human being to such baseness that one had to be ashamed to belong
to the race. They even laugh about it [air-raid casualties] and they put this laughter
on the air and broadcast it all over the world. I thought of James Joyce's prediction:
"A day of reckoning is in store for mighty England on account of her crimes." And
a day of reckoning is in store for Washington—just wait and see.[87]

The counteroffensives in the Soviet Union and North Africa during the
winter of 1941–42 were touted by Koischwitz's Allied counterparts as the
turning point of the war. Mr. O.K. challenged this contention immediately.
"From privileged information I know that this withdrawal was planned before
the Russian offensive began . . . that the Russians could have occupied these
sectors without firing a shot," O.K. argued, "instead of which they have
won them at the cost of tremendous losses." In Libya, no military decision
had been reached, despite Churchill's assurance that the Africa Corps represented a disorganized mob. "Was this," he asked rhetorically, "worth the
loss of the *Prince of Wales* and *Repulse*, of Hong Kong, Malaya, Luzon, Guam,
Wake, etc." As conditions worsened for the Reich High Command during
the summer of 1942, O.K. resorted, on June 5, to sowing seeds of discord,
suspicion, and jealousy within the Allied camp.

"If we could send 20,000 bombers over Germany," says the B.B.C., "she would be
out of the war tomorrow." There is a German saying: "If my grandmother had wheels
she would be a bus." This British propaganda aims at alleviating British disappointment over a Soviet victory. And with it has gone the possibility of a second front.
They had expected U.S. Forces to land in France, but Washington has abandoned
the whole idea of a second front, and the British feel left in the lurch. And the BBC
soothingly says that a good second front is not necessary, the big air offensive is a
sufficiently good Ersatz.[88]

Still armed with a rapier wit at this juncture, Koischwitz concealed the
Wehrmacht's early reversals by alluding to the victories of its allies.

The talk of the town is the Japanese landing on U.S. territory. Americans said the Japanese were in flight after the Midway battle. In America, Midway was described as the U.S. Navy's rehabilitation after Pearl Harbor. Strangely enough, the fleeing Japanese arrived in the Aleutians. Perhaps their navigation instruments suffered so much that they went the wrong way. Remember [Frank] Knox saying the Japanese Navy would be knocked out in 90 days. Now 190 days have passed, and they are still around. The Japanese fled to Hong Kong, to Singapore, the Philippines, Rangoon, and Mandalay, and now they have even fled to Alaska![89]

The first U.S. planes with all-American bomber crews were shot down over the Continent in early July 1942. Koischwitz seized upon this theme in hopes of strengthening pacifist sentiment in the United States. On December 22, he observed:

The other day I saw a letter which was found in the pocket of an American pilot who met his death on the way to the Rhineland. . . . In that letter . . . an American mother writes to her son. It's one of those tender, motherly letters which to read publicly over the radio would be out of place. But there is one short passage I'd like to quote: "While I'm writing you this letter . . . Roosevelt is speaking over the radio and I can't help thinking of all his pledges." Many American mothers will feel the same this Christmas season.

He informed troubled parents the following summer that should their sons' bombers be hit by the fire from pursuing Messerschmitt fighters at heights of 20,000 feet or more, those inside would be "blown to bits" by sudden exposure to low air pressure. Death would come in many ways to U.S. airmen ordered on terror raids over Germany, snapped Koischwitz, and still the Allies continued these suicidal missions. Scores of brave crew members were hopelessly shipwrecked in the inaccessible glaciers of the Alps. Telescopes revealed these doomed flyers alive but stranded, "awaiting death in a hell of ice!"[90]

For those civilian Americans about to enjoy their first wartime Thanksgiving holiday, Koischwitz offered an especially cheerful message.

Today is Thanksgiving Day. Be thankful for having reaped some of the glory of Britain's defeats in the Far East; for the disaster of Pearl Harbor, for the heavy losses of the U.S. Navy in the Pacific, for the losses of U.S. merchant ships in the Caribbean, the Atlantic, the Arctic. Be thankful for rising prices, higher taxes, and a lower standard of living; for increased working hours, oil restrictions, limitations of individual freedom, the muzzling of American liberty. Be thankful for U.S. cooperation with Bolshevism. Be thankful that American boys sit in Iceland, or Northern Ireland, or die 1,000 miles away from home in every corner of the world. Don't forget the main thing: be thankful that between you and Stalin stands the German Army![91]

For the servicemen who spent their first Christmas in some remote theater of operation, O.K. painted a depressing picture of isolation, death, and lifelong dependence:

You may be glorified as heroes right now, but when you get home you will have a tough time getting a job, and, should you go back without a leg, or without an arm, they'll tell you . . . So sorry, but cripples can't walk up the stairs! All your patriotism will count nothing. . . . Better a coward for a couple of minutes than a cripple for the rest of your life.[92]

Convinced beyond doubt that Germany's defeat would usher in the Eschatol, Koischwitz approached his work with the energy of a zealot. He convinced himself that an Allied victory would bring about a quarrel among "the United Nations" concerning "the world of tomorrow." Britain would seek to regain its hegemony in Europe through a political network of small states weakened by mutual hatred and distrust. The United States aspired to colonize Europe with its own officials and perhaps a few obsequious British functionaries in the pay of U.S. corporate interests. The Soviet Union, however, meant to "liberate" the masses of Europe and "swallow" the Continent at the opportune moment. Unfortunately, in the postwar period the former Allies would be too indifferent and war-weary to check Soviet adventures. The final results would be limited conflict, global chaos, and world annihilation through a constant series of class wars. On June 22, 1943, preoccupied with this doomsday scenario, Koischwitz willingly accepted state excesses in defense of nazism:

If National Socialism adopted certain dictatorial measures, it simply took up some of those weapons by which the whole civilized world was threatened from the U.S.S.R. But the Soviet Union is using these weapons to destroy western civilization; National Socialism to save it. For Germany dictatorial measures are an emergency; for the Soviets a permanent institution.[93]

Koischwitz's commitment to the holy bonds of matrimony survived his allegiance to the United States by scarcely three years. If ever there was an opportunity for him to philander, it came with his first major promotion. American broadcasters were routinely paid solely by German radio, but Koischwitz drew an additional paycheck as a writer-commentator for the Reich Foreign Office. Good fortune continued in the spring of 1943, when his superior was sent to a concentration camp for shoddy editorial work. Koischwitz inherited the post as head of Subsection IX (U.S.A. Zone) of the Radio Political Department of the Foreign Office.[94]

The object of O.K.'s amorous attentions was a 43-year-old American expatriate, Mildred E. Gillars, whose star-crossed career defies the imagination. Available sources reveal nothing of his family. Did Erna Koischwitz approve of her husband's politics or his castigation of her native land? Although she remained loyal to him, their marriage withered. When Koischwitz declared his love for Gillars, his wife was pregnant with their fourth child. Gillars learned of the expected child the day before its birth. Frau Koischwitz subsequently perished in the bombing of a Berlin hospital.[95]

Mildred Gillars was born in Portland, Maine, on Thanksgiving Day, 1900. Her mother divorced Vincent Sisk when Mildred was seven and eventually married a dentist, Robert Bruce Gillars, whom Mildred disliked. He drank.

After high school, she attended Ohio Wesleyan University because it had an excellent drama department. Mildred studied under Professor Charles M. Newcomb and took a leading part in the college's dramatic productions. When forced to decide between marriage and the stage, she jilted her suitor. A period of privation followed, during which she took a host of odd jobs and studied theater at night. Since her tuition and daily maintenance consumed most of her earnings, she lived on astonishingly little.

Falling short of graduation, Mildred's next stop was New York City's Greenwich Village. True to her profession, despite her financial circumstances, she pulled out of a musical comedy, explaining: "I didn't feel my career was being helped by playing that sort of part . . . I hoped to get something with the Theater Guild or . . . more serious producers." Gillars' dream of stardom never materialized. In 1928, a Mrs. Barbara Elliott of Camden, New Jersey, advertised that she was pregnant and wanted her wayward husband to return home. Informing the press that she had never been formally married, she staged a melodramatic suicide attempt. The authorities discovered that (1) Ms. Elliott was Mildred Gillars, (2) she was neither married nor pregnant, and (3) the hoax was designed to promote a movie called *Unwelcome Children*.

In 1933 Gillars went to Algiers to meet a gentleman in the British consulate there whom she knew "rather fleetingly." After this fling, she covered Europe, landing in Germany in 1934. Toward the end of her tour Gillars arranged to meet her mother in Budapest, and the mother had agreed to finance Mildred's dramatic studies in Dresden. On the eve of her departure for Hungary, her mother wrote that she could not honor her promise of support. Stranded and alone, Mildred managed to eat by selling her jewelry. In time she finagled an instructorship in the Berlitz School in Berlin, where she translated, tutored, attempted interpretative dancing, and established a fragile bond with the German film colony.

When the Wehrmacht invaded Poland, Gillars was again unemployed. In May 1940 she got a job with "Bremen Sender," a European broadcast under the direction of the German radio system. Mildred started as an announcer at 180 marks a week, later rising to the station of mistress of ceremonies for entertainment programs.

During her postwar treason trial Gillars allowed that her government had asked her to return to the United States. "Go home to what?" she sneered, "to poverty again?" An unsympathetic U.S. vice-consul had confiscated her passport in the spring of 1941. Caught between nations, ideologies, and loyalties she not altogether understood, Gillars lived a precarious existence. The Gestapo reputedly offered her passage home in exchange for detailed information on the Wright aircraft factory in Dayton, Ohio. Gillars refused.

Following the Japanese attack on Pearl Harbor, she caused a scene in the Rundfunk. Her racial invectives directed against the Reich's Eastern ally nearly landed her in prison, a fate she quickly avoided with a pledge of allegiance to Germany.[96]

What qualities could have attracted Koischwitz and Gillars to one another? Perhaps it was her flair for the dramatic that intrigued him, and perhaps he empathized with her difficult life and frustrated career aspirations. Professor Halle infers that Koischwitz had a weakness for women his senior who might act as surrogate mothers.[97] Obviously, Gillars enjoyed the company of so erudite and debonair a figure as Koischwitz. In time her ability to control this influential, yet naive, servant of the Reich would infuse her with a sense of false security: "I feel that if Professor Koischwitz had not been in my life," mused Gillars in her trial testimony six years later, "I would not be fighting for my life today. . . . I consider him to have been my man of destiny." Koischwitz began their relationship by pestering Gillars to appear with him on political broadcasts beamed to U.S. troops in North Africa. She claimed that his insistence became "a constant source of discord" because of her desire to avoid the U.S.A. Zone. Undeterred, Koischwitz used his influence with von Ribbentrop's staff to have her transferred. The professor wooed Gillars in his "letters from Silesia." Mr. O.K. had gone there early in their courtship because "there was a particular mountain in Silesia which had played a fateful role in his life since his youth." Gillars testified that "every time he had a problem he'd go to what he called his 'Mount Olympus' and confer with himself concerning his problem. When he realized, in the spring of 1943, what was happening to him (his growing infidelity), he reverted back to his boyhood habits at Mount Olympus and brought the answer 'that God gave him to life.' " In these missives from his ancestral home, Gillars recalled, "he wrote me many letters about philosophy and life and the influence of the German landscape on his character. It molded his character and he considered character analogous with destiny. He'd return to Germany each year with his children as they came along."[98]

Due to Koischwitz's machinations and the popularity of her bedroom voice among Allied troops, Gillars soon commanded top salary ($800-$1,200 per month) at the Reichrundfunk. Her shows "Home Sweet Home," "Midge-at-the-Mike," and "Medical Reports" were prized for their entertainment value.

Despite her growing popularity in the enemy's camp, Mildred warmed slowly to her new job. Many of Midge's German colleagues resented Koischwitz's interference on her behalf and Gillars' hollow protestations of love for the United States. She detested Horst Cleinow, head of the Radio Section of the Rundfunk, who frequently threatened his broadcasters with the line "One false utterance and you'll be put away." Guards patrolling the broadcasting studios intimidated her.[99] Gillars blatantly refused to read German newspapers for fear of being influenced by Nazi propaganda. Consequently,

Koischwitz supplied his paramour with American magazines with which she might focus her broadcasts. Finally, there was Midge's bout with an imposter. She learned through Koischwitz that a woman broadcasting from Rome was using the name "Axis Sally." Mildred complained to the Reich Foreign Office that she could not be responsible for another's actions. Moreover, Gillars wanted no confusion after the war as to who said what. Midge informed the imperious Cleinow that either he squelch the Italian fake or accept her resignation. Koischwitz's prima donna won the day at the cost of her few remaining supporters.[100]

The "Home Sweet Home" program, hosted by Mildred and Fritz (Koischwitz), was designed to "cheer" U.S. troops in North Africa. On June 24, Gillars imagined thousands of GIs asking themselves: "Gee, what in the world am I doing over here in the Dark Continent? However did I let myself get roped into Churchill's and Roosevelt's war business? After all, God can save the King. Americans don't need to bother about him." Fritz congratulated Midge on her many admirers in North Africa. One soldier wrote an American newspaper that Gillars "sounded like the girl next door," and that he and his buddies wanted to know her name. For the remainder of the broadcast Fritz, between music and humorous stories, attempted to describe Midge, which she, feigning embarrassment, continually prevented.[101] Midge was always "thinking of the boys" and sympathizing with them "in their odious task of having to carry out the orders of Roosevelt, Churchill, and the Jewish gangsters." She forgave her countrymen, however, for they were but pawns in a bigger game.[102] Gillars drummed on the themes of isolation, betrayal, and lifelong dependence:

While you are over in French North Africa fighting for Franklin D. Roosevelt and all his Jewish cohorts, I do hope that way back in your home town nobody will be making eyes at honey. (September 19, 1943)[103]

Songs: "Can I Forget You"; "Somebody Stole My Gal"; "Never in a Million Years."

Well, boys, I guess all of you have felt the same about some girl. Well, you've parted now, and you may dislike my repeating this to you, but it's the truth, especially if you boys get all mutilated and do not return in one piece. I think then you'll have a pretty tough time with your girl. Any girl likes to have her man in one piece, so I think in any case, you've got a pretty hard future ahead of you. (November 26, 1943)[104]

Collaboration with the enemy enabled Mildred to represent captured U.S. servicemen, or so she swore six years later inside a Washington, D.C., federal district courtroom:

I'd had various talks with Professor Koischwitz starting in the spring of 1943, when we were doing "Midge-at-the-Mike." We very often talked about America. I told him I felt my only reason for being was to go to prisoner-of-war camps. I told him the only thing that would give me some happiness in the chaos of war was to feel I'd be of some service to the people of the United States.[105]

Obviously Gillars was playing to her audience long before war's end, for she knew that Koischwitz had employed POW camps as an issue with significantly different results. His former broadcasts had spoken to the impossible heterogeneity of the Allies' armed forces as reflected within these detention centers. On May 22, 1941, in the wake of Hitler's Greek campaign, Koischwitz observed:

I have been visiting the biggest prisoners-of-war camp in Greece. British officers avoid everyone except English. They despise the Jews, whom they call a dirty pack; they dislike the Arabs; they hate the Serbs and they ignore the negroes. Some of the British officers don't get on so well with the Australians and New Zealanders. One [British officer] told me that in a couple of weeks the Germans would be driven out of Africa. Another assured me that the Doughboys would recover Greece. By Doughboys, he meant you, the Americans. The overwhelming majority of prisoners, however, are convinced of the inevitable British defeat and hope for a speedy end to the war.[106]

Over a year later Koischwitz toured a POW camp in northern France where soldiers had been interned following the disastrous Dieppe raid. The camp impressed him as "a place of shyness, inexperience and Boy Scoutish suspicions, nourished by cheap war novels and magazines." Canadian farmers conscripted as ersatz soldiers exhibited a "refreshing naturalness," while their British cousins displayed false bravado with unconvincing *V* for Victory gestures. Toward the end of his inspection, the professor chortled that after a few weeks in England and a few hours on the Continent, most Canadian and GI prisoners were ready to get back home. He closed the broadcast by describing the funeral of two Americans who died of their wounds.[107]

After six months of political maneuvering Koischwitz managed authorization for "Midge's Medical Reports," which were transmitted as messages and interviews with U.S. internees. Accompanied by Mr. O.K. and several technicians, Gillars motored from camp to camp. "We discussed America and Dr. Koischwitz did a great deal to bring a sort of understanding between the captors and their prisoners," she recalled for the benefit of 12 incredulous jurors in 1949. "He delighted the prisoners by drawing pictures." America's alliance with the Soviets preyed on Koischwitz's mind. His traveling companion recalled that in transit between camps one afternoon he stormed out, in regard to the subject of Soviet aggression, that "if Spengler's *Decline of the West* were in every American home perhaps 'we' could still be saved, even though 'we' have lost China to the Communists." Despite this disillusionment, Midge insisted that she and O.K. continually resisted ministry demands that "Medical Reports" be used for strictly propaganda ends.[108]

Koischwitz and Gillars were "amazed" by the friendly treatment afforded to the prisoners. A few Jewish inmates told Koischwitz of "bad situations," but he attributed their reaction to the influence of anti-German atrocity propaganda rampant in the United States. Each internee was permitted to send home a message of 25 words, with the understanding that it would be aired at the earliest possible date. The professor good-naturedly confessed that unexpected prisoner response had led to an embarrassing backlog of communications. Loved ones were advised to send their men parcels of coffee, chocolate, and cigarettes. German chocolate, apologized Koischwitz, went to frontline soldiers, expectant mothers, and children. The remainder was parceled out to the general population "exposed to Allied air raids." Furthermore, it was his impression that many POWs were addicted to tobacco: "Personally, I'd ask for a few tins of Prince Albert or Half and Half, but the Doughboys want Camels and Lucky Strikes, so send them."[109]

Koischwitz's accounts of the conditions in these camps and the collaborative spirit of the inhabitants differed sharply from the recollections of former POWs who testified during Gillars' postwar trial. The twosome's visit to Stalag 11–13 near Hammerstein proved alarmingly typical. They were introduced by the camp commandant as Red Cross representatives there to interview the men and relay their brief conversations back home to family and friends. Suspicious of this strange pair, the prisoners drove Gillars and Koischwitz from the camp, taunted by "vile names" after they failed to produce official U.S. authorization. Prior to their hurried departure Mildred had asked for an American cigarette. Minutes later she requested another. Finally, a Chesterfield carton was offered as a good-will gesture. Gillars was pleased, until she opened it and discovered horse manure inside. When the troops asked how an American could run free in Nazi Germany, she replied that she was an "idealist." GI Michael Evanick accused Gillars in postwar testimony of assuming alluring poses in his camp as enticement to participate in her show. He remembered that Midge, sans undergarments, had seated herself on a cot opposite him, crossed her legs above the knee and proceeded to open a bottle of brandy. Koischwitz's fiancée, who claimed ownership to a solitary summer frock in 1943, heatedly denied that she would ever have taken a seat on a filthy cot. Moreover, she forbade drinking during her interviews.[110]

Despite growing dissatisfaction from the Propaganda Ministry and the prisoners alike concerning the camp interviews, O.K. and Mildred continued to portray the stalags as ideal communities inhabited by naive boys and supervised by overly indulgent guards. One such institution in northern Germany allowed too much latitude, as U.S. enlisted men went so far as to demand wages for work performed. Koischwitz and the camp commandant were surprisingly tolerant of this display of Yankee impertinence: "It was refreshing to find that some of the Americans had their own ideas on the subject [required labor from prisoners]. It showed that the American tradition of liberty and individualism was still alive despite Roosevelt's dictatorial measures."[111] During their tour of Stalag 7A on June 6, 1943, the Rundfunk's roving ambassadors of good-will met Mickey Gressell, star big leaguer for the Chicago White Sox. Koischwitz teased Gressell about his membership in the AWCRFE, which stood for "Americans Who Couldn't Run Fast Enough." His June 13 description of this camp and a subsequent installation almost exceeds the bounds of credibility.

Stalag 7A reports sunny days for prospective tans. A few gaudy umbrellas and some Fräuleins, and the area would resemble a beach; but no Frauleins are allowed . . . the art exhibit in Barracks 18, sponsoring the works of Joe Demarre and Bert Green, is attracting a crowd.

Last week Camp Marlock Moor complained that private parcels had failed to arrive for some weeks, and that the boys were getting tired of American Red Cross parcels No. 8, and the monotony of sardines and corned beef. . . . Another camp reports spectacular progress in cooking research. The most startling discoveries made in that camp are these: a piece of clove candy will remove the scorched taste from a pudding or cake; a bit of coffee takes away the sour taste of black bread in a pudding. How about an American housewife trying the clove candy idea? Maybe it works even in the U.S. If it does, it seems to me that "Good Housekeeping" should give a prize to the P.O.W. camps for the recipe.[112]

When not inspecting these "model communities," Koischwitz remained behind in Berlin to help edit *The Overseas Kid*, a thin weekly published for GI prisoners inside the Reich. His contributing column entitled "German Lesson" seldom took the intellectual high ground, and it was usually replete with anti-Semitic humor.[113]

Koischwitz's *piece de résistance* as a multi-dimensional propagandist came in the spring of 1944, with the prospect of a second front looming just beyond Europe's horizon. Less than a month prior to the Normandy Invasion, he wrote, produced, and directed a play depicting the military operation as an Allied disaster. Few of Koischwitz's colleagues were surprised when he starred Gillars in the leading role. *Vision of Invasion* (May 12, 1944) graphically detailed the bloody events of June 6, 1944, but even Koischwitz shrank from predicting the outcome of that fateful day.

Scene #1

A gong strikes. The menacing noise of ship's engines is punctuated by the cry of D Day. Two voices continue in question and answer: "Why D Day? D stands for Doom and Disaster; for Defeat and Death; for Dunkirk and Dieppe." The commentators discuss Dieppe. A big landing boat washed ashore with the whole crew burnt to death looking like roasted geese. A smaller craft with fifty dead men aboard—all killed before reaching land. And a big hay wagon travelling between the beaches of Dieppe and an improvised cemetery, for two days carrying loads of dead to the grave.

Scene #2

Engine noises from a ship ready to sail from an English port. In tense, expectant voices they [the radio players of the U.S.A. Zone] discuss her name and cargo. The tanks, the guns, the food and "the boys" all come from the U.S.A. "The U.S.A. leads the whole invasion." One soldier is questioned about his destination, and southern France or Holland is suggested. He replies: "Military secret. I received a letter; I can open it on the high seas. But I have a premonition—this is the last time that I shall take her out."

Men aboard ship talk about their lives. Apprehension and fear break through the conversation. "You know, Bob, I have a feeling that I shall never see the States again. I was just thinking what mother will be doing now."

Scene #3

The scene shifts to an American home; dance music is heard from the radio. The program is interrupted by a news flash announcing the invasion of the Continent. An hysterical mother [Gillars] screams "Turn that damn thing off. I just can't stand it any longer; it gets on my nerves." The mother shouts at her husband that their son, Alan, is somewhere in Europe and nobody seems to care. She continues that the invasion will be suicide, that between 70 and 90 percent of the boys will be killed or maimed for life.

The husband advises her that nothing could be done about the invasion. "We could have done a lot about it," she shouts. "Have we got government by the people or not? Roosevelt had no right to go to war. If I had my way Alan would never have put on a uniform." The husband advises her to guard her tongue and to think of Dorothy Thompson who said: "I would be glad to sacrifice a million American boys in Europe." This leads to a retort that Thompson had not sacrificed her own son, and that Roosevelt's son, sunning himself in Miami, told reporters that he could do this because his old man had a lot of money. The mother claims that she is in telepathic communication with Alan. The beleaguered husband puts his distraught wife to bed.

The scene returns to the invasion craft. Alan asks his friend next to him to visit his mom after the war and tell her how he died. There is a loud crash and the sound of escaping steam. This din mingles with the voice of Alan's mother counting sheep to get to sleep. She asks her husband if he thinks Alan will be in the first wave ashore. He tells her not to think about their son's possible fate; to think of him as a boy and their many activities together. His words fade into the sinister sounds of battle.

Scene #5

Alan speaks to his mother and tells her that he has come to be with her always. She is happy. The whistling sound is heard and he says that it is the steam in their boiler room. She moans: "I was dreaming, but you are so real, Alan, I'm so happy." "It's no dream, mother, our ship is sinking. I only came to say farewell." Alan's voice rises to a despairing wail: "Mother." His mother screams, "Alan." The woman awakens to the sound of church bells announcing "D Day." She laments, "The dead bells of Europe's bombed cathedrals are tolling the death knell of America's youth."[114]

German opposition to the landings along the Normandy beachhead was strong in all sectors except Utah Beach, and it was particularly fierce at Omaha. Nevertheless, by nightfall of the first day the Allies held the coastal perimeter. During the succeeding days no serious counterattacks developed, for Hitler anticipated the main invasion farther north, in the Pas-de-Calais area, and he assembled his panzers there to counter the enemy. By July 1, the Allies had landed nearly 1 million men and had cleared most of the Cotentin Peninsula. The town of St.-Lô fell to the Americans on July 18.

Berlin dispatched Koischwitz to the forward areas in hopes of explaining this unfolding military crisis. What possible strategy could he adopt to concede with honor the reality of a second front? Reporting from unnamed towns and villages within earshot of approaching Allied artillery, Koischwitz presented a bright picture of conditions behind German lines. On June 13 he denied that the French population rejoiced in its prospective liberation or that sabotage activities were rampant. In fact, he concluded:

In Rouen . . . the first long processions of battleworn U.S. prisoners were not greeted with demonstrations of joy, but showered with curses. To the French people "liberators" spells "killers." Not freedom, but the sinister spectre of war rears its ugly head behind the invasion armies.[115]

Parisians went about business as usual, mindful that the "United Nations" would transform their city into a battlefield. The following day Koischwitz complained that fog and enemy smokescreens prevented a clear visual of the invasion front. "All reports agree," he chirped, "that the human tragedy is overwhelming."

When news of the invasion broke I was in Berlin. The people there were electrified. Everywhere they expressed satisfaction that the day of reckoning was at hand after U.S. and British fliers had waged a cruel war against civilians. Here [French countryside], however, the news frightened, depressed and paralysed the people at first, but since the invading forces are making no tangible progress . . . the people watch developments with calm confidence. They do not speculate on defeat or victory— they all talk about the human side of it. They just wonder how anybody in the world could take the responsibility for this carnage.[116]

Koischwitz spoke to an American audience from Holland on June 15, reminding his listeners of Dutch opposition to Operation Overlord and of Germany's determination to protect its loyal ally. "War profiteers on the London and New York exchanges go wild with joy," charged the speaker, "Whilst tens of thousands of bodies litter the beaches of northwestern France waiting in vain for a decent grave."[117]

From New York City, columnist William Shirer informed his readers with mock ceremony of Mr. O.K.'s new position as a "roving" war correspondent.

Otto Koischwitz . . . long ago discontinued his breezy broadcasts under the name of O.K. Goebbels, for some reason, sent the professor to the firing line as a "front-line reporter." His specialty was broadcasting eye-witness accounts from the various battle fronts on which the Americans were facing Germans. Since General [Omar] Bradley's Americans began their race through France, I have not been able to catch any more broadcasts by him. Presumably he began moving too fast to allow for a pause at the microphone.[118]

Channel coast residents were awed by Germany's new flying bomb, exulted Koischwitz on June 20. "Sympathy for Germany in the Western Occupied Territories has been rising steadily," he continued, "since the application of the new weapon." Crews of German reconnaissance aircraft had informed him that the thick smoke blanket over southern England suggested that the entire region was ablaze. People in Rouen spent their evenings watching the red glow from burning English cities just over the northern horizon. With Britain's military schedule in shambles, massive raids were being flown against northern France in a desperate gamble to locate and destroy the missile-launching sites.[119]

When Germany's super weapons failed to alter the war's course, Koischwitz sought salvation in the collective genius of the Reich High Command. He compared the victorious Allied armies swarming inland to a mindless insect being drawn into the Wehrmacht's web:

Nobody believes that the invasion army is simply going to march into France now. Eisenhower knows that to advance beyond the range of protecting guns of the big battleships might be fatal. If Germany had defeated the Americans at Cherbourg she would have deprived herself of the opportunity of beating the invasion armies in a decisive battle."[120]

Koischwitz's concluding broadcasts from Paris dealt with the supposed deterioration of Franco-American relations. Frenchmen by the thousands were seeking war production work in Germany, confided Koischwitz, despite harassment from an anemic underground movement. Anti-American sentiment was so prevalent in Paris that he and Gillars were accosted by an angry French mob for conversing in English. Koischwitz continued this theme in his final recorded broadcast on July 26: "They [Frenchmen] are becoming better Europeans, realising that Bolshevism would be the sole beneficiary of an Allied victory."[121]

With the guns of the triumphant Americans being heard more and more clearly in Paris, Koischwitz left for Berlin. Before his departure, however, he obtained the promise of a Reich Foreign Office official, Werner Plack, to see Gillars safely from the French capital. However, Plack's dislike for Gillars prompted him to leave the city without his charge. "When I telephoned Berlin [for Koischwitz's assistance] I had a feeling something had happened," Gillars subsequently recounted. "I asked for Dr. Koischwitz and at that moment I knew I'd never hear his voice again. . . . I heard a voice say, 'Professor Koischwitz is dead.' " He had committed suicide. Fleeing from Paris on August 15, Gillars first went to Holland, entrained there for Germany after bribing a conductor with coffee for passage, and arrived in Berlin in time for her lover's funeral on September 4, 1944. Despite press reports of Koischwitz's "suicide," FBI reports show that he expired in the Berlin-Spandau municipal hospital in the early morning hours of August 31, 1944. Death was attributed to tuberculosis of the lungs and heart failure.[122]

Arrested by Allied authorities after the war, Mildred Gillars was sentenced to 12 years in a federal prison for women. She won parole in 1961. After teaching German, French, and music in a suburban Roman Catholic convent in Columbus, Ohio, she returned to Ohio Wesleyan and completed her bachelor's degree in speech in 1973 at the age of 72. Living quietly for another 15 years, Axis Sally would pass away on June 25, 1988.

Koischwitz's checkered career represented a paradox when compared to his more predictable U.S.A. Zone compatriots. A German academician who came to national socialism through his emotions rather than his intellect, Koischwitz blamed his undistinguished career on the frozen political system and class structure of his adopted country. A visionary who returned to Germany in 1940 for the purpose of spiritual regeneration, he nevertheless prospered under Hitler for the first time in his life. Enmeshed in his own discipline, Koischwitz chafed that America's unevenly educated mass society refused to accept nazism as a manifestation of the German psyche in the evolution of a nation's epic saga. He viewed the world—with its prevailing rationalist and materialistic ideologies of capitalism and communism—as ripe for the purifying fire of Hitler's twentieth-century romantic movement.

How ironic that both Koischwitz and his cause were hoisted upon the petard of historical determinism. Time had never been kind to Koischwitz; it had robbed him—at least in his own mind—of his ideals, illusions, and aspirations as an intellectual and a scholar. Death may have been, after all, the only way out of a tragic life over which he possessed little control and for which he assumed no responsibility. Perhaps, too, during the chaotic summer of 1944, Koischwitz experienced remorse for the course of his brief life. Professor Louis Halle postulated of his old friend and mentor:

None of us, after all, know whether Lucifer, who had originally been a noble angel, ended by regretting his revolt. . . . By the time he [Koischwitz] had tasted, at last, the apple of the Tree of Knowledge, there was no longer any turning back. As the consequences of his fall approached, as the ring closed upon him, he may well have thought with Macbeth in like circumstances: "I have supped full with horrors." He must have welcomed the release of death.[123]

4

Robert H. Best, Alias Mr. Guess Who

News of Bob Best's indictment for treason (in absentia) by a federal grand jury reached his home town of Pacolet, South Carolina, in late July 1943. Predictively, the tarnished reputation of the expatriate distressed those who preferred to remember Best, not as Radio Berlin's "Mr. Guess Who," but rather as a bright young journalist in Europe. They could only wonder what circumstances abroad possessed Best to defect, a question as enigmatic to them today as then.

The personality of Robert Henry Best was substantially molded during his youth as the son of an itinerant Methodist minister. Born April 16, 1896, Best was subjected to early years of privation and regular adjustments to new communities. Before his family finally settled in the Piedmont mill town of Pacolet in 1912, Albert Hartwell Best had served a dozen pastorates within 25 years. Existence was further complicated for Best and his four siblings by the death of their mother the preceding winter.[1]

Best's early appetite for learning surpassed local offerings. To meet his educational needs, Best was sent on horseback to a neighboring town, where he divided his time between a field school and private religious instruction. Acceptance at Wofford College's fitting school in nearby Spartanburg ended this arrangement. The 16-year-old rapidly advanced into the Methodist institution's senior collegiate ranks by finishing the two-year preparatory phase of his education in half the time.[2]

For the remainder of Best's college career he juggled finances with his studies. Although awarded a modest scholarship, Best paid his way through college by waiting on tables in the dining hall, by collecting laundry, and

This chapter has been adapted with permission from John Carver Edwards, "Bob Best Considered: An Expatriate's Long Road to Treason," *North Dakota Quarterly* 50, no. 1 (Winter 1982): 72–90.

by working at a variety of jobs from textile worker to salesman.[3] Not one
to whom good grades came easily and somewhat of a loner, Best compensated
with an intensity and aggressiveness that some of his peers found disagreeable. Still, Best posted commendable marks, distinguished himself as president of the prestigious Carlisle Literary Society, and managed to play varsity
football.[4]

Following graduation in 1916 with both A.B. and A.M. degrees, Best
taught school in Spartanburg County until the United States plunged into
the Great War. Despite strong pacifist leanings, Best volunteered and was
sent to Officer's Training School at Camp Oglethorpe, Georgia. The volunteer rashly expressed enthusiasm for the air service to his commanding
officers and quickly lost his commission. Best subsequently enlisted at Fort
Moultrie, South Carolina, as a coastal artilleryman, only to be transferred
to the Balloon Corps, where he finally received a commission as second
lieutenant. After the Armistice Best chose to remain in the United States
Army as an artillery officer temporarily detached to the air service. During
this tour he helped formulate an innovative coastal defense scheme based on
radio-controlled aircraft. According to Best, this work resulted in a jealous
rivalry between the air service and his former superiors in the Artillery Corps.
Best claimed the latter branch demanded his return, which he refused. In
1920 he defiantly resigned his commission.[5]

From the army, Best, inspired by collegiate literary success, went directly
to New York City in pursuit of a career in journalism. Although his collegiate
themes were more rhetorical than substantive, more borrowed than original,
Best's earnestness and forceful narrative gained him acceptances and encouraged him to enter Columbia University School of Journalism. Following
his 1922 graduation, a Pulitzer Traveling Scholarship entitled him to ten or
more months of study and travel in Europe.[6]

The ebullient Pulitzer recipient sailed for Europe on June 22, 1922. Once
abroad Best headed for Geneva, where he divided his time between language
classes and coverage of the League of Nations for the *Independent*, a nationally
known magazine. At the league's assembly proceedings Best met Conrad
Hoffman, general secretary of the European Student Relief, who persuaded
him to adopt student relief as his scholarship thesis. Best canvassed various
youth movements on the Continent during the next ten months as Hoffman's
unofficial representative.

From Geneva Best went by way of Paris to London and there contacted
England's student relief strategists. He tried unsuccessfully to infect this
circle with his plan to earmark Allied relief funds for the establishment of a
European-American student exchange program. Rebuffed but undaunted,
Hoffman's volunteer pestered league delegate Lord Robert Cecil with a similar program to be subsidized by enemy reparations. These reparations had
been exacted by the Entente to punish Germany, Lord Cecil reminded his
idealistic petitioner, rather than as a means to revive the Kaiser's progeny.

Crestfallen, Best abandoned his paradigm for world peace and continued what must have seemed a hopeless crusade.

Best toured the capitals of central and southwestern Europe in the ensuing months, and from every quarter he observed near panic among the people concerning the probability of a Bolshevik takeover. In Berlin he witnessed a resuscitation of the old Red Spartacus leagues, and in Prague Czech Communists told him of their plans to dominate the Balkan bloc with Soviet support. Czechoslovakia's political instability so upset Best that he warned government officials to strengthen their ties with the West, particularly the United States.[7]

On Christmas Eve, 1922, Best reached Vienna with an expired scholarship, little money, and less enthusiasm for student relief. Swayed to remain in postwar Europe by a taste for continental living and the allure of political intrigue, the Carolinian took a room at a *Studentenheim* on Strozzigasse 15 and looked for work. Best unearthed a plan by United Press (UP) to establish a news listening post in Vienna to cover central and southeastern Europe for its Berlin bureau. Following brief negotiations with the news agency in May 1923, Best agreed to affiliation on a string basis.[8]

In time Best accepted his secondary association with UP. Although his station denied him the professional sanction he coveted, at least it afforded him the chance to seek outside assignments. Aside from his UP connection, Best performed substitute duty for such British and U.S. organs as the Westminster *Gazette*, Manchester *Guardian*, *Daily Express*, New York *Evening Post*, Chicago *Daily News*, *Time*, and *Newsweek*. In addition, ghost-written columns published under the bylines of prominent journalists provided substantial retainers for the young journalist.[9]

Vienna's cafe Louvre became Best's unofficial office as well as the meeting place for many of the world's foremost journalists: Dorothy Thompson, William L. Shirer, Sinclair Lewis, John Gunther, M. W. Fodor, Edgar Mowrer, Whit Burnett, George Seldes, Frederic Scheu, and Vincent Sheean. Located just a few steps from the Journalistenzimmer, the cafe provided journalists with a convenient forum for gathering information while sipping coffee. As an added bonus the establishment was handy for the messenger boys from the Balkan news agencies.

Best cut a flamboyant figure at his reserved table in the Cafe Louvre. A broad-brimmed Stetson capped his 220-pound frame, and his high-laced shoes and wretched German were familiar to other habitués of Ringstrasse. In professional status Best fell short of his celebrated guests, perhaps a reality he never digested. The popular stringer rather commanded respect through his news brokerage service fed by an army of tipsters. Today this talented constellation has offered a kaleidoscopic view of Best in their correspondence, reports, autobiographies, and even in autofictional accounts. William Shirer's *Traitor* (1941) and John Gunther's *Lost City* (1964) are excellent personality studies of Best through the use of fictional surrogates.[10]

Between the wars, peer characterizations of Best ran the gamut. The fledgling expatriate impressed Dorothy Thompson as a callow youth wholly devoid of field savvy and important contacts.[11] Best's folksiness and clever ability as a storyteller revealed to Bill Shirer the inbred charms of a dyed-in-the-wool Southerner.[12] Others observed a change in Best over time, possibly due to his gradual absorption into Vienna's baroque lifestyle. By the early 1930s he had earned the reputation of an eccentric from the coffee house regulars. UP president Hugh Baillie described meeting his unorthodox employee on a tour of his European bureaus:

He came one evening to the Hotel Bristol to pick us up for dinner, dressed in the regalia of an Alpine guide, complete to spiked climbing shoes. I can still hear the sound of his spikes clattering on the Bristol's marble floors. We could never find him when we wanted him—at the office or at his home—but somehow he always knew where we were, and would show up suddenly to join us at places way the hell-and-gone out from the center of Vienna. . . . Sometimes I wondered what they made of him and his fancy costumes.[13]

In retrospect Vienna's American community has linked Best's downfall to his involvement with a notorious White Russian émigré. Veteran journalist George Seldes, who left Austria in 1928, insists that even then this mysterious woman (Countess N. V. Deroye) had already exposed Best to Nazi propaganda. While covering the Balkans for the Philadelphia *Public Ledger*, Dorothy Thompson sadly witnessed the countess' influence on her paramour:

This woman, who was, she said, a Countess, and who was many, many years older than young Mr. Best, became the center of his life during the most impressionable years. . . . The relationship was well known to his companions in Vienna, who both despaired of it, on his behalf, and admired his strange and utter devotion to a woman whose years seemed quite unsuitable to such a liaison, and whose penury was, we knew, a great tax on his very niggardly income. In addition to this, the woman like very many Russian émigrés who having lost all in war and revolution, saw no future whatsoever, assuaged her despair in drink and drugs, which eventually unbalanced her mind and led to her confinement in a sanitarium. I believe this first passionate attachment . . . had a profound and embittering influence on his attitude toward the Soviet regime.[14]

Austrian newsman Frederic Scheu knew of the countess' morphine addiction and discovered from the Stammtisch crowd that "Bob might have fallen prey to this device."[15] Gunther's portrayal of the union in his novel suggests a domestic hell for the beleaguered stringer. The countess resented her dependence on Best, and this bitterness usually boiled over into violent altercations. She possessed a coarseness that was habitually exhibited in the cafe, to Best's mortification. The countess once explained her lover's constancy as follows: "You are curious why I stay with Drew [Best]? Because fat men are so grateful." Another of Gunther's fictional characters thought otherwise. "No, he's a southern boy . . . and it flatters him to be living with a Countess. To show chivalry to her, no matter how horrible she is, gives a lift to his own ego."[16]

Best masterminded a local news service aimed at breaking governmentally controlled press monopolies in the Balkans. This small enterprise quickly mushroomed into a major cartel. Membership in Best's clearinghouse brought extraordinary benefits to its subscribers. The ground rules stipulated that news stories would be considered as common property. Each journalist with an exclusive would allow himself one hour's lead time. That way, his newspaper would have the scoop before the competition. After that time, however, the Cafe Louvre would be called and the information given to an "orderly." Best's representative would then contact all other member correspondents. Ironically, the appearance of so many releases similar in wording and substance tended only to certify the original submission. This unique enterprise, which lasted for several years, was held together by a coalition of Vienna's U.S. press corps and foreign news reporters.[17]

British and U.S. journalists forged a separate press union on June 24, 1930, with Best, Marcel Fodor, and John Gunther as principal architects. Chancellery records showed Best as president and administrative caretaker of Ampress.[18] Few contemporaries criticized Best for the energetic way he attacked the job during those early days, but some observers began to suspect his professional integrity. It was rumored that Best's press association had accepted unusually high retainers from the banking cartel Credit-Anstalt in exchange for both an information service and a favorable press. The name of Best's business manager, Ladislaus Benes, was discovered by government officials on the Credit-Anstalt's payroll, and the South Carolinian was assumed guilty by association. Despite the fact that Benes and Best were subsequently cleared by the Austrian press and the Ministry of Justice, doubts continued to linger. Fellow Ampress officer and auto-novelist John Gunther attributed Drew's (Best's) predicament to desperation rather than greed. Maintaining that his personal remuneration went to satisfy a gambling debt incurred by one of the countess' ex-husbands, Gunther admitted in *The Lost City* that the other Anglo-American Press Union members finally came to suspect Best's culpability, but for the sake of their organization, the membership closed ranks and effected their colleague's exoneration.[19]

Frequenters of his cafe forums agree that Best was surprisingly apolitical during his early expatriation. Occasionally pressed as to his former party affiliations in the United States, Best facetiously countered that as a native Southerner, he naturally "was against Negroes and Republicans."[20] In an unguarded moment he might offer grudging praise for a local Social Democratic candidate or castigate Vienna's Socialist city government for its high taxes, but these remarks lacked ideological conviction. The rise of Prince von Starhemberg's Fascist Heimwehr army sparked Best's political interest, however, and prompted him to endorse openly the prince's political fortunes. Even as his champion lost ground in the scuffle for power, Best held to the Dollfuss-Schuschnigg brand of clerical fascism, "with only occasional lapses into wondering whether there wasn't something in the Nazi business."[21] In Gunther's *Lost City* James Drew (Best) began to move among Nazi circles in 1932, a point Best himself later broached over Radio Berlin. The charge of collaboration, he maintained, arose among his colleagues only after his dogged insistence that Hitler would come to power in Germany.[22] At UP's New York headquarters, President Hugh Baillie tolerated Best's politics for the sake of his Balkan contacts:

Of course we watched his copy for any signs that he was slanting it pro-Nazi, but he never did. He was too foxy for that. He never made the mistake of coloring his dispatches which would have ended his career with us. And his news sources were excellent. So we kept him on . . . under surveillance, you might say.[23]

On the evening of the Anschluss (March 11, 1938) William Shirer found Best at his table scribbling dispatches. Suddenly Best was called to the telephone, and when he returned he proudly announced to edgy news reporters that "Schuschnigg had returned as chancellor and that the Nazis were out." "This was typical of his reporting," Shirer noted, "but there was no doubt that he was happy about his 'tip.' Things are not over yet, he kept saying to me. At that time, he was not Nazi." There were additional signs hardly characteristic of a crypto-Fascist.[24] Nearly half of Best's European newspaper cronies were Jews, and that fateful night he appeared genuinely concerned for their safety. In a morbid scene at the Cafe Louvre Best tried to persuade an old Jewish tablemate to foreswear suicide in the face of certain German occupation. Best also concealed at UP headquarters a German-Jewish staffer wanted by the SS and, with the help of the U.S. embassy, designed elaborate plans for smuggling the fugitive across the Hungarian frontier. Another news agency employee, Elizabeth Thurg, was arrested by the Gestapo for illegal political activities. Best applied every pressure to effect this Socialist's release—at no small danger to himself—even though she had directed a secret propaganda mill on the bureau's premises.[25]

"I believe Best started going Nazi after I left Vienna on 9 June 1938," Shirer opined, "that is, three months after Hitler took over."[26] Only weeks after the Anschluss Hugh Baillie confirmed those suspicions that had tantalized his curiosity for so long: "One night at dinner he gave us the full treatment, enthusiastically explaining the Nazi idea of brotherhood. From others we heard about his liaison with . . . the most extreme local Nazis." During this period Best was seen frequently with Baron von Han, who was at that time the head of the DNB (a German news agency) and known to be the person distributing money for the Nazi government in Vienna. It was also whispered that Best consorted with Gestapo agents, but this was never

proven.[27] United Press' Joseph W. Grigg was flabbergasted by his colleague's
rabid pro-Nazi sentiment: "He talked as a convinced Nazi and I quickly
came to the conclusion there was no point in arguing with him about politics.
I will say, however, that he was sufficiently professional so that this strong
pro-Nazi bias did not appear to color his news coverage."[28] As fellow staffers
hurried their departures following the Anschluss, Best opted to stay behind
"to cover events in the city." UP tried to entice Best elsewhere with a more
attractive post. When this stratagem failed, the home office relented with
the prophetic admonition that Berlin would censor all substantive dispatches.
Best remained unpersuaded, as he plainly meant to subordinate his craft to
private considerations that bound him in Vienna. Southern journalist Ralph
McGill remembered Best at this juncture in his column for the Atlanta
Constitution.

He was drinking coffee. Around him were two or three men and next to him was a
very pretty girl who looked very much like the actress, Louise Rainer. In all those
17 years he rarely left Vienna. He never came home, even for a short vacation. He
became almost entirely European. He was something of a lotus eater who ate daily
of the comfort, the pleasantness and the delight of Vienna. . . . I remember one night
when a group of us were sitting in the Cafe Louvre watching the bully boys of the
Nazis drinking and dining with their girls, there was a fist fight in one corner between
two young men of about 20. Blood flowed from a cut lip. I recall Best saying, "The
fools, to think they believe they can go through the world with men like that. . . . "
And now Best, a South Carolinian, has joined them. I don't think it is the girl, even
though she was lovely. . . . I think it was just that Best, who didn't care much about
money, but who wanted only his corner in the Cafe Louvre, his conversation, and
his ease.[29]

The countess' eventual mental breakdown left Best free to pay court to
Carinthian Erna Maurer, an attractive Associated Press stringer and fervent
Nazi. Shirer weighed this obscure woman's influence heavily on Best's ultimate decision. With equal conviction Shirer averred that his old friend had
remained too long abroad and that he had gone European.[30] German freelance
writer Margaret Boveri dismissed Shirer's explanation of Best's ideological
shift as well-intentioned Western propaganda that glossed over the traitor's
petty opportunism. In Boveri's definitive work on twentieth-century treason,
the author concludes that Best was a "cheap crook" and "petty swindler . . .
far too hollow as a human being to suffer" from mere geographical displacement.[31] Dorothy Thompson coined these same unkind sentiments much
earlier in her personal statement of excommunication against Best "on behalf"
of the U.S. press corps (1942):

Bill Shirer says . . . it's [Best's defection] because you stayed too long in Europe and
went European. With all due respect to Bill, I think that is hooey. You went Nazi
and going Nazi isn't going European. Nazism is as anti-European as it is anti-

American. Lots of American correspondents lived for years on end in Europe and became much more "Europeanized" than you ever did, Bob Best. Why, you never even properly learned the German language. They did, and read European history and philosophy, sociology and psychology, and entered deeply into European culture. . . . No, Bob, that doesn't explain you. The truth is that you remained after 20 years as intellectually lazy and just about as ignorant as you were when you arrived.[32]

It must have been small consolation to Best that after 15 years of pioneer service to United Press he now stood as bureau manager of a defunct office. His past efforts to advance had been stymied by superiors who saw him as nothing more than a low-echelon conduit between native stringers and a parade of bureau chiefs. The tiresome cycle of impossible deadlines and abbreviated dispatches allowed Best few creative challenges and slowly strangled his professional enthusiasm.[33]

Of the original native American correspondents who were stationed there [Vienna] when Robert Best arrived, all, without exception, passed on to more influential and remunerative positions, and many attained a degree of fame. . . . But Robert Best seemed bogged down at a miserable salary. . . . He became an expatriate, a discouraged man, living in a discouraged community, with only transient American friends, increasingly dependent for any form of participation in the life of the country and society in which he found himself. . . . His citizenship had become . . . reduced to a passport and an ill-paid job that had furnished him no advancement in all the years.[34]

Colleagues with careers in similar mid-life doldrums might blame their callous bosses or a competitive occupation, but Best fancied himself the victim of Jewish interests:

Over the past years there has been an increase in the number of non-Jewish correspondents who after cynically taking cognizance of the situation [Jewish takeover of magazine and newspaper industries] chose to covet favor of the Jews as a certain road towards notoriety and, therefore, towards a small fortune. They chose to do this instead of telling you the truth. In my own 19 years as a journalist in Europe in various American and British news enterprises, I chose, I am proud to say, an uncompromising stand, and I remained, in consequence, comparatively unknown to the wider public in America and Britain, as well or absolutely unknown to the monied aristocracy of the world in general.[35]

The Southerner's anti-Semitism must have chagrined Vienna's American community, many of whom remembered Best as the grateful protegé of Europe's premiere Balkan correspondent—a Jew. Marcel W. Fodor taught Best much of what he knew about eastern Europe, telegraphed his copy whenever Best was away on assignment, entertained the young American in his home, and occasionally advanced him money. This parasitic relationship gradually cooled, however, due to Best's prejudice and the embarrassment connected with rumors that Fodor had mercifully covered stories carelessly ignored by Best.[36]

Little information survives on the whereabouts of Best during the next three years. United Press historian Joe Alex Morris places him at the Munich Conference in late September of 1938, where he covered Allied appeasement through German news sources.[37] One suspects that this reporter took grim satisfaction in Czechoslovakia's certain demise. Best was in Bratislava during the summer of 1938 to confirm rumors of a bloody revolution. He found no sign of violence, but his investigations led to his arrest by agents of the Benes government. The Czech secret police interrogated Best in a highly provocative manner; one of them kept loading and unloading an automatic pistol in the prisoner's face.[38] This sacrificial effort went unrewarded as UP unceremoniously demoted Best for "non-performance." Best had been employed as a regular staffer since 1934, and before then he recorded 12 years as a productive stringer. In 1939, as Europe stood on the brink of another war, the news agency's wayward correspondent was dropped to his old station with an assured nominal salary. After 1940 Best was paid only for news stories accepted by the wire service.[39] What rankled him, however, was the assumption gleaned from copyroom gossip that he had been fired outright. Best would later utilize his wartime broadcasts to correct what he perceived to be at best a careless mistake and at worst calculated libel.[40]

Germany's military victories should have provided any remaining U.S. journalist with plenty of saleable copy. In Best's case, UP's apprehension about Nazi censorship and the chance of tainted dispatches compromised the stringer's effectiveness. On September 13, 1940, Best wrote his brother, Eugene, that his few assignments confined him to Vienna and the Balkans. He mentioned news broadcasts that he had made for Radio Vienna, a personal tour to Greece on the eve of Mussolini's ill-fated invasion, and random assignments in London and occupied Paris.[41] The summer of 1940 marked the nadir of Best's European term. In addition to his vocational woes, word came of both his father's death and the forced closing of Cafe Louvre. Together these events must have presented the middle-aged Best with an uncomfortable sense of self-displacement, of having irretrievably lost his own past.

Pearl Harbor propelled Best into the anxious role of enemy alien. Gestapo agents brought him the unwelcome news on the evening of December 7, 1941, took him into custody, and deposited their bewildered prisoner in "a common criminal jail."[42] Berlin mercifully concluded Best's ten-day incarceration with orders for all U.S. journalists and diplomatic personnel to report to a resort spa near Bad Nauheim. The camp's 145 guests ate dumplings and sauerbraten *ad nauseam*, nearly froze to death, and were bullied daily by the Gestapo. To fight boredom the internees founded "Badheim University" and offered a curriculum of drama (UP's Fred Oechsner), Shakespeare and phonetics (Chicago *Tribune*'s Alex Small), and scientific bridge (UP's Pat Conger), with miscellaneous courses ranging from tap dancing to philosophy.[43]

At first Best stayed on the periphery of camp life, studiously avoiding the orchestrated activities. His reclusive demeanor caught the attention of both his former chief, Frederick Oechsner, and a member of Nauheim's diplomatic circle, Francis Cunningham:

He did not participate in group activities, was a quiet, passive individual who was considered eccentric by the others. . . . Best was not attached in any way to the group of fine Berlin Unipressers. There was no outright exclusion, but he just didn't belong umbilically.[44]

I recall Best as an internee assiduous in recycling cigarette butts. . . . I realized that he seemed preoccupied or worried. I supposed his anxiety arose chiefly from wondering whether so long absent from the U.S.A., he could find a job back in this country.[45]

When Best emerged from his shell in early February 1942, tempers quickly flared. He made no secret of his petition to the Reich Propaganda Ministry for permission to remain in occupied Europe. Best astonished Leland M. Morris, former chargé d' affaires in Berlin, with assurances that he would mend "the broken ties" between his country and Germany. He went further, attributing his long self-exile to his repugnance for Jewish domination of American society and its government. Correspondent Louis Lochner and Best nearly traded blows over the latter's insistence that Lochner's marriage to a German national obliged him to support Adolf Hitler.[46] The German Foreign Office granted Best's appeal for wartime residence none too soon, and on March 2 he quietly entrained for Berlin.

Once in Berlin Best was directed to Werner Plack, head of the Radio Division of the Nazi Foreign Office and liaison with the Ministry for Propaganda and Enlightenment. Plack's interest in Best as a potential Reichrundfunk broadcaster grew from the American's earlier association with Radio Vienna. During preliminary negotiations Plack persuaded Best that only Germany could offer him a forum from which to address the political and social ills of his country. He unconsciously offended Best by receiving him as a common job applicant. Best stiffly informed Plack that he had offered his services as a means to unite their countries against world communism and international Jewry. He admitted to virtual destitution but added that as a volunteer he would require only nominal living expenses. Plack readily agreed to Best's generous terms, ordered him suitable lodgings and personally escorted him to the Rundfunk for orientation.[47]

Best assailed his work with a neophyte's enthusiasm. In mid-March Radio Berlin boosted the debut of an American microphone personality, to be known simply as Mr. Guess Who. Enamored with Goebbels' artifice to build him an audience, Best trumpeted in his first broadcast on April 10, 1942:

"Who are you anyway? This is one of many questions which many would like to put to me at this moment. But unfortunately, I must remain for you merely 'Mr. Guess Who,' your self-appointed correspondent for the New World Order."[48] Conclusive knowledge of Guess Who's true identity hit as a bombshell among friends and family alike. The Jewish correspondent whom Best rescued from the Nazis caught his benefactor's broadcast at the New York City Listening Post of CBS. "Suddenly he dashed into my office," Shirer remembered. "He was in tears. . . . 'There's someone talking from Berlin who calls himself "Guess Who," ' he cried. 'It sounds like Bob Best. Come and see.' " "I always figured he was an eccentric," exploded another angry journalist, "but I never thought he was a son of a bitch." Back in South Carolina, the Sumter Chamber of Commerce questioned a *Time* editorial that described Best as a native son of the low-country town. Needless to say, the chamber's policy of disassociation did not apply to the Best family. Embarrassed by their brother's defection and apprehensive about small-town prejudice, the whole family feared they would be blamed in some way. Eugene Best even offered to relinquish his promising future as a local banking executive—a magnanimous gesture predictively refused by his superiors.[49]

Best's broadcasts continued to blast the alleged enemies of Germany with unbridled vehemence. He ranted against "funny Frankie," FDR, as the dupe of America's Jewish interest, inveighed against the Semitic takeover of Masonic lodges in the United States (Best was a thirty-second-degree Mason), and recounted lurid tales of Soviet cannibalism on the eastern front.[50] Coarse and unstructured texts such as these irked Dr. Heinrich Fritsche, political controller of German broadcasting, who rebuked Best for the inclusion of extraneous issues in domestic copy.[51] Signs of an estrangement between Best and management soon appeared in the newsroom. He clashed with Fritsche over two words, "Christocrat" and "Jewdocrat," used in his series, "Best's Berlin Broadcasts." Fritsche cancelled a scurrilous "BBB" commentary on the Archbishop of Canterbury's ancestry and, as a precaution, ordered the series preceded by an unusual caveat, "Although he [Best] enjoys the privilege of this station, his views are not necessarily identical with our own."[52] Best sought to have unfriendly news editors assigned to the Russian front, and when this stratagem backfired, he entertained an equally bizarre exile for himself. Miffed by what he considered petty opposition to his work, Best wrote Goebbels: "Am I supposed to think that my superiors at the radio are fools or saboteurs? I cannot get along with such persons; that is evident. I would rather dig out potatoes, or I would rather apply for service in the International SS in Arms. It is enough to drive me to despair."[53] The Propaganda Ministry's troublemaker sulked until early July 1942, when he deserted the Rundfunk for a two-month honeymoon with his new bride, Erna Maurer. Fritsche, disconsolate that he lacked the authority to fire Best outright for his "cheap, bombastic terminology," nevertheless engineered his removal as assistant editor of the German news service.[54]

Back on the wireless, Best's offerings became even more extreme. In October Guess Who enacted the farce of running for Congress. "Elect me to Congress as your protest candidate," he urged, "and I shall do my best to bring about peace before America has fallen into a state of complete chaos and Jewish slavery." Every correspondent should be "a soldier of propaganda," Best maintained, referring to himself as "the alarm clock of America's sleeping conscience." Past administrations had ignored George Washington's sage opposition to involvement in foreign wars, Best lamented, and this indifference cost the lives of "tens of thousands of the country's youth." He announced that BBB clubs were being organized throughout the United States to support his candidacy in the 1944 presidential election. Best pledged as Roosevelt's successor to recall U.S. arms from Europe and to liquidate "one Jewish gangster" for every American lost in combat.[55]

The New Year—1943—presaged a succession of Axis military reversals too disastrous to explain away. In late January Best bade farewell to the beleaguered German defenders at Stalingrad:

The disengagement of the Caucasus divisions and their withdrawal to positions suitable for an offensive later in the year . . . is a feat which ranks with Xenophon's. Similarly, the German troops sacrificing their lives in a defense of civilization are making Stalingrad a new Thermopylae. They recently became hopelessly trapped but they never considered retreat. They died to save the world from the Jewish evils of communism and Plutocracy. My mission is to rouse you to action to end this holocaust of the International Jew.[56]

Best cautioned that a Soviet breakthrough in the east would mean Germany's systematic annihilation of her Jewish minorities. On January 22 Goebbels' hagridden spokesman sarcastically noted:

U.S. newspaper and radio editors have been trying to deceive you [the American public] with announcements concerning the alleged plan of Churchill and Roosevelt to open up a real Second Front in the near future. Any time you hear it spouted out you should shout "The Judocrats should first take Tunis," and then talk.[57]

Tunis, Hitler's last bastion in North Africa, fell to the Allied armies on May 13, 1943. Closer to home, he denounced Allied bombing raids on Berlin as too criminally unique "to compare to Germany's onslaughts on Warsaw and Rotterdam," and that such comparisons "required the logic of a moron."[58] To the south, Mussolini's regime toppled, and on September 9 Marshall Pietro Badoglio's provisional government accepted surrender unconditionally. Hitler struck immediately, rescued an imprisoned Duce in a daring raid on September 12, and within days formed a puppet government with Mussolini as his new Roman *gauleiter*. Best managed a private interview with the raid's chief architect, Haupsturmfuhrer SS Otto Skorzeny, and then beamed the "substance" of their conversation to the United States:

Eisenhower had a whole airborne division poised and ready for a dramatic occupation of Rome. The General lost his nerve when he learned from the traitor Badoglio that some Germans had arrived from the sky. . . . The Jews and Jewdocrats behind the Allies were arranging "a cheap publicity stunt." Mussolini was to go to Palermo on September 14, to Gibraltar on the 15th and then on to New York City on the 16th. Pressmen were to cover a tour of a shackled Mussolini led by a Jewish Rabbi.[59]

Indications are that Best spent an unhappy 18 months in Berlin. Rundfunk officials wearied of his unguarded language and unpredictable behavior. For one who professed fealty to the New Order, Best avoided membership in the Party; shunned Nazi uniforms and emblems; habitually refused to carry state identification cards; and readily acknowledged allegiance to a quintessential United States.[60] He got along badly with U.S.A. Zone staffers on several points. First, Best projected a holier-than-thou image at work, refusing to allow any form of light entertainment on his broadcasts because of the "importance" of his messages; second, he always affected an indifferent attitude toward monetary compensation for service rendered, a nonchalance diagnosed by his colleagues as being disingenuous.[61] Royal Air Force sorties and acute food shortages scarcely elevated Best's dour spirits; on March 5, 1943: "In the terror-raid on Berlin my own house got hit by a fire-bomb. 'Serves the dirty traitor right!' I can hear various Jewdocratic listeners saying in America, but it won't worry me. Raids act as a tonic and will hasten the New Order's victory."[62] On March 29, 1944: "I used to tip the scales at well over 200 lbs. I say, 'used to' because four and a half years of wartime rations have tended to reduce my figure to something like that of Dracula rather than that of Fatty Arbuckle."[63] Best also bore the psychological strain of his impending indictment for treason. He raged against Allied magazines, which almost gleefully anticipated legal action, and on May 9, 1943, Best threw down his gauntlet to Attorney-General Nicholas Biddle: "Not only is the Department of Justice powerless to arrest me but no executioner could be found in America so low as to kill a man who has dedicated his life to saving America from the Jews."[64] A federal grand jury indicated Goebbels' radio traitors on July 27, a move Best heralded as a Rooseveltian smear tactic designed to compromise his U.S. presidential candidacy.[65]

The Rundfunk veiled Best's return to Vienna in late autumn of 1943 with prerecorded commentaries. Only six months away from Operation Overlord, the transplanted BBB programs extolled Germany's Atlantic wall as impregnable. When the events of June 6, 1944, dispelled this confidence, Best fell back on the Reich's *Vergeltungswaffe* (vengeance weapon) program:

D-Day will begin a flow of death from Europe to Britain and the U.S.A. . . . The new flying projectiles which are being launched against England are stacked not in mere hundreds of thousands, but in tens of hundreds of thousands. . . . Nothing in the nature of a V.1 catastrophe can ever even approach the U.S.A., but catastrophes of another and even worse kind can and will some day strike our country hard. . . .

So far V.1 has been doing more practice shooting than otherwise and by the time it reaches its climax, V.2, V.3, V.4, etc. will be ready to step into the ring with deadlier punches.[66]

A fortnight after the Normandy Invasion Best aired a tour of new buzz bomb factories—several of which were under aerial attack during his visit—to heighten the psychological terror of Hitler's secret weapon.[67]

Nazi technology did nothing to check the Allied war effort, however, and at the beginning of August 1944 Germany seemed to be in imminent danger of a total collapse. Best's last favorable combat report came on October 6 in reference to the Battle of Arnheim (Operation Market-Garden). Three Allied airborne divisions had been parachuted behind enemy lines at Arnheim, Holland, on September 17 to secure bridges across the Meuse, Waal, and Lower Rhine rivers for a strike by the British Second Army into northern Germany. This 9,000 man invasion contingent was surprised by a superior German force, and on September 25 only 2,000 battered survivors managed to slip back across their own lines. Best toasted Hitler's generalship and expressed hope that the Arnheim fiasco would serve as a "graphic" example to his countrymen.[68] Five hundred and forty miles from Berlin and increasingly distracted by Soviet eastern advances Best seldom mentioned the war's progress after Arnheim—not even Germany's winter counteroffensive in the Ardennes. On January 17, 1945, the day Warsaw fell to the Red Army, he entreated the United States to allow "Europe" to pursue its own destiny. Best praised Hitler as one who would "settle the hash of the Bolshevik beast" and would be "a valuable partner to the U.S.A. in the fruitful exchange of cultural and material values."[69]

On April 13 Soviet soldiers occupied Vienna, and in Berlin the Rundfunk announced that Best's program would not be carried as scheduled. Best fled his Vienna apartment, carelessly forgetting a cache of personal papers that would eventually help to convict him. Taking Erna Maurer with him, he disappeared into the British-occupied zone of Austria. He remained at large until February 10, 1946, when British security police discovered him living on his wife's farm near Villach. Best, who by that time had grown a full beard for disguise, claimed that any recognition must have been through a suspected Communist informant. Once arrested, Best was turned over to the U.S. authorities, who interned him for a period at Camp Marcus Orr near Salzburg. Best remained at Salzburg ten months before leaving the camp to join fellow radio traitor Douglas Chandler in Frankfurt, Germany, for their flight back to the United States.[70]

Best was tried in Boston, because a provision in the treason law stipulates that persons accused while abroad must be tried in the district where they reenter the United States. In Best's case, the plane bringing him and Chandler from Germany was forced down at Westover Field, Chicopee, Massachusetts, by inclement weather. The pair spent several days at FBI headquarters in

Washington, D.C., and returned to Boston's East Cambridge jail on January 4, 1947. At his arraignment Best told the court, "I need no defense. I have counsel in the Holy Trinity—the Father, the Son and the Holy Ghost." Such irrational outbursts were overlooked by a team of psychiatrists, who declared the defendant sane and able to stand trial on March 29, 1948.[71] Best requested a change of venue and subpoenas for 22 character witnesses, among whom were Franz von Papen, Field Marshal Albert Kesselring, Hans Joachim Riecke, the former Nazi under-secretary of state, and one Englishman, the controversial Twelfth Duke of Bedford. Judge Francis J. W. Ford refused the motions. The court did allow a host of prosecution witnesses, however, which included Messrs. Shirer, Lochner, and Oechsner plus numerous radio officials from Reichrundfunk and Vienna.[72]

For an entire week prosecutor Tom DeWolfe's witnesses linked Best directly to the Nazi war effort. Werner Plack testified that the accused's broadcasts were designed to combat world communism. This testimony buoyed Best, who remarked to his court-appointed lawyer, "That makes a different story, doesn't it?"[73] Beginning April 13, Best favored the jury with a three-day rambling colloquy on communism and international Jewry, and the influence of these movements on the Roosevelt administration: Yes, he admired Hitler and thought Germany could win the war; yes, he had worked with William Joyce—Lord Haw Haw—who was hanged by the British as a traitor; yes, he had collected $700 a month while broadcasting, cognizant of his allegiance to the United States. Finally unnerved by DeWolfe's probing cross-examination, Best shot back, "I would prefer to be denounced as a traitor by people who were traitors themselves, rather than actually be a traitor."[74] On April 16 the court observed Best's fifty-second birthday with a verdict of guilty. At the presentencing hearings the defense counsel portrayed his client as a "fanatic, a crusader, doing what he thought best for his country." Judge Ford disagreed: "A fanatic can do as much harm to his country as any other person" and added, "He knew what he was doing—when a man intends to betray his country, his motive is immaterial."[75]

Six weeks after his conviction, Best was sentenced to life imprisonment and fined $10,000. There followed a two-year appeals process, a tedious period for Best brightened only by his wife's arrival in the United States. The U.S. Circuit Court affirmed the traitor's conviction on July 7, 1950. Still unresigned to his fate, Best wrote President Harry S. Truman from his cell:

As one who has been battling against Soviet Communism unremittingly for almost thirty years . . . I beg herewith to offer my services in any desired capacity to you as our Chief Executive. . . . And, now that the Korean action of the Comintern . . . has awakened you to at least partial appreciation of the fact that the Soviet Union has been a war-to-the-death enemy . . . [m]ay you never again "backslide" into the errors of understanding such friends as Stalin.[76]

Eight months lapsed before the High Court notified Best of its refusal to hear the case. After suffering a cerebral hemorrhage in August 1951, he was transferred from the federal penitentiary in Danbury, Connecticut, to the Medical Center for Federal Prisoners in Springfield, Missouri. He died on December 16, 1952, and his body was sent to South Carolina for burial in Pacolet's Methodist Community Cemetery.[77] Robert Henry Best had come home at last.

Although Best's defection will always remain a puzzle to those who knew him, retracing his life provides insight into the circumstances influencing his decision. A review of Best's early years shows that he had not anchored his roots too firmly into his native soil of Piedmont, South Carolina. Memories of his hard youth and the anticipation of a highly competitive job market in the United States discouraged his return home. Viennese life, according to Dorothy Thompson and Frederic Scheu, also took its toll, both intellectually and professionally. His stringer status gave him a peculiar role in the community he delighted in and found impossible to relinquish. Concomitantly, Best became frustrated by the limitations of his station and the upward mobility of his more fortunate colleagues. He failed to see, or would not admit, that his stagnant career bore a direct relationship to his irregular life style and casual administrative procedures, his unfortunate choice of women, and his questionable connections within the city's seamier circles—all of which adversely influenced UP management. During the 1930s Best had gravitated toward national socialism through his endorsement of the Clerical Fascist administrations of Engelbert Dollfuss and Kurt Schuschnigg, and by the time of the Anschluss his ideological leap was not quantum in size. Pearl Harbor put a name to his conversion—treason—and he could no longer evade the charge. To be sure, there was an element of opportunism in Best's decision. Without working for the Nazis his choices were either deportation or incarceration. Ironically, this misfit fared no better with the Reichrundfunk than with the United Press.

Mildred (Axis Sally) Gillars

Nurse Constance Drexel in war-torn France

E D WARD
DELANEY

- was -

Behind the
Iron Curtain

When it Fell

He Tells All!!

In His Revealing and
Dramatically Presented Lecture

SEVEN YEARS BEHIND THE WAR FRONT!

Internationally known novelist, speaker, publicist, foreign correspondent, news commenator and world traveler, Edward Delaney is now disclosing for audiences throughout the country his on the spot observations and personal experiences during the war and the subsequent period of 'peace'. Many of the vital topics of our times are dealt with — plainly and forcefully.

Although born in America, he has resided abroad for almost two decades; four years in Asia, Australia, British India, Dutch East Indies and two years in Africa, followed by extensive stay in Central America and several years in Europe. During the war his fact-finding travels were from the Baltic Sea to the Balkans, from Paris to Poland, in Germany, Italy, Rumania, Bulgaria, Yugoslavia, Hungary and Czechoslovakia when the 'Iron Curtain' fell.

WHY WERE FACTS ABOUT EUROPE'S REDS SUPPRESSED?

Why were the pieous pleas of besieged Prague ignored and the city never liberated? Why did we wait three years to protest the Red 'grab' of Czechoslovakia? Why was it not revealed that Soviet slave camps existed in Central Europe two months after the armistice of 1945? Why did we permit the partition of Europe? Why was there a Morganthau Plan — which spawned the Marshall Plan? His talks spotlight incidents, facts and symptoms of political trends that answer some of these vexing questions.

IS ANOTHER WAR INEVITABLE?

We can judge the future by the record of the past. As one of the original commentators on radio networks in the United States and abroad, this speaker presents some timely and pertinent observations on past and current events and what they mean to us. He reported the first eye-witness comments of the war from Berlin the day it began — last and only personalized story of its ending in Prague — nearly six years later.

"Not to have heard his inside story of Europe, means having missed an amazingly candid word picture of things as they were — and not as they were often reported."—N. Whitehead, Financial News, London.

E. L. Delaney lecture poster
Source: FBI files

The Georgia Peach
Source: Joan Givner. Used by permission

Jane Anderson and the Conrads at Capel House
Source: John Conrad, *Joseph Conrad: Times Remembered* (New York:
Cambridge University Press, 1981). Used by permission

Otto Koischwitz at Hunter College
Source: Hunter College Archives. Used
by permission

Examples of Mr. O.K.'s pen drawings

Adolph Busse
Source: Hunter College Archives. Used by permission

Robert Best (top row, fourth from the left) as a member of the Wofford College Engineering Club (1916)
Source: Archives, Wofford College, Spartanburg, S.C. Used by permission

Best and Chandler in custody

Donald Day circa 1942

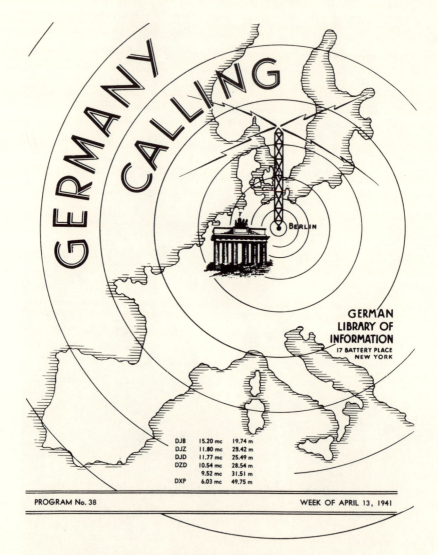

GERMANY CALLING

BERLIN

GERMAN
LIBRARY OF
INFORMATION
17 BATTERY PLACE
NEW YORK

DJB	15.20 mc	19.74 m
DJZ	11.80 mc	25.42 m
DJD	11.77 mc	25.49 m
DZD	10.54 mc	28.54 m
	9.52 mc	31.51 m
DXP	6.03 mc	49.75 m

PROGRAM No. 38   WEEK OF APRIL 13, 1941

German Library of Information Graphic (New York City)

Program for the Week of April 13 to April 19, 1941

EVERY DAY

6:00 A. M. — 4:50 P.M.

D J B — 19 m

EST A.M.	PST A.M.	
6:00	3:00	Call, Early Bird Concert
6:30	3:30	**News in English**
6:45	3:45	"Action Reports from the Front" (Monday, Wednesday, Friday) Rieder Talk — (Tuesday, Thursday, Saturday)
7:00	4:00	Music
8:00	5:00	**News in German**
8:15	5:15	Music
8:30	5:30	**News in English**
8:45	5:45	SILENT
11:30	8:30	**News in English**
11:45	8:45	SILENT
P.M.		
12:30	9:30	**News in English**
12:45	9:45	SILENT
1:30	10:30	**News in English**

D J Z — 25 m

3:30	12:30	**News in English**
3:45	12:45	**News in French**
4:00	1:00	SILENT

D Z D — 28 m

4:30	1:30	**News in English**

11:05 P.M. — 1:00 A.M.

D X P — 49 m

11:05	8:05	Late Music
11:15	8:15	**News in English**
11:30	8:30	Late Music Continued
Midnight		
12:00	9:00	**News in English**
A.M.		
12:15	9:15	Concert of Light Music by a Regional Broadcasting Orchestra
1:00	10:00	Sign Off until 6:00 A.M. (3:00 A.M. PST)

Sunday, April 13

D J D — 25 m; 31 m; D X P — 49 m

EST P.M.	PST P.M.	
4:50	1:50	Call, German Folk Songs
4:55	1:55	Program for the Day
5:00	2:00	"The Easter Hare"
5:30	2:30	The Zeesen Women's Club
5:45	2:45	**News in German**
6:00	3:00	**News in English**
6:15	3:15	German Folk Concert
7:00	4:00	"From the German Heart"
7:15	4:15	(a) News Review in French (b) Topical Talk in German
7:30	4:30	"Today in Germany"

D J D — 25 m; D Z D — 28 m; 31 m; D X P — 49 m

8:00	5:00	**News in German**
8:15	5:15	**"America Asks — Germany Answers"** (Answers to Questions from American Listeners)
8:30	5:30	"LORD HAW-HAW"
8:45	5:45	Sunday Evening Program
9:00	6:00	Rear-Admiral Lützow
9:15	6:15	Economic Review
9:20	6:20	"Action Reports from the Front"
9:30	6:30	"Anchors Aweigh"
10:00	7:00	"Easter Bells are Ringing"
10:15	7:15	**News in German**
10:30	7:30	**News in English**
10:50	7:50	Talk in English

Monday, April 14

D J D — 25 m; 31 m; D X P — 49 m

4:50	1:50	Call, German Folk Songs
4:55	1:55	Program for the Day
5:00	2:00	Chamber Music
5:45	2:45	**News in German**
6:00	3:00	**News in English**
6:15	3:15	Music of the German Countryside
7:15	4:15	Topical Talk in German
7:30	4:30	"Today in Germany"

U.S.A. Zone offerings

D J D — 25 m; D Z D — 28 m; 31 m; D X P — 49 m

EST P.M.	PST P.M.	
8:00	5:00	**News in German**
8:15	5:15	**"America Asks — Germany Answers"** (Answers to Questions from American Listeners)
8:45	5:45	"Dear Harry": Fred Kaltenbach
9:00	6:00	"O. K. SPEAKING"
9:15	6:15	Economic Review
9:20	6:20	E. D. WARD
9:30	6:30	Notions Club
10:00	7:00	Music
10:15	7:15	**News in German**
10:30	7:30	**News in English**
10:50	7:50	"Listen and Judge for Yourself"

Tuesday, April 15

D J D — 25 m; 31 m; D X P — 49 m

4:50	1:50	Call, German Folk Songs
4:55	1:55	Program for the Day
5:00	2:00	Light Music
5:30	2:30	"Happy Family"
5:45	2:45	**News in German**
6:00	3:00	**News in English**
6:15	3:15	Berlin Philharmonic Orchestra
7:15	4:15	PRESS REVIEW BY HANS FRITSCHE
7:30	4:30	"Today in Germany"

D J D — 25 m; D Z D — 28 m; 31 m; D X P — 49 m

8:00	5:00	**News in German**
8:15	5:15	**"America Asks — Germany Answers"** (Answers to Questions from American Listeners)
8:30	5:30	"LORD HAW-HAW"
8:45	5:45	Variety Entertainment
9:00	6:00	"O. K. SPEAKING"
9:15	6:15	Economic Review
9:20	6:20	"Action Reports from the Front"
9:30	6:30	Scenes from "Aimee"
10:15	7:15	**News in German**
10:30	7:30	**News in English**
10:50	7:50	Fred W. Kaltenbach: German Contributions to Making America

Wednesday, April 16

DJD — 25 m; 31 m; DXP — 49 m

EST P.M.	PST P.M.	
4:50	1:50	Call, German Folk Songs
4:55	1:55	Program for the Day
5:00	2:00	Soldiers' Songs
5:30	2:30	"Through a Woman's Eyes"
5:45	2:45	**News in German**
6:00	3:00	**News in English**
6:15	3:15	Musical Program
6:45	3:45	"Eine Kleine Nachtmusik" (Mozart), conducted by Wilhelm Furtwängler
7:15	4:15	Topical Talk in German
7:30	4:30	"Today in Germany"

DJD — 25 m; DZD — 28 m; 31 m; DXP — 49 m

8:00	5:00	**News in German**
8:15	5:15	**"America Asks — Germany Answers"** (Answers to Questions from American Listeners)
8:30	5:30	**"Interview of the Week":** Dr. Erika Schirmer
8:45	5:45	"Thoughts and Things"
9:00	6:00	"O. K. SPEAKING"
9:15	6:15	Economic Review
9:20	6:20	E. D. WARD
9:30	6:30	Dance Music and Carbaret
10:00	7:00	Music
10:15	7:15	**News in German**
10:30	7:30	**News in English**
10:50	7:50	Talk in English

Thursday, April 17

DJD — 25 m; 31 m; DXP — 49 m

EST P.M.	PST P.M.	
4:50	1:50	Call, German Folk Songs
4:55	1:55	Program for the Day
5:00	2:00	Irish Concert Hour
5:30	2:30	**Program Preview for the Week of April 27 to May 3**
5:45	2:45	**News in German**
6:00	3:00	**News in English**
6:15	3:15	Request Concert for the Army
7:15	4:15	PRESS REVIEW BY HANS FRITSCHE
7:30	4:30	"Today in Germany"

DJD — 25 m; DZD — 28 m; 31 m; DXP — 49 m

8:00	5:00	**News in German**
8:15	5:15	**"America Asks — Germany Answers"** (Answers to Questions from American Listeners)
8:30	5:30	"College Hour": Dr. Otto Koischwitz
8:45	5:45	Orchestra Concert
9:00	6:00	"O. K. SPEAKING"
9:20	6:20	"Action Reports from the Front"
9:30	6:30	"The Struggle for Tin"
10:15	7:15	**News in German**
10:30	7:30	**News in English**
10:50	7:50	"Jim and Johnny"

U.S.A. Zone offerings

Friday, April 18

DJD — 25 m; 31 m; DXP — 49 m

EST P.M.	PST P.M.	
4:50	1:50	Call, German Folk Songs
4:55	1:55	Program for the Day
5:00	2:00	"Praise be to Music"
5:30	2:30	Concert Program
5:45	2:45	**News in German**
6:00	3:00	**News in English**
6:15	3:15	Viennese Music
7:15	4:15	Topical Talk in German
7:30	4:30	"Today in Germany"

DJD — 25 m; DZD — 28 m; 31 m; DXP — 49 m

8:00	5:00	**News in German**
8:15	5:15	**"America Asks — Germany Answers"** (Answers to Questions from American Listeners)
8:30	5:30	"LORD HAW-HAW"
8:45	5:45	Concert Program
9:00	6:00	"O. K. SPEAKING"
9:15	6:15	Economic Review
9:20	6:20	E. D. WARD
9:30	6:30	Music by the Great Masters: Franz Liszt
10:15	7:15	**News in German**
10:30	7:30	**News in English**
10:50	7:50	**Program Preview for the Week of April 20 to April 26**

Saturday, April 19

DJD — 25 m; 31 m; DXP — 49 m

EST P.M.	PST P.M.	
4:50	1:50	Call, German Folk Songs
4:55	1:55	Program for the Day
5:00	2:00	Musical Cabaret
5:30	2:30	Concert Program
5:45	2:45	**News in German**
6:00	3:00	**News in English**
6:15	3:15	Dance Music
7:15	4:15	PRESS REVIEW BY HANS FRITSCHE
7:30	4:30	"Today in Germany"

DJD — 25 m; DZD — 28 m; 31 m; DXP — 49 m

8:00	5:00	**News in German**
8:15	5:15	**"America Asks — Germany Answers"** (Answers to Questions from American Listeners)
8:30	5:30	"Mirror of German Progress"
8:45	5:45	"Military Review": Fred W. Kaltenbach
9:00	6:00	Talk in English
9:15	6:15	Economic Review
9:20	6:20	"Fritz and Fred, the Friendly Quarrelers"
9:30	6:30	Dance Music and Cabaret
10:15	7:15	**News in German**
10:30	7:30	**News in English**
10:50	7:50	"Hot Off the Wire"

A.M.		
12:15	9:15	**Program Preview for the Week of April 20 to April 26 for the Pacific Coast**

5

Douglas Chandler, Alias Paul Revere

Douglas Chandler was born in Chicago on May 26, 1889, the son of Walter Gardner Chandler (March 29, 1859), who hailed from Douglas, Massachusetts. Little is known of his mother, Carrie Barbour Chandler (August 21, 1859), a native of Lancaster, Wisconsin. Walter Chandler attended Phillips Andover and graduated from Brown University. In his subsequent studies Chandler pursued a master's degree at the University of Wisconsin and at Cambridge, England. More than an academician—a student of the classics—Chandler was an aspiring entrepreneur who tried everything from sheep raising in Florida to the establishment of a girls' school.[1]

Chandler's family came to Baltimore, Maryland, in 1895 when small, exclusive schools were in vogue to succeed Dr. Edward Daves as teacher of English and Latin in Hall House. Five years later he organized the Arundel School at the southwest corner of St. Paul and Madison streets. The elder Chandler remained headmaster there less than two years. From this post he went on to finance several brass works in Greensboro and Asheville, North Carolina, lost his proverbial shirt in the deal, and was forced to borrow money from his wife to make good the losses. "My father had a feeling of insecurity because of his father's attitude," remembered his son. Douglas' mother and maternal grandmother repeatedly supplied the funds for these wild schemes. Despite his shortcomings, Walter Chandler was generally a liked person, optimistic, kindly, tolerant, and above all sociable. A periodic drinker, he would occasionally disappear for days or weeks and "have to be located."[2]

Illness in the boy's extended family only served to exaggerate the problems incurred by Walter Chandler's business ventures. Douglas' great maternal aunt had been institutionalized for a mental condition, and his mother's brother died in an asylum. His maternal grandmother's long affliction with crippling arthritis made a permanent impression on the child. Perhaps this family atmosphere induced the insomnia that plagued Douglas during his adolescence. Down through this troubled lineage, young Chandler regarded his grandfather Barbour as a beacon, the personification of America's pioneer spirit. He relished stories of how the old patr arch had migrated to Wisconsin as a lad, carving out for himself a homestead and a career in law. "He was one of the handsomest men I ever saw," proclaimed Chandler in later years. "In his will he forgave all who owed him."[3]

Upon graduation from a Baltimore private school, Douglas bypassed college for New York City and a career in advertising. He also saw brief, if undistinguished, service in the United States Navy during the closing months of World War I.[4] Chandler was not popular with other navy personnel. He affected an air of superiority and always talked about poetry, art, and music. Quite often he was the butt of cruel jokes from his shipmates.

Chandler's addiction to the byline led him into the newspaper business and freelance writing for popular magazines. For a time the Baltimore *Sunday American* carried an obscure weekly news roundup column entitled "This and That," which issued from Chandler's pen. During the interwar years his contributions would appear in the *National Geographic* magazine, not as a staff writer (a position he deemed altogether appropriate), but rather as a contributor. He also contributed to the old *Life* magazine when it was a humor publication—"before it degenerated into a vulgar photoweekly," Chandler confided to agents of the FBI following his capture in 1946. There persisted in Chandler's writing a strain of undisguised contempt for America's mass society and unleavened culture. The typical American, according to Chandler, was a "sophmoron" who possessed a "thin and brittle veneer of culture," condemning this shallow Babbitt to mistake "isms" for reasoned ideology and "cults" for the collective pursuit of philosophical truths. A postwar issue of *Newsweek* researched Chandler's early editorials and congratulated him on such a brilliant self-portrait.[5]

On August 27, 1924, Chandler married Pittsburgh heiress Laura Jay Wurts in a quiet ceremony at Bar Harbor, Maine. The great granddaughter of John Jay, the first chief justice of the United States; the niece of George Guthrie, former ambassador to Japan; and the daughter of Alexander Jay Wurts, the brilliant Carnegie Tech professor of electrical engineering and inventor, Laura Wurts represented wealth and social position. There is no record as to what Laura's family thought of her new husband, although Chandler complained in later years that his brother-in-law, Thomas Childs Wurts, had shown little "understanding" in his executorship of her inheritance. As a struggling stock broker in New York City, Chandler naturally assumed responsibility for his new bride's wealth—which amounted to several annuities and a bank account of approximately $200,000. During the ensuring five years, however, Chandler discovered that the availability of venture capital was no guarantee of success on the stock market. The Depression of 1929 and his own risky investments conspired to seriously compromise Laura's small fortune.[6] Despite limited resources, the couple entertained regularly in their cramped flat on West 58 Street. An old acquaintance recalled:

She asked my husband and me to cocktails. The small room was jammed. One of the guests was I believe Sinclair Lewis—Laura rather fancied herself as a "saloniste." . . . The baby—I suppose Laurette—was in a baby carriage in the bathroom at the rear of the apartment. . . . Laura told me he [Chandler] had been in a firm in Wall Street; let go after the 1929 Crash; could get no job. So she went to work with Princess Obolenski in her dress shop. Laura said the better she did in business the sicker he became till he went to bed with his face to the wall.[7]

Acceptance of his own professional shortcomings would have broken Chandler, and the prospect of reliving his father's sad existence menaced his sanity. Under the care of a "nerve specialist" who had diagnosed him as "a walking nervous breakdown," Chandler confided to friends on several occasions: "I am a perfectionist-defeatist (one who aims for perfection but is always defeated). . . . My capacity for happiness is great. My capacity for suffering is greater. My forebodings of suffering to come have tormented me."[8] Filled with frustration and resentment, Chandler, his wife, and two daughters—five-year-old Laurette and two-year-old Patricia—sailed for France on September 3, 1931. Aside from references to his declining health, he described his decision to go abroad as "the sloughing off of inhibited provincialism."[9]

The expatriates headed for a small village on the French Riviera, Vence Alps Maritimes. There the family remained for 18 months. In March 1933, the Chandlers crossed into Germany for the first time. Chandler rented a villa near Munich on Starnberger See. Seemingly by chance he met Rolf Hoffman, who was attaché in the Nazi Press Department and contact for the foreign journalists under Press Chief Erst (Putzi) Hanfstaengel. Hoffman developed an attachment to the Chandler household. Both he and Hanfstaengel went to great lengths to expose their American guests to the Reich's many welfare organizations. Desirous of making the couple feel at home, Hoffman and associates introduced them to a bevy of British and U.S. journalists who were visiting Munich in 1933. While in Starnberg Chandler made the acquaintance of Robert Dudley Longyear, who was consul general in Munich. Longyear's residence was in Starnberg, and the two were frequently together.

Before making the trip to Germany my wife and I had been warned by the United States consul at Nice against our plan inasmuch as he claimed there was a reign of terror going on and that we would be subjecting ourselves to great physical danger. Two acquaintances in Vences . . . told us that this was nonsense and that we would find quiet and harmony existing. We accepted their advice. . . . On the contrary, whereas in the first few weeks there were daily many beggars at our gate, as the weeks advanced such signs of poverty ceased and a general contented attitude was observable among the population.[10]

Chandler's new friend monopolized his calendar. Longyear invited him on an official inspection of Dachau. They toured the prisoners' mess and witnessed inmates building an outdoor swimming pool. Both men found the barracks and physical layout to be "wholesome and adequate." Longyear wryly observed to his guest that he could not report "the account of horrors which would be expected of him." "All these factors and the incident of the Nice Consul's warnings," concluded Chandler, "lead my wife and I to the conclusion that there was some deliberate effort on the part of our authorities to color and distort the actual existing conditions in Germany." By summer's end the Chandlers had moved from Starnberg into Austria, renting a cottage in Sanct Wolfgang, where they remained until April 1934.[11]

The pro-German sentiment reflected across Austria surprised Chandler. For instance, during a local school Christmas drama his youngest daughter strode center stage and gave the Nazi salute, saying "Heil Hitler." Before he could admonish the child, the director took him aside and said, "Don't bother about that, Mr. Chandler. We all say that here. Those are our sentiments."[12]

Everywhere he looked during this phase of his European sojourn, the ominous specter of bolshevism manifested itself. During the winter of 1934 the Chandlers made several excursions to Vienna and Budapest with letters of introduction. These documents kept them confined to pro-Nazi circles. From those they met, Chandler learned of widespread Red subversion in Vienna and "horrible details of the Bolshevik putsch and the reign of terror under Bela Kun in Hungary." Their fact-finding trip through the Balkans that spring revealed similar conditions. Returning from Greece in June 1934, the Chandlers settled for the summer in Bohinska Jazero, a mountain resort in the northwestern corner of Yugoslavia. Chandler reported that Communist agitation in the region had completely unnerved the countryside. Back to the Balkans in the fall, the couple lingered on the island of Corfu for eight months. This time without their children, they criss-crossed Greece, documenting the flimsiest rumor on Soviet activities. In June 1935 they returned to Austria, spending several months in Innsbruck before entering Germany.[13]

At this point Rolf Hoffman again contacted Chandler, inviting him to a convention of journalists at Frankfurt am Main. While at the conclave Hoffman conducted Chandler through newly constructed workers' dormitories, schools, hospitals, and model factories. The contributions made by the Women's Labor Organization, volunteers who substituted for expectant mothers in these plants, impressed Chandler as much as the Reich's new maternity program. Herr Hoffman materialized at Chandler's new Freudenstadt residence in September with tickets to a forthcoming Nuremberg Party Congress. As before, it was important to Hoffman that Chandler mix socially with the Anglo-American delegation represented there. Later that fall Hoffman asked Chandler to an anti-Comintern convention. A week in length, the convention was attended by 50 delegates representing 14 countries. There were long sessions daily in which these representatives outlined in tedious detail the overt and covert activities of bolshevism in their respective countries. So taken by these proceedings, Chandler observed in retrospect:

The effect of this detailed and personal presentation of the havoc wrought by Soviet Bolshevik aggression on my mind was deep and lasting and undoubtedly contributed much to the decision which I made six years later. . . . I formed a few real friendships among these men with two or three of whom I corresponded for several years.[14]

In April 1936 the Chandlers spent a fortnight on the Riviera en route to North Africa. They were the guests of Consul General Longyear during their stay in Marseilles. Several weeks were spent traveling in Algiers and Morocco, and then a week in Tangier, where the U.S. minister furnished Chandler with a letter of introduction to a prominent shipowner in Malaga, Spain. Although the Spanish Civil War was in the offing, the couple was not informed by any of the diplomatic representatives in Tangier. They crossed to Algeciras, rented a car, and drove down the coast to Malaga. On the way, the Chandlers witnessed gatherings of unruly citizens, and plastered on many roadside buildings were crude symbols of the hammer and sickle. Chandler's shipping magnate friends in Malaga, the Petersons, warned him to leave for Gibraltar at once and take a ship to France. The Americans left Spain immediately, only days before their host's murder. Once in France, they called on an old acquaintance of the Wurts family, Donald Bigelow, who served in the diplomatic corps. The twosome informed their government, through Bigelow, of the deteriorating situation in Spain. Following a brief rest, Douglas and Laura returned to Freudenstadt.[15]

During his early days in Freudenstadt, Chandler discovered the Ikon camera and bought one. A course in photography went with the camera and, over a period of time, he developed into an excellent photographer. Laura silently begrudged her husband's expensive hobby, but as it was the first diversion to pique his interest since their expatriation, she said nothing.[16] Chandler took hundreds of snapshots while in North Africa. He sent several hundred of these photographs to Oliver La Gorce, associate editor of the *National Geographic*, an old acquaintance. A number of these illustrations were accepted for the *Geographic* archives, and this transaction proved the opening wedge for Chandler's association as a contributing correspondent several months later.[17]

La Gorce contacted Chandler in mid-summer 1936, asking him to survey the city of Berlin and prepare an illustrated article for the magazine. During the next three years he undertook several assignments, covering the Baltic and Scandinavian countries, Belgium, the island of Barnholme, Turkey, Yugoslavia, and Albania. In Riga, Tallin, and Helsinki Chandler discussed the likelihood for Bolshevik aggression with veteran newspaper correspondents. "These grateful Baltic countries," he wrote home, "gave full credit to Germany for having rescued them from their Soviet aggressors back in 1919 and the early 20's." While in the region Chandler called on Donald Day, the Russophobic Baltic correspondent for the Chicago *Tribune*, whose unbridled commentaries would lampoon the Kremlin for 23 years. Awed by Day's personal sacrifices to Soviet intrigue and his anti-Communist rhetoric, Chandler adopted this controversial journalist as his champion.[18]

Perennial Nazi-watcher George Seldes pronounced Chandler's connection with right-wing elements of the Fourth-Estate as blatant and longstanding, beginning with Hearst's Baltimore *American*, ending with *National Geographic*, and interspersed with such dubious characters as the *Tribune*'s Donald Day, who brought him to nazism. In a wartime article Seldes would charge that the *National Geographic* had fired Chandler (July 31, 1943) solely because he had accepted under-the-table payments from Berlin.[19] Political commentator Elmer Davis maintained that this same hypocritical sense of moral outrage had, in the final analysis, served to convict an otherwise pathetic figure.

Other men throughout the war were writing in American newspapers things not much less virulent than what Best and Chandler were saying but they were in the clear. . . . What made Best and Chandler traitors was that Goebbels paid them to say it. The distinction may seem illogical; more harm can be done by a widely circulated American newspaper than by short-wave broadcasts of known enemy origin. . . . But it was merely to preserve that distinction that the Founding Fathers wrote their definition of treason, and to obliterate it would probably create far more evils than it would cure.[20]

The benefit of seven years' hindsight revealed to Seldes a hidden agenda behind the collaborative efforts of Chandler and La Gorce. Right on page one of Chandler's "Berlin" essay (February 1937) a prim matriarch lauded Hitler's new revolution in the field of art known as realism, which repudiated degenerate impressionism. Photographs of Berlin festooned with swastikas were "indisputable evidence" of the editorial board's pro-Nazi attitude. Berliners, according to Chandler's copy, avoided faddish apparel and spurned consumerism and self-promotion. Without class distinctions there were few society columns in the city's newspapers. Urbanites pursued outdoor recreation, which accounted for the vitality and self-reliance of Aryan youth. Germany's mammoth industrial cartels had eradicated slum life with the construction of modern worker communities. Beneficiaries of the Reich's Winter Relief charity campaigns drew direct assistance inexpensively and without bureaucratic delays. Berlin's *zeitgeist* struck Chandler as evidence of Germany's impending greatness as a world power.

At the close of my last day in Berlin, I stand on the north end of a bridge facing the curve of the Spree. A bent old man stops at the bridge rail, opens a paper bag, and, taking out small lumps of bread, flings them one by one out over the river. With childish delight he watches as gulls swoop and pluck the morsels from the air. Across the bridge returning from an outing, marches a group of small boys wearing the uniform of the Hitler Youth. . . . They are singing in accurately pitched, youthful treble that moving modern national song, the Horst Wessel Lied.[21]

It followed that Chandler's literary depiction of the Soviet Union was far more severe and far more subtle than his accounts of Nazi Germany. Limited by the basic editorial restrictions of *National Geographic* magazine, he nevertheless cleverly managed to convey his message. In a 1938 article, "Flying around the Baltic," Chandler used humor as a weapon during an innocent tour of Riga's zoo.

I visited the zoo. Rather shamefacedly the custodian showed me around the meager exhibit. "During the five terrible months of the Communist invasion in 1919 when 5,000 of our inhabitants were murdered, 8,500 died of starvation, and 30,000 were imprisoned, we were forced to eat the menagerie," he explained.

Seeing my shocked expression, he continued in a lighter vein, "The elephant fed a crowd of hungry people for weeks. It was the porcupines and armadillos that yielded the least nourishment—there was a shortage of gloves and can openers at that time."[22]

In November 1936, the Chandlers took lodgings in the university city of Goettingen near Hanover. They moved to divorce their children from the Swabian dialect in Freudenstadt. During their year's residence in Goettingen, they visited Berlin several times as the guests of U.S. military attaché Truman Smith, another old friend of Laura's family.[23]

The son of a career officer killed in the Philippine insurrection, Smith graduated from Yale University before enlistment. He saw action at Chateau-Thierry and Meuse-Argonne during World War I. After the Armistice he was assigned to Germany as a military observer. He spent time in Bavaria in 1922, and during that time he managed an interview with Hitler. Impressed by the Austrian's charismatic personality, Smith nevertheless doubted the rabble-rouser's ability to hold his unruly movement together. Following a succession of drab assignments in the United States, the colonel's career peaked in August 1935, when he once again returned to Berlin as military attaché.

As attaché, Colonel Smith reported on the growth and deployment of the Nazi war machine. Because his estimation of the Luftwaffe was far above that of the RAF air attaché in Berlin, his superiors in Washington urged more caution and less hysteria. In November 1936, Smith flew home to defend his estimates before U.S. Military Intelligence, but he won little ground. He next arranged to have Field Marshal Herman Goering acquaint Colonel Charles A. Lindbergh with Germany's military prowess. The famous aviator substantiated Smith's contentions. Critics held that both men were virtually fifth-columnists, deliberately attempting to foster isolationism.

Suspicion and innuendo dogged Smith's heels throughout the remainder of his career in Berlin, which ended in March 1939. He left the service in September 1941, rejoined the Intelligence Division of the United States Army's general staff the next year, and again retired in June 1946. Several months later the colonel ran for Congress and lost. He died in October 1970.[24]

Through Smith, the Chandlers became acquainted with two influential families—the Bülows and the Schirmers. Ulrich von Bülow, an ardent Nazi and geologist, served with Hoffman as the editorial board for the ministry's propaganda sheet, "News from Germany." With his American heiress wife as the go-between, von Bülow met and, in selected cases, actually recruited members of Goebbels' U.S.A. and British overseas departments, including William Joyce, Jane Anderson, and Chandler himself. Herr von Bülow helped sustain Joyce's morale during reoccurring periods of melancholy, and on the eve of World War II the German couple were with Lord and Lady Haw-Haw.

We [Joyce and wife Margaret] went to tea with some friends whose name is famous in German history. They too felt no emotion except surprise and regret. We talked of England: and my host was so inspiring in his eloquence on the subject of what England might have achieved in friendship with Germany that, as I looked out on the twilight enshrouding the Kurfürstendamm I could think of nothing to say but Marlowe's famous lines: "Cut is the branch that might have grown full strait. And burned is Apollo's laurel bough!"

In Chandler's case the von Bülows would pirate him away from the Foreign Office and personally negotiate his salary with the Propaganda Ministry. This distinguished academician, together with Erika and Hans Schirmer, son and daughter of a prominent German general and American mother, would play a major role in Chandler's decision to work for the Reichrund-funk.[25]

From spring through autumn of 1937, Chandler undertook commissions from La Groce for articles on Belgium, the Baltic, and the Scandinavian countries. Following these assignments he accepted yet another Hoffman invitation to a Party congress in Nuremberg. At this assemblage he renewed old bonds with the same English and Scottish gentlemen he had encountered there the previous year. War seemed probable at this juncture, and the majority of Chandler's colleagues viewed appeasement as the way to peace. Professor Charles Sarolea, the eminent French scholar at Edinburgh University, kept close company with Chandler, and following the proceedings he asked Douglas to his home in the interest of Anglo-German relations.[26]

Sarolea's invitation lent an air of respectability to the Chandler mission and its Berlin sponsors. A native Belgian, this brilliant linguist had pursued his discipline at the universities of Liege, Paris, Palermo, and Naples. The University of Edinburgh awarded him a newly created chair of French in 1918, a post from which he retired in 1931. During his career the professor acted as Belgian consul for Edinburgh (1901); founder, editor, and proprietor of the journal *Everyman* (1912–17); war correspondent for the *Daily Chronicle* (1914); fundraiser for Belgian relief; and political advisor to King Albert of Belgium.[27]

In January 1938 the Chandlers sailed from Hamburg to Edinburgh. House guests of the Saroleas for a fortnight, Hoffman's emissaries offered afternoon lectures on their impressions of Germany and how better Anglo-German relations might be effected. From Edinburgh the Americans proceeded to London, where they were entertained by Sarolea's Nuremburg companions. This company included such proponents of appeasement as Sir Arnold Wilson and Sir Barry Domville, a retired British admiral. It was Domville's admiration for Hitler's social program that prompted him to establish an intercountry exchange organization, "The Link." Chandler's lecture circuit concluded in the homes of Domville's friends, Davidson Hewston and John Alexander Walker, proprietor of the famous Johnny Walker distilleries.[28]

Domville and Wilson were Hoffman's indirect links with a widening circle of British fellow travelers. Throughout the Great War Domville had served with Admiral Sir Reginald Tyrwhitt of the Harwich Force, rising in the early postwar period to an important post on the British Admiralty naval staff. From 1922 to 1925 he was stationed with the Mediterranean Fleet, and in 1927 Domville rose to the rank of rear-admiral (director of Naval Intelligence). Promotions came regularly to him; first as rear-admiral and then as vice-admiral he commanded the Third Cruiser Squadron, Mediterranean Fleet. During the early 1930s he was president of the Royal Naval College, Greenwich, and vice-admiral commanding the War College. King George V made him Knight Commander of the Most Excellent Order of the British Empire in 1934. Several years later, at 58, Domville retired with the rank of admiral.

Domville had stumped England on behalf of appeasement. As a means to check Japanese aggression in the Pacific, he advised accommodation with the Germans. The admiral went so far as to suggest an alliance with the Nazis. In a 1935 trip to Berlin he was courted by Reichsfuhrer Heinrich Himmler, lunched with the officers of the Adolf Hitler SS Regiment, took the salute at a Berlin parade, and inspected Dachau. All facets of his German stay impressed him. In 1940 the British government ordered Domville to Brixton Prison for his pro-Nazi sympathies.[29]

A surprising number of MP Arnold Wilson's constituency believed that a dictatorship was the salvation for England's loss of a sense of national purpose. He brazenly expressed his admiration for the Reich's vitality, its absence of class distinctions, and the patriotism of its youth. A devotee of Houston Chamberlain's racial theories, Wilson found much to his liking during a peregrination through Germany in the spring of 1934. Hitler had proven himself a providential catalyst for his country, proclaimed Wilson, who would oversee the nation's racial heritage. German hegemony should be allowed in Europe, with British supremacy acknowledged in Africa and round the Indian Ocean. This benign "Third Force" would stand as a buffer between the materialistic tenets of Marxism and the avariciousness of Wall Street capitalism. In intellectual lockstep Wilson accepted the remilitarization of the Rhineland, the Falangist takeover in Spain, and the Sudeten grievances in Czechoslovakia. The Czech invasion and the subsequent threats against Poland would meet his approbation, as long as Parliament continued its drive for a military buildup. In time the German-Soviet Non-Aggression Pact and its resultant partition of Poland altered Wilson's perspective. Betrayed and alone, heartsick that his seven years in Parliament had ended in failure, he sought atonement. Doubtless Chandler never knew that, at 55, Sir Arnold Wilson served as gunner with a squadron of Wellington bombers, or that he lost his life over France on the night of June 1, 1940.[30]

Once back in Goettingen Berlin's good-will ambassador won another commission from *National Geographic* to prepare an article on the Kemel Attaturk regime. The family moved its residence to Potsdam in February 1938, and Chandler left for Turkey the month of April. His manuscript completed, Chandler sought the companionship of the von Bülows, the Schirmers, and the Truman Smiths at his new Potsdam villa. The fall brought more writing projects in Yugoslavia and Albania. Chandler and Laura took the occasion to explore the island of Korcula on the Dalmatian coast. He became infatuated with Yugoslavia's "Black Corfu" and its exotic attractions. The overabundance of jackals provided sport for furloughed British naval officers, and children trapped mongccsc for sale abroad. While there the couple discovered an old house with an ancient battlemented tower attached. This structure had been purchased as a partial ruin by a former Yugoslavian minister in Belgrade, repaired, and modernized with electricity. Recalled Chandler:

In the remaining few days of my allotted six weeks I revisited old scenes of delight: Lumbarda with its blue-gunwaled boats . . . brown-legged laughing girls stomping grapes to pulp . . . donkeys taking surreptitious sips of the nectar. . . . Then, one bright day, passing a house in Korcula town, an ancient house from the top story of which ran a covered bridge to a 15th century tower, someone whispered in my ear, "That house can be bought." I hesitated and was lost.[31]

In January of 1939 the Chandlers took possession of their prize. Chandler commuted regularly between Korcula and a Westphalian boarding school where his daughters resided. During spring recess he brought the children to Korcula, where they benefited from a private tutor. There the family remained, aside from minor trips around the Adriatic, until mid-August 1940.[32]

Chandler's idyllic respite on Korcula quickly took on the aspect of a night-mare. In early August 1940, the Yugoslavian government denied him a residence permit and demanded that he leave the island before September 1. The local Jewish community, according to Chandler, regarded him as a Nazi. This group was suspicious of his numerous trips to Germany while on the island and his alleged close ties with the Italian Fascists. Its malevolent designs ran the gamut from destroying Chandler's credibility with *National Geographic* to complete expulsion from Yugoslavia. The target of this alleged discrimination complained to Under-Secretary of State Sumner Welles in voluminous correspondence that his unenviable predicament had resulted from a social snub. He charged that his indifference to a New York Jewish physician and resident of Korcula had culminated in "a most fantastic scandal of international dimensions." Through a rather labyrinthine process Chandler claimed that this prominent surgeon had cajoled a former Austrian minister into persuading the State Department that he was a political undesirable. On the eve of his expulsion this conspiracy had grown in Chandler's mind to include the U.S. consul in Zagreb, and even Welles himself, whose re-luctance to communicate had shown him to be "in thickest *Verbindung* with the Roosevelt gang."[33]

Laura Chandler became ill and Douglas suffered from nervous exhaustion. Consequently, the family migrated to Florence, Italy, where Chandler re-sided from the end of August 1940 to March 1941. Once accustomed to the city, the couple found that their social circle expanded as their health im-proved.[34] George Otto Edward von Lilienfeld, a German foreign service official, and Chandler developed a friendship during this interim. It was to von Lilienfeld that the American expressed his dread of the worldwide Jewish conspiracy, the loss of central Europe to the Bolsheviks, and the subversion of the United States by these twin evils. Mussolini had gently rebuffed his services, reported Chandler, as a result of Zionist pressure.[35] The wife of a member of America's diplomatic corps evoked a painful recollection of Chan-dler's frame of mind for this author:

I remember being at the Chandlers' house in I think Potsdam. At one moment I was alone with Douglas on the terrace. He asked me how I liked that school in Switzerland where I had sent my daughter. . . . He said his two children had finished the Catholic school to which they had been for several years and that he must find another school— I said I liked [deleted] very well but I said "Why don't you send them home to America to make friends there and to be Americanized?" He replied, "I am not at all sure I want them to be Americans. I am thinking of becoming a German citizen." I was dumbfounded. I said, "Are you out of your mind? You are treated favorably by the Government because you speak for them at your own expense. Once you are a German citizen you will come under all the very oppressive socialist laws." "Well," he said, "I do not want them to live in a country run by the Jews." I said, "You must be mad to think of staying here. The war will come very soon." "We can go

to Luxembourg," "Luxembourg! That will be run over in a few minutes. Go home."
And I left. I did not see him or Laura again.[36]

Chandler observed that the American colony in Florence was greatly disturbed by President Roosevelt's growing involvement in the European war.
He felt himself urged from all sides to employ his "talents" and his "name" to
thwart any possible attempt at intervention by the Washington government:

As I look back upon it, my alarm assumed the dimensions of a morbid and perhaps
quasi-psychopathic sense of urgency for me to speak to the people of America and
pass on warnings gleaned from my accumulated knowledge during years of European
travel.

Chandler wrote the von Bülows in Berlin, and also Rolf Hoffman in
Munich, asking if they could suggest any way by which he could work
effectively for the "preservation of peace." Von Bülow responded that he
had explored a means whereby Chandler could speak over the German Broadcasting System.[37]

During the winter of 1940–41, the U.S. consul in Florence notified all
U.S. citizens to return home. Chandler balked, pleading his wife's precarious
health and his own fierce determination to keep his native land nonaligned.
Through von Bülow's influence he received a *Fremdenpass* (alien identity card)
and entrained for Berlin on February 15, 1941. On arrival Chandler went
straightway to see his old friend, Dr. Hans Schirmer, who was the head of
the Radio Broadcasting Department of the Reich under the Foreign Office.
To further his hopes for U.S. neutrality, Chandler offered to speak over
Radio Berlin as a "freelance commentator without compensation." Chandler's
altruism sprang from his wife's sizeable inheritance. Laura Chandler, at her
father's death in 1932, became co-beneficiary with her brother, Thomas
Childs Wurts, in an irrevocable trust fund administered by the Peoples
Pittsburgh Trust Company of Pennsylvania. The book value of the securities
in this trust was approximately $400,000. Laura's income amounted to
$13,000 annually. In addition, she had on deposit $40,000 in gold.[38]

Schirmer dismissed Chandler's generous offer as unworkable. Reichrundfunk management would never permit him such latitude, he insisted, and neither would it condone the American's services without payment. Taken
aback, Chandler contacted the von Bülows about this unexpected rebuff. The
German couple scolded him for approaching a representative of the Foreign Office, instead of the Propaganda Ministry. Said von Bülow:

You are a quixotic and impractical dreamer, Douglas. Although you will bring funds
for your family's maintenance with you into Germany if you undertake this work,
you have no assurance that those funds might not become in the course of time
valueless and that you will find yourself . . . in a strange land, cut off from your own
country without the means to live.

Unbeknownst to Chandler, von Bülow had already contacted Dr. Hans Theodore Froelich, intermediary for foreign journalists in the Press Department of the Propaganda Ministry, concerning his friends' dilemma. Eighteen hundred reichsmarks struck these self-appointed negotiators as a sufficient annual income for Chandler's family. The von Bülows introduced their somewhat bewildered American comrade to Froelich—almost as an afterthought—and the pair spent an afternoon discussing Chandler's possible microphone identities. During the next several days Chandler became acquainted with the Reichrundfunk and its U.S.A. Zone personnel. A tentative contract was tendered by Froelich's office, and Chandler carried the document back with him to Florence for his wife's inspection. Thrilled by the course of events, Laura observed in her diary: "Thank God Douglas has this wonderful opportunity to serve the U.S.A.!"[39] On March 20, 1941, the Chandlers motored over the Brenner Pass into Germany. Chandler located a boarding school for his children in the Black Forest—far from Allied air attacks—and proceeded to Berlin.[40]

For the first few weeks Chandler spent time in the offices of the Drahtlosen Dienst (Wireless Service) formulating various copy trends and approaches to his broadcasts. It was suggested by Froelich that he employ a studio identity. Chandler wanted to preserve his real name, which would be associated with his literary contributions in the States. A compromise was struck whereby Chandler agreed to adopt a microphone alias in exchange for the right to reveal his true identity within a month's time. "The selection of the name Paul Revere," he said, "was then peculiarly appropriate as the British were so intensively organized in their propagandistic battle in the United States for American participation in the war. Someone conceived the idea of employing as a sort of 'trade mark' an introduction and sign-off of galloping horses' hoofs and 'Yankee Doodle' played with flutes." By coincidence, the anniversary of Paul Revere's famous ride (April 18) was only five days away when Chandler completed the text for his initial airing.[41]

When Chandler appeared at the Reichrundfunk for his April 18 debut, he was refused permission to broadcast. Unaccustomed to such bureaucratic insensitivity, Chandler cooled his heels for eight days while awaiting his superior's pleasure:

Thus through this opposition encountered my talks were launched, in an atmosphere which was strangely unfriendly and disappointing to me. I must state that subsequently, throughout my entire activities in the Berlin station, I encountered unceasingly this attitude of unwilling cooperation.

Working conditions gradually worsened. He had been promised an office and a private secretary to assist him in preparing a daily digest of the world's news and to help in translation work. Several weeks after Chandler joined the U.S.A. Zone the Drahtlosen Dienst ceased to exist, and "Paul Revere"

received none of the amenities promised. Management required him to work
in a bullpen environment with "chattering" colleagues and "clattering" type-
writers. Moreover, he was instructed to read as a preface to his own commentaries a digest of latest news items. Without typewriter, secretary, or
office, Chandler arranged to do his work at home. He would read over the
material supplied each afternoon by Karl Schotte, the U.S.A. Zone chief.
Then came the distasteful task of adapting Goebbels' material to his own
idiom:

Within the first hour I would be seized by a violent nervous paroxysm which centered
in my solar plexus and caused me during the time of writing (it took me four to six
hours to write the talks) a violent diarrhea each day. I was suffering from acute
headaches and experienced great difficulty with my eyes.

Neither the broadcasting station, the Propaganda Ministry, nor the Foreign
Office made the slightest effort to locate an apartment for the Chandlers.
These same officials took no responsibility for the transportation of their new
recruits' valuables and furniture from his Yugoslavian residence to Berlin.
Chandler griped to his bosses that he considered himself an "undesired step-
child" in their organization. For his first three months of work no pay was
forthcoming. Complaints to Dr. Froelich resulted in a lump-sum payment;
then for the next three months the Reichrundfunk again declined to meet its
obligation. His initial contract ran for six months and called for six talks per
week. Overwrought by this daily pace and the bureaucratic maze in which
he found himself, Chandler found it increasingly difficult to walk the razor's
edge between continued employment, German censors, and the formulation
of convincing messages to his countrymen back home.[42]

   In his inaugural broadcast Chandler focused on his country's pro-British
bias:

Tonight I, an American observer, come galloping on the radio. With bloodshed and
agony we freed ourselves from England. Are we going to enslave ourselves today?
. . . Among the melting-pot medley of American people are untold thousands of
descendants of the minute men whom Paul Revere electrified into action. But the
word "minute" is undergoing a change of pronunciation. Today these descendants
are apparently "minute" men because of their impotence in deciding national issues.[43]

On May 20 he sneered that America's palsied chief executive had chiseled
seven billions (lend-lease) from U.S. taxpayers, "a sum which Downing
Street now says is only the first installment." Answering an indictment from
a distant family member on the air, Chandler boomed:

My Baltimore relative is the mother of a fine and talented son, but she is willing to
gamble his life for a muddling monarchy. . . . What have you to say to this, my
passionate pro-Brit, you and your pseudo-intellectual liberal leftist friends; can you

not grasp the reason for Europe's determination to hack off Britain's shackles? It was America who first set the fashion.[44]

William Joyce, he proclaimed on May 26, "is clad in chain armour—a protagonist cast in the heroic mold." Chandler found grim satisfaction that the author of *Twilight over England* (Berlin 1940), a former victim of John Bull's vicious caste system, now took his revenge from a broadcasting studio at Kaiserdamm 77—Berlin.[45] Laura wrote a friend on September 20: "D. is forever at it. Do you ever listen in? He gets lots of fan mail which takes about six weeks by ordinary post. . . . I like Lord Haw-Haw better than anyone we know. He is such a likeable fellow." How Chandler relished trafficking with the British Empire's incendiaries, individuals such as India's Chandra Bose, a fugitive from British justice who mocked his colonial masters.[46] Chandler pummeled Whitehall to the end, and when his frontline reports became either stale or all too embarrassing, he retreated to personal anti-British testimonials. On March 31, 1944, he confessed:

I, Paul Revere, remember the hatred to which the U.S.A. was subjected by its Allies at the end of the last war. I was an ensign in the U.S. Navy, and after the armistice for many months we brought back shiploads of U.S. men and officers whose bitterness against the British was of hurricane proportions.[47]

Following his first term of employment, Chandler asked for a leave of absence for medical reasons. He inferred to Froelich that he might not return to the microphone unless conditions improved. Douglas and Laura then retired to Hinterzarten in the Black Forest, where their children were in school. They spent several weeks near them, then vacationed in the Alps until late November. On their return to Berlin Chandler discovered that he had allowed the lease on their apartment to lapse, so the couple took lodging in the Pension Continental, where the von Bülows were living. At this juncture the Japanese attack on Pearl Harbor drew its Axis partners into the war against the United States.

This [occurrence] naturally made the further continuance of my broadcasting a more complicated matter. The point of view taken by my wife, myself, and such advisers as we had in Berlin was that the difference was purely a technical one; that since Roosevelt's orders of several months previous to fire on German ships there had actually been an undeclared war in existence. . . . At the end of the war when I go home, if the Democrats are still in power, I will be definitely *persona non grata* with officialdom but will be acclaimed by the masses of the people. . . . I was as shocked as any other American at the dastardly blow struck at Pearl Harbor, but this did not alter the underlying facts as regarded making war against Germany; Germany through its pact with Japan was technically forced to issue its declaration of war, but it was my opinion then and remains my opinion that Germany's greatest wish was to preserve an amicable relationship with the United States.

In late January 1942 Chandler returned to work. He was presented with three contracts. The first contract between him and the Deutscherkurzwellensender (January 7, 1942) provided for his duties as a commentator at a salary of 1,000 reichsmarks per month. The second binder (January 31, 1942) with the anti-Comintern provided for the duties of "Paul Revere" in the Foreign Language Propaganda Section at the monthly remuneration of 750 reichsmarks. The Fremdsprachendienst matched this sum on the same date. Additional concessions included "full official support in matters of daily existence" and a reduction of weekly broadcasts by half. Chandler pressed his luck by demanding of Karl Schotte regular daily meetings to resolve disagreements over matters of subject content and political censorship.[48]

The Paul Revere broadcasts continued uninterrupted until the death of Laura Chandler on July 26, 1942. At that time Chandler took another furlough, secluding himself on the Isle of Ruegen. He returned to his studio on September 10. Everyone on the U.S.A. Zone staff knew of Chandler's excessive devotion to his spouse. It had been her influence and her character, he insisted, that brought him to Germany's cause. The subject of suicide became a constant refrain from Laura's death until war's end. He frequently debated aloud to himself whether he should employ poison or a pistol for that end. Peeved by these constant morbid soliloquies, an unsympathetic associate observed that either instrument of dispatch should prove equally fatal.[49]

A full office calendar and the awful prospect of being indicted for treason undermined Chandler's already fragile constitution. His reputation for eccentric behavior preceded him among Berlin's American colony and Reichrundfunk personnel. For instance, on the eve of Germany's invasion of Poland, Chandler converted his cash reserve in France into gold and deposited it in a Luxembourg bank. Beset with nagging doubts, he soon withdrew his gold from Luxembourg and transferred it to banks in Switzerland. Still unsure, he changed his mind again, converted his savings into reichsmarks, and moved the family's wealth to Germany. Acquaintances knew of Chandler's offer to work without pay, and of Laura's vigorous opposition to such a ridiculous notion. Perhaps in time they would appreciate his publicized impatience with Goebbels' dilatory payrolls. When he included his daughters on one of his broadcasts, Chandler demanded that they be fully compensated. His bluster irritated several station officials, who were constantly at the point of calling his bluff in the civil courts.[50]

Chandler harped about the many technical flaws inherent in Rundfunk offerings. He denounced the poor announcing and the playing of jazz music both preceding and concluding his shows. Moreover, station supervisors did not provide him suitable script material, recording dates were unwelcome, and travel allowances to certain events—that he desired to cover and report on—were sparse. He cast aspersions on other U.S.A. Zone productions, and he especially disliked the work of E. D. Ward (Edward Leo Delaney). "We should avoid any kind of sketches of the so-called Delaney type," he said, "which were always very dirty in character and . . . we should rather build up a program which would be on a higher level. . . . I personally would like to contribute to this program reading poetry of a classic nature."[51] Assuming the mantle of the curmudgeon, Chandler repeatedly abused the reputation of his boss, Karl Schotte, as well as that of Horst Cleinow, head of the Overseas Service. A vexing dearth of information on the United States and the Allied war effort in the Propaganda Ministry library drove him to alternative sources. He liked to haunt the Foreign Press Club in Berlin, where correspondents kept him abreast of developments back home. When all else failed, Chandler visited the Radio Section of the Foreign Office, officially to meet with Schirmer and von Lilienfeld, but actually to help himself to a large assortment of U.S. periodicals and newspapers. Ministry representatives did not receive Chandler's constructive criticisms kindly. They told him that if it came to a showdown between Goebbels' agency and himself, they would choose the ministry. He would have to go.[52]

Chandler was not an easy person to befriend or to supervise. Professional competitors, administrators, and strangers usually met an "icy reserve" coated over with a veneer of civility. His thought processes worked rapidly, and during any given conversation he might change topics any number of times. Furthermore, his memory seemed erratic. At certain times he could quote long passages of verse remarkably well; on other occasions he appeared lost, quite unable to remember simple details of transactions or meetings. Spells of nervousness plagued him before each show, and the preparation of scripts frequently brought on bouts of diarrhea. Months before the Japanese attack on Pearl Harbor, Chandler had consulted a renowned psychiatrist in Karlottenburg. After delving into his patient's former life, his habits, his family relations, this physician prescribed an alteration in Chandler's pattern of living.[53]

The anti-rationalist view of life intrigued Chandler. "He thought that man was a mere cockleshell," recalled a comrade, Edward V. Sittler, "who was tossed about by his own emotions or the happenings of his surroundings, at any given time. . . . Once he asked me if I, as a philosopher, believed that the tongue controlled the mind, or that the mind controlled the tongue. I told him I was the conservative type, that I believed the mind controlled the tongue. He said I was a young man yet, and had a lot to learn—that some day I would learn that the tongue babbles along and that the mind follows as best it can, to excuse the tongue."[54] He naively regarded Germany as a perfect crucible in which to exercise his complete freedom of expression. It was Chandler's passion to chauffeur his cohorts around Berlin in a big maroon Mercedes with a large U.S. flag painted on its side. After Pearl Harbor, the Gestapo confiscated the vehicle. Friends seldom saw him without the Third Reich emblem in his lapel—a Nazi swastika centered among crossed flags. "They are the flags of all the Axis nations," he proudly explained.[55]

Those who knew Chandler well partially attributed his manic-depressive state to an unregimented home life. An insomniac, even black market sleeping pills usually brought him only fitful rest. During the day he drank to excess, without displaying the slightest sign of intoxication. Chandler took pride in his fully stocked bar, although he opposed drinking in principle. Regrettably, the children suffered from their father's periods of depression. He fumed that his eldest daughter had been spoiled by the preparatory school she attended. Laurette would not obey his commands, stormed Chandler, nor would she refrain from overwinding her phonograph. As punishment, he hired her services as a charwoman to a very poor family. In a fit of rage Chandler publicly paddled his youngest teenage daughter. In reprisal, Patricia refused to communicate with him for some time thereafter. On the air, however, Paul Revere changed his tune. Offering to match his daughters against "any pair of youngsters producible at home," Chandler contended that credit for their upbringing must be attributed to national socialism.[56]

Chandler received his instructions by way of a bureaucratic jungle. Policy was formulated at daily high-level staff conferences conducted by Josef Goebbels. The propaganda minister took orders from no one. Periodically he consulted with his Fuhrer. Their discussions encompassed the current military and political situation on the basis of press telegrams, published material, and other miscellaneous intelligence. The radio chiefs for each sector met next, and the director of the Radio Division of the Propaganda Ministry chaired these conferences. Discussion centered on procedural problems, news manipulation, and the formulation of a daily propaganda line. Those attending included the director's associates, the different European Services bureau leaders, officials of the shortwave station, regional European station chiefs, and all zone heads of the overseas stations. Finally, the head of the U.S.A. Zone met with the commentators. Censorship was performed informally. Five times a week Chandler presented the U.S.A. Zone chief's secretary with his prepared scripts. She, in turn, sent these submissions up the chain of command for political and military scrutiny. When the corrected copies filtered back, she gave them to Chandler to be recorded and broadcast.[57]

The Paul Revere broadcasts were undeniably treasonous. Chandler's view of his own culpability, however, was quite another matter. His pronouncements sought to promote disunity among the Allies while fomenting social and economic discord within each nation. Members of the North American Zone talked about their country's inability to win the war, about economic ruin that would follow in the attempt, about the sheer folly of a second front, and about the average GI's lack of commitment to a European struggle. Chandler and associates attempted to drive a wedge between the American public and the Roosevelt administration through appeals to isolationism and defeatism, and through charges of racial intolerance and class prejudice in the United States.[58]

In late fall 1942, and again during the winter of 1942–43, Chandler broached the possibility of his indictment by a federal grand jury. The topic even surfaced during a round-table commentators' conference. When this long-awaited sword of Damocles fell in the summer of 1943, Chandler dismissed the news as a "natural consequence of the ideological war he [Chandler]... was fighting against the New Deal and the hidden forces in the United States."[59]

Those "hidden forces" in Chandler's logic came down to the Jewish issue, which was, as a Rundfunk employee subsequently observed, the "crystallization point" of his mental processes. Different families of international Judaism controlled the Soviet Union, Britain, and the United States, explained Chandler, and each tribe had direct ties to western European cells, masterminding repeated attempts to overthrow Nazi occupation. The Russo-German pact had unnerved him in 1939, and he made no secret of his relief when the invasion of the Soviet Union commenced. Returning German soldiers persuaded him that the Soviet Union's military arsenal, coupled with the ideological zeal of its leaders, posed a threat to Christendom.[60]

Many of Paul Revere's messages targeted what he perceived as a minority-dominated government in Washington manipulated by Jewish advisers. For him this patchwork of alien interests found expression in America's New Deal policies. Reports of depressed economic conditions and labor violence there convinced him that the United States was ripe for a Communist takeover. Perhaps this eventuality could be avoided, he observed, but only through more stringent immigration laws.

In 1936, I visited an American consul in a German town, and found him despondent. He and his staff were greatly overworked trying to cope with the applications from Jewish emigrants for visas to America. He showed me a letter from an official in the Immigration offices in America, urging him not to be so careful in his scrutiny, and to hurry along with the business. . . . I remembered two things [from the conversation]—one, the difficulty experienced by many perfectly good Nordic Scandinavians in getting visas to the States; and two, the unemployment in the U.S.A. (June 7, 1941)[61]

He, himself, had been the victim of talmudic agents in prewar Europe. On eight separate broadcasts Chandler recounted how international Jewry had driven him from Korcula, wrecked his career as a writer, and suborned Roosevelt's State Department to deny him redress—even as its henchmen pursued him across Europe.[62]

The Jewish community had undermined civilization in every quarter of the globe, thundered Chandler, and distracted world attention through charges of Gentile persecution. The very term "anti-Semitism" was a Jewish invention, and pogroms were first organized by rabbis for "rounding-up" their non-orthodox brethren. Germany's Nuremberg Laws (1938), complained the speaker, had driven Jewish immigration westward, and Americans must be prepared to repulse this tide.[63]

Chandler's broadcasts suggest that he knew of and condoned Hitler's "Final Solution" policies in regard to minorities.

Yes, by all means let Pearl Harbor be avenged, but not upon the Japanese, who have been forced into a struggle for their national existence; no, not upon the Japs, but upon the real authors of this war, the Jews. The day is not far off the horizon when the Yankee cry will be for a plentifully purging pogrom, and the measures employed by the Reich will seem child's play in comparison. (February 22, 1942)[64]

The terrible fate of Atlantis compares favourably with the fate prepared for America by Jewry: the ruthless Bolshevisation of the American Continent. Roosevelt, himself an offspring of Spanish Jews—is a mere tool of the Jewish conspiracy against all Nordic Aryans. . . . Only through the letting of Jewish blood can America be set free. (March 10, 1942)[65]

On April 16, 1942, Chandler produced a play set in the year 2042. The scene opens with a youngster inquiring of his teacher about Roosevelt's war for the Jews and its failure. The boy is told that the American public's indifference to the truth was responsible for "the tragedy of 1942." Asked "How did America get rid of Roosevelt and the Jews?" his mentor describes the ravages of runaway inflation, unemployment, and wage slavery, and the government's evil attempts to right the floundering ship of state "on the battlefields of the Antipodes." Suddenly the instructor's face brightens as he recalls how the people rose and swept America "clean of its Jewish despoilers." Chandler's drama closes with the teacher's proud boast, "In our day every man, woman, and child of the Jewish nation has been dealt with in a manner which eliminates for all time their intrusion into our national life" (Act III).[66] On assignment in Poland during the early spring of 1943, Chandler discovered his dream come true:

In Cracow I had further opportunity to see the progress that every town experiences as soon as it is rid of the contaminating influence of the International Jews. Cracow's ghetto is today free of Jews, its former inhabitants being removed to the Polish Jewish Settlement of Lublin. I found plenty of good food in the restaurants at prices which were just about the same as in the German Reich. Eggs were the special treat. After the very strict egg rationing in Berlin, I smacked my lips over the portion of six scrambled eggs at my first breakfast.[67]

The American public's refusal to underwrite similar policies with respect to its own Jewish population depressed Chandler. Precisely four months prior to the invasion of Europe, he sadly confided to his audience:

The USA stands today at the gates of peril, with 130 odd million citizens of 48 states mobilized for the destruction of Europe's spiritual values. Ellis Island was a springboard for the scourings of every ghetto of Europe. The leering face of the Jew shows itself in the Government, in the professions, in every stratum of our cultural and economic structure. Politics became the monopoly of alien immigrants. Now it is too late to save America, except through the blood-letting of internal revolution. The only hope for Americans to get their country back is to align themselves with the heroes of Western Europe in their fight against Bolshevism.[68]

With Hitler's Ardennes offensive in shambles and the Soviets closing on Warsaw, Chandler fired a final salvo against his old foe on January 11, 1945: "I curse the geographical impediments that made it impossible for me to attend the World Jew Conference at Atlantic City. What could the eaves-droppers not have heard about the plans for capturing the war-befuddled world for world Jewry and their allies, the Bolsheviks."[69]

The temperance of Chandler's remarks bore an inverse relationship to the success of Axis arms. Royal Air Force bombers over German cities and Soviet counteroffensives along the eastern front persuaded him to drum the tandem themes of individual resolve and national unity:

They [Jewish-controlled U.S. press] are building up a false picture of the European situation today. . . . Allied bombing has produced the opposite effect to that intended. The best the plutobrits and their American brothers-in-arms can hope to do is tem-porarily to delay the recrudescence of an autonomous Europe. (January 12, 1944)[70]

The Allies have started a whispering campaign . . . that Germany is now prepared to discuss terms. This is no cafe rumor, but was started by good old Reuter. A five days tour through bombed areas of the Reich convinced me of the people's continued solidarity. The Winter Help Collection was nearly 100 percent up on last year's total. The rumormongers must have failed to take into account the Special Communiques of the last two days with their combined total of over 200,000 tons of shipping sunk. To Roosevelt's war cry of Unconditional Surrender Germany's answer is Total War. (February 9, 1943)[71]

On March 9, 1943, Chandler noted that many of the cure resorts in the Greater Reich were currently being used as army hospitals, sanitoria, and homes for evacuated children. It pleased him to discover that in one such facility "a spirit of Pan-European understanding" pervaded every ward. The following month he spent time among the laborers of a large munitions plant in Germany. There he was struck by the cosmopolitan group housed in the factory village. A Spaniard, who had fought with Franco's Blue Division in Russia, expressed consternation over America's alliance with the Bolsheviks. This insane coalition, appended Chandler, "was a shocking demonstration of the power of the Jews in America."[72] How long would the women of the United States stand idly by and allow their European sisters to hold the line against bolshevism, snorted Paul Revere on May 18, 1943:

Total war has touched the depths of the great soul of Europe's composite woman. . . . Long grueling hours of labor, short hours of sleep, whipping up the courage of those less strong, day after day the women of the Pan-Europe Axis bloc toil with indomitable courage awaiting the day when peace will again smile over the world.[73]

Adversity had elicited similar manifestations of courage from Germany's allies. After touching on the fine points of Roman valor and the Samurai's code of Bushido, Chandler then read a letter from Tokyo, written by Englishman Lafcadio Hearn, describing life in wartime Japan. The communication rambled on about the stoical qualities of the Nipponese and their superhuman accommodation to war, and only at the end did he reveal that the document had been penned in 1904.[74]

Stalingrad taxed Chandler's ingenuity to the limit. Following a frenzied series of commentaries extending over nine days on the impending collapse of Hitler's Sixth Army, Chandler wearily resigned himself and his listenership to the inevitable: "Today, in spite of the spiritual undertow of Jewish engendered iconoclasm, heroism stands immutably as the leitmotif of our sick world." Not even enemy propagandists, contested Chandler, viewed the tragic end of this epic siege as a providential turning point in the war:

When that day comes [the extirpation of bolshevism] the realisation will be borne in upon you [Americans], that the troops of Stalingrad died for you, as well as for their Fatherland. In view of this would it not be wholly fitting that you also pause for a minute at noon on Thursday and Saturday [Nazi decree] to reflect on the bravest of the brave. (February 4, 1943)[75]

Chandler talked incessantly about his distinguished forbears and those of his wife's lineage. He and Laura had come to Europe as Americans; they had criss-crossed the Continent as Americans; and they would continue to live as Americans inside the Reich. Whatever the cost, the couple vowed never to hide under German citizenship. Chandler's closest associate, Edward Sittler, recalled:

And he said to me that he [Chandler] . . . considered himself in a certain sense as a pioneer in Berlin, and even he said, as an advance unit; that is, that he was a force working for American interests which was moving in advance even of the American armies, and that sooner or later they would catch up to the position in which he was.

Denaturalized German-Americans on the U.S.A. Zone earned his rebuke, and he was contemptuous of William Joyce, who had secured German citizenship papers. Chandler compared himself to the reformer Karl Schurtz, who was attacked in the U.S. Senate in 1870 by Mugwump partisans. Charged with being a disloyal American, Schurtz declared, "My country, right or wrong; if right, to be kept right; if wrong, to be set right." The charge of treason would be Chandler's cross for serving as his homeland's conscience, and he would pay the martyr's price should Germany fail in its geopolitical aspirations. A Soviet military reversal, however, might discredit the Roosevelt government, drive the United States from the Allied group, and set it on an isolationist course.[76]

Ever since his Baltimore *American* apprenticeship, Chandler had perceived himself as a reform critic of American culture. Now he "could only blush for shame that his country was . . . doing battle against . . . the philosophy of Goethe and Schiller."[77] The lack of professional opportunities back home embittered him, the shallowness of its aesthetics bored him, and the manipulators of its wealth—those who had driven him to Europe—he regarded as pickpockets. The United States had blessed him with a moderately wealthy spouse, and little else. Chandler expressed contempt for Keynesian monetary theory and relief that while his countrymen struggled to free themselves from Rooseveltian economics, the peoples of 14 Axis nations had united behind a powerful Euro-Japanese trade bloc. This common market, he threatened, would drive the Allies to financial ruin.[78]

On the battlefield, American soldiers apparently lacked the spiritual and physical stamina to prosecute a grueling war. Said Chandler, on March 22, 1942:

When I talk of the American way of life I mean the Founding Father's way, the frontier man's way. Flabbiness abounds among politicians, but one would expect to find something better in the Army. Yet look at that milksop MacArthur's panic flight to Australia. The handsome deserter's abandonment of his comrades would have been branded by the heroes of Valley Forge as cowardice.[79]

Chandler fancied himself as a historical anachronism, a patriotic throwback to the precarious beginnings of the United States.

My wife's family and my own are both products of America's colonial settlers. My hearers in Roosevelt's Jew-dominated Empire have the right to know this. They must know that the family of Paul Revere the Second is by birthright qualified to fill the role of its elected namesake. The B.B.C. has referred to me as "that self-styled American." Judge for yourself whether your messenger and his beloved wife have by right stood in the ranks of America's front fighters. (September 13, 1942)[80]

Glimpses of Chandler's life in the Reich's embattled capital and other stations were preserved for postwar American prosecutors through the trial testimony of his former working colleagues. Of those individuals who befriended Chandler, perhaps Edward V. Sittler was closest to him. A native Ohioan, Sittler returned to the Fatherland in 1937; he received his German citizenship three years later. The product of several universities, and physically unfit for military service, Sittler spent the war as an irregular student at the University of Berlin. He earned a modest living as translator at the U.S.A. Zone, where he met Chandler.[81]

Their relationship began in the late summer of 1941 when the Sittlers invited the Chandlers to dinner. After the meal both men motored to the

University of Berlin, where they addressed a class. Following his host, Chandler told the students that any consideration of the U.S. political situation would revolve around the personality of Franklin Roosevelt. Roosevelt had forged a foreign policy alien to the welfare and traditions of his people, concluded Chandler, and had beguiled them into accepting his bastard creation.[82]

At times only a determined effort held the families together. On a professional basis Sittler frequently sat with Chandler in official conference meetings. Not only had he witnessed many Paul Revere broadcasts, but he had taken a voice role in several as well. By the time the radio staff moved to Koenigswusterhausen to escape Allied bombing in mid-August 1943, Laura Chandler had died and had been replaced by Mia, Chandler's Belgian wife, who gave him two additional daughters. On several occasions Sittler showed up at the new Chandler residence in Bavaria, already overcrowded with Chandler, wife, and four children. The visiting Sittlers numbered six, having four children of their own. They were known to come for an evening and remain a week. During these convivial interludes Laurette and Patricia would sing old German folk songs while their father accompanied them on his guitar. Sometimes both families came together in impromptu musicals. Afterward, Chandler and Sittler plotted broadcasting strategy and program content, or perhaps Chandler would harangue his friend about the Jewish agents who continued to vex him. Sittler was reminded that his comrade's account of the Korcula episode had been published in the *German News Letter*, a mimeographed publication issued by Rolf Hoffman. Furthermore, there were Chandler's articles to *National Geographic*, texts that told of widespread Bolshevik subversion, as well as tales of Soviet misdeeds against its own populace. Were these insider reports appreciated by the magazine's Jewish staffers? No! Rather, Chandler was curtly notified that political statements were not to be included in his submissions. To complicate matters, Sittler's undisguised indifference toward his friend's ramblings infuriated Chandler, who retaliated by humiliating his companions on the most unexpected occasions.[83]

Margaret Sittler recalled a dinner party that took place at Chandler's Berlin apartment. The host ranted and raved against Roosevelt and his Jewish advisors, who had ruined his journalistic career. When Margaret tried to change the subject, Chandler rebuked her severely and referred to her husband as an "insufferable boor." Initially, she broke down in tears. "But he was all right again afterwards," Frau Sittler brightened and added, "You see, we knew him and made allowances." Another persistent theme was the total unacceptability of the Sittlers in polite circles. During a ridiculous disagreement over whether or not a passing oxcart driver might be accepted into German society simply by donning a tuxedo, a circumstance Chandler thought likely, he referred to Margaret Sittler as a "caged lioness." He was known to refer to Sittler as "a snarling dog" and "a backwoodsman" in public.[84] In the spring of 1943 Sittler left his daughter overnight at the Chandler house. At approximately midnight he unexpectedly returned to the flat to retrieve his child. He was met at the door by Chandler. For 15 minutes the sleepy Chandler assailed his colleague, informing him that he was, indeed, "a miserable character," "a villainous personage" who would take every liberty with a friend. Following a few additional insults, Chandler declined to fetch the girl and informed him to return in the morning— slamming the door in his face.[85] Chandler once reflected that his long association with the German people—despite intermittent periods of productive harmony—always ended in betrayal and broken promises. He concluded that this penchant for duplicitous behavior was a flaw in their national character. Sittler took instant exception to his comrade's slur and a violent argument erupted.[86]

Chandler's childish antics had offended nearly everyone on the Reichrundfunk staff by the spring of 1943. His picayune complaints drove even stolid supervisors to distraction. He repeatedly clashed with U.S.A. Zone chief Karl Schotte and the director of German Radio, Horst Cleinow, in the winter of 1942–43. It was even rumored that with Chandler the possibility of physical violence was always present.

In the spring of 1943 Chandler and Margaret Sittler exchanged critical views on the operation of the station. Such candid discussions in the Chandler home among Douglas, Edward, and Margaret led to Sittler's presentation of remedial suggestions to the agency's officialdom. As a result, both men were suspended without pay. Their German supervisors in Berlin, on receiving the list of complaints and proposals, had agreed to meet with them and to permit a frank exchange of views at a private conference in the Hotel Adlon. But without informing these grumblers, the executives took care to include a Gestapo agent in the conversation. When the meeting convened, Chandler unwisely suggested that the problems in the system were the work of sabotage. He proceeded to mention the names of a few suspects. On the advice of the disguised Gestapo operative, both Sittler and Chandler were temporarily suspended as security risks and troublemakers. These outcasts, meanwhile, threatened a suit in their demands for a ministry board of review. They were notified in the fall to report to Koenigswusterhausen to discuss reinstatement. Both men complied; they were greeted at the new broadcasting facility by Otto Koischwitz, who was acting head of the U.S.A. Zone. Following a brief discussion, all parties entered Horst Cleinow's private office. Chandler dominated the conversation. He thought it strange that he had been suspended without cause and that now, after a lapse of months, he had been reactivated without explanation. There would be a price, he said, for his return to duty: (1) He would be allowed to make broadcasts in the south of Germany; (2) he would have the privilege of certain reading materials in the preparation of his broadcasts; and (3) Rundfunk officials must meet certain obligations to him as a professional. His superiors agreed to the demands, and Chandler returned to work.[87]

No sooner had Chandler emerged from one embroglio than he drifted into another. At the time of Laura Chandler's death in July 1942, a professional acquaintance, Gerdt Wagner, voluntarily assisted Chandler in the details of his wife's burial. From that point on the men became close friends.

Wagner had emigrated to the United States in 1924 and entered the mosaic business in New York City. Twelve years later he became a U.S. citizen. Happenstance dictated that his profession should bring him in contact with a satellite group of the *Oberkommando Der Wehrmacht* (OKW), an adjunct of the German High Command and, ultimately, a part of the twentieth of July movement aimed at the overthrow of the Nazi regime. His business and OKW assignments took him to Germany, Italy, Yugoslavia, Turkey, Austria, Mexico, Canada, and the Baltic states on a regular basis. Suspicious of Wagner, the U.S. government withheld his passport in 1939. The following year he was allowed to repatriate to Germany on condition that he surrender his U.S. citizenship. Departing for Germany immediately, Wagner set his sights on a promised career as radio news editor at the Reichrundfunk. It did not take him long to meet the U.S.A. Zone's most controversial personality.

Early in their association Chandler offered to give Wagner "expert instruction" in anti-Semitism. On the eve of an official visit to Italy in mid-February 1943, Chandler suggested to his colleagues that he contact a certain countess in Rome who was an "expert" on the Jewish problem. When Wagner expressed his disinterest in this topic, Chandler became upset. The woman, according to Chandler, was an authority on the "documents of the Elders of Zion." In truth, Wagner admitted that he wrote such pulp for the Propaganda Ministry, but he went on to say that he considered it nonsense. His friend's flippancy on this important subject made an indelible impression on Chandler.[88]

Soon thereafter Wagner returned from the Baltic Sea area following a fact-finding tour. He related to Chandler how his investigation of the ghetto in Vilna and its environs had revealed the liquidation of 160,000 Jews. Chandler became enraged, insisting that no German soldier could commit such an atrocity. Disinformation concerning alleged Nazi excesses had been spread throughout the world by the Jewish press, he rebutted.

In every journalistic woodpile, you will find not a Nigger, but a Jew. Not that the actual ownership of the paper will rest in Jewish hands—Ah, no. That is a rarity, but the control on editorial policies rests on the sale of white space, or advertising space. Look into the social connections of the advertising managers of your daily papers, and you will discover that the case rarely exists where the advertising manager is not enjoying perquisites that come to him solely through his Jewish connections.

It was Wagner's opinion that Hitler and his lieutenants should be incarcerated after the war and forgotten. Shocked by his friends' disloyalty, Chandler admonished Wagner to exercise caution.[89]

The incident troubled Chandler, however, and he eventually consulted others about Wagner's poor attitude. Sittler believed him guilty of sedition, as did Herbert John Burgmann, alias Joe Scanlon, an American radio traitor on the U.S.A. Zone. Rolf Hoffman urged Chandler to betray his comrade before he himself became enmeshed in Wagner's plots. Finally, Chandler approached Maurice Gagnon, an officer of the Radio Political Department of the Reich Foreign Office. Gagnon went straight to the Gestapo. The following day Paul Revere found himself heralding Wagner's disaffection over luncheon at the Hotel Adlon. The security police allayed their informer's discomfort and promised him an investigation of the charges. Days passed before Chandler and his fiancée were instructed to report to the police. In the interim, on May 19, 1943, Chandler attended a special commentators' conference at Zeesen, a suburb of Berlin. After the meeting Karl Schotte asked Chandler and Wagner to remain behind. The U.S.A. Zone's chief enquired of Chandler whether or not he had denounced his colleague to the security police. Chandler responded in the affirmative. Schotte snapped, "I asked you this question because I won't stand that my organization, in my zone, somebody denounces somebody else to the Gestapo." Chandler apologized to Wagner, but informed him that he had only performed his duty— and then left the room.

Minutes before his appointment at Gestapo headquarters, Chandler glimpsed Schotte and Wagner in the inspector's outer office. To his disbelief, Chandler learned that the radio officials were there on his behalf. The smug authorities told Chandler that Wagner's role had been that of *agent provocateur*, and that his involvement was a mistake. For his loyalty to the Reich, Schotte awarded Chandler a four-month extension of his suspension. As for Wagner, he was promoted to war reporter for his part in this elaborate charade. Paul Revere's superiors did permit him to relocate in Schloss Seuftenegg, near Vienna. His recordings were to be sent by courier to Berlin from Vienna, then up to Koenigswusterhausen for transmission.[90]

The obvious weakness in Chandler's character—namely, pride and a towering ego—provided Wagner with an opportunity for delayed revenge. Believing himself a brilliant script writer and program director, Chandler prepared a policy outline for one of his radio spots to U.S. troops in North Africa that read:

This program must be so arranged that it doesn't stink of propaganda. We must make them absorb our propaganda teaspoonful by teaspoonful. Give them jazz and schmaltz. Don't arouse their sales resistance. . . . Give them news disguised as confidential gossip. . . . Make it breezy so they'll want to tune in. Give them readings from standard American poets like Walt Whitman and Tennyson.

Wagner connived to produce Chandler's show and broadcast it from Paris. He persuaded ministry brass that a production from such a dangerous locale would command more respect in the United States than one from Berlin. Baiting his trap, Wagner suggested that Chandler recite American poetry selections and perhaps also take part in round-table discussions with Bob Best and Fred Kaltenbach—as he had done in an earlier installment with William Joyce. Chandler professed to like the idea, but he refused to move to Paris. When pressed for an explanation, Chandler responded that in Paris he and his family would be endangered by "American military progress."[91]

Historian Nathaniel Weyl suggests that Chandler's administrative troubles grew out of a vendetta between Joachim von Ribbentrop's Foreign Office and the Propaganda Ministry. Aware of Chandler's temper, his unpopularity among personnel in both agencies, and his initial preference for ministry work, Foreign Office tricksters—including Hans Schirmer—may have chosen him as the instrument of Goebbels' discreditation. Perhaps it was no coincidence that the gentleman who unilaterally contacted the Gestapo on Chandler's behalf, Maurice Gagnon, worked for the Foreign Office's radio division. The final locus of Wagner's true allegiance remains a mystery.[92]

Cologne's martyrdom at the hands of the RAF's first 1,000-plane sortie on May 30, 1942, infuriated Chandler. Assessing the cost effectiveness of the raid, he estimated that the British had expended $13.5 million (the loss of 45 bombers) for the satisfaction of murdering 200 of the city's innocent victims: "That's what it cost Humpty Dumpty Churchill to kill 200 industrious, peace loving Cologne inhabitants. . . . The two German attacks on Canterbury have been the answer to Churchill's latest atrocity and for every German eye extinguished Albion will pay in kind."[93] While attending a convention in Vienna in late February 1944, Chandler found himself in the midst of an air raid. His hotel took a direct hit, and he managed to salvage but a single valise and his Bible. En route to Koenigswusterhausen, Chandler stopped on the outskirts of Vienna to inspect a stricken four-motor Lancaster and its mangled crew. It occurred to him that a few mementoes of that grisly interlude might serve as effective reminders in his next show.

On the desk beside my microphone, they lie—a handful of machine-gun cartridges found beside the machine's shattered tail, blood and human hair plastered over the wreck of the gun, a scrap of uniform with the name and address of a London army tailor, a few strands of copper wire from the timing mechanism of the bomber's motor, and three fragments of aluminum alloy from the aircraft's framework. I collected these ghastly souvenirs, not for any morbid interest, but because I felt that some of my listeners in America might care to know what happens when an air bomber has dropped its eggs of death on a sleeping city and then has received its own death blow from the city's air defenses. . . . I have many relatives at home in the U.S.A., including three nephews of military age. One I know gained his commission before 1941 as reserve flying officer. Perhaps it had been his fate to end his joyous life as a crumpled mass. (March 1, 1944)[94]

Sensing an imminent Allied invasion and fretting over the prospect of its horrible cost, Chandler claimed spiritual kinship with America's prewar exponents of isolationism. For nearly a quarter century these tragic heroes—at the price of their reputations—had worked for peace and against the secret machinations of a jingoistic government. Operation Overlord persuaded him to alter his scripts. He would play the kindly Dutch uncle who mourned for GI dead and prayed for their comrades who must still face the Wehrmacht's crack veterans. When German reserve divisions gave ground to Allied Expeditionary Force advance columns, Chandler graciously afforded the families of these proud liberators a sneak preview of the destructive power of Hitler's V.1 and V.2 missiles.[95]

On August 1, 1943, the Chandlers moved to Vienna. There they remained for several months before relocating in Schloss Seuftenegg, from where every fortnight Chandler entrained for Vienna to record his shows. These recordings were immediately dispatched via courier on wax records 450 miles to either Berlin or Koenigswusterhausen, a suburb of the German capital. On receipt of these wax discs, technicians transferred the program contents to a magnetophone band for transmission.

Chandler's broadcasting duties were interrupted in the spring of 1944 for several months due to nervous exhaustion brought on by Nazi military reverses and his own deteriorating lifestyle. Toward the end of June he resumed his radio talks. The Allied invasion of Europe, however, served to reduce Chandler's appearances and refocus his scripts. Paul Revere's postinvasion offerings, such as his broadcast of December 27, 1944, became far more temperate and softened by classical music and poetry recitations:

With the landing of the American troops on the European Continent I realised that the purposes for which I had made my broadcasts were in vain . . . in the progression of events which marked the invasion of Europe . . . I realised that perhaps my continued adherence to my course of action had been the result of colored thinking. My only thought during this period had been for . . . the continued existence of what we called the American way of life.[96]

In truth, his commentaries on the world of arts and letters bespoke the innocence of a dilettante unequal to the complexities of the discipline. He initially employed this subject as just another entree on his propaganda menu, but when Hitler's military fortunes plummeted, he embraced the topic to soften his rhetoric and deflect criticism away from the democracies. He believed this approach would add variety and sophistication to his airings. Perhaps, too, these scripts would help distance him from the gallows should Germany capitulate. During the summer of 1942, Paul Revere toured several music and art festivals in Weimar and Munich.

Perhaps it may be that wartime has called for a more heroic expression of the artistic impulse, akin to that strange biological fact that in times of war the proportion of male children outnumbers that of the females born. The God of Mars is a cruel god, but he is at least robust and forthright and has no part with the affectations and degeneracy to be observed among the art extremists of Democracy's Jew-inspired artists. That sort of thing was systematically scoured out of the German art galleries back in the prewar days, and later sold to gullible faddists in London, Paris and New York.[97]

On February 20, 1944, he launched his series on American poetry that lasted for the remainder of the war. In this segment Chandler enlisted the aid of colleagues—even his daughters—to assist him with readings and sessions on criticism. To be sure, this new program did not entirely free Chandler's rhetoric of its old bellicosity, but it did signal the possibility of negotiations leading to a separate armistice with the United States. "Poets and musicians were the ultimate peacemakers," mused Chandler, "for in troubled times they provided mankind with that central ingredient to international understanding—love of beauty" (February 20; May 14, 1944).[98]

Chandler's exhausting schedule slowed after October 1944, when he was transferred to Durach in Allgane. From Durach he commuted to Munich's radio station. Due to poor road and rail connections as a result of Allied air strikes, however, Chandler made the trip only on token occasions.

On February 28, 1945, Edward Sittler appeared at Chandler's door unexpectedly with a message from Horst Cleinow. The superintendent of the Reich Radio demanded Chandler's return to work in Koenigswusterhausen. Incensed by Cleinow's summons, Chandler magnified his old friend's discomfort by observing that the Soviets had nearly overrun the town. He pleaded his family's safety at this delicate juncture. Chandler suspected betrayal, particularly since most of his fellow commentators had been assigned to the city of Landshut, well beyond the Soviet advance. Reading further, he took umbrage at a sentence in the communication that implied dismissal as punishment for disobedience. With Germany near collapse, it struck Chandler as darkly amusing that his boss should threaten his livelihood, especially since he had not drawn a payroll voucher in months.[99]

World War II ended raggedly for most of the radio traitors, and Chandler's case was no exception. Within a matter of weeks following V-E Day the United States Army uncovered him still living in Durach with his family. Chandler's first interrogator, Captain Aldo Cesarini of the U.S. military government, found his unwilling host to be a most difficult subject. For 15 minutes Chandler simply stared at the captain, before abruptly delving into a one-sided discussion about his career as Paul Revere. Warming to the subject, he wanted to know how his program was received in the United States. Rhetorical questions concerning the American public's perception of his disenchantment with nazism, his vain attempts to guard his native land from the horrors of war, and the reality of the Bolshevik menace to western

Europe, all came in rapid succession. Who would deny him the opportunity to return to the United States to defend his motives and actions?

Cesarini listened politely to Chandler's protestations of good intentions, jotted down notes, and left him to his own devices. Other military interrogations were equally unproductive—if surprisingly sympathetic. On July 12, one questioner noted:

That Chandler is telling the truth and is fundamentally honest admits of little doubt. That he is precisely what he declares himself to be—"a sentimentalist"—is amply proven in the quotations above. He is essentially a very naive person who meant well within his misguided and warped framework of ideas; so much so that to this day he is unable to see that he was more than just "an unmuzzled Isolationist" after December 7, 1941.

Time passed. On February 28, 1946, Chandler greeted a special investigator of the FBI, John Eldon Dunn, at the door of his small cottage in Kempton, Bavaria. Taken into custody, he was hustled away to the United States Army detention center at Oberursel, Germany, on the first leg of his journey back home. During this lonely hiatus in his life Chandler unwisely agreed to provide bureau agents with a 48-page autobiographical sketch, culminating in his wartime activities.

Several weeks prior to Chandler's arrest the authorities seized Robert H. Best in Austria. Best was detained near Salzburg, and it was ten months before he and Chandler were reunited in Frankfurt, Germany, for their flight home. The aircraft negotiated the Atlantic Ocean successfully, but subsequent engine trouble forced it down at Chicopee, Massachusetts. Thus fate dictated, through a technicality in the treason law that stated that prisoners be tried in the district where they first entered the United States, that Chandler and Best would have their day in Boston's federal district court.[100]

While the accused faced FBI questions in Washington, D.C., a federal grand jury in Boston heard the incriminating testimony of 11 witnesses, personnel of the Reichrundfunk, who had been flown to Massachusetts to help convict their old associates. These former supervisors and technicians of the U.S.A. Zone performed well, and on December 30, 1946, the jurors returned indictments against both men. The pair were returned to Boston on January 4. Ever the hypochondriac, at his arraignment several days later Chandler recited to Judge Francis J. W. Ford the extent to which his army jailers had permitted his health to deteriorate in Europe: "I do not feel capable of organizing my defense unless hospitalized or given an opportunity to repair my physical condition." The court remained impassive, but Judge Ford did allow the defendant a continuance to secure counsel.

Oscar R. Ewing, the vice-chairman of the Democratic National Committee, was Attorney-General Tom Clark's choice as prosecutor. The Department of Justice sent along Tom DeWolfe and Clyde E. Gooch to assist Ewing and tapped local assistant U.S. attorney Gerald J. McCarthy as part of the team. Washington assigned Boston attorneys Clyde B. Cross and Edward C. Park to defend Chandler.

Psychiatric examinations were ordered on Chandler in early March. Meanwhile the defense moved to dismiss all charges, as Chandler had done nothing more than exercise his First Amendment right of free speech in Berlin. Besides, held Cross, the accused's allegiance to the United States had become diluted through his protracted residency in Germany. "Propaganda is a weapon of war," countered Ewing. Chandler had willingly served a hostile war machine bent on the destruction of his own country.[101]

Chandler's sanity hearings dominated the Court's calendar for the last half of April, and when the proceedings ended, he was deemed sufficiently coherent to stand trial. Judge Ford set the date for June 5.

For three weeks (June 6–27, 1947) in Boston's federal district court, 12 jurors sat and observed the defendant fidget uneasily in his chair. The gaunt, nervous prisoner did not make a favorable impression. Reporter William Schofield of the Boston *Globe* recalled: "As I remember Chandler, he was a foppish poseur of extremely soft character, a weakling whose sole gift seemed to be that of self-adoration."[102] Author Nathaniel Weyl captured the drama's main protagonist in even less flattering tones:

At first glance the shrunken, somewhat cadaverous man who stood before the Court seemed like a startled rabbit. Those who had expected a satanic presence were disappointed. Chandler's shoe-button eyes were framed by dark eyebrows, which tilted upward in an alarming manner to create the impression that their possessor was in a state of chronic astonishment. His head was abnormally small and undistinguished. . . . His mouth was straight and fleshless. This was the face of a man who had renounced the sins of the flesh for those of the spirit. . . . If Chandler represented anything at all, he illustrated the poetic truth of the Platonic doctrine that evil is incompleteness of being.[103]

Impatiently Chandler listened as 16 of his former German colleagues testified against him. Toward the end Chandler tried to repudiate his statement to FBI agent J. Eldon Dunn in Germany. "Dunn, the blond beast, possessed hypnotic powers," he insisted.

One might expect that Chandler's arrogance and aloof demeanor would irritate Judge Ford, and it did. The court refused to accept defense's contention that Chandler was "a true paranoiac" due to his anti-Semitic views. Four psychiatrists held that Chandler's detestation of the Jewish people did not stem from a self-created delusion, a necessary determinant of "true paranoia." Anti-Semitism, continued Ford, was a worldwide phenomenon. There were external causative forces that shaped his poisoned beliefs concerning so-called international Jewry.[104] Chandler sat mute until moments before judgment was rendered. Coming to his feet, he hurled his defiance at those who presumed to comprehend his motives and measure his patriotism: "My counsel thought me insane. I am, of course, not insane, but I have permitted them to defend me on the grounds they chose. It is the tragedy of my life that the warnings I gave my country were not and are not yet accepted. Time, however, will vindicate me."[105] Failing to convince the jury of his altruism, Douglas Chandler drew a sentence of life imprisonment and a $10,000 fine. His lawyers appealed the conviction on the grounds of "natural" territorial allegiance and free speech to the U.S. Supreme Court, an exercise which, of course, availed them nothing.

On January 15, 1962, the attorney-general's office informed the White House that the 74-year-old Chandler would be released from Lewisburg Penitentiary on condition that he return to Germany as his daughter's charge.[106] Simple justice dictated this course. Mildred Gillars had been paroled from her 10- to 30-year sentence in 1961. Iva Toguri d'Aguino (Tokyo Rose) was released in 1956 after completing her ten years behind bars. Both Robert H. Best and Herbert J. Burgman (Joe Scanlon) died in prison. The host of "Station Debunk," Burgman had refused repatriation after Pearl Harbor while serving as a U.S. embassy employee in Berlin. The only commissioned officer sentenced as a radio traitor, Martin J. Monti, was known as "Martin Wiethaupt, an American officer," during his broadcasting days. Monti plead guilty to treason in 1949 and was released from his 25-year sentence in 1960.[107]

In April, Chandler's release bogged down over whether or not he should pay the $10,000 fine levied by Judge Ford. Since he was destitute, the question appeared moot. During the spring of 1963, Sylvia Chandler flew to the United States to escort her father home. Washington's bureaucratic delays had undermined his health, and she feared the worst.[108] On July 31, an Episcopal minister in Philadelphia appealed to President John F. Kennedy on Chandler's behalf. The Reverend Walter M. Hanshatter had known Douglas Chandler for five years as a correspondent and a communicant in his church. He understood from the authorities that Chandler's behavior had been exemplary while incarcerated at Danbury and Lewisburg penitentiaries, and that he was currently serving effectively as prison librarian at the latter facility.[109] Five days later President Kennedy commuted the sentence of America's last radio traitor.

6

Donald Day, Goebbels' Final Recruit

Nazi Germany's development of radio as an international propaganda vehicle made the overseas broadcaster an indispensable part of its war machine. As early as 1933 Propaganda Minister Josef Goebbels established the U.S.A. Zone of the Reichrundfunk and subsequently staffed it with American expatriates. During the early phases of World War II these foreign broadcasters were asked to cajole their countrymen into supporting U.S. neutrality legislation. When the Japanese attack on Pearl Harbor triggered global war, Goebbels directed his American announcers to weaken Uncle Sam's resolve to fight. Their compliance resulted in a United States federal grand jury indictment on July 26, 1943. Undaunted by the actions of their government and mounting German military reverses, the U.S.A. Zone's radio traitors grew in number through late 1944 with the final employment of Donald Day.

Ironically, Donald Day's brief tenure as a Nazi propagandist proved far less controversial than his career as the Baltic correspondent for Colonel Robert McCormick's Chicago *Tribune*. For 20 years Day's partisans had defended his embattled reputation by alluding to his able coverage of major world events. Day's alleged use of journalistic license was attributed to deadline pressures and face-value acceptance of information from unreliable tipsters. There were other members of the press community, however, who charged that Day falsified his dispatches to enrich himself financially, to gain notoriety, and to satisfy a consuming hatred for the Soviet Union. When, in the summer of 1942, he abandoned his post to bear arms for Germany's ally, Finland, journalist George Seldes branded Day's aberrant course as the final dissolution of a scoundrel's career:

The fact that Donald Day . . . has joined the Finnish army to fight against Russia is of no importance. The important fact is that Donald Day faked the news for more than 20 years and that Colonel McCormick knew that Day lied and printed his lies because he liked those lies. . . . The U.S. press lied about Russia from 1917 onward, and the most persistent liar of all was Donald Day of the Chicago *Tribune*.[1]

Seldes, a former *Tribune* colleague of Day, represented a contingent of foreign correspondents who were convinced that Donald Day had for decades subjected a gullible American public to anti-Soviet propaganda. They were hardly surprised to learn near war's end that he had found common ground with bolshevism's most implacable foe, Adolf Hitler.

Donald Day, the elder scion of a newspaper family, began his apprenticeship as a fledgling journalist early in life. He was born in Brooklyn Heights, New York, on May 15, 1895, the first of five children, three boys and two girls. His parents were John I. Day and Grace Satterlee, the father being racing editor of the New York *Morning Telegraph*. Sam Houston, the second Day offspring, was destined to become a prominent executive with the New York *Journal American*. The third child of this union of an erstwhile Congregationalist father and an Episcopalian mother was Dorothy Day, the Catholic lay activist, who founded the New York newspaper the *Catholic Worker* and St. Joseph's House of Hospitality for the destitute. Donald's youngest brother, John, became a newsman with the Hearst organization in New York.[2]

John I. Day was born in Cleveland, Tennessee, in 1870. His great-great-grandfather was James McElwee, a Revolutionary War veteran who fought in the battles of King's Mountain, Musgrove's Mill, and Guilford Courthouse. The hardy McElwee was a kinsman of Daniel Boone and had accompanied the pathfinder on one of his trips west of the Alleghenys. Donald's paternal grandmother, Mary Mee, married Sam Houston Day, a doctor in Cleveland, Tennessee. Born on a farm in Bradley County, Tennessee, on September 10, 1839, Sam Day graduated in medicine from New York University in 1861, just as the Civil War began. Returning home, he enlisted in the Confederate army and served as a surgeon in General Joseph Wheeler's army. In the last year of the war, Sam Day was wounded three times and spent the last 40 days of the conflict in a prison camp.

A native New Yorker, Grace Satterlee was born in Marlboro in 1870. Her great-great-grandfather Satterlee had come from England as the captain of a whaler, settling in Wappinger Falls, New York. Her father, Napoleon Bonaparte Satterlee, joined the Union army during Lincoln's first call for volunteers—an error in judgment the Day clan never forgave. Satterlee contracted tuberculosis in service and was never well after the war. He became a chairmaker and reared six children, Grace included. When Grace was nine years old (1879), her father died and she was reduced to employment in a shirt factory. Fortunately, a concerned aunt secured her brother's military pension for the benefit of the Satterlee children and Grace returned to school. In time, she gained admittance to Eastman's Business School in New York City, and it was there that she met John Day.[3]

Family fortunes and surroundings changed whenever John Day assumed new posts as sports journalist and editor. The Days lived in Bath Beach, Brooklyn, until Donald was eight, at which time the family moved to California. In Berkeley, the Days took a furnished house until their furniture could be brought around the Horn. When their belongings arrived, the Days moved into a bungalow in Oakland near Idora Park, where John Day would work as a racetrack reporter. Day kept his own horse stabled at the Oakland track and took Donald and Sam there frequently.[4] On April 18, 1906, the San Francisco earthquake destroyed the elder Day's newspaper plant and ended the family's residence in California. Unwilling to accept charity, the proud patriarch liquidated and transported his clan to Chicago. The first year in Chicago was a period of trying readjustment for the family. The Days lived over a saloon on Thirty-seventh Street. For lunch Donald ate potato soup, and for supper, bread, bananas, tea, and jelly. The boy's mother salvaged cast-off remnants, made dining room and living room curtains out of them, and hung them over fishing rods. Grace created furniture from orange crates and nail kegs. John Day could not find employment, so he undertook writing a novel. His manuscript never sold, but he did manage to peddle articles on racing and racetrack gossip.[5]

These financial and spiritual doldrums took an awful toll on Donald's parents. Always the stern disciplinarian, John Day's dictates grew ever more extreme as conditions worsened. He permitted no "trash" in his children's reading, and they were not allowed to interfere with his daytime regimen of writing by having friends in the house. With the exception of Sunday dinner, Day refused to take his meals with the children. Regrettably, even that weekly event became a source of great strain to everyone, as Dorothy later observed in her first book, *The Eleventh Virgin* (1924):

Mr. Henreddy [John Day] must hate his children, June [Dorothy] often thought. As long as she could remember, the only time they ever sat at the table with him was on Sunday at the midday meal. Even when the boys [Donald and Sam] had started to work nights as telegraphers, getting up at ten when he also arose, he would not eat breakfast with them but insisted that Mother Grace serve his meals separately. ... None spoke at the Sunday noon meal; all ate in gloomy silence. They could hear each other swallow and the strain to eat quietly was so great that by the time the dessert was brought on, appetites had fled.[6]

This parental reserve must have haunted the Day children, especially Dorothy, who pursued the issue in her autobiographical account, *The Long Loneliness* (1952):

There was never any kissing in my family, and never a close embrace. There was only a firm, austere kiss from my mother every night. . . . We could never be free with others, never put our arms around them casually, lean against others companionably as I see Italian boys do. . . . We were always withdrawn and alone.[7]

For the most part both Grace and John Day had ignored the subject of religion in the presence of their children. Both seemed to feel that talking about religion was undignified. Neither parent ever went to church, and none of the children were baptized. In fact, John Day enjoyed the role of the village atheist, who affirmed nothing save the racetrack, the bottle, and his wife. During his New York days, "Judge Day" had enjoyed the company of such influential people as New York Giants manager John McGraw and state politico Al Smith, not to mention his drinking associates. Now, living in Chicago in relative obscurity—except for the bill collectors—Day could only vent his frustration on his hapless family. One evening Grace Day's usually serene demeanor cracked under the stress. It was after supper, while doing dishes, that Grace broke into hysterics and, one by one, slammed the dishes to the floor. Despite John's efforts to calm her, the slamming and screaming continued, while brother Sam herded all the children into the bedroom for prayer. They obeyed, except Donald, who sat grim-faced and pretended to read. In most cases, however, Grace managed to face the grimness of her daily life with the aid of leisurely hot baths and ginger ale highballs.[8]

Young Donald escaped the bleakness of Thirty-seventh Street in the many diversions of childhood. It was his custom to invade Dorothy's room by window and door in order to seize and read aloud her diary. When Dorothy took after him with the bread knife, Donald ran to his mother in apprehension of his life. Brother and sister never got along well, a worrisome detail Dorothy recalled as an adult:

She would have loved her brothers [Donald and Sam]—but they were ashamed of being fond of their sister, and would suffer no expression of love from her. They were cold and aloof to each other, except when drawn together in times of storm; the poverty-stricken tenement on the South Side, and the time Mother Grace became hysterical and broke everything in sight—these colossal things made them run together and clutch each other.[9]

In adolescence Donald worked nights as a telegrapher and spent his spare daytime hours in the backroom of the Emery Street saloon—prizefighting. Despite his marked face and a broken thumb, Donald successfully kept this extracurricular activity from his mother. Dorothy, however, uncovered the source of her brother's extra income and blackmailed him for months.[10]

When Donald was 12, John Day got a job as the sports editor of a Chicago newspaper, the *Inter-Ocean*. Shortly thereafter the family moved into a better neighborhood, first on Oakwood Boulevard and then to a house on the North

Side. Several years later the Days relocated to a large house on Webster Avenue, near Lincoln Park. Judge Day always believed that Donald would be the success story in the family, with his strapping physique, quick mind, and thirst for adventure; and early signs seemed to bear out his conviction. In 1912 the 17-year-old began his newspaper career on a journalistic experiment called *The Day Book*. The dime-novel-size book recounted the struggles of labor in the Chicago area and elsewhere, and its editorials were pro–Eugene Debs, Industrial Workers of the World (IWW), and the Haymarket anarchists. *The Day Book* carried no advertisements, thereby freeing its staff to expose unfair labor practices without fear of economic reprisal. Carl Sandburg, who sat on the publication's copydesk, inspired Donald to "look on the people as he did, with love and hope of great accomplishment." Although Sandburg was 34 and Donald a mere teenager at the time, both mentor and protégé were children of the Progressive Era. It was an exciting period of social fermentation when politicians talked of reform and the intelligentsia mobilized to alleviate human suffering. Who could doubt that Donald Day understood poverty or that he was a product of the contemporary political current?[11]

The first of the three Day children to graduate from the Robert Waller High School in Chicago, Donald pursued his journalism career on the staffs of the City News bureau of Chicago, the *Inter-Ocean*, and the Chicago *Journal*. By the age of 23 Day found himself in the position of sports editor of the New York *Morning Telegraph*, a prized assignment partially won through his father's connections. The lure of World War I prompted Donald to enlist as an observer in the naval aviation service on August 13, 1917. From the Montauk Point airdrome, Day's flimsy craft patrolled off New England's coast in search of enemy submarines. He emerged unscathed from three airplane crashes, all of them in the sea. Following the war Day surfaced in New York City as a labor reporter for the *World*. The plight of the urban working class intrigued him far more than the sporting world of his father, and apparently he enjoyed a good rapport with many of the city's labor personalities. Time and again Day drew on his former Chicago experiences with *The Day Book* and the *Tribune* (1916), when he and Floyd Gibbons covered strikes and unruly IWW rallies, to produce his best work. Small wonder that the ambition and flair of this newcomer caught the competition's notice.[12]

In 1920 publisher William Randolph Hearst and Donald Day shared a single obsession, namely, firsthand knowledge of Russia's domestic scene following the Bolshevik revolution. At home misinformation abounded as the purveyors of America's Red Scare cast the Russian Socialist Federated Soviet Republic as an evil empire bent on immediate world revolution; conversely, an equally vocal minority touted the new social experiment as a rising utopia. Despite the fact that newspaper reporters were barred from the Soviet Union, which was still in the throes of bloody civil war, Hearst insisted that his syndicate be the first one represented in Moscow. Accordingly the Hearst interests contacted Day and made this deal with him: If he should finagle his way into the Soviet Union, he would be placed on the payroll at $100 a week; however, if he failed, he would be fired. After every conceivable scheme collapsed, Day resolved to make the Hearst assignment as the spouse of a Communist deportee. In this bizarre affair Day's lady-in-question worked for Professor Ludwig K. Martens' controversial Soviet bureau.[13]

To be sure, Day knew Martens, given the reputation of this colorful middle-aged revolutionary and his New York City organization. In 1896 the professor had been imprisoned for subversive activity against the Czar and, following a three-year jail sentence, was deported to Germany. In 1906 Martens, an engineer by profession, emigrated to England; and on January 2, 1916, he arrived in New York as representative of the Demidoff Steel Works of Perm, in the Soviet Union. In May 1917, shortly after the Czar was ousted, Professor Martens was made a citizen of the new Russia. When the Bolsheviks came to power, he aligned with them. Later he announced he had been named ambassador to the United States and was authorized to use $200,000,000 in trade contracts. Within a few months, however, an anti-radical hysteria swept the country and the local authorities began inquiries. New York police raided Martens' headquarters. A federal warrant was issued for his arrest, and 13 hearings in his case were held in New York and Washington, D.C. It was during this unsettling hiatus that Day wooed and married Etta Fox, a member of Martens' staff. Counsel argued for several weeks before William B. Wilson, secretary of labor, who authorized a deportation order on December 16, 1920. On January 22, 1921, Martens and family, together with 46 men and women from the Soviet bureau, were deported to the Soviet Union. The names of Mr. and Mrs. Donald Day appeared on the passenger list of this so-called "Soviet Ark."[14]

Even today there is some ambiguity as to what actually transpired on the Latvian-Russian border. Day subsequently offered himself as the hapless victim of Soviet capriciousness:

In December 1920, a representative of the Soviet government in New York invited me to go to Russia with him; he was being deported. I got as far as Riga only to find that Moscow had changed its mind. I received a telegram telling me I would not be permitted to enter Russia. "All right," I said, "I'll stay here."[15]

According to George Seldes, however, a dejected Day confided quite a different version of his rebuff. Seldes met his colleague by chance in 1922 during a trip through Riga to cover the Litvinov-Hoover treaty negotiations leading to America's aid to millions of Russian famine victims. "The man I knew in Riga was a crude, uneducated, tough guy with the mind and feelings say of a policeman," Seldes remembered. Apparently during their visit Day

bemoaned his most recent setback. It was at the border station that the Cheka
examined each of the deportees closely; and although everyone professed
devotion to bolshevism and the Soviet Union, several of the train passengers
were detained, and one was sent back to Riga. That unfortunate soul was
Day; and, to make matters worse, his wife and the Martens party resumed
the journey to Moscow.[16]

The Soviet police claimed to have pried from their unwelcome guest the
purpose of his counterfeit marriage, and they branded him as the agent of a
corrupt capitalist press. He, of course, denied the charge and spent several
months in Riga protesting his innocence. When Day exhausted his chances
of getting to Moscow, Hearst dismissed him. Day feigned bewilderment
concerning his status and petitioned for a modest living allowance while in
Riga. When no reply was forthcoming, he offered to represent the International News Service without compensation if allowed to retain the Hearst
letter of credential. The stranded American reported that Louise Bryant,
Hearst writer and widow of American Communist John Reed, was a member
of the Cheka. One of her colleagues had provided Day with this information
in the hope of recruiting him for espionage work inside the U.S. mission in
Moscow. Moreover, Bryant had commented negatively to the secret police
on several of her Hearst associates, one of whom had advanced her ship fare
back to the United States. As a parting shot Day wrote his ungrateful former
employers: "Of course you may already know of this and perhaps the ends
justify the means in getting news out of the Soviet Union. But I am afraid
Miss Bryant has stepped a little out of her way in order to queer things for
other correspondents." Penniless and alone, he desperately sought employment. Fortunately, the London *Daily Mail* retained him as a stringer, paying
him a pound for every item he contributed. When Colonel Robert Mc-
Cormick read Day's pieces in the *Daily Mail*, he hired him as a regular
correspondent at $25 a week.

Twenty years later Seldes would write that Day tried to pen a dispatch
every day in order to survive, even if he had to manufacture a story. Through
trial and error Day had realized that no factual, objective or balanced treatment of the Soviet Union was wanted; every such item was refused, whereas
sensational accounts were printed. With this idea firmly in mind, Day was
able to deliver about three stories a week for Lord Northcliffe's paper, some
so crude that he dared not peddle them to the *Tribune*.[17] Foreign correspondent William L. Shirer remembered the speculative nature of these dispatches
as an embarrassment to many of Day's associates: "As I recall, he spent most
of his time in the Chicago *Tribune* office in Riga faking stories about the
outbreak of revolution in Moscow. Unfortunately for him and the *Tribune*,
it was very easy in those days to call up Moscow, talk to a correspondent
like Walter Duranty and find out the truth."[18] Quite often Day came to the
Soviet consulate with copies of his fakes and tried to negotiate, saying that
if he were permitted to enter the Soviet Union he would write the truth,

but so long as he was being denied a visa, he would continue to send fabrications. Seldes insisted that Day's campaign was no secret, as he had boasted to Floyd Gibbons, director of the *Tribune* news service, of his vendetta with the Soviets and his questionable ploy for getting a visa. Gibbons' cable to Colonel McCormick about Day's irregular activities brought neither censure nor remedial action.[19]

The former chief of the *Tribune*'s Washington bureau, Walter Trohan, challenged Seldes' portrayal of Day. In his 1981 introduction to Day's memoir, *Onward Christian Soldiers* (1942), Trohan defended Day's record while attempting to discredit his old friend's accuser:

Through 21 years Day sought regularly to get the once promised visa. Almost as regularly he was approached by Red agents, who told him he would get the visa if only he would write favorable articles for some months and if he would agree to report on the activities of governments with which he was familiar. This Day would not do. He considered the invitation one to join the Soviet espionage apparatus . . . these [Baltic] countries allowed Day to write without censorship, where in Russia correspondents were required . . . to report to the foreign office every three months for consideration of the extension of their visas. If they displeased the Soviets, their visas were withdrawn. For this reason, the *Tribune* elected to withdraw George Seldes, its Soviet ingratiating correspondent, from Moscow and leave the coverage of Russia to Day in Riga.[20]

In fairness to Seldes, the facts show that he was expelled from the Soviet Union in 1923 for using the American Relief Mission diplomatic pouch as a way to smuggle uncensored copy out of the country. Angered by Trohan's words, Seldes would write after 63 years:

I question any writing by Hearst and *Tribune* men who did what their bosses told them to do. It was one of the most despicable situations in American journalism history—and the passing of the Press Lords, in my opinion, is one of the great reasons the American Press today is a great, good press as compared to what it was then. . . . I never faked and I never slanted or colored or distorted a factual news item— which is what Day did with 80 or 90 or perhaps 100% of the items he sold.[21]

Whether or not Day actually loved Etta Fox and shared her left-wing political views is subject to debate, although he repeatedly professed his earlier adoration for both woman and cause. What is indisputable, however, was Day's preoccupation with being among the first U.S. journalists inside Communist Russia and the awful price he would pay in pursuit of this goal. Having been unable to get into the Soviet Union through marriage, Day divorced Etta Fox and wed a White Russian émigré. For years John Day had good-naturedly counseled Donald to marry a rich widow instead of pursuing such a high-risk, low-salary profession as journalism. Right after the nuptials, Day cabled his father: "Dear Dad: Have followed your advice.

Have married a widow, but she isn't rich." Edit Day made a favorable impression on Donald's parents as well as her husband, with whom she lived for the rest of his life. The elder Day believed that Donald was "still the most unsophisticated East Tennessee kid of all of them. He's six foot two inches tall and weighs 240," Judge Day would subsequently observe, "married to an educated, high-class Russian, who has taught him a lot of languages, and who never had and never will have any children. Mother Day and Della have both been over there and spent several months with them, and Donald had her over here two years ago, and we thought she was really sweet." Still, Day groused, he wished that Donald had "married that Baxter girl of Nashville."[22]

Conditions in Riga scarcely mitigated Day's sense of despondency following his rebuff at the Soviet border. He discovered that the Russian famine had taken its toll in the Baltic states. Riga's thoroughfares were lined with boarded shops and the citizenry survived on contributions from the American Red Cross and the American Relief Administration (ARA). The city's customs houses overflowed with merchandise meant for Soviet markets, which would later be sold in Latvia at deflated prices. In February 1921 the starving sailors of the Kronstadt garrison revolted and defied the Red Army before Petrograd. From the unwelcome safety of his Riga bureau Day wrote Colonel McCormick that, ironically, the same seamen who had killed so many of their countrymen during the revolution were themselves its victims. A few weeks later Day covered the suppression of an uprising of Don and Kuban cossacks.[23]

The United States responded to Russia's famine appeals with more than $60 million in food and medical supplies. Maxim Litvinov and W. B. Brown of the ARA met in Riga to sign the terms of agreement. No sooner had the ink dried than Day charged the Soviets with violation of the accord, maintaining that Moscow had bullied the ARA into releasing large quantities of supplies to feed Soviet railroad personnel. One condition of the agreement was fulfilled, however, when five Americans were released from Soviet prisons. Day was present during the June 1921 repatriation of these "spies" at Narve, an Estonian town on the Soviet frontier. He wired Chicago that these "living skeletons" had confirmed the stories emerging from the Soviet Union of a terror campaign led by the Jewish-controlled Cheka.[24]

By the end of 1921 Day had convinced himself that Maxim Litvinov was the author of his misfortunes. Day believed that Litvinov's dislike for him stemmed from an alleged incident that occurred during the summer when the Russian, as minister to Estonia, negotiated with a firm in Holland for the purchase of $2.5 million worth of old German uniforms. Day happened to be at quayside when Soviet officials opened the cases to discover that the uniforms were bloody and filthy beyond description. It amused him that the Bolsheviks had been duped in one of their first foreign business transactions. Moscow recalled Litvinov for an explanation of the swindle. On the eve of

Litvinov's departure Day haunted the Soviet embassy in Tallin seeking permission to cover the arrival in Leningrad of the first U.S. shipments of food for Russian famine victims. Litvinov put Day off, and when he returned to Litvinov's office the next day the minister became hysterical, ordering Day from his office. Several days following Litvinov's departure his secretary, who also had been summoned to Moscow, confessed to Day his fears that Litvinov might shift the blame to him for the bogus shipments. The young man told Day that he would contact Day again if he reached Moscow safely and was not arrested. Minister Litvinov's assistant disappeared, Day wrote, and weeks later rumors circulated in Moscow that his boss had persuaded the secret police of his innocence. Day knew too much and he realized that Litvinov had a long memory. McCormick's embattled reporter cabled headquarters that as long as Litvinov was *persona grata* in Washington, D.C., he would be *non grata*.[25]

In Day's eyes Deputy Commissioner of Foreign Relations Litvinov could deny a troublesome correspondent a visa for whatever reason, and the Russian's Jewish lineage made him even more an object of suspicion. After a few visits to the Soviet legation Day's expectations soured and his encounters with its staff ran the gamut from feigned outrage to silent resignation. His skewed remembrance of one such meeting revealed Day's growing irritability and pronounced anti-Semitism:

Visiting the Soviet legation, I filled out the long questionnaire applying for a Soviet visa. The official was a Whitechapel Jew from London who told me his name there had been Marshall. When he went to Russia to help the revolution he changed it to Markov. Ganetzski, the minister, was also a Jew. When I asked where the Russians were they told me they were back in Russia.

A fortnight later Day received a denial of his application from a functionary in Litvinov's office. Further investigation supposedly showed to Day that the bureaucrat's name was Nuorteva, a Finnish Jew who had embezzled money from Ludwig Martens' old Soviet bureau in New York City. Day reportedly betrayed Nuorteva's former talent for creative bookkeeping, and several weeks later word came of the Russian's removal from office and disappearance. He made another application. After the customary delay, another negative response came. This time it was signed by Gregory Weinstein, whom Day recognized as having been another one of Professor Martens' employees. In his next application Day incorporated nonsensical information designed to antagonize its reviewer. When Weinstein perused Day's application, he became angry and drafted a letter to the Soviet press chief in Riga, vehemently denouncing the *Tribune* and its correspondent. The press chief, in turn, confronted Day with these charges and foolishly permitted him to copy the communication. Day sent Weinstein's indictment to his paper. It was published, creating a small scandal in Moscow that resulted in Weinstein's untimely transfer to Leningrad. Desirous of further revenge, Day wrote Weinstein on the *Tribune*'s stationery, regretfully informing him that there was no possibility of his obtaining a visa to enter the United States. He further expressed sympathy for Weinstein's homesickness for New York City and suggested that if he really meant to desert the cause, he should obtain a Canadian visa and then slip into the United States. As Day anticipated, the GPU (the State secret police) intercepted the letter and arrested Weinstein. It took him several weeks to persuade the Soviet authorities that the whole affair was a hoax. Unhappy with his lieutenant's performance, Litvinov downgraded Weinstein's station once again from Leningrad to Ankara.[26]

During the early 1920s Day took pride in the fact that the *Tribune* was the only American newspaper or news agency to keep a staff correspondent north of Berlin. As approximately 80 papers published the news collected by the *Tribune*'s Foreign Press Service, Day believed that his uncensored stories about the evils of bolshevism helped to stiffen U.S. resolve against recognition of the Soviet regime. Denied access to the Soviet Union, he frequently employed Latvian journalists to cover assignments inside Soviet territory. He gave these men $500 to cover expenses, agreeing to pay an additional $23 for each acceptable article they wrote after their return. The Soviet Foreign Office tried to counter Day's network by warning travelers against granting interviews in Riga. Later the single sleeping car on the train from Moscow to Riga was disconnected at Drinski and routed through Lithuania to the German frontier. The railway connections over Warsaw were improved, and many passengers were given permission to leave the Soviet Union only through Poland.

Day wrote Colonel McCormick on February 24, 1926, that the Bolsheviks had taken a sudden interest in the *Tribune*. A Soviet representative named Valdemer Anine had materialized in Riga to ferret out the sources of the Soviet Union's bad press. When Day pressed the Russian about his inability to secure a visa, Anine informed him that Moscow believed him to be an agent of the U.S. State Department. Anine's special trip to Riga flattered Day, who seemed to relish their meeting:

I informed him the only way they could change my views would be to give me a visa to enter Russia where the censor could control my stories. I said I would continue to write as before. . . . From what I have heard there is little doubt but what Anine made the trip to Riga especially to investigate the *Tribune*. The strength of our news syndicate and the stories I have been writing about, they admit, is delaying the recognition of Russia by the United States.

Shortly thereafter Anine supposedly made Day Moscow's best offer. The coveted visa would be his if he agreed to write "objectively," abstain from anti-Soviet espionage activities, and establish a few Red operatives in selected

Baltic legations and consulates. Perhaps Day took a particular delight in apprising Colonel McCormick of his value to the opposition:

My payroll could run as high as $500 per month and I was to turn over to him all the information I could get about the present negotiations between Russia and the Baltic States regarding separate neutrality pacts. Since these facts are of very little importance I think he figured I could rake off about $400 per month for myself and begin to shade news in their favor. I told him spying was not my line and left.

On another occasion Comrade Umanski, press chief in the Russian Foreign Office, presented Day with a new deal. First, he should cable the *Tribune* only news manufactured by Riga's Soviet press attaché. If Day complied for three months, he would be rewarded with a visa, an apartment, and an automobile in Moscow, where he would be awarded the station of official *Tribune* correspondent. Again Day declined Moscow's generosity. This time Communist agents were dispatched to Riga to assassinate him. In self-defense, Day carried a pistol and arranged for police protection.

In 1928 the press chief of the Latvian Foreign Office, Alfred Bihlmans, was appointed minister to Moscow. No sooner had Bihlmans assumed office than he asked Day to Moscow, promising the correspondent a visa if he made the trip. Day was suspicious and delayed his trip pending word from McCormick. The *Tribune* responded that if Day went, he would go at his own risk. In the meantime Day and his wife had their fortunes told on a street corner in Riga. The gypsy warned Day not to undertake the trip. "She then passed her fingers across her throat and repeated her warning," he subsequently recalled in his memoir. The old woman then gave Edit Day an accurate reading of her past, concluding, "This is your second husband and twice in your life you have really wept." Day's wife later told him that she had cried on two occasions: first, when her baby died of starvation in Petrograd during the Bolshevik famine in the winter of 1918–19; and second, when her first husband was murdered during the Red occupation of Riga. Day chose to remain at home. Three weeks later the Soviets placed three conditions on the Latvian parliament as a prelude to a new trade treaty. They asked that 55 White Russians, whose names were mentioned, be arrested and expelled from the country; also, that the Russian newspaper *Serodnja*, published in Riga, be closed; finally, that Day be deported. The Latvians found these demands to be excessive and the treaty failed.[27]

Even aside from the Russophobic campaign, Day's daring career typified the glamor of the Richard Harding Davis school of foreign correspondence. In January 1923, Day learned that a band of Lithuanian irregulars had somehow mobilized with the intention of seizing the Memeland. He immediately contacted John Dared, a Latvian cinematographer for *Pathe News Weekly*, and the two entrained for Memel. The next morning Day awoke to find his compartment guarded by a Lithuanian soldier. The train car was empty, having been sidetracked at Krettingen. Managing to overpower his jailer, Day forced the soldier to take him to the station commandant. The newsmen asked to join the Lithuanian insurgents. The captain agreed, and together they located the commander and his ragtag army having breakfast at Bajoren's railway station.

Budrys, the leader of the guerrillas, had been a former sergeant in the German river police. At that moment his assault on Memel had stymied because the French garrisons were offering resistance. Clearly, these sunshine patriots did not want to clash with the French, who had armed the German policemen in Memel and had put them forward to stop Budrys' advance. Day warned the Lithuanians that they must take Memel before the arrival of British and French warships. The two newsmen tagged along with the Lithuanians after promising Budrys favorable coverage. Prisoners were taken outside Memel, and with the irregulars staging a march-by in the background, the journalists filmed 14 dejected French and German captives as a center-piece. The ensuing battle of Memel cost both sides 8 killed and 15 wounded. The French garrison of two infantry companies withdrew to the western suburb of the town and entrenched around their barracks.

Several days later the British cruiser *Caladon* arrived. Terrified, Budry's motley contingent came to Day for advice. Day's thoughts, however, were on good film footage:

I suggested to Budrys that as soon as the cruiser made fast he should stage a little parade of his troops along the quayside. Dared was able to get a film of the shabbily clad Lithuanian forces as they marched down the dock alongside and past the British ship and disappeared around the corner of some warehouses. In order to impress the newcomers properly with their numbers, the infantry marched past twice but their single troop of cavalry appeared only once as I was afraid the horses, which were strikingly bad, might even be recognized by the sailors as being the same nags.

The British dispatched their consul general from Danzig for negotiations. Budrys refused the Englishman's demands to withdraw in compliance with the League of Nations and the Guarantors of the Memel Convention. Later Day, whose association with the putschists appeared suspicious, was summoned to the British consulate, where he endured the consul general's bad temper. He shocked his host by suggesting that he alone could arrange to have the Lithuanians withdraw back across a small river that flowed through Memel. This maneuver, according to Day, would enable the *Caladon* to land a detachment of marines that could control the western half from the river to the barracks where the French were entrenched. After the expected French destroyers arrived, the French troops could embark; then, after a face-saving interval, the British marines could embark and the town could be left to the Lithuanians. The consul general rejected this American upstart's proposal and stalked from the room. Ten days elapsed and he cabled the story to.

Chicago, where it was published in the *Tribune* under the headline *"Tribune Man Memel Peacemaker."*[28]

Following this political melodrama, Day visited Kaunas before returning to Latvia. He observed that the Lithuanian government was sponsoring public agitation for the return of the Vilna province once held by Lithuania but now lying within Polish borders. A government spokesman tried to persuade Day that the Memel putsch had been a spontaneous uprising. Furthermore, he was informed that Lithuania was not appeased by the annexation of Memeland and that the government would never resume diplomatic relations with Poland until Vilna's return. Angered by the Lithuanian's crassness, Day wired Colonel McCormick a stinging rebuke of the Kaunas government:

I began by reporting that once upon a time the Lithuanians had been a great tribe of people, but they had not progressed much farther than the tribal stage. In describing my experiences in Memel and Lithuania, I reported that Lithuanians had as much right to govern the Memeland as the Apache Indians had to govern Arizona.

Colonel McCormick surprised his correspondent by publishing Day's communication on the front page of the *Tribune*. This ill-advised move spoiled his paper's relations with the Lithuanians for some time. Hitler's annexation of Memel on March 21, 1939, brought Day a measure of satisfaction after 16 years:

I was in Danzig when I heard of the intention of the German government to reannex Memel territory. . . . En route I saw an inn where a crowd of brownshirted SA men had gathered. We halted and I bought them a round of beer and asked what they had been doing. From the talk of some it seemed they had been busy all night beating up Lithuanians. . . . It was announced that Hitler would address a mass meeting. . . . Memel not only contained many Lithuanians, but there were also many Jews and communists in the town, enemies of Nazism. Despite this, Hitler stood up in an open car. . . . I stood on the sidewalk and was only six feet from him when the car passed. . . . Memel became again a small unimportant German provincial town, but its culture and economic future is secured.[29]

On November 11, 1924, approximately 100 members of Estonia's Communist party were arrested and put on trial in Tallin. The possibilities of the story so intrigued Day that he journeyed from Riga to report the proceedings. During the trial one of the defendants, who showed disrespect for the court, was summarily shot as an example to the others. The surviving prisoners were found guilty of attempted insurrection and drew long prison terms. After the trial Day telegraphed McCormick that the political atmosphere in Tallin remained charged and that he meant to stay on temporarily. His cable was relayed back to the press of the Baltic states from the Paris edition of the *Tribune*. Latvia's largest daily, the *Jaunakas Sinas*, blasted Day for spreading such a malicious misrepresentation about the region and recommended his expulsion.

On the evening of November 30, Day and friends had dinner at the Linden Restaurant in Tallin. During his meal Day was made uneasy by the presence of so many Estonian officers in the dining hall. At 5:00 A.M. he was awakened by the hotel porter, who told him that a revolution was in progress. Hearing gunfire in the streets, Day got dressed, armed himself, tied a white handkerchief around his arm, and headed for Tallin's telegraph office. Halfway there he encountered a delegation of Estonian officers. The ranking member of this cortege disarmed Day but agreed to accompany him to his destination. The bloody events of that morning fascinated Day, who graphically detailed them in his memoir:

General Podder was the first to enter the telegraph office. On the stairway was standing a man with a rifle who raised it and leveled it at the general. . . . General Podder then made one of the best shots I ever saw. When he glimpsed the man aiming his gun he shot him over his left shoulder. The bullet hit the red in the chin and penetrated up to his brain and he fell dead. I accompanied the officers when they went through the telegraph office. They found five other reds there and shot them all dead. Two of them were busy sending messages to Russia asking for aid when they met death. . . . We then proceeded to the railroad station where we arrived in time to participate in the charge of the cadets who bayonetted a number of communists and seized other prisoners. The cadets surprised the putschists at the moment they were preparing to execute a number of Estonian officers who had arrived on an early train. . . . Some twenty policemen, soldiers and private citizens were murdered by the putschists before order was restored. Investigation revealed this plot had been organized and directed from Russia. . . . The Estonian authorities showed no mercy. Everyone of the reds captured in the Tallin putsch was shot.

It was only after this attempted insurrection, Day noted with satisfaction, that Estonia followed the example of the other Baltic states and outlawed the Communist party.[30]

Throughout his checkered career as one of Colonel McCormick's ace eastern European correspondents, never once did Day seek to improve his bad relations with Poland's government. In late January 1926 he arrived in Warsaw to cover an assignment of several weeks' duration. While there he accidentally met delegates from the Guarantee Trust Company and Dillon, Reed & Company, both of New York, who were negotiating a $40 million loan. Day cabled the *Tribune* a series of articles about Poland's rocky financial situation and its corrupt ministries. His stories were published, and the loan negotiation temporarily collapsed. The Polish Foreign Office ordered the secretary of its legation in Washington, D.C., to visit Chicago, call on Colonel McCormick, and inform him that Day was both a drunkard and a liar. McCormick offered to send another journalist to corroborate Day's series. The Polish secretary agreed, and McCormick instructed John Clayton, the paper's correspondent in Berlin, to visit Warsaw in March. Clayton's reports were even more damaging than his colleague's, since the Polish economy had dipped alarmingly during the intervening weeks. The Polish loan fell through, and five weeks later Marshal Joseph Pilsudski came to power.

Another incident occurred in 1933 when a member of Pilsudski's government concocted the idea of calling a World Congress of Poles in Warsaw. Elaborate preparations were made and the congress convened in the summer of 1934. The World Polish Alliance Charter was to be kept confidential until its ratification. Day surreptitiously obtained a copy of the charter, however, and persuaded himself that the document's real purpose was to secure for the Pilsudski government control of all Polish organizations in the United States. Two such organizations, the Polish National Alliance (PNA) and the Polish Roman Catholic Union, were fraternal insurance companies with funds amounting to millions of dollars. Both sent delegates to Warsaw. Apparently Day persuaded John Cudahy, the U.S. ambassador to Poland, to summon the leaders of these Polish-American societies and warn them of Pilsudski's scheme. The congress assembled in the hall of the Polish parliament. Foreign Minister Joseph Beck and the Polish cabinet were in attendance. John Kwick, president of the PNA, told those gathered that the American contingent considered themselves to be Americans of Polish descent and not Poles, that their aim was to attend the conclave but to transfer no allegiances. Day reported that the entire congress appeared thunderstruck. The ceremony scheduled for the signing of the charter was cancelled. Day interviewed Kwick before cabling the story to Chicago. His dispatch caused a stir among Polish groups in the United States and Kwick, before he left Poland, denied his interview with Day. Colonel McCormick ignored the denial and ran an editorial lauding the position of the delegates. Day claimed that a bitter Polish government turned its attention to the two men who foiled its machinations: "The intrigues were continued but were now directed against Mr. Cudahy and myself. After many unpleasant experiences we both left Warsaw. Mr. Cudahy became American minister to Ireland and I returned to Riga. We were both happy at the change."[31]

In the summer of 1934, Day ran afoul of the Polish Foreign Office again. The affair began with a journalist named Stefan Klecgkowski who had been a reporter on the staff of the *Kurjer Warszawski*. During his association with this paper Klecgkowski was asked to serve as a propagandist at the Polish legation in Washington, D.C. When he arrived, however, his prospective employees informed him that they were unable to pay his salary. Without funds, he worked for several years as editor of a Polish paper in New York City that opposed the Pilsudski regime. When Klecgkowski returned to his homeland, he immediately became a marked man. No sooner had Day employed the Pole as a translator than the Polish Foreign Office demanded Klecgkowski's dismissal. Day stood his ground. In gratitude, Klecgkowski introduced his boss to General Ladislaw Sikorski. Through Sikorski, who was out of favor with the Pilsudski circle, Day gained a valuable pipeline to Polish military and political camps. Although Sikorski was kept on the active list, he received neither post nor duties. Day forwarded some of the general's writings and interview transcriptions to the *Tribune*. The two men disagreed over the best course for Poland. Sikorski believed his country's future lay with France, while Day insisted that Warsaw must cooperate with Berlin.

Perhaps it was inevitable that this friendship should mire Day even deeper into Polish political intrigue. One morning the general telephoned Day and asked to see him immediately. Within 15 minutes Sikorski was showing Day the corpses of two would-be assassins on his villa's grounds. The Polish officer maintained that he knew the identities of the men who were trying to kill him. He anticipated another attempt, and he thought it best to tell Day his story should worse come to worse. Day recommended that Sikorski write an account of the bungled assassination attempt, his invitation to Day to inspect its aftermath, and of those conspirators involved. In this note the general would authorize his friend to publish the story in the *Tribune* should another attempt on his life occur. Sikorski penned the document and signed it. Day sent the contents of Sikorski's note to Chicago. The account, without the names of the conspirators, merited front-page coverage. As a temporary resident of Warsaw at this juncture, Day anticipated the price for his actions. He knew that the Polish-American newspapers back home would pick up the report and republish it, that it would be branded a falsehood, and that there would be an attempt to expel him. In his book Day has bequeathed a rich account of his confrontation with the Polish press chief:

The press chief smiled maliciously for we were not on friendly terms. He asked if I knew why he had phoned. I said I expected him to inform me that I had to leave Poland. He said this was correct and I must do so immediately. I replied I had no intention of obeying this order and told him to inform Colonel [Josef] Beck, the foreign minister, that General Sikorski had given me the before mentioned note which was already in Berlin and if the Polish authorities dared to arrest me and expel me across the frontier I would publish the entire story and the names of those involved in the assassination plot. The press chief turned pale and quickly left the room. Returning in a few minutes he asked me to please forget the entire matter, it had all been a regrettable mistake.[32]

Day never missed an opportunity to insinuate that Beck was behind the attempt on Sikorski's life. He took pride, however, in the fact that there were no more plots to kill the general. Marshal Pilsudski's death in 1935, nevertheless, distressed Day because he was convinced that Poland's last chance for an accord with Germany perished with its head of state. He knew that the vacillating Colonel Beck would prove no match for Sir Howard William Kennard, the British ambassador, and Leon Noel, the French ambassador. According to Day, these conniving diplomats, together with their paid Polish agents, engineered the appointment of the pro-Western Marshal Edward Rydz-Smigly, thereby sealing Poland's doom.

In 1933, when President Franklin Roosevelt appointed William Bullitt as ambassador to Moscow, Day received instructions from McCormick to use Bullitt's good offices to procure a Soviet visa. He met Bullitt at the home of John Cudahy, the U.S. ambassador to Warsaw. Bullitt promised to pursue the matter and to communicate with Day either through Cudahy or the U.S. minister in Riga. After the passage of several months and no visa, McCormick ordered Day to forward a story about Bullitt's activities as ambassador in Moscow. Several weeks passed and still another wire arrived from the colonel. For Day there was no mistaking its implication: "I hear Bullitt is making a fool of himself in Moscow. Make a report." The following morning Day reported that he was withdrawing some cash from the Bank Americanski when he noticed in front of him a messenger of the U.S. embassy. Ambassador Cudahy's courier was there presenting a check to be cashed. "I knew the bank clerk and reached in and took the check," Day recalled. "It was for two thousand dollars drawn on Bullitt's personal account in the Philadelphia General Trust Company and made out to our ambassador John Cudahy and endorsed by him." Somewhat suspicious, Day memorized the check number and interrogated the embassy messenger. He learned that Bullitt frequently sent such checks from the Moscow embassy. According to Day, Warsaw embassy personnel were instructed to cash these checks for dollars and with this money purchase Soviet rubles and chervonetz from Jewish *valnts mechlers* (currency black marketeers) in the ghetto.

Further investigation disclosed that the official Soviet state bank rate of exchange was one ruble, 13 kopeks for one dollar. Day claimed, however, that the Soviets instructed Bullitt to seek his money in Warsaw. He even suggested that the ambassador had boasted of this East-West arrangement. His research further disclosed the activities of lower-echelon Western diplomats who purchased from GPU-sponsored secondhand shops the belongings of murdered Russian aristocrats "for prices which enabled them to obtain a handsome profit on their investments abroad."

In his report Day contended that Bullitt had bought so many rubles on Warsaw's black market that the price rose to 30 rubles for the dollar. This action outraged the American colony in Moscow. Day's next step was to confront Cudahy with his findings, tell him of McCormick's desire to have inside information on Bullitt, and apprise Cudahy that he meant to do a story on the U.S. ambassador-turned-ruble-smuggler. The smug newsman portrayed Cudahy as the horrified public servant who was insistent that the whole matter be reconsidered. The Polish ambassador would be protected, Day notified his employer, even though Cudahy had been an unwitting accomplice. Day was subsequently disappointed to learn that his exposé had generated little news sensation among the American public, although "it did kick up a considerable row in the State Department."

In less than a fortnight a former *Tribune* employee who had been fired by Day salvaged the Bullitt story from McCormick's columns and gave it front-page exposure in the Warsaw press. This individual, Michael Nowinski, also wrote that the U.S. government intended to conduct an investigation of the whole incident, a fact Day vehemently denounced as untrue, and that McCormick's correspondent was to be recalled because he could not substantiate his story. Unfortunately, Day became embroiled in a war of words with several of the Warsaw dailies. In the midst of this unpleasantness Count Potocki, head of the Anglo-American Department of the Polish Foreign Office, expressed his regrets to Ambassador Cudahy that Day should go unpunished. He reminded the U.S. ambassador that if a native journalist had ever written such a feature on a Polish diplomat, he would receive at least five years' imprisonment. It went without saying, Potocki concluded, that Day would no longer be welcome in the Polish Foreign Office. Cudahy relayed the Count's words to Day, who, after obtaining official sanction, angrily confronted his accuser:

Mentioning there was considerable difference between American and Polish correspondents and since I could prove my charge against Bullitt I said no action would be taken against me by either my government or the Polish government. As for his statement that I was *persona non grata* I had felt I had been that ever since 1926 when I frustrated Poland's attempts to obtain a forty million dollar loan in the United States. In conclusion, I suggested to Count Potocki it might be advisable for him to mind his own business in the future and leave me out of his discussions. Our language became rather heated and I am afraid I punctuated some of my remarks with profanity.

Day's profane remarks signaled the end of the newsman's involvement in the Bullitt affair, but not his bitterness. He never forgave Franklin Roosevelt for papering over this alleged scandal by recalling Bullitt from Moscow, only to appoint him ambassador to France a short time later.[33]

The research of Bullitt scholar Beatrice Farnsworth contradicts Day's image of the ambassador as a ruble smuggler. Her findings suggest that the Soviet government had refused to provide the U.S. embassy with sufficient paper rubles at reasonable prices with which to operate, despite prior assurances to the contrary. When Bullitt pressed the Soviets for an explanation, he was told that the government could not show partiality toward his delegation. It is possible that Bullitt drew on his own account during his early days in Moscow in order to keep the embassy solvent. Perhaps Day witnessed one of these transactions and placed the darkest interpretation on the ambassador's immediate need for rubles. Bullitt's third secretary, George Kennan, subsequently observed that his boss was mortified by Commissar Litvinov's suggestion that he purchase Soviet currency on the "Black Bourse."[34]

Moscow's archenemy continued to besmirch the world image of communism. On March 31, 1929, Day revealed in the *Tribune* that the Soviet Union's nationalized industries were virtually bankrupt due to widespread alcoholism among the workers. On the eve of bolshevism's fifteenth anniversary, Day reported the Red Terror's liquidation figure at 3,883,891 lives and its political exiles at nearly twice that figure. Perhaps Colonel McCormick's audience was amazed to read that Day had taken as his authority a 1922 casualty list prepared by Alfred Rosenberg, spiritual godfather of the national socialist movement.[35] In the basement of the Gertrude Lutheran Church in Riga, Day interviewed volunteers who collected clothing and food parcels for German refugees stranded in the Soviet Union. On occasion he was permitted to review the "pathetic" communications from these unfortunates, some of which were fabricated from wrapping paper and birchbark.[36] When Premier Stalin announced his First Five-Year Plan in 1928, it was discovered that the secret police had decimated the country's reserve of scientists and technicians. Unable to resurrect their best minds from the grave or from long-forgotten gulags, the Russians opted to employ American engineers. This opportunity seemed tailor-made for Day, who proceeded to milk his transplanted countrymen for unique copy about doings inside the Soviet Union. When the U.S. newspaper establishment criticized Day's professionalism and the *Tribune*'s policy of covering the Soviet Union without a news bureau in Moscow, McCormick struck back editorially:

Censored reporting has given not only an inadequate but a radically deceptive account of the extent and gravity of conditions created by communist rule, but such doubts as were thrown upon uncensored service through the publication of officially permitted reports can no longer survive. . . . The American public has a right to know the facts of communist rule, especially at a time when there is much callow propaganda for the transformation of our social order and much inevitable discontent with American conditions.[37]

The *Tribune* never forgave Franklin Roosevelt for his recognition of the Soviet Union in November 1933. Its editors were further outraged over the appointment of the individual significantly responsible for Moscow's diplomatic victory, William C. Bullitt, first U.S. ambassador to the Soviet Union. An ardent New Dealer, Bullitt's ambassadorship was anathema to the *Tribune*'s publisher. McCormick could scarcely forget that as a member of President Woodrow Wilson's Peace Mission of 1918, young Bullitt had advocated official recognition of the Soviet Union. Then, in 1923, Bullitt compounded his sin by marrying Louise Bryant Reed, widow of American Communist John Reed.[38] Hardest hit was Day, however, who blamed the president for betraying his life's mission of isolating the contagion of communism. For him there was more than a fragile connection between bolshevism and New Deal liberalism.

Defenders of Bolsheviks are mentally degenerate. This unintelligentsia throngs into Soviet representations abroad on revolutionary holidays to partake of caviar, vodka and other delicacies provided by the new Jewish rulers of Russia. It accepts subsidized journeys to Russia and permits various agencies of the Soviet regime to stuff its pockets with money. . . . The unintelligentsia in their secret hearts are also revolutionaries. They are dissatisfied with the makeup of society in which they live and wish to change it.[39]

The *Tribune*'s foremost theme during the presidential election of 1936 was its attempt to link the White House with international communism. After three frustrating years how fortunate for Day that McCormick's editorial campaign, coupled with a train of random circumstances, permitted him a measure of revenge against Roosevelt.

On May 29, 1936, the Communist party of Illinois held a convention at Chicago's Ashland Auditorium. Among the speakers was Earl Browder, secretary of the American Communist party, who spoke on "Issues of the 1936 Election Campaign." The secretary's presentation reeked of defeatism, a litany of failed political strategies. His party had attempted unsuccessfully to forge a coalition with the Socialists and the Farmer-Labor party in order to present a popular front against both Roosevelt and the GOP's Alf Landon. Browder's plan for a "united front" met its greatest opposition from Norman Thomas, whom he quoted over the radio. The Socialist leader had said: "The Roosevelt administration is probably as liberal as any capitalist administration in America is likely to be. . . . Those who want reforms better stick to the Roosevelt administration." Despite Thomas' coolness, Browder hoped to salvage the American Communist party's fortunes by claiming his Communists could "enter such a united front with workers who support Roosevelt." He denied, however, that his approach constituted a surrender to Rooseveltian liberalism. Said Browder: "Our position toward Roosevelt is clear. We do not cancel a word of our criticism of Roosevelt. We do not and will not take any responsibility for him."

Browder repeated his position in a public address in New York City. He then incorporated the same language in a signed article that appeared in the *Communist International*, published in Moscow in August 1936. A voracious reader of Soviet material, Day soon came across the Browder piece and recognized its potential. After rewriting a paragraph in the article, Day cabled the *Tribune* that instructions had been sent by the Comintern for the support of Roosevelt's candidacy by the American Communist party. McCormick's artful reporter attributed to the Comintern the pivotal passage he had redrafted from Browder's essay:

The decision of the Comintern to join the workers' organizations in supporting Roosevelt is not because we endorse his policies or intend to stand responsible for his actions. We are going to work for the election of Roosevelt because we wish to strengthen our influence among America's many radical groups.

The *Tribune* ran Day's sensational story under the headline "Moscow Orders Reds in U.S. to Back Roosevelt." The *Tribune* in editorials accepted Day's contribution in its entirety. It maintained that "a bulletin issued by the Communist International headquarters in Moscow states the reasons why the Communists desired the reelection of Mr. Roosevelt." There was no such bulletin. There were no orders. The publisher went so far as to print a page advertisement with the banner "He Hurled a Bombshell 4,000 Miles." The "he" was Donald Day. "It was a notable news beat," declared the *Tribune*. "From the publication of this news in the *Tribune* has sprung the outstanding issue in the presidential campaign."

The Chicago *Times* not only branded the *Tribune* story of August 8 a lie but offered $5,000 as a challenge to McCormick to substantiate Day's submission or retract it. The colonel declined to rise to the bait. When the Republican State Committee of Wisconsin flooded the state with reprints of the Day "creation," Robert LaFollette's Progressive party added another $5,000 invitation to document or retract. There were no takers. Although McCormick shrank from employing the Day article again for political ends, the Hearst syndicate reran the now familiar dispatch on election eve. A turncoat in Hearst's employ alerted Steve Early, FDR's press secretary, to the potential danger, and Early adroitly defused the issue in a press conference.[40]

While Europe rehearsed for war, Day prepared himself for life under German occupation. In correspondence written between April and August of 1939, he bade farewell to his friends at the *Daily Mail*, expressing sorrow that Britain's government and most Englishmen had not come to appreciate the "terrific vitality" of Hitler's new Reich. He attributed Germany's bad press in England to the influence of Jewish advertisers. Day ratified his break with the British Empire by allowing his membership in Riga's British Club to lapse.[41]

The Polish authorities signified their break with Day by annulling his visa in March 1939. Barred from Warsaw and unable to report on "the Polish persecutions of the German minority during the late summer crisis," Day settled for the Prussian-Polish frontier. He arrived in Koenigsberg and proceeded to the Polish Corridor, where he was permitted to interview German refugees. It appeared to him that the Polish authorities "had gone mad." He returned to Koenigsberg, filed his stories, and telephoned Sigrid Schultz, the *Tribune*'s Berlin correspondent. Schultz mocked Day's theory that the Nazis and Soviets were about to sign a political accord. She predicted that an alliance would result from the British-French-Soviet negotiations taking place in Moscow. The morning paper of August 24 brought news of the German-Soviet Non-Aggression Pact as Day prepared for an interview with Gauliter Erich Koch, president of East Prussia. During their discussions Koch maintained that all displaced Germans from Poland would be resettled following that country's defeat. Day confided to Koch his knowledge of an

Allied war plan in which the British fleet would occupy Libau, while the Polish army struck across Lithuania from the Vilna Corridor toward Libau. He assured Koch that under these circumstances, despite the appalling unpreparedness of Lithuania and Latvia, both countries would fight. Would the German High Command support these naive governments in the event of an Allied military adventure? Gauliter Koch pledged the use of German arms in the protection of the Baltic region.

That evening Day attended a banquet at the Koenigsberg Fair in the Park Hotel. In the middle of dinner word came that Foreign Minister von Ribbentrop would be stopping over en route to Moscow. Although the foreign minister's room adjoined Day's and Reichmarshal Herman Goring was expected, the entire Nazi delegation departed early the next morning before Day had an opportunity to conduct interviews. Following lunch he dispatched his story with a colleague to be delivered to the official Latvian government newspaper *Brive Zime*. By chance Day encountered von Ribbentrop that evening in a Koenigsberg restaurant reading the wireless he had supposedly sent earlier in the day. The foreign minister approved the dispatch, but the Gestapo forbade Day's passage to Danzig to witness the beginning of the war. Fearful that the Poles would invade Lithuania and cut him off from Riga, Day immediately left for home. Once inside Latvia, Day reported scores of Polish pursuit aircraft on every airfield he passed. The fighters had deserted from airdromes in the Vilna Corridor without firing a shot.[42]

After his return from Koenigsberg in September and reporting on the Nazi invasion of Poland from Riga, Day decamped for Helsinki early in October. Of concern to him were some anti-Finnish articles in the *Leningrad Pravda* and the *Krasnaija Gazet*. As these publications seemingly enjoyed the sanction of the Foreign Affairs Commissariat, Day surmised that the Soviet Union would use the protection of its new non-aggression accord with Germany to pressure Finland. On October 5, the Finnish minister of foreign affairs was invited to Moscow for consultation. In the ensuing discussions Stalin ordered the Finnish delegation to sign a mutual assistance agreement and cede several outlying garrisons to the Soviet Union for the defense of Leningrad. These conditions were rejected, and by mid-autumn relations between the two countries verged on war. Uneasy over the certainty of Soviet military adventures, Day countered with the only weapon at hand—disinformation.

Toward late November, Day tried to persuade Finland's foreign minister, Elias Erkko, to provide Moscow with the bogus news that his country would accept a $100 million loan from the United States. To his amazement, he learned from Erkko that Prime Minister Risto Ryti was actually negotiating a $60 million advance from Washington. Day lost no time in appealing to the prime minister's better judgment. Realistically, Finland could not expect aid from the Americans, argued Day. First, FDR's Jewish secretary of the treasury, Henry Morgenthau, would do nothing to compromise Soviet ambitions; second, "world Jewry" considered Finland an anti-Semitic country because its government had opposed large-scale Jewish immigration. Day asked Ryti's permission to publish Finland's desperate need for U.S. aid. The prime minister balked, despite his guest's ardent wish to arouse American public opinion. Day agreed to temporarily honor Ryti's position, but he eventually released the story in a February 1940 issue of the *Tribune*. In this exclusive he demonstrated how Roosevelt purposefully slowed assistance to Finland, and how he finally agreed to a $30 million appropriation only after Finland had been overrun.

A lull in the diplomatic crisis persuaded Day to return to Riga for the Thanksgiving holidays. He was home less than a week when word came that the Finns had shelled Soviet positions. The Soviets bombed Helsinki in reprisal. Within 24 hours Day had embarked on a small steamer for Stockholm, escorted by two Estonian torpedo boats. His voyage was not without incident. The Soviet fortification at Baltioport caught his ship in its searchlight beams and the vessel was stopped and searched by a Soviet warship. In Stockholm the next day, Day transferred to a Swedish steamer en route to Turku. He discovered Finland in a state of total mobilization.[43]

From the beginning, Day's unswerving devotion to Finland's cause prejudiced his dispatches. On December 4 he reported that Soviet bombers, fueled with gasoline from California, were leveling the civilian districts of every major Finnish city.[44] In Helsingfors, Day overheard several Italian observers excoriate Soviet pilots, who wantonly "machine-gunned invalid women and children" in flight from burning towns. Captured Soviet prisoners told him of special GPU detachments that stayed behind the Red advances to liquidate defectors. Atrocity stories filtered into Helsingfors from the Mannerheim defense line that the Bolsheviks were using refugees to clear enemy mine fields.[45]

When the Soviet Union's military juggernaut began to overwhelm Finland's precarious defense network, Day journeyed to the Petsamo-Salmijarvi front to report on Finnish morale. In subfreezing weather where a minor wound could mean death, he witnessed hundreds of ill-clad, half-starved Russian soldiers surrender in exchange for warmth. Along the route of withdrawal Day observed Finnish demolition squads performing their ruinous work, and he chanced on a young sniper who had killed over half a company of Soviet troops.[46] Day reported his greatest moment in journalism came on February 5, 1940, in Sortavala, a small commercial center on the northwest corner of Lake Ladoga. When he arrived, the town had just undergone a severe aerial bombardment. In due course Day volunteered as part of a salvage crew. Halfway through this work a small boy came running up to say that no one should fire because some Finnish planes would soon be over Sortavala:

We watched and waited expectantly. At noon 86 Soviet bombers had attacked Sortavala. During the afternoon, squadrons of 32, 18 and 16 planes had dropped bombs.

We waited for the Finnish machines. At last we heard a motor. One lone fighter plane crossed Sortavala en route to Pitkaranta where they were fighting. Just one airplane. Not a single person thought of the odds against the Finn. They were as confident in him as they were in themselves. . . . That was the fighting spirit of Finland I saw that afternoon. I felt myself a better man because of my contact with it.[47]

On the night of February 5, the Finns surrounded and destroyed a battalion of Russians in a forest near Kitela. Since the engagement occurred on a moonless night, Day inquired of a corporal how his comrades managed to avoid killing one another. The soldier quipped, "We all wore our rucksacks, and when we discerned a man we slapped him on the back. If he had no rucksack he got the knife." The aftermath of a Finnish ambush near Lake Ladoga offered Day's readers a grisly insight into combat in an arctic environment:

On both sides of the road were tanks and cannons and cars and sleds. Russian bodies were lying everywhere—under the wagons, in the trenches and half out of the tanks, their faces frozen blue-black. At one point on the road, the Finns had placed a number of [Russian] bodies upright in the snow, making a ghastly group of figures which looked as though they had been turned to stone while running for shelter.[48]

By early March the Finnish army was in full retreat on the Karelian Isthmus. The British offered limited military assistance, but Day lobbied influential circles in Helsinki to resist John Bull's generosity. He diagnosed London's concern as a ruse to sever Germany's access to Sweden's rich ore fields. England, he argued, wanted to draw the Nazis into Sweden and trigger a confrontation between Berlin and Moscow. With Finland as the cat's-paw, Churchill would sacrifice Scandinavia, including many of its excellent harbors, to the Bolsheviks in return for a military alliance. Embittered over Finland's dilemma, Day's reports hinted at an international conspiracy afoot to save the Soviet Union's Jewish oligarchy from "ignominious defeat." During his frequent trips to the front he wrote of Soviet POWs carrying meat tins packed in Chicago. When irate Finnish soldiers cornered Day about these findings, he blamed the Roosevelt administration for provisioning the enemy. His surveys showed that Finland's people were no less disaffected by the United States' indifference to their fight for national survival. The results of this indifference, concluded Day on March 14, were the defeat of a proud people and the displacement of 450,000 Finns.[49]

Scarcely had the first Russo-Finnish War ended than Day learned of German landings in Calo, Trondheim, Narvik, and other Norwegian ports. From Sweden's capital he interpreted Norway's war effort as one riddled with defeatism and fifth-column treachery. What's more, he wired Chicago that Hitler's occupation of Norway successfully checked Moscow's designs in Scandinavia.[50] Day entrained for Ostersund, Sweden, arriving there on April 25, 1940. A small group of Norwegian volunteers recently demobilized from the Finnish army appeared on the Swedish side of the Fjallnas Pass several days later. These men were eager to join their compatriots who were in flight before the advancing Germans. Day happened by and watched the Norwegians shovel snow in order to join the remnants of their army. When the pass was cleared, however, the soldiers discovered that they had opened the way for the last stage of a panicky retreat. One of those fleeing the Nazi Blitzkrieg, a colonel, told Day of British duplicity and betrayal. He avowed that his fellow officers regarded the British as invaders and wished to repel them. Many of the Norwegian conscripts, according to the colonel, either could not use their weapons or refused to engage the Germans. Skotgarden, a forward Norwegian outpost, attracted Day's interest. There he encountered a demoralized company of Norwegian soldiers who had replaced their commanding officer with the cook. In this unstable situation Day and his companions were suspected by the troopers of being saboteurs and barely escaped with their lives.[51]

By early May, Day's primary mission of reaching Norway's King Haakon VII and party seemed dashed. As a consolation prize the Swedish government managed to get Day to Trondheim, a city under German occupation. In Trondheim, Day toured a hospital attending British POW wounded. The condition of England's fighting men shocked him, as he recalled years later:

The British soldiers were undernourished, stunted, sickly looking boys, nineteen, twenty and twenty-one years of age. They were weak and undersized compared with all the other soldiers I had seen in Finland, Norway, Sweden, and the Baltic States and Germany.... They had about as much chance against the properly equipped German soldier as a cow would have to win a race against a thoroughbred horse.[52]

There was no war hysteria or bitterness in the ballroom of the Trondheim Hotel where German troops and Norwegians intermingled freely. The Wehrmacht regulars Day interrogated that evening told him they were in Norway to fight the British and French, not the Norwegians. Trondheim's merchants were grateful that the Germans were under orders to spend only a small number of reichmarks, continued Day, and that they were consuming their own provisions in lieu of pillaging local shops. When General Nikolas von Falkenhorst unexpectedly hosted the arrival of a delegation of Axis correspondents in Trondheim, the German commander asked Day to return to Sweden. From there he returned to a Latvia under Soviet control.[53]

On June 16, 1940, the Latvian government capitulated to an ultimatum from Moscow demanding a change of government and the right of the Red Army to occupy Latvia's chief centers. Large Soviet garrisons had already been established in the vicinity of Riga. American minister John C. Wiley notified Day that several cabinet members, including Foreign Minister Wilhem Munters, had fled to Moscow. Mistrustful of Munters' reported left-wing affiliations and perceived Svengali-like hold on Latvia's president, Karl

Ulmanis, Day welcomed rumors of Munters' subsequent promotion to the
Soviet Commissariat for Foreign Affairs. The first Soviet armor rumbled
into Riga on the afternoon of June 17. Day wrote that a crowd of 3,000
cheering Jews tried to mob the procession. Jubilant demonstrators boasted
to Day: "Now the Germans will never come here." Suddenly the Soviet tank
crews opened fire on their rowdy allies and summoned Latvian army troops
to help restore order. Delighted with these proceedings, Day published his
report under the headline "Riga Reds Battle Police: Ten Slain as Soviets
Occupy Latvia." Although Day blamed the riot on local Jewish Bolsheviks,
the *Tribune* expunged the word "Jewish" from the report.[54]

Life in the Baltic states changed rapidly. The Soviets monopolized the
press and radio, introduced commissars into the army, outlawed rival political
parties, and arrested those who complained. The country's gold reserves and
foreign holdings compensated Soviet monopolies that supplied raw materials
to Latvian industries. In late July the parliaments of Estonia, Latvia, and
Lithuania requested membership in the Soviet Union. Dejected over Moscow's effortless victory, Day aired his frustration on the front page of the
Tribune:

Thus about 5,500,000 people, 95 percent of whom are Christians and all of whom
have been living under the capitalistic system of government, are being absorbed
without resistance by the atheistic, anti-capitalistic Soviet government and the imperialistic world revolutionary organization, the Communist International, all of
which are ruled by Dictator Josef Stalin.

In explicit detail he recounted how innocent citizens were mysteriously deported, murdered, raped, tortured, and otherwise victimized on a routine
basis.[55]

On the evening of July 24, several Latvian security police appeared at the
Riga bureau with state authorization for Day's expulsion from the country.
Having little hope of obtaining an extension of the 24-hour grace period, he
spent most of the night burning the bureau's files. The following morning
Day notified the U.S. ministry of his plight. He also appealed to the Latvian
premier, Professor August Kirchenstein, but without success. The premier's
aide explained that the expulsion order had been ratified by the entire Latvian
cabinet in response to the correspondent's editorial distortions. During the
afternoon Day polled several old police friends, who urged him to go abroad
immediately, saying they had orders to arrest him on sight after the deadline,
and hinting that he could be killed in the process of apprehension. Day and
his wife started for the Estonian frontier. On the outskirts of Riga, the couple
passed a Red armored contingent encamped in a forest. Suddenly an escort
of security policemen emerged from the roadside military depot and began
trailing the correspondent's automobile. Unperturbed, Day led his pursuers
on a harrowing chase before eluding them and slipping across the Estonian

border. Once safely in Tallin, Day received instructions from McCormick to move his Baltic bureau to Helsingfors, Finland.[56]

News of the progressive disintegration of Moscow's pact with Berlin and dictated peace with Helsinki filled Day's columns for the remainder of the year. On October 18, Day reported that Stalin's decisions to curtail German trade with the Baltic countries, limit grain shipments to the Reich, and encourage Soviet ambitions in central Europe had chilled Nazi-Bolshevik relations. Foreign Ministers Halifax and von Ribbentrop were pursuing a quiet peace initiative at the expense of the Soviets. In early December the correspondent's dispatches hinted that an alliance between the Soviet Union and the United States was in the offing, despite Moscow's concern about America's state of military unpreparedness. By Christmas Eve, however, Day unexpectedly announced that the Russo-German accord was stronger than ever, primarily due to England's anticipated collapse. When Britain endured with U.S. assistance, Day reverted to exploring the dire ramifications of Roosevelt's undisguised involvement in a European war. With the Luftwaffe's spring offensive against England in shambles, Day asked rhetorically whether or not Hitler would betray his Soviet allies.[57] On April 19, 1941, he acknowledged that a showdown was imminent. German informants persuaded Day that the Reich High Command had already drafted invasion plans, and he learned that Red commissars in the Baltic states were calling for a people's war on fascism. Eyewitness accounts inside the Soviet Union suggested to Day that Stalin might be the aggressor. His proxies swore that the premier had cleared the frontier regions of valuable heavy machinery and skilled laborers, while amassing thousands of offensive aircraft along Germany's border. The newsman wired McCormick on June 14 that the Wilhelmstrasse had presented Moscow with a new set of demands that included the following: (1) Bessarabia returned to Rumania, (2) Nazi control over a large section of the Ukraine and a portion of the Baku oil fields, (3) removal of the Red Army from the Baltic states, and (4) the revision of the Soviet Union's border with Finland. Day notified Chicago that a rift had developed in Moscow between the political bureau of the Communist party, which continued to push for negotiation, and the army. *Tribune* subscribers read that an escalation of this crisis could result in another civil war between Stalin's GPU guard and Marshal Semyon Timoshenko's regulars. A scheduled broadcast by Day over the Mutual Broadcasting System was abruptly terminated in Helsingfors only 48 hours prior to Hitler's invasion of the Soviet Union.[58]

Finland's domestic ills mushroomed during the winter of 1940–41. The Ryti government experienced acute food shortages exacerbated by England's naval blockade. President Ryti warned Day's readership that any national policy aimed at depriving Finland of necessary foodstuffs would be considered an unfriendly act. The Soviet Union, meanwhile, nervously contemplated Berlin's use of Finland as a convenient avenue to occupied Norway.

On December 7 Hitler aggravated Moscow's paranoia by conveying his congratulations on the twenty-fourth anniversary of Finland's independence. When appeals for Anglo-American assistance went unfulfilled, President Ryti signed a $74 million trade agreement with the Germans. It struck Day that this backlash to Allied indifference might push Finland into the Nazi orbit. The citizens of Helsingfors concurred in his survey of May 31 by overwhelmingly supporting a "European solution" to the current hostilities. Day warned his brother on April 24, 1941, that the BBC's silly propaganda efforts threatened the survival of Europe because it masked the Bolshevik menace and gave false hope to the Allies: "The latest anecdote from Berlin is: Germany is fighting herself to death, the British are bragging themselves to death, Italy is running herself to death, and the Russians are laughing themselves to death." His letter rebuked England's puny commitment to the Baltic region. "It is just as though a New York grammar school should organize a football team and challenge Illinois University for a game on its home grounds," he analogized. Rosy predictions of a quick German victory, a generous armistice with Britain, and an Anglo-German crusade against the Bolsheviks filled Day's paragraphs. The Roosevelt administration, he asserted, would accommodate itself to this new reality, especially after John Bull blamed the United States for its past errors. "I'm known among them [Riga's English community] over here as being anti-British," he boasted, "a sort of renegade. . . . When the war began I dropped into the [British] Club in Riga and they all said: 'Now you are with us, aren't you, Donald?' I replied, 'No,' that it was a war between hooligans and hypocrites, and that I thought the hypocrites didn't have even a remote chance to win." National socialism represented more than street hooliganism, pressed Day, for it carried within its message "the persuasive powers of a religion"—one of economic stability, social and governmental efficiency, and a national commitment to social reform. Best of all, Hitler had freed Europe of its minority problem, a national scourge that had been imported to his homeland by the U.S. government.[59] Hitler's invasion of the Soviet Union on June 22, 1941, carried Finland across the Rubicon, and as Axis armies swept forward, Day seemed caught up in the momentum of history:

The Europe of the future is expected by Finnish leaders to develop along Nordic lines. Germany has declared itself a Nordic nation. German policy has been directed to help the other Nordic countries. Despite all propaganda to the contrary, Finland and the Scandinavian states and Germany are growing closer together. . . . I have not yet met a Finnish or Swedish military authority who believes Germany can be defeated. These military men further believe the German conquest of Europe will not be ended before the Communist government of Russia has been destroyed and the disintegration of the Soviet completed.[60]

Following a dangerous tour of the Hango front on the southern tip of Finland—where the Finns had closed on a Soviet peninsula fortification in a protracted siege—Day headed northward to join the invasion effort.[61] From the Russo-Finnish border it took him 24 hours of steady travel by automobile, motorboat, and truck to reach the battlefield. There Finnish and German officers briefed him that they were advancing in several sectors—in the north, toward Murmansk, the Arctic port; in the south, around both sides of Lake Ladoga toward Leningrad. Day was "privileged" to accompany the Finns in a major sector, the central eastern front. The objective was Kemi, a key point on the White Sea and the Leningrad-Murmansk Railroad. After 19 months Day's derring-do combat stories once again made front-page news. As always, he viewed this continuation of Finland's winter war from his old Manichean perspective. Colonel McCormick grumbled that Day's communiques were too subjective—and then proceeded to raise his reporter's salary.[62]

The Finns used Day to translate prisoner interrogations and, in return allowed him access to most forward positions. After the bloody battle of Aajualahti on the western shore of Lake Kuitti—which cost the Soviets 1,000 killed—he caught his victorious supermen swimming in the nearby Pisto River. Always the graphic storyteller, Day indelicately pictured the remainder of his compatriots at lunch in a field of dead Russians.[63] Accounts of Finnish losses, however, were treated with understatement and reverence:

A few minutes ago one of the older men working around the field kitchen . . . was called by an officer who pointed to an open rucksack and asked him if he recognized the contents. "Yes," said the veteran, "they belong to my son." The officer silently offered his hand. Nothing more was spoken.[64]

Between trips to the eastern front, Day covered Soviet reverses in the Baltic region. From Helsingfors he reported that in Lithuania German liberators had freed numerous political prisoners, and that thousands of panicky Jews had accompanied their Bolshevik allies into the Soviet Union. Kaunas' radio station declared the country rid of enemy occupation on June 24 and ready to enter Europe's New Order. Soviet resistance in Estonia lasted until late summer when Moscow ordered Tallin burned. On August 24, Day witnessed the aurora of the conflagration from a distance of 60 miles. In a fortnight German guides toured him about the ruined city. The authorities charged that 19 months of Soviet occupation had resulted in the death or disappearance of over 150,000 Estonians, and they showed their guest documentary proof of their claims.[65]

Returning home, Day proceeded to the siege of Leningrad and the promise of rattling good copy. In anticipation of a reasonably short siege, Berlin commenced the beleaguerment of Leningrad on September 4, a state of partial investment destined to collapse after 17 grueling months. The misplaced enthusiasm of those around him appeared in many of Day's early dispatches, such as this one of September 17, 1941:

Towards midnight there was a lull. Leningrad's burning factories and buildings cast their glow up into the sky. . . . Less than 30 miles to the east about 2,000,000 women and children were starving in a besieged city without hope of rescue or reinforcements. . . . There was no merriment [in the Finnish lines]. All were watching the southeastern sky in the direction of Leningrad.[66]

All along the front brave Finnish soldiers, stalking the enemy in dense forests, came to regard the killing of inexperienced Russian conscripts as great sport. The bravado of these natural hunters appealed to Day's imagination.

While Leningrad is tottering, the Finnish front along the Karelian Isthmus is never still. Soviet sharpshooters dressed in dark gray . . . perch at the top of pine trees and watch for Finnish patrols penetrating the lines. The Finns make great sport of their hunts for these snipers. Keen eyes and woodsmanship are needed to bag them and the Finns are disappointed if the sniper's expensive rifle with its telescopic sights is damaged in a fall. (September 21, 1941)[67]

Typhus and typhoid are killing thousands of adults in Leningrad; measles, diphtheria and scarlet fever are killing an equal number of children. The Soviet "diggers" are preparing mass graves instead of trenches in the suburbs of Leningrad. (October 28, 1941)

One elderly woman from the city told Day that half a million people had died in Leningrad. Riots before government bread shops had been dispersed by the GPU with an appalling loss of life. The homeless were sleeping in Leningrad's five great railroad stations.[68] On November 7, Day wrote his last byline from the embattled metropolis atop an observation tower: "I can see Leningrad burning. Without field glasses I can see a wide wall of smoke mounting from its southern suburbs. Through an extra powerful pair of binoculars I can see tongues of flame eating up whole blocks of buildings. . . . As I watch from the tower, batteries of heavy German siege guns are bombarding both Leningrad and Kronstadt. There is no answering fire from the Russians. . . . Everywhere there is a feeling of cheerfulness and hope," he concluded, "despite the pressure being applied by England and America" to forestall a Russian defeat.[69]

Leningrad endured, however, and Soviet resistance stiffened along the front. Germany's sputtering winter campaign perplexed Day, who sought explanations among Sweden's High Command. His military contacts explained that Hitler, now supreme commander, was replacing his regular officers with fanatics who were sacrificing thousands of men in defense of indefensible perimeters. Unwilling to vouchsafe Hitler's generalship, neither would Day condemn the Nazi leader's crusade against a common foe.[70]

Through interviews and commentaries on local press editorials, Day implied that Roosevelt's allies were pursuing a hidden agenda foreign to the best interests of the United States. On February 21, 1942, he warned that Sir Stafford Cripps' induction into the British cabinet would spark the demand for an Anglo-American expeditionary force to Murmansk. Day was persuaded that Germany would meet this threat by invading Sweden in order to provision its armies in Finland, thereby dragging the United States into a Scandinavian theater of operations.[71] One particular wire, in which Day claimed that Finnish troops had cut the Murmansk Railroad, outraged George Seldes. This involved story began when the Chicago correspondent of a Copenhagen paper saw Day's revelation in the *Tribune* and sent it back to Denmark, whereupon the U.S. newsmen in Copenhagen, crediting it to a reliable Danish newspaper, recabled the dispatch to all U.S. papers.[72] Day reported that the Allies' naval blockade would produce a generation of malnourished Scandinavian children and that the virus of communism had taken root in America's labor movement.[73] On March 9, he dropped the following bombshell on the American public:

There were persistent rumors in Stockholm about negotiations between the Soviet and German governments which may lead to a truce on the eastern front. . . . There is a lack of faith on both sides, but there is a mutual understanding of the advantages which both have to offer from a temporary truce. There is also a mutual respect developed by eight months of ferocious fighting. The Soviet government was the first to make the advances now said to be under discussion. The chief reason for Moscow's proposals was to pressure the Allies into opening up a Second Front on the continent of Europe.[74]

The March 18, 1942, edition of New York City's daily *P.M.* blasted Day as a traitor.

What is the purpose of *Tribune* Publisher Robert McCormick and his associates in printing such stuff as that dispatch from Stockholm? . . . If he doesn't know that Stockholm is the source for Axis propaganda; if he doesn't know that the above story is a message which Berlin-Tokyo-Rome is trying to dump on us; if he doesn't yet know that the Axis "Divide and Conquer" strategy is designed to split England, Russia and the United States . . . his paper should be suppressed for the duration. . . . Neither Freedom of Speech nor Freedom of Press permits McCormick or any political Quislingist to drive a wedge between the United States and its Allies. He, and his *Tribune*, and "his allies" have gone too far this time.[75]

Cordell Hull's State Department shared *P.M.*'s indignation. In August 1942, the U.S. minister to Sweden, Herschel Johnson, demanded Day's passport. Taken aback, the correspondent stalled and referred all criticism of his work to Colonel McCormick. He planned a return to Finland to close his bureau and settle personal affairs. The minister, however, petitioned Day's detention and made preparations for his return to the United States. It was then that Day decided to enlist in the Finnish army. He asked the *Tribune* for indefinite leave without pay, or to place him on its pension list. The paper's management refused and discharged him. Robert E. Lee, city editor for the *Tribune*, informed an FBI agent that he would have fired Day long ago had he not been willing to work in "that hole" (Latvia and Poland). In Helsinki, the U.S. minister, Arthur Schoenfeld, again pressed Day to go home. Resentful, Day charged that his recall had been plotted by the State Department and his old enemy, Maxim Litvinov, the current Soviet ambassador to the United States. Unable to change Day's mind, Minister Schoenfeld did persuade Helsinki that the expatriate's induction into the Finnish army would be considered "an unfriendly act." His passport having lapsed, Day, so far as the United States was concerned, became a man without a country.[76]

It is uncertain what vocation Day pursued during the next two years. There is evidence that he did some translating work for the Finnish government after 1942 while completing his political testament, *Onward Christian Soldiers*. He also contacted the German Foreign Office's press attaché in Helsinki about employment. Day promised to write favorable articles for the U.S. press, propaganda which might be filtered through American reporters in Sweden. The chief of the Press Department of the Reich Foreign Office, Paul K. Schmidt, was confused by Helsinki's background report on Day. The Nazi bureaucrat suspected him of being an Abwehr agent (counterintelligence, the Foreign Intelligence Service of the OKW), and that the Abwehr wanted to establish the American in Helsinki at Foreign Office expense. Possibly Schmidt learned that as part of Hitler's planned invasion and occupation of England in 1940, the Gestapo meant to arrest Day—if discovered on British soil—along with hundreds of other notable politicians, intellectuals, industrialists, and journalists. Evidently the SS singled out this relatively unknown correspondent as a courtesy to Moscow.[77] In any case, Day's application was denied. Meanwhile, Soviet military and diplomatic victories during the summer of 1944—from the rescue of Leningrad to the penetration of Finnish defenses along the Karelian Isthmus—further plagued Day's peace of mind. Neither did he warm to the half-hearted peace overtures that Helsinki kept floating across certain Kremlin desks. Since a weakened Germany could no longer guarantee the territorial integrity of Finland, Day sought his own safety inside the Reich. Some time between July and August he quietly assumed residency in Berlin.

The Foreign Office, mindful of the misgivings of its own Press Section, nevertheless saw Day's potential as a broadcaster and hired him. The Radio Department welcomed this fresh personality who apparently supported national socialism so near its end and who spoke so convincingly of the Bolshevik menace. Day's professional stock skyrocketed during the next eight months, even as Berlin was being reduced to ashes. Both he and Anglo-American propagandist William Joyce, alias Lord Haw-Haw, were among the six highest-paid employees on the Reichrundfunk payroll. Wartime bookkeeping records of the radio station showed that Day earned a salary of 1,500 marks a month plus a bonus of 6,000 marks, which before the Nazi collapse amounted to $3,000 monthly. Joyce earned the same salary, but with a monthly bonus of only 5,000 marks. According to postwar military investigators, the retainers commanded by Day and Joyce were ten times those received by the average German functionary and enabled them to live sumptuously. They occupied ornate suites in the Reichrundfunk and took their daily propaganda directives personally from Goebbels. All other foreign commentators were briefed by underlings from the Propaganda Ministry.[78]

On August 31, Radio Berlin erroneously introduced its new recruit as a "twenty-year veteran correspondent for the Chicago *Herald Tribune*," who had placed himself on Europe's side in the fight against bolshevism. In his maiden broadcast the following evening, Day charged that FDR and Stalin were in league to destroy the Baltic states and to "Bolshevise" Europe. What followed was a rambling commentary on Finnish runner Heino, who had broken four world records, and how this Nordic competitor had never admitted defeat either on the athletic field or the battlefield.[79] In a September airing Day cast himself as one who, for several decades, had been the target of Soviet intrigues abetted by the United States, Poland, and Lithuania: "Of course, it is only natural that over here an American sees things differently from what you do over there. . . . Just consider me as a veteran U.S. newspaper correspondent whom Mr. Roosevelt and his friends have placed, through their intrigues, on the other side of the fence."[80]

Life in Berlin was far from bleak, intoned Day on October 7. He denied the existence of a black market there "because money could not corrupt justice in Germany as it did in the democracies." The average German ate well, and the country's superior social legislation covered most illnesses and war-related injuries.[81] By late February 1945, however, Day's spirits bottomed as conditions worsened:

Owing to [the] Red Army's advance into Upper Silesia, Berlin hotels and private homes are without heat and hot water. Eight weeks' food coupons must last for nine weeks, and we must make-up with un-couponed vegetables. The horrors of life are enhanced by the air raids, and the need to dress in a cold room at every alert. . . . I thought so little of Berlin had been left to bomb that these large-scale raids would cease; but I was mistaken. . . . Sleeping in a room with no windows in freezing weather is not pleasant. Life would be unendurable, but for the unostentatious heroism of everyone. (February 24, 1945)[82]

The Wehrmacht has decided to confer a special decoration upon General [Carl] Spaatz, the Commander of the U.S. bombing forces in England. This special decoration is the Order of the White Feather. Spaatz earned this decoration when he sent over a fleet of nearly 1,000 U.S. bombers to lay a carpet of bombs across Berlin. . . . Spaatz was deserving of this decoration for acts of exceptional cowardice in bombing German cities filled with pitiful refugees [fleeing from advancing Soviet armies]. (February 17, 1945)[83]

On January 13, 1945, Day challenged the credulity of the American public during one of his more extreme presentations. He told his audience that U.S. prisoners of war were "pretty sore" about FDR's lies concerning Nazi tyranny. On the contrary, his personal observations suggested that the German army, when unhindered by Jewish-Bolshevik agents, "always maintained order in the occupied areas." He continued:

Did you know that Roosevelt is using Jewish-Bolshevik-Communist terrorist methods to intimidate U.S. P.O.W.s; that political commissars of the U.S. Army land in Germany by parachute to be captured and placed in P.O.W. camps, so they can terrorize U.S. soldiers there? The prisoners are threatened with courtmartial after the war just because they complain of the Bolshevik regime in Russia or the imperialistic British.[84]

Frustrated over Germany's prostration and embittered by his homeland's involvement in its accomplishment, Day assumed the mantle of the apocalyptist on March 29, 1945:

It is hard to believe that a Christian people should gang with a barbaric nation to try to exterminate another Christian nation, solely because the victim of this conspiracy expelled the Jews from its country. . . . The Jews will not return to Europe because no European country wants them. That is why the Jews are determined Europe shall be destroyed.[85]

When Soviet troops laid siege to Berlin in mid-April, Day and his wife fled to Bavaria. In June he reported voluntarily to U.S. military officials, who released him after four days of interrogation. The United States Army elected to rearrest him in March 1946, however, and for the next nine months he was confined to the Intelligence Service Interrogation Center at Oberursel, near Frankfurt. Not until October would the authorities permit Day to correspond with his family in the United States, and his diet was so bad that he lost 30 pounds. On December 23, the army announced that Day would be released because the Department of Justice was "no longer interested in his case."[86] Several months later, on February 21, 1947, Dorothy Day received an unexpected communication from a military chaplain:

Yesterday Donald knocked at my door and told me who he was. I spent last evening at his home here in Bad Tölz where we are stationed. I had a long talk with both Donald and his wife and I know you will be glad to know that they are both well, and are living fairly comfortably, if frugally. . . . At the moment it is difficult for him to write anything for publication in the U.S., as it must first pass through military censorship . . . and I fear that some of the things he would have to say would shock some of these delicate appeasers! . . . Who should run such articles or a series of such? . . . The *Tribune* should be the one but we will have to wait till its staff can gather its wits and consult its conscience.[87]

Gratified by the anti-Communist hysteria sweeping the United States at this time, Day gave Senator Joseph McCarthy the benefit of his wartime experiences in battling a Red-infested State Department. In the winter of 1950 he informed the Wisconsin senator that the pin-striped leftists there had done everything from the censoring of diplomatic and military mail pouches, to the wholesale issuance of visas and travel permits to known Communist agents ("beekeepers"), to the termination of his job with the Chicago *Tribune*. There is no record of a response.

Prohibited by the military from returning to the United States, the Days remained in southern Bavaria until late 1953, when Day got permission to go to Finland. On July 20, 1953, Day contacted Hearst journalist Kurt Von Wiegand about a stringer position in Helsinki. Rolf Hoffman of Scandinavian Airlines—who had been Reichrundfunk press attaché and erstwhile recruiter for the U.S.A. Zone—suggested Von Wiegand as an employment contact. Day offered no apologies for his past, concluding that in recent years he had worked for the *Daily Press* in Ashland, Wisconsin, and for Stockholm's *Fria Ord*. With time to spare, he frequently wrote Della in defense of his life's course. How could anyone accuse him of treason or of being a Jew-baiter? "We came to Germany as refugees and only after the Finns told me to leave as quickly as possible." In Berlin, he said, "I spoke against Bolshevism, not against the Jews, and I shall always fight them [the Communists] as long as I live. The Nazis were bad enough, but the communists are worse." On May 17, 1957, Secretary of State John Foster Dulles ordered the U.S. embassy in Helsinki to use all means at its disposal to exclude Day from membership in the Western Foreign Press Club. Failing this objective, the staff was instructed to shun him. Day underwent surgery for cancer in early 1962, and many of his colleagues urged consideration for him. The following year U.S. ambassador to Finland Bernard Gufler, who had known Day for over three decades, helped him apply for a new U.S. passport. Through the efforts of Gufler and several *Tribune* veterans, Day was rehired by the newspaper as a $50-a-month stringer in Helsinki. The aging newsman established a warm and solicitous correspondence with Dorothy, and soon many of their former differences were resolved. In Day's last letter to her on August 3, 1966, he lamented the U.S. government's inability to contain the menace of communism: "I shudder at the thought of what our dark future will bring." Donald Day died of a heart attack on September 30, 1966.[88]

As a cub reporter in postwar Europe, Donald Day had shared the American people's guarded enthusiasm for Russia's new social experiment. Somehow, he believed that he would gain access to this workers' paradise and establish the first Western press bureau in Moscow. One can imagine Day's embarrassment and disillusionment when the Soviet Foreign Ministry shattered his dream at an obscure frontier checkpoint and then proceeded to toy with his expectations through 30 subsequent visa applications. With neither wife nor the promise of a brilliant career, Day joined the Communists in battle during the ensuing two decades as a correspondent for the Chicago *Tribune*.

From his Riga bureau Day wired home verifiable reports and unsubstan-

tiated rumors alike, provided by the city's large White Russian population
and his own paid informants operating inside the Soviet Union. These dispatches invariably portrayed Russia's governing oligarchy as the pariah of a
civilized world. Only his freedom from Bolshevik censorship and bribery,
Day contended, allowed him to expose the evils of communism. His more
skeptical colleagues, however, attributed Day's biased journalism to a potent
combination of unrequited ambition and a morbid obsession with Soviet
imperialism.

For years Day had identified with Germany's sense of national purpose
and the early rhetoric surrounding its quest for racial purity. The popular
Nazi slogan "Ein Volk, Ein Reich, Ein Fuhrer" conceptualized a mystical
sense of national community that he believed to be a remedy for Europe's
ills. In his book, Day pictured a Europe led by a coalition of Aryan nations,
which included Germany, Scandinavia, and the Baltic states, whose leaders
would enthrone their own ethnic group and cultural standards at the expense
of all others. More importantly for Day, this idealized brotherhood of nations
would stand as a bulwark against the further spread of bolshevism. He had
glimpsed the possibilities of such a Nordic concert during the Finnish-
German siege of Leningrad.

Nazi Germany's impending *Gotterdammerung* drove Day from safe harbor
to safe harbor until, in April 1945, his old enemy stood poised at the outskirts
of Berlin. Once again he eluded his would-be Soviet executioners, preferring
instead the spartan accommodations of an army detention center. The U.S.
Department of Justice would eventually judge Donald Day innocent of treason on the basis of his short-term contributions to the propaganda effort and
the alleged innocuousness of his broadcasts. Army investigators ignored the
issue of personal intent. With growing Soviet expansionism throughout the
world, Day's exoneration went unchallenged in the United States. After a
quarter century he had become, for the heralds of McCarthyism, a prophet
with honor in his own country.

Epilogue

To be sure, all of these expatriates had extremely fragile emotional ties with the United States. Best, Day, and Chandler abandoned their homeland in the 1920s and 1930s never to return. Family funerals, births, and holidays went unobserved. Kaltenbach came back to Iowa once, only to become embroiled in a bitter local altercation. Without immediate family, Delaney's prewar trips to America's east and west coasts were purely of a commercial nature. Koischwitz and Drexel left in 1939—the former in high dudgeon—never to recross the Atlantic until war's end. At the time of her death in Connecticut in 1956, Drexel was planning to relocate in Europe.

One might easily apply sociologist Robert E. Park's concept of the marginal man to the subjects of this study, an interpretation which, while not excusing the awful implications of their poor judgment—if not criminal in behavior in all cases—still seems to partially explain a motivating factor of their actions.

The marginal man . . . lives on the margin of two cultures—that of the country of his parents and that of the country of his adoption, in neither of which he is quite at home. We know . . . that this so-called marginal man is likely to be smart, i.e. a superior though sometimes a superficial intellectual type. . . . The Christian convert in Asia or Africa exhibits many if not most of the characteristics of the "marginal man"—the same spiritual instability, intensified self-consciousness, restlessness, and malaise.

Early life proved scarcely the tie that bound these nomads to their native/ adopted land. The lack of any information on Delaney's youth speaks volumes, and by his late teens this Irish-American was indeed a citizen of the world. Fräulein Drexel's trans-Atlantic visitations between parents scarcely grounded her in the American experience. The hectic ministry of Reverend Albert Best left little time for Robert, who fled a mill town existence for greener pastures in Europe. Young Jane Anderson arrived in London about then, the neglected offspring of southern gentility and western self-reliance, and the poorer for her experiences. Koischwitz described the United States as a country without a soul, uncultivated geographical expanses and people who cared little for his genius. Day and Chandler were the progeny of dreamers who could scarcely provide for their needs. In their cases, as in the formative years of Anderson, Best, and Gillars, it seemed that the family's marginal existence proved more devastating than actual privation; for the lack of food and shelter demands remedial action on the part of the community and state, whereas an unhappy family environment may be the subject of neighborhood gossip and nothing more. Unconsciously, at least, expatriation may have had to do as much with their search for a more congenial extended family atmosphere as with the quest for opportunity.

How did these radio traitors regard the concept of personal freedom? Surely they did not share the same perspective as their fellow countrymen, and in this singular way, they had indeed become "un-American." Those liberties vouchsafed in the U.S. Bill of Rights they regarded as inapplicable to Hitler's expanding New Order, and clearly without relevance in their own daily lives. They had generally come to believe—in the face of Nazi aggression—that the strict hierarchical-organization structure of the Wehrmacht might eventually provide the best means for overcoming and replacing the divided, pluralistic, and fractious interests that had afflicted many European governments since the Great War. Perhaps this convoluted reasoning constituted nothing more than an attempt to assuage a nagging conscience. Enter first the paramilitary Free Corps thugs into local government, followed by the Fuhrer's idealized "community of the front," which represented government by the military desperado on a grand scale. It would be nothing more than a historical phase in retrospect, they may have naively assured themselves; this brotherhood of the gun would, in its time, influence and direct the orderly reconstruction of Europe into a national community of spirit and purpose.

Clearly, these Americans cherished another laundry list of freedoms: freedom from privation; freedom from the threat of political street violence as only a dictatorship can ensure; freedom to pursue a lifestyle or occupation painstakingly fashioned during the interwar years; and freedom to prosper under a totalitarian regime that promised a new beginning for the alienated, the disinherited, and the loser. In this last aspiration each failed miserably. These individuals suffered not only from a geographical and cultural marginality but from a historical disassociation as well. These expatriates grew up in a society that had institutionalized regionalism, racism, social stratification, the entrepreneurial buccaneer, and the confining tenets of white

Anglo-Saxon Protestantism. Yet Goebbels billed them as interpreters of the social and economic revolutions in the United States and Germany. How could these products of the nineteenth century be expected to decipher the growing complexities of twentieth-century government and its control over a mass society? In the end, they rebelled against all aspects of statism from Roosevelt's alphabet agencies to the menacing arms of the SS.

Contemporaries of Anderson, Koischwitz, Delaney, Drexel, Kaltenbach, Best, Chandler, and Day have portrayed them as little more than ciphers, third-rate opportunists who seized the prizes afforded by the Propaganda Ministry and the Foreign Office as a means of staying afloat professionally inside the Reich. Opportunists they may have been, but these individuals were far from parasites leeching upon the benevolence of Goebbels and von Ribbentrop. Without question, Anderson, Best, Drexel, and Day came to Berlin with proven track records as journalists, and Koischwitz and Kaltenbach could have found employment as teaching faculty at many colleges and universities in the United States. Perhaps only Chandler truly fits the mold set by correspondents Shirer, Seldes, Thompson, and others. Granted, for their Nazi recruiters the question of personal morality and ethics took a back seat to the skillfully prepared propaganda menu, but this deficiency as seen in a free society in no way compromised the potential usefulness of these people in German eyes. What problems arose—and these hitches proved disastrous to the viability of the North American Service—literally stemmed from personality conflicts. Gillars, Kaltenbach, Chandler, Delaney, and Anderson were to experience serious brushes with the authorities over matters of professional style, working conditions, script content, and lapses of individual enthusiasm for national socialism and its global allies. Best and Drexel, due to their eccentric behavior and irregular personal lives, came to be considered by Promi officials as ungovernable cranks. Koischwitz enjoyed a measure of success although he, too, as temporary head of the U.S.A. Zone, was forced to continually defend his paramour from the jealousy of fellow broadcasters. Moreover, much of his time was spent fending off distasteful propaganda strategies and issues demanded by his superiors.

True, these turncoats carried into adulthood the racist views of a nineteenth-century America, but several of them seemed most uncomfortable with Nazi racial ideology. Anderson's scripts were not laden with anti-Semitic invective, and both Best and Koischwitz had shown a penchant for abstracting Jewish friends from their religious and cultural antecedents, and on occasion mounting impressive defenses on their behalf. While Chandler was a dedicated anti-Semite, Delaney preferred to direct his verbal darts against British class snobbery, and in his postwar autobiographies he attacked Hitler's extermination policies against Russian minorities on the eastern front as a tactical error. Day's references to a Baltic Aryan brotherhood of nations scarcely underwrote Heinrich Himmler's mad program of genocide. Once aboard the Nazi bandwagon, however, they soon learned that their new employers would not permit the dispensing of racial ideology in doses, nor would its henchmen stay the horrible results of this hate mongering.

A sense of personal betrayal suggests itself as a partial explanation for the treasonous behavior of these subjects. Despite her many precedents in the field of reporting, Drexel saw her early journalistic career subjugated to the whims of a male-dominated profession, her social standing and constitutional guarantees undermined by the wishy-washy leadership of America's women's movement, and her culture tainted by fad and superficiality. Best and Day languished in UP's and Colonel Robert McCormick's least desirable jour-nalistic outposts, without hope of advancement. Koischwitz's impressive cur-riculum vitae bore little relationship to his scholarly standing and paycheck, and Kaltenbach's academic aspirations never left the ground. It was clear to the Marquesa de Cienfuegos that Roosevelt's support of the Loyalist cause during the Spanish Civil War threatened her husband's ancestral fortune and therefore her very being. Whether or not one is tempted to allow this spiritual descent into paranoiac self-pity as an unavoidable corollary of their lives, and if the reader will pardon the author's anti-Manichean world view, it is clear that these radio traitors struggled with the darker forces within them-selves and lost.

Did these American propagandists champion Hitler's New Order as a revolutionary movement or as the guarantor of the status quo in Europe? Obviously, they made much of Nazism as the world's only bulwark against the rapaciousness of Western capitalism and the economic determinism of communism; but what they really envisioned was the comfortable provin-cialism of interwar Europe. It never occurred to the romantic Koischwitz that his Fuhrer meant to march far deeper into German history than he himself wished, and to invoke a neo-barbarism that would eventually engulf half the world. For one who professed to enjoy the transcendental view, Koischwitz naively followed a leader whose gaze never left the battlefield and the death camp. Journalist William L. Shirer maintained that these people simply went native in their conversion to national socialism; his colleague, Dorothy Thompson, countered that to become European in thought and deed did not necessitate a conversion to Nazism. Common sense and personal perspective, however, dictated to these subjects that they must accommodate themselves to the New Order or perish.

Whether the reader agrees with the findings of this study or not, one salient fact remains: that these eight wartime American broadcasters for the Reichrundfunk were definite liabilities to the Nazi propaganda effort.

Consideration of the U.S. government's motives behind the prosecution of its radio traitors is worthy of a final digression. Attorney General Francis Biddle recalled his introduction to the career of these individuals in his autobiography, *In Brief Authority* (1962).

Robert Patterson, the Under Secretary of War, called me up one day to ask if . . . I ever listened to any of the programs and commentators? . . . I told him that I had never listened to any—I thought most radio news comments were a bore. . . . I said to Patterson that I knew the Axis line, it was very much like the cranks and isolationists here: scurrilously anti-Jewish and anti-Roosevelt, pro-Hitler, defeatist. Only a few nuts paid any attention to it. But, Bob thought we ought to take action—if we branded this talk as criminal it would stop people listening to it. But why stop them, I said. It just made them [the American public] mad, and probably was helping the war effort . . . but I promised to take a look at it.

It appears that Washington's option to prosecute these irritating broadcasters constituted a military decision instead of the response to a nation's outraged cry for justice. The War Department saw their speedy indictment and ultimate conviction as an issue of national security and pledged its untiring efforts toward that end.

All in all, America's treason laws proved an ineffective vehicle in the prosecution of enemy spokespersons, domestic and foreign. Blatant critics of the war effort on the home front could not be shown to be "adhering" to the Axis threat. Americans by birth who went abroad and attacked U.S. interests could elude punishment by simply forfeiting their citizenship. Because the law considered intent, rather than motive, the subtler members of the U.S.A. Zone got off scot-free, while a few representatives of its lunatic fringe went to prison following rather theatrical trials and charged newspaper copy. Those borderline commentators who managed to escape the courts lost little time in enlisting in Senator Joseph McCarthy's war on communism—either in this country or overseas.[1]

Notes

CHAPTER 1

1. "History of the German Radio System," Jane Anderson Files, Doc. No. 119863, pp. 13–15, FBI, Department of Justice, Washington, D.C.

2. *Nazi Conspiracy and Aggression: Office of U.S. Chief of Counsel for Prosecution of Axis Criminality* (Washington, D.C.: Government Printing Office, 1946): I, 328–339; Michael Balfour, *Propaganda in War, 1939–1945: Organizations, Policies and Publics in Britain and Germany* (London: Routledge & Kegan Paul, 1979): 11–52.

3. Louis L. Snyder, ed., "Radio in the Third Reich," *Encyclopedia of the Third Reich* (New York: McGraw-Hill, 1976): 279.

4. E. H. Gombrich, *Myth and Reality in German Wartime Broadcasts* (London: Athlone Press, 1970): 3–4. Also see "Propaganda Techniques of German Fascism," in *Modern English Readings*, eds. Roger S. Loomis and Donald L. Clark (New York: Rinehart & Company, 1949): 312–332.

5. Ross Scanlan, "The Nazi Party Speaker System," *Speech Monographs*, vol. XVI, No. 1 (August 1949): 82–89; ibid., "The Nazi Party Speaker System," *Speech Monographs*, vol. XVII, No. 2 (June 1950): 134–148; ibid., "The Nazi Rhetorician," *Quarterly Journal of Speech*, vol. XXXVII, No. 4 (December 1951): 430–440; Charles H. Wilson, "Hitler, Goebbels, and the Ministry for Propaganda," *Political Quarterly*, vol. X, No. 1 (January-March 1939): 99.

6. Gombrich, *Myth and Reality in German Wartime Broadcasts*, 10.

7. Robert Edwin Herzstein, *The War That Hitler Won: The Most Infamous Propaganda Campaign in History* (New York: G. P. Putnam's Sons, 1978): 176–177; *Nazi Conspiracy and Aggression—Opinion and Judgment* (Washington, D.C.: Government Printing Office, 1947): 161–163.

8. *Nazi Conspiracy and Aggression* vol. VI (Washington, D.C.: Government Printing Office, 1946): 174–194.

9. Herzstein, *The War That Hitler Won*, 183; Douglas M. Kelley, *22 Cells in Nuremberg: A Psychiatrist Examines the Nazi Criminals* (New York: Greenberg Publisher, 1947): 81–85; Florence R. Miale and Michael Selzer, *The Nuremberg Mind: The Psychology of the Nazi Leaders* (New York: New York Times Book Co., 1975): 52–57.

10. Snyder, "Radio in the Third Reich," 279; W. A. Sinclair, *The Voice of the Nazi: Being Eight Broadcast Talks Given between December 1939 and May 1940* (London: Collins Publishers, 1940): 52–58.

11. Z. A. B. Zeman, *Nazi Propaganda* (London: Oxford University Press, 1964): 104–117; Edwin Muller, "Waging War with Words," *Current History* (August 1939): 24–27; John B. Whitton, "War by Radio," *Foreign Affairs*, vol. 19, No. 3 (April 1941): 584–596.

12. Harold N. Graves, Jr., *War on the Short Wave* (New York: Foreign Policy Association, 1941): 21–32; Gordon Skilling, "Organising Hatred," *Dalhousie Review*, vol. 23 (April 1943): 11–22.

13. Werner Schwipps and Gerhart Goebel, *Wortschlacht Im Ather: Der Deutsche Auslands Rundfunk in Weltkreig* (Berlin: Hande and Spenersche, 1971): 70–71; Harold N. Graves, "Propaganda by Shortwave: Berlin Calling America," *Public Opinion Quarterly* (December 1940): 601; Joseph C. Harsch, *Pattern of Conquest* (New York: Doubleday, Doran & Co., 1941): 271–287; Arvid Fredborg, *Behind the Steel Wall: A Swedish Journalist in Berlin, 1941–43* (New York: Viking Press, 1944): 1–24.

14. Graves, *War on the Short Wave*, 32; Schwipps and Goebel, *Wortschlacht Im Ather*, 70.

15. Charles J. Rolo, "Radio War on the U.S.A.," *American Mercury*, vol. 52, No. 205 (January 1941): 67–74; S. K. Padover, "How the Nazis Picture America," *Public Opinion Quarterly*, vol. 3, No. 4 (October 1939): 663–669.

16. "News Release/Department of Justice" (May 26, 1943), Frederick W. Kaltenbach Files, FBI, Department of Justice, Washington, D.C.

17. BBC, *Monitoring Service*, August 20, 1940.

18. Ibid., April 24, 1943.

19. "News Release/Department of Justice" (May 26, 1943), Frederick W. Kaltenbach Files, FBI; "Former Newsman among 8 Indicted for Treason by U.S.," *Editor & Publisher* (July 28, 1943).

20. F. W. Kaltenbach, *Self-Determination 1919: A Study in Frontier-Making between Germany and Poland* (London: Jarrolds Publishers, 1938): 8, 14, 17, 23, 39–40, 46, 52, 59, 60, 82–83, 113, 132–133, 138–139.

21. Charles J. Rolo, "Germany Calling!" *Current History & Forum*, vol. 52, No. 2 (October 22, 1940): 28.

22. BBC, *Monitoring Service*, January 2, 1940.

23. Ibid., February 13, 1940.

24. Albert Parry, "Short-Wave Traitors," *Cosmopolitan*, vol. 114, No. 4 (April 1943): 59; Graves, "Propaganda by Shortwave," 602–605; Rolo, "Germany Calling!" 28.

25. Rolo, "Germany Calling!" 28.

26. William L. Shirer, *Berlin Diary: The Journal of a Foreign Correspondent, 1934–1941* (New York: Alfred A. Knopf, 1942): 442; ibid., "The American Radio Traitors," *Harper's*, vol. 187 (October 1943): 402–403; Harsch, *Pattern of Conquest*, 287–288.

27. Harwood L. Childs and John B. Whitton, eds., *Propaganda by Short Wave* (Princeton, N.J.: Princeton University Press, 1943): 273.

28. BBC, *Monitoring Service*, June 30, 1940.

29. Ibid., July 3, 1940.

30. Ibid., January 23, 1940.

31. Ibid., August 27, 1940.

32. Ibid., July 31, 1943.

33. Ibid., September 30; November 30, 1943.

34. Ibid., April 8, 1944.

35. Ibid., October 9; November 23, 1943.

36. Ibid., April 18, 1944.

37. New York *Times*, November 22, 1945; May 16; July 21, 1946.

38. New York *Times*, July 27, 1943; August 29, 1956; New York *Herald Tribune*, August 29, 1956; Waterbury *Republican*, August 29; August 31, 1956; Waterbury *American*, August 28, 1956; "News Release/Department of Justice" (May 26, 1943), Constance Drexel Files, FBI, Department of Justice, Washington, D.C.

39. Constance Drexel, "The Woman Pays," *Delineator*, vol. 87, No. 1 (July, 1915); "Our Family Album," *Ladies Home Journal*, vol. 43 (January 1926): 26.

40. New York *Times*, August 5, 1916; Woodrow Wilson to Constance Drexel, January 10, 1917, Woodrow Wilson Papers, Series 3 (Presidential Papers Microfilm); Constance Drexel to W. H. Taft, January 30; W. H. Taft to Constance Drexel, February 5, 1917, W. H. Taft Papers, Series 3 & 8 (Presidential Papers Microfilm).

41. Constance Drexel, "The Woman behind the Gun," *Delineator*, vol. 87, No. 19 (November 1915): 19; ibid., "German Women Active in Political Affairs," New York *Times*, August 24, 1924.

42. "News Release/Department of Justice" (May 26, 1943), Constance Drexel Files, FBI; New York *Times*, July 27, 1943.

43. Ishbel Ross, *Ladies of the Press: The Story of Women in Journalism by an Insider* (New York: Harper & Brothers Publishers, 1936): 514; Genevieve J. Boughner, *Women in Journalism* (New York: D. Appleton Century, 1942): 251–252.

44. "Our Family Album," 26.

45. Constance Drexel, "Feminism More Effective in Europe Than America," *Current History*, vol. 24, No. 2 (May 1926): 211; ibid., "Have Women Failed as Citizens?" *Collier's*, vol. 71 (May 12, 1923): 5–6; ibid., "The New Woman—Power in Europe," *Harper's*, vol. 149 (June 1924): 73–81.

46. Ibid., "Bananas across the Sea," *Collier's*, vol. 73, No. 9 (March 1, 1924): 31.

47. Ibid., "The Foreign Correspondent," *New Republic*, vol. 37 (January 30, 1924): 252–254.

48. Ibid., "The Munitions Traffic," *North American Review*, vol. 236, No. 1 (July 1933): 64–72; ibid., "Are We Our Brothers' Keepers? How Our Country Is Fighting the Drug Evil," *Harper's*, vol. 149 (November 1924): 736–43; ibid., "The Continuing Curse of Opium," *Ladies Home Journal*, vol. 42 (July 1925): 6, 58, 60.

49. Ibid., "A Brief Outline of Efforts to Control the Manufacture and Sale of Munitions and Implements of War," in "International Traffic in Arms and Munitions," *Reference Shelf*, vol. 9, No. 9 (New York: H. W. Wilson Company, 1934): 49–57; ibid., "Armament Manufacture and Trade," *International Conciliation*, No. 295 (Worcester, Mass.: Carnegie Endowment for International Peace, 1933): 5–27; ibid., *Disarmament, Security and Control: A Draft of Convention for Disarmament, Security, and Control Based on the Kellogg Pact*, Senate Document No. 33, 74th Congress, 1st Session (Washington, D.C.: Government Printing Office, 1935): 1–26.

50. "News Release/Department of Justice" (May 26, 1943), Constance Drexel Files, FBI.

51. *In Fact*, vol. 8, No. 4 (November 1, 1943): 1; vol. 9, No. 9 (June 5, 1944): 1; see Richard Harold Waldo in *The National Cyclopaedia of American Biography*, vol. 32 (New York: James T. White & Co., 1945), 123; *Who's Who in America*, vol. 22 (Chicago: A. N. Marquis Company, 1942): 2252.

52. "Former Newsmen among 8 Indicted for Treason by U.S.," *Editor & Publisher*, July 28, 1943.

53. "News Release/Department of Justice" (May 26, 1943), Constance Drexel Files, FBI.

54. Charles J. Rolo, *Radio Goes to War* (New York: G. P. Putnam's Sons, 1942): 104.

55. Harsch, *Pattern of Conquest*, 290.

56. Harry W. Flannery, *Assignment to Berlin* (New York: Alfred A. Knopf, 1942): 167.

57. William L. Shirer to Author, April 16, 1987; ibid., "The American Radio Traitors," 397; ibid., *Berlin Diary: The Journal of a Foreign Correspondent, 1934–1941*, 422–423.

58. Parry, "Short-Wave Traitors," 119; Rolo, "Germany Calling!" 30–31; Graves, "Propaganda by Shortwave," 614.

59. New York *Times*, August 18, 1945.

60. New York *Times*, August 29, 1956.

61. New York *Times*, October 2, 1946; April 14, 1948.

62. Constance Drexel, "Unpublished Letters of F.D.R. to His French Governess," *Parents' Magazine*, vol. 26, No. 9 (September 1951): 30–31, 80–84.

63. Edward Leopold Delaney, *Five Decades before Dawn* (Pasadena, Calif.: Deljon Publishers, 1969): 1–49; "Nazis' Radio Spieler an Ex-MG P.A.," *Variety* (May 25, 1940), E. L. Delaney Files, 97–21, FBI; "News Release/Department of Justice" (May 26, 1943), E. L. Delaney Files, FBI; "Mr. Wisecrack," *Time* (May 20, 1940): 52–54.

64. New York *Times*, June 3, 1934. A State Department memorandum concluded on July 9, 1942:

His connection with M.G.M. may well be responsible for his present anti-Semitic outlook and resultant willingness to propagandize for Berlin. This would appear to be the case since he left his position with M.G.M. with some bitterness, claiming that room was being made for a relative of one of the heads of this firm at his expense.

E. L. Delaney Files, File No. 65–26534–11, FBI.

65. Delaney, *Five Decades before Dawn*, 52–57.

66. Ibid., 61–75.

67. Ibid., 68; BBC, *Monitoring Service*, January 4, 1940.

68. Delaney, *Five Decades before Dawn*, 72.

69. BBC, *Monitoring Service*, April 13, 1940; Delaney, *Five Decades before Dawn*, 72; "Mr. Wisecrack," 53.

70. E. L. Delaney, *False Freedom* (Los Angeles, Calif.: Sequoia University Press, 1954): 26; ibid., *Five Decades before Dawn*, 73.

71. Harsch, *Pattern of Conquest*, 288–290; Joseph C. Harsch to Author, April 10, 1985.

72. Delaney, *Five Decades before Dawn*, 76–78.

73. BBC, *Monitoring Service*, June 19, 22, 25, 1940.

74. Rolo, "Germany Calling!" 30.

75. Delaney, *Five Decades before Dawn*, 80–88; Whitton, "War by Radio," 591.

76. BBC, *Monitoring Service*, July 27, 1940.

77. Delaney, *False Freedom*, 30.

78. BBC, *Monitoring Service*, February 29; September 26; December 28, 1940; March 8; October 29, 1941; February 3, 1942.

79. Ibid., August 13; September 12, 1940; January 14; April 26, 1941; Graves, *War on the Shortwave*, 36.

80. BBC, *Monitoring Service*, August 8; November 13, 1940; June 26, 1941.

81. Graves, "Propaganda by Shortwave," 617–618.

82. Delaney, *Five Decades before Dawn*, 91; ibid., *False Freedom*, 36.

83. Delaney, *Five Decades before Dawn*, 100–101.

84. Flannery, *Assignment to Berlin*, 327–337.

85. Delaney, *Freedom's Frontier* (Sacramento, Calif.: H. A. Nickel Co., 1964): 136–137.

86. BBC, *Monitoring Service*, August 27; November 19, 1941; Delaney, *Five Decades before Dawn*, 105.

87. BBC, *Monitoring Service*, July 23, 1941. By the year of his death in 1975, at the age of 93, Pelham Grenville Wodehouse had been knighted by Queen Elizabeth II. He also had been awarded a doctor of letters degree by the University of Oxford. Wodehouse wrote 98 books and collaborated in the production of some 75 plays, musical comedies, and film scripts. Iain Sproat, *Wodehouse at War* (New Haven, Conn.: Ticknor & Fields, 1981): 7, 11, 13, 31, 33, 71, 102; ibid., "Wodehouse's War," *Encounter*, vol. 59 (September-October 1982): 98–100.

88. Delaney, *Five Decades before Dawn*, 110–113. Censored correspondent to Director J. Edgar Hoover, January 31, 1942, E. L. Delaney Files, File No. 65–26534–4, FBI.

89. Delaney, *Five Decades before Dawn*, 115; ibid., *False Freedom*, 62.

90. BBC, *Monitoring Service*, December 18, 1941. On August 27, 1942, Oscar R. Ewing, the special prosecutor who sent American Fascist leader William Dudley Pelley to prison for 15 years, called for indictments and the death penalty for all the radio traitors—including Delaney—on conviction. The indictments would take nearly a year to hand down. Washington *Post*, August 28, 1942.

91. Delaney, *Five Decades before Dawn*, 120.

92. Flannery, *Assignment to Berlin*, 22.

93. Parry, "Short-Wave Traitors," 59; Shirer, "The American Radio Traitors," 397–398.

94. American Legation (Bern) to the Division of Foreign Interests of the Federal Political Department, July 28, 1943, B.24.USA(2)3—Delaney, HE/CT, Department of State, Washington, D.C.; Interrogation of Edward Delaney, March 28, 1946, E. L. Delaney Files, File No. 146–28–240, Division of Records, Department of Justice, Washington, D.C.

95. Delaney, *Freedom's Frontier*, 109.

96. Ibid., *Five Decades before Dawn*, 129–133.

97. Ibid., 140–153.

98. Washington *Post*, June 20, 1945; Delaney, *Five Decades before Dawn*, 155; ibid., *False Freedom*, 104–108.

99. G. W. Hickman, Jr. (Chief, Claims and Litigation Division) to E.L. Delaney, October 11, 1948, E. L. Delaney Files, File No. 65–26534–188, FBI; Delaney, *Five Decades before Dawn*, 163–167.

100. J. E. Miloses to D. M. Ladd, August 8, 1947, E. L. Delaney Files, File No. 65–26534–146, FBI; Delaney, *Five Decades before Dawn*, 170; Raymond P. Whearty to James M. McInerey (General Asst. to Asst. Attorney General), July 24, 1947, Delaney Files, File No. 146–28–240, Criminal Internal Security Section, Department of Justice, Washington, D.C.

101. Richard B. Vail (Congressman, 2nd District, Illinois) to Tom Clark, July 9, 1947, E. L. Delaney Files, File No. 146–28–240, Office of the Attorney General, Department of Justice, Washington, D.C.; Delaney, *Five Decades before Dawn*, 174.

102. "Bureau Telephone Call," August 7, 1947, E. L. Delaney Files, File No. 65–26534, FBI; Reyton Ford (Acting Asst. to the Attorney General) to Senator Francis J. Myers, December 18, 1947, E. L. Delaney Files, File No. 146–28–240, Office of the Attorney General, Department of Justice, Washington, D.C.; Delaney, *Five Decades before Dawn*, 183–185; New York *Times*, August 29, 1947; Los Angeles *Times*, August 29, 1947. Interestingly enough, one month earlier, on July 28, T. Vincent Quinn (Asst. Attorney General, Criminal Division) wrote Douglas McGregor (Asst. to the Attorney General) that the Delaney case should be closed. He based his decision on the lack of two witnesses to the defendant's overt acts of treason (Haupt case) and the "qualitative weakness" of Delaney's broadcast material. A dismissal of charges and the issuance of Delaney's passport to him for emigration to the U.S. was approved by the three attorneys assigned to his case. E. L. Delaney Files, File No. 146–28–240, Communications Section, Department of Justice, Washington, D.C.

103. "Enclosure," N.D., E. L. Delaney Files, File No. 65–26534–163, FBI; Los Angeles *Times*, March 2, 1948.

104. Congressman John Phillips to Director J. Edgar Hoover, August 15, 1949, E. L. Delaney Files, File No. 65–26534–195, FBI.

105. SAC, San Diego, to Director J. Edgar Hoover, July 26, 1949, E. L. Delaney Files, File No. 65–26534–196, FBI.

106. Arizona *Daily Star* (Tucson), August 1, 1951; Tucson (Arizona) *Daily Citizen*, August 2, 1951.

107. Arizona *Daily Star*, August 3, 1951; SAC, Phoenix, to Director J. Edgar Hoover, November 29, 1951, E. L. Delaney Files, File No. 65–26534–202, FBI; "Enclosure," *Guardian*, October 27, 1951, E. L. Delaney Files, File No. 65–26534–203, FBI.

108. E. L. Delaney to J. Howard McGrath (U.S. Attorney General), August 24, 1951, including enclosure of newspaper clipping from the Arizona *Register* of the same date, E. L. Delaney Files, File No. 146–28–240, Office of the Attorney General, Department of Justice, Washington, D.C.: E. L. Delaney to President Harry S. Truman, August 8, 1951, E. L. Delaney Files, File No. 146–28–240, Criminal Division, Department of Justice, Washington, D.C.

109. Thomas J. Jeffers, Jr., to Author, November 6, 1986; Vivian Glaus (Personnel Director, *Ledger*) to Author, June 17, 1987; Beverly Place Chance (Reporter, *Ledger*) to Author, March 22, 1987; Burton H. Wolfe (Editor, *Californian* [San Francisco]) to Author, November 27, 1961, E. L. Delaney Files, File No. 146–28–240, Records Branch, Department of Justice, Washington, D.C.; Barbara R. Boyd (Special Collections Librarian, Glendale Public Library) to Author, July 12, 1986.

110. Delaney, *Five Decades before Dawn*, 202–203; ibid., *Freedom's Frontier*, 145.

111. Ibid., *Freedom's Frontier*, 44, 72, 154; *Congressional Record*, vol. 95, Part 13, 81st Congress, 1st Session (March 14, 1949–May 10, 1949): A2319; *Congressional Record*, vol. 95, Part 15, 81st Congress, 1st Session (July 5, 1949–August 25, 1949): A4551.

112. Delaney, *Freedom's Frontier*, 164; ibid., *False Freedom*, 168–171.

113. Delaney, *Freedom's Frontier*, 73; ibid., *False Freedom*, 167–173.

114. Delaney, *Five Decades before Dawn*, 235–249.

115. Glendale (Calif.) *News-Press*, July 3; July 5, 1972; Certificate of Death—E. L. Delaney, File No. 72–086715, July 1, 1972, Vital Statistics Branch, Department of Health Services, Sacramento, Calif.

CHAPTER 2

1. Franklin M. Garrett, *Atlanta and Environs: A Chronicle of Its People and Events*, vol. I (Athens: University of Georgia Press, 1954): 381–382; William L. Shirer, "The American Radio Traitors," *Harper's*, vol. 187 (October 1943): 402; William G. Schofield, *Treason Trail* (New York: Rand McNally & Company, 1964): 203–204.

2. John Pomian, ed., *Joseph Retinger: Memoirs of an Eminence Grise* (Sussex, England: Sussex University Press, 1972): 37–39; Atlanta *Constitution*, January 20, 1942; Atlanta *Journal*, January 20, 1942; Jess G. Hayes, *Sheriff Thompson's Day: Turbulence in the Arizona Territory* (Tucson: University of Arizona Press, 1968): 24–25; Dan L. Thrapp, *Al Sieber: Chief of Scouts* (Norman: University of Oklahoma Press, 1964): 390–391; Schofield, *Treason Trail*, 205.

3. Atlanta *Constitution*, January 20, 1942; Emily Hahn, *The Soon Sisters* (New York: Garden City Publishing Co., 1945): 59–62; Elmer T. Clark, *The Chiangs of China* (New York: Abingdon-Cokesbury Press, 1943): 50–51.

4. Joan Givner, *Katherine Anne Porter: A Life* (New York: Simon and Schuster, 1982): 114.

5. Atlanta *Journal*, January 20, 1942; Schofield, *Treason Trail*, 205. Most of Jane's stories dealt with her Arizona period: "The Gift of the Hills," *Harper's Weekly*, October 21, 1911; "The Keeper of the Well," *Harper's Weekly*, April 23, 1910; "The Burying of Lil," *Harper's Weekly*, August 13, 1910; "The Spur of Courage," *Harper's Weekly*, January 13, 1912; "El Valiente," *Harper's Weekly*, June 22, 1912.

6. Atlanta *Constitution*, January 20, 1942; Schofield, *Treason Trail*, 205; "Looping-the-Loop over London," in Jane Anderson and Gordon Bruce, *Flying, Submarining and Mine Sweeping* (London: Sir Joseph Canston & Sons, 1916): 13.

7. Dame Rebecca West to Author, October 4, 1982.

8. Givner, *Katherine Anne Porter*, 115; Schofield, *Treason Trail*, 206.

9. Jane Anderson Taylor to H. G. Wells, October 12, October 16, 1915, H. G. Wells Collection, University Library, University of Illinois at Urbana-Champaign.

10. West to Author, October 4, 1982.

11. Roger Tennant, *Joseph Conrad* (New York: Atheneum, 1981): 219.

12. Frederick R. Karl, *Joseph Conrad: The Three Lives, A Biography* (New York: Farrar, Straus & Giroux, 1979): 162.

13. Jessie Conrad, *Joseph Conrad and His Circle* (London: Jarrolds Publishers, 1935): 196–197.

14. Robin Douglas, "My Boyhood with Conrad," *Cornhill Magazine*, vol. 139 (London: John Murray, Albemarle Street, 1929): 25.

15. John Conrad, *Joseph Conrad: Times Remembered* (Cambridge: Cambridge University Press, 1981): 108–109.

16. George Seldes to Author, May 15, 1982.

17. Tennant, *Joseph Conrad*, 220.

18. Jessie Conrad, *Joseph Conrad's Letters to His Wife* (London: Privately Printed, 1927): 13–14.

19. Ibid., 21–22.

20. Conrad, Jessie, *Joseph Conrad and His Circle*, 207.

21. Tennant, *Joseph Conrad*, 222; Borys Conrad, *My Father: Joseph Conrad* (London: Calder & Boyars, 1970): 119; Dale B. J. Randall, *Joseph Conrad and Warrington Dawson: The Record of a Friendship* (Durham, N.C.: Duke University Press, 1968): 95.

22. Joan Givner to Author, September 27, 1982; J. H. Retinger, *Conrad and His Contemporaries* (New York: Roy Publishers, 1943): 98.

23. Conrad, Borys, *My Father*, 120–122; Tennant, *Joseph Conrad*, 222.

24. Karl, *Joseph Conrad*, 162–169; Gary Geddes, *Conrad's Later Novels* (Montreal: McGill-Queen's University Press, 1980): 116–119.

25. George Seldes to Author, April 29, 1982. Brigadier General R. E. Lee, U.S. Army (Acting Assistant Chief of Staff G–2) to Lt. Col. J. E. Hoover (Chief, FBI, January 7, 1942, Doc. No. 65–36240–9, Military Intelligence Division G–2, War Department.

26. Jane Anderson to Katherine Anne Porter, June 6, 1918. Katherine Anne Porter Collection, Box 4, McKeldin Library, University of Maryland, College Park; Joan Givner to Author, September 15, 1982.

27. Givner, *Katherine Anne Porter*, 121–122; *Rocky Mountain News*, July 8, 1919; Dame Rebecca West would have most likely categorized Jane Anderson as being a psychotic, "the condition of being at war, not with one's self, but with one's environment . . . the desire to enjoy life spiced by danger and reckless pleasure without having to pay the tab." Motley F. Deakin, *Rebecca West* (Boston: Twayne Publishers, 1980): 116.

28. Gilbert Seldes, "Geometry," chapter from an unpublished memoir (New York, 1967): 60–62. Original in the possession of George Seldes.

29. Pomian, ed., *Joseph Retinger*, 38–39; Seldes, "Geometry," 61–62.

30. Jane Anderson to H. G. Wells, October 6, 1932, Wells Collection. "Memorandum," November 14, 1942, Doc. No. 65–36240–36, Jane Anderson Files, FBI, Department of Justice, Washington, D.C.

31. Jane Anderson to H. G. Wells, April 8, 1933, ibid.

32. Schofield, *Treason Trail*, 210–211.

33. Jane Anderson de Cienfuegos, "Horror in Spain," *Catholic Digest* 1 (1937): 69–74.

34. *New York American*, May 16, 23, 30, June 13, 1937; H. Edward Knoblaugh, *Correspondent in Spain* (New York: Sheed & Ward, 1937): 194.

35. Schofield, *Treason Trail*, 219.

36. *Foreign Relations of the United States*, Diplomatic Papers (Europe), 1936, vol. II (Washington, D.C.: Government Printing Office, 1934): 745; New York *Times*, October 11, October 15, 1936.

37. New York *Times*, September 28, 1937.

38. Ibid., February 28, 1938; *In Fact*, March 13, 1944, 3; September 3, 1945, 3; Fred Taylor, ed., *The Goebbels Diaries: 1939–41* (New York: G. P. Putnam's Sons, 1983): 26.

39. Nathaniel Weyl, *Treason: The Story of Disloyalty and Betrayal in American History* (Washington, D.C.: Public Affairs Press, 1950): 375; *Time* (January 19, 1942): 30. Despite Anderson's Herculean efforts, the sentiment of the American people would never coalesce on the Spanish question. J. David Valaik, "Catholics, Neutrality and the Spanish Embargo, 1937–1939," *Journal of American History*, vol. 54, No. 1 (June 1967): 73–85.

40. Kitty Barry Crawford to Katherine Anne Porter, March 13, 1940, Katherine Anne Porter Collection, Box 45, McKeldin Library, University of Maryland, College Park.

41. John Roy Carlson, *Under Cover: My Four Years in the Nazi Underworld of America* (New York: E. P. Dutton & Co., 1943): 456–459; "Merwin K. Hart," *Current Biography*, 1941, 367–369; Marquis W. Childs, *I Write from Washington* (New York: Harper & Brothers Publishers, 1942): 137–138; Thomas J. Hamilton, *Appeasement's Child: The Franco Regime in Spain* (New York: Alfred A. Knopf, 1943): 16; Weyl, *Treason*, 375.

42. BBC, *Monitoring Service*, April 21, 1941; Taylor, *The Goebbels Diaries*, 357.

43. BBC, *Monitoring Service*, September 8, 1941; January 10, 1942; Derrick Sington and Arthur Weidenfeld, *The Goebbels Experiment: A Study of the Nazi Propaganda Machine* (New Haven, Conn.: Yale University Press, 1943): 187–188.

44. BBC, *Monitoring Service*, April 14, 1941.

45. Ibid., October 24, 1941.

46. Ibid., February 9, 1942.

47. Ibid., October 13, 1941.

48. Ibid., December 22, 1941.

49. Ibid., August 8, 1941.

50. Ibid., November 14, 1941.

51. Ibid., December 29, 1941.

52. Ibid., November 21, 1941.

53. Ibid., May 5; July 25, 1941; January 19, 1942. An American monitor noted, "If her microphone hysteria is any clue to her personality, she is probably mentally unhinged." See Charles J. Rolo, *Radio Goes to War* (New York: G. P. Putnam's Sons, 1942): 106; Harold Ettlinger, *The Axis on the Air* (New York: Bobbs-Merrill Company, 1943): 53.

54. BBC, *Monitoring Service*, December 26, 1941.

55. Ibid., January 23; February 23, 1942.

56. Ibid., March 6, 1942.

57. Weyl, *Treason*, 376; Schofield, *Treason Trail*, 222.

58. New York *Times*, October 28, 1947; Katherine Anne Porter, *The Collected Essays and Occasional Writings of Katherine Anne Porter* (New York: Delacorte Press, 1970): 212–213; Field Report, April 26, 1945, Doc. No. 65–36240–131, Jane Anderson Files, FBI; Frederick Ayers to J. E. Hoover, July 26, 1945, Doc. No. 65–36240–140, Jane Anderson Files, FBI; Madrid Legation to State Department, June 26, 1947, Doc. No. 65–36240–164, Jane Anderson Files, Division of Communication and Records, Department of State; Cable, April 1, 1948, Doc. No. 40–0–4089, Jane Anderson Files, Division of Communication and Records, Department of State.

CHAPTER 3

1. BBC, *Monitoring Service*, May 5, 1942; *Editor & Publisher*, July 31, 1942, 40; New York *Times*, July 27, 1943.

2. Max Otto Koischwitz, *Staff Personnel Record*, Hunter College Archives, Hunter College, New York City, New York; Koischwitz, "Der Theaterherold im deutschen Schanspiel des Mittelalters und der Reformationzeit Germanische," *Studien*, No. 46 (Berlin: E. Ebberring, 1926): 102.

3. Federal Writers' Project, *New York City Guide* (New York: Octagon Books, 1970): 287. Prepared summary on M. O. Koischwitz and Erna Keller Koischwitz, December 5, 1942; M. O. Koischwitz Files, FBI, Department of Justice, Washington, D.C.

4. Louis J. Halle, "O.K.," *Virginia Quarterly Review*, vol. 51, No. 2 (Spring, 1975): 214.

5. Horace Coon, *Columbia: Colossus on the Hudson* (New York: E. P. Dutton & Company, 1947): 212–225.

6. Max Otto Koischwitz, "Our Textbooks and Kulturkunde," *German Quarterly*, vol. 1, No. 3 (May 1928): 107–115.

7. Max Otto Koischwitz, "A New Method of Testing Extensive Reading in Contemporary Literature Classes," *German Quarterly*, vol. 7, No. 1 (January 1934): 9–18.

8. Halle, "O.K.," 215–216.

9. Louis Halle to Author, November 14, 1984.

10. Halle, "O.K.," 216.

11. Ibid., 217.

12. Ibid., 214–215; Field Reports, March 17, 27; May 28; September 14, 1943. M. O. Koischwitz Files, FBI.

13. Max Otto Koischwitz, *Staff Personnel Record*, Hunter College Archives; New York *Post*, September 24, 1940.

14. New York *Post*, September 24, 1940; Field Report, April 16, 1943. M. O. Koischwitz Files, FBI.

15. Halle, "O.K.," 218.

16. Max Otto Koischwitz, *Faculty Performance Report*, Hunter College Archives.

17. Max Otto Koischwitz, *Academic Vitae*, Hunter College Archives.

18. Ibid.

19. *German Quarterly*, vol. 6, No. 4 (November 1933): 185–186.

20. Ibid., vol. 9, No. 1 (January 1936): 32.

21. Ibid., vol. 10, No. 2 (March 1937): 151–152.

22. Louis Halle to Author, March 10, 1984.

23. Max Otto Koischwitz, *Staff Personnel Record*, Hunter College Archives.

24. BBC, *Monitoring Service*, July 4, 1941.

25. Ibid., July 1, 1943.

26. Max Otto Koischwitz, Files of the Hunter College Retirement System, Hunter College Archives.

27. New York *Post*, September 24, 1940.

28. Max Otto Koischwitz, *A German-American Interprets Germany* (Milwaukee: Gutenberg Publishing Co., 1935): 10.

29. Ibid., 17.

30. Ibid., 36.

31. Ibid., 42–47.

32. Ibid., 89–98.

33. Koischwitz, Files of the Hunter College Retirement System, Hunter College Archives; William L. Shirer, "The American Radio Traitors," *Harper's*, vol. 187 (October 1943): 403.

34. *P.M.*, August 11, 1941.

35. Ibid. In the summer of 1941 Koischwitz returned to the subject of Thomas Mann:

When you arrived in the U.S.A. seven years ago you said: "Wherever I am is Germany." The Americans might with reason, therefore, suspect you of being a spy in Germany's pay, although you profess to admire Roosevelt. You are, in fact, a tangle of contradictions—a kind of dual personality whose opinions change with every passing whim. You have no philosophy of life and belong nowhere—a tragic fate.

BBC, *Monitoring Service*, July 11, 1941.

36. Ward B. Lewis, *Eugene O'Neill: The German Reception of America's First Dramatist* (New York: Peter Lang Publishers, 1984): 79–83, 159–161; Otto Koischwitz, *O'Neill* (Berlin: Junker and Dünnhaupt, 1938).

37. *Books Abroad*, vol. 13 (Winter 1939): 58–59.

38. Max Otto Koischwitz, "German Readers Turn to Foreign Countries," *Books Abroad*, vol. 13 (Winter 1938): 431–434.

39. Hunter College *Yearbook*, 1938.

40. *P.M.*, August 11, 1941; New York *Post*, September 24, 1940; Field Report, April 16, 1943. M. O. Koischwitz Files, FBI.

41. Max Otto Koischwitz, "Echo from Abroad: American Letter," *Literatur* (August 1939): 555–557.

42. G. Egerton Harriman to James Marshall, August 10, 1939, Hunter College Archives.

43. Pearl Bernstein to Ordway Tead, August 17, 1939, Hunter College Archives.

44. George N. Shuster to Ordway Tead, August 31, 1939, Hunter College Archives.

45. Sam Glane to "Gentlemen," September 5, 1939, Hunter College Archives.

46. "Hitlerite Teaches German in New York's Hunter College," *The Hour*, No. 9 (August 30, 1939): 9.

47. New York *Post*, September 24, 1940; *P.M.*, August 11, 1941.

48. Ordway Tead to George S. Messersmith, December 29, 1939, Hunter College Archives.

49. "Action to Be Taken in the Case of Koischwitz," *The Hour*, No. 13 (September 30, 1939): 3; "Koischwitz Broadcasts Nazi Propaganda to America," Ibid., No. 54 (July 20, 1940): 3; "Secretary," Hunter College, to "My dear Dr. Koischwitz," January 29, 1940, Hunter College Archives; Harold N. Graves, *War on the Short Wave* (New York: Foreign Policy Association, 1941): 33; Field Report, April 16, 1943. M. O. Koischwitz Files, FBI.

50. Charles J. Rolo, "Radio War on the U.S.A.," *American Mercury*, vol. 52, No. 205 (January 1941): 69; "Facts in Review," *German Library of Information*, vol. 11, No. 27 (July 1940): 291.

51. BBC, *Monitoring Service*, January 19, 1940.

52. Ibid., March 19, 1940.

53. Ibid., August 14, 1940; Harold N. Graves, "Propaganda by Shortwave," *Public Opinion Quarterly* (December 1940): 605. John O. Rennie, "Dr. Goebbel's Awkward Squad," *Atlantic Monthly*, vol. 172 (September 1943): 107.

54. BBC, *Monitoring Service*, August 1, 1940; Charles J. Rolo, "Germany Calling," *Current History*, vol. 52, No. 2 (October 1940): 30.

55. BBC, *Monitoring Service*, July 17, 1940; Gordon Skilling, "Organising Hatred," *Dalhousie Review*, vol. 23 (April 1943): 11–22; John B. Whitton, "War by Radio," *Foreign Affairs*, vol. 19, No. 3 (April 1941): 584–596; Edwin Muller, "Waging War with Words," *Current History*, vol. 50, No. 6 (August 1939): 24–27.

56. BBC, *Monitoring Service*, August 14, 1940.

57. Ibid., August 22, 1940.

58. Ibid., June 29, 1940; S. K. Padover, "How the Nazis Picture America," *Public Opinion Quarterly*, vol. 3, No. 4 (October 1939): 663–669.

59. BBC, *Monitoring Service*, June 27, 1940.

60. Ibid.

61. Ibid., August 17, 1940.

62. Ibid., December 10, 1940.

63. Ibid., March 18, 1941.

64. Ibid., October 17, 1941.

65. Ibid., September 11, 1942.

66. Ibid., July 6, 1943.

67. Ibid., January 16, 22, 1941.

68. Ibid., July 5, 1941.

69. Ibid., July 19, 1941.

70. Ibid., June 4, 1941.

71. Ibid., October 31, 1941.

72. Louis Halle to Author, June 5, 1986.

73. BBC, *Monitoring Service*, July 12, 1941.

74. Ibid., November 13, 1943.

75. Ibid., September 29, 1942.

76. Ibid., July 29, 1941.

77. New York *Times*, April 24, 1941; BBC, *Monitoring Service*, August 1, 1941.

78. BBC, *Monitoring Service*, August 12, 1941.

79. Dorothy Thompson, "Who Goes Nazi?" *Harper's*, vol. 183 (August 1941): 237–242.

80. BBC, *Monitoring Service*, September 19, 1941; Derrick Sington and Arthur Weidenfeld, *The Goebbels Experiment: A Study of the Nazi Propaganda Machine* (New Haven, Conn.: Yale University Press, 1943): 186–187.

81. BBC, *Monitoring Service*, February 6, 1941.

82. Ibid., May 15, 1941.

83. Ibid., May 29, 1942.

84. Ibid., August 19, 1942; July 20, 1943.

85. Ibid., September 16; October 2, 1942.

86. Ibid., November 7, 1942.

87. Ibid., August 12, 1943.

88. Ibid., January 21; June 5, 1942.

89. Ibid., June 12, 1942.

90. Ibid., July 7; December 22, 1942; June 26, 1943; March 2, 1944.

91. Ibid., November 27, 1942.

92. Ibid., February 23, 1943.

93. Ibid., December 9, 1942; June 22, 1943.

94. O. John Rogge, *The Official German Report: Nazi Penetration 1924–1942, Pan-Arabism 1939–Today* (New York: Thomas Yoseloff, 1961): 311; Washington *Post*, January 27; February 1, 1949.

95. Washington *Post*, February 25, 1949; Erna Koischwitz perished on August 24, 1943, only nine days after the birth of the Koischwitzes' only son, Otto, who died within hours of birth. Enclosure, N.D., M. O. Koischwitz Files, FBI.

96. Nathaniel Weyl, *Treason: The Story of Disloyalty and Betrayal in American History* (Washington, D.C.: Public Affairs Press, 1950): 376–379; Margaret Boveri, *Treason in the Twentieth Century* (London: MacDonald, 1956): 180–181; *Time* vol. 53, Pt. 1 (March 7, 1949): 27; Washington *Post*, February 24, 1949.

97. Louis Halle to Author, June 7, 1984.

98. New York *Times*, February 25, 1949; Washington *Post*, February 25, 1949; Weyl, *Treason*, 379–380; Richard H. Rovere, "Letter from Washington," *New Yorker*, vol. 25 (February 26, 1949): 77–82; *Federal Reporter*, vol. 182 F. 2d (St. Paul: West Publishing Co., 1951): 967.

99. Washington *Post*, February 22, 1949.

100. Ibid., March 1, 1949.

101. BBC, *Monitoring Service*, June 24, 1943.

102. Ibid., July 22, 1943.

103. Ibid., September 19, 1943.

104. Ibid., November 26, 1943.

105. Washington *Post*, February 25, 1949.

106. BBC, *Monitoring Service*, May 22, 1941.

107. Ibid., August 28, 1942.

108. Washington *Post*, February 25, 1949.

109. BBC, *Monitoring Service*, April 18, 25, 1943.

110. Washington *Post*, February 17; March 1, 1949. Also see Col. Albert Smith, "The Little Brown Hen at Stalag 11-B," *Saturday Evening Post*, vol. 218, No. 10 (September 8, 1945): 34. David Foy, *For You the War Is Over* (New York: Stein & Day, 1984): 65; Francis L. Sampson, *Paratroopers Padre* (Washington, D.C.: Catholic Unit of America Press, 1948): 92–108.

111. BBC, *Monitoring Service*, May 9, 1943.

112. Ibid., June 6, 13, 1943.

113. William L. Shirer, "What the Germans Told the Prisoners," *Harper's*, vol. 189, No. 1134 (November 1944): 537–538; Foy, *For You the War Is Over*, 86–87; William L. Shirer to Author, May 12, 1986; U.S. Postal Censorship Sheet, March 2, 1945, M. O. Koischwitz Files, FBI.

114. BBC, *Monitoring Service*, May 12, 1944; *Federal Reporter*, vol. 182, 968–970.

115. BBC, *Monitoring Service*, June 13, 1944.

116. Ibid., June 14, 1944.

117. Ibid., June 15, 17, 1944.

118. William L. Shirer, "Propaganda Front," Undated and unidentified clipping

located in the Robert H. Best folder in the Vertical File Section of the Department
of Special Collections, South Carolina Division, University of South Carolina.

119. BBC, *Monitoring Service*, June 18, 20, 25, 1944.

120. Ibid., June 30, 1944.

121. Ibid., July 8, 26, 1944.

122. Washington *Post*, March 1, 1949; Enclosure, September 4, 1945, M. O.
Koischwitz Files, FBI.

123. Halle, "O.K.," 220–221.

CHAPTER 4

1. Joseph M. McLaughlin to Author, January 27, 1980; Spartanburg *Herald*, May
13, 1940; Boston *Herald*, April 14, 1948; *Minutes of the Upper South Carolina Conference
of the Methodist Church, 1940*, 89–90, South Carolina Conference, Methodist Church
Archives, Wofford College, Spartanburg, South Carolina; Albert Deems Betts, *History of South Carolina Methodism* (Columbia, S.C.: Advocate Press, 1952): M.C.A.,
514, 524; E. O. Watson, *Builders: Sketches of Methodist Preachers in South Carolina with
Historical Data* (Columbia, S.C.: Southern Christian Advocate, 1932): M.C.A., 41,
49.

2. Records of the U.S. District Court for the District of Massachusetts, Record
Group 21, Criminal Case No. 17666, Stenographic Record, vol. X, Federal Archives
and Records Center, Waltham, Massachusetts, 952–953. Hereafter cited *Best Deposition*; Wofford College Fitting School: *Grade Book*, 1907–1916. *Rooms and Waiters*,
1912–1916, Wofford College Archives, Wofford College Library, Spartanburg, South
Carolina.

3. *Best Deposition*, 954; *Editor & Publisher*, June 6, 1942, 38.

4. Joseph M. McLaughlin to Author, January 27, February 12, March 31, 1980;
Carlisle Literary Society *Minutes*, October 26, 1905; April 1, 1921, 329; *Bohemian*,
1916, 18, 55, 137, 149, 156, 163, 191, 201. Surviving classmates polled include John
L. Bennett, (Dillon, S.C.), William H. Crews (Greenville, S.C.), Jarvis E. Thompson
(Coral Gables, Fla.), Edwin F. Moseley (Chapel Hill, N.C.), Joseph M. McLaughlin
(St. Cloud, Fla.); *Wofford College Journal*, October 1914, 45, Wofford College Archives;
Field Report (Baltimore, Md.), December 19, 1942, Doc. No. 100–103780–42, Robert
Best Files, FBI, Department of Justice, Washington, D.C.

5. BBC, *Monitoring Service*, September 16, 1942; *Best Deposition*, 955–962; *Official
Roster of South Carolina Soldiers, Sailors and Marines in the World War 1917–18*, vol. I
(Columbia: South Carolina General Assembly, 1929): 170. Found in Spartanburg
County Library, Spartanburg, South Carolina.

6. *Best Deposition*, 962–964; New York *Times*, May 22, 1922. For a sample of Best's
writing see the *Wofford College Journal*, November 1914; April, November 1915;
February, March, 1916; *Old Gold and Black*, January 12, 1923. Wofford College Archives; Herbert Brook, ed. *The Blue Book of Awards* (Chicago: Marquis—Who's Who,
1956): 132; Boston *Daily Globe*, April 13, 1948.

7. *Best Deposition*, 965–977; Boston *Daily Globe*, April 13, 1948. For a distillation
of Best's research, see Best, "Old World Sees Something New" and "Student Internationalism in Austria," in *Reconstruction* (June–September, 1923): Nos. 47–54.

8. *Best Deposition*, 977–982; Boston *Daily Globe*, April 13, 1948; Robert W. Desmond, *The Press and World Affairs* (New York: D. Appleton-Century Company, 1937):

280–284; Austrian Federal Press Department, ed. *The Austrian Year Book*, 1931 (Vienna: Manzsche Verlags–Und Universitats–Buchhandlung, 1931): 225–233; BBC, *Monitoring Service*, June 16, 1943.

9. *Best Deposition*, 983–986.

10. George Seldes to Author, September 5, 1979; William L. Shirer, *Midcentury Journey: The Western World through Its Years of Conflict* (New York: Farrar, Straus and Young, 1952): 53–54; W. L. Shirer, "The American Radio Traitors," *Harper's*, vol. 187 (October 1943): 397; Friedrich Scheu, *Der Weg Ins Ungewisse: Osterreichs Schick Salskurve, 1929–1938* (Vienna: Verlag Fritz Molden, 1972): 18–19; John Gunther, *Behind the Curtain* (New York: Harper and Brothers Publishers, 1949): 287–288; Whit Burnett, "Hunting Headlines in the Balkans," *American Mercury*, vol. 30, No. 117 (September 1933): 42–49.

11. Dorothy Thompson to Charles W. Bartlett, April 12, 1948, Dorothy Thompson Collection, George Arent Research Library, Syracuse University, New York. Xerox copy in possession of the Author.

12. William L. Shirer to Author, August 27, 1979.

13. Hugh Baillie, *High Tension* (New York: Harper and Brothers Publishers, 1959): 127.

14. George Seldes to Author, September 5, 1979; Dorothy Thompson to Charles W. Bartlett, April 12, 1948, Dorothy Thompson Collection.

15. Scheu, *Der Weg Ins Ungewisse*, 19.

16. William L. Shirer, *The Traitor* (New York: Farrar, Straus and Company, 1950): 97; John Gunther, *The Lost City* (New York: Harper and Brothers Publishers, 1964): 171, 57, 93, 104, 119.

17. Scheu, *Der Weg Ins Ungewisse*, 23.

18. Ibid.

19. Shirer wrote in 1943, "His [Best's] financial state never seemed to worry him very much except possibly during one period when there arose what Dorothy Thompson called the other day 'those doubtful affairs around Credit Anstalt Bank' the details of which I've forgotten." "The American Radio Traitors," 397; Gunther, *The Lost City*, 53, 56, 59, 281–282, 287, 294, 297, 334–335; Scheu, *Der Weg Ins Ungewisse*, 97–98; Louis P. Lochner, *What About Germany?* (New York: Dodd, Mead and Company, 1942): 326; Unfortunately, the whispers of corruption surrounding Best's professional activities did not end in Vienna. Louis Lochner recorded that the Nazis coaxed him into treason with the promise of quick riches in Germany's lucrative black market trade. Shortly after Best's defection, he wrote his former colleagues still interned at Bad Nauheim and offered to provide foodstuffs and other necessities to their relatives inside the Reich for a price. On October 13, 1943, Best denied that he was "running" the German black market, promising that despite his business activities he would be no richer after the war. BBC, *Monitoring Service*, October 13, 1943. FBI files show that Best believed that a story was the property of the journalist, to treat as he or she pleased. Aside from suppressing stories, he would fabricate them for a price. Field Report, January 26, 1943, Doc. No. 100–103780–55, Robert H. Best Files, FBI.

20. Scheu, *Der Weg Ins Ungewisse*, 19.

21. Shirer, "The American Radio Traitors," 398. Field Report, January 9, 1943, Doc. No. 100–103780–48, Robert H. Best Files, FBI.

22. BBC, *Monitoring Service*, May 13, 1942.

23. Baillie, *High Tension*, 12.

24. William L. Shirer, *Berlin Diary: The Journal of a Foreign Correspondent, 1934–1941* (New York: Alfred A. Knopf, 1942): 81; John Hohenberg, *Foreign Correspondents: The Great Reporters and Their Times* (New York: Columbia University Press, 1964), 327–328; Douglas Reed, *Insanity Fair* (London: Jonathan Cape, 1964): 374–375; United Press correspondent Harold Ettlinger and New York *Tribune* reporter George Seldes agree that Best did not exhibit pro-German sympathies prior to the Anschluss. Harold Ettlinger, *The Axis on the Air* (New York: Bobbs-Merrill Co., 1943): 48; George Seldes to Author, September 5, 1979; Seldes, *Tell the Truth and Run* (New York: Greenberg Publisher, 1943): 222.

25. Shirer, "The American Radio Traitors," 399; Ettlinger, *The Axis on the Air*, 49; Scheu, *Der Weg Ins Ungewisse*, 298.

26. William L. Shirer to Author, August 27, 1979.

27. Baillie, *High Tension*, 127; Field Report, January 26, 1943, Doc. No. 100–103780–55, Robert H. Best Files, FBI.

28. Joseph W. Grigg to Author, March 27, 1980.

29. Scheu, *Der Weg Ins Ungewisse*, 298; Atlanta *Constitution*, June 18, 1942.

30. Shirer, *Midcentury Journey*, 53–54; Shirer, *The American Radio Traitors*, 399; Shirer, *20th Century Journey: A Memoir of a Life and the Times* (New York: Simon and Schuster, 1976): 439–441.

31. Margaret Boveri, *Treason in the Twentieth Century* (London: MacDonald Publishers, 1956): 178–200.

32. Columbia (S.C.) *State*, June 8, 1942.

33. For accounts of the hardships and callousness of the trade, see Theodore Edward Kruglak, *The Foreign Correspondents: A Study of the Men and Women Reporting for the American Information Media in Western Europe* (Geneva: Librairie E. Droz, 1955): 50, 61; Eugene Lyons, "Why Foreign Correspondents Go Home," *Saturday Review*, vol. 16, No. 18 (August 28, 1937): 4, 17; George Seldes, "The Poisoned Springs of World News," *Harper's*, vol. 169 (November 1934): 719, 731; John Gunther, "Dateline Vienna," *Harper's*, vol. 171 (July 1935): 198–208.

34. Dorothy Thompson to Charles W. Bartlett, April 12, 1948, Dorothy Thompson Collection.

35. BBC, *Monitoring Service*, September 18, 1942.

36. Columbia (S.C.) *State*, June 8, 1942.

37. Joe Alex Morris, *Deadline Every Minute: The Story of the United Press* (New York: Greenwood Press, 1968): 218.

38. BBC, *Monitoring Service*, March 31, 1944.

39. Boston *Daily Globe*, April 2, 1948.

40. BBC, *Monitoring Service*, June 2, 1943.

41. Charleston *News and Courier*, January 12, 1941.

42. *Best Deposition*, 253–254.

43. *Editor & Publisher* (June 6, 1942): 3, 4, 30, 32, 38; "Back from the Axis," *Time*, vol. 30, No. 24 (June 15, 1942): 69.

44. Frederick Oechsner to Author, April 25, 1980.

45. Francis Cunningham to Author, March 26, 1980.

46. Boston *Daily Globe*, April 1, April 6, 1948; New York *Herald Tribune*, April 2, 1948; BBC, *Monitoring Service*, May 28, 1943; A classmate recalled for the FBI that even as a college student Best had always had the compulsion to pull off "one

big coup." It was his belief that Best's decision to remain in Europe was part of this compulsion. Field Report, July 6, 1945, Doc. No. 100–103780, Robert H. Best Files, FBI.

47. *Best Deposition*, 253–259; Washington, D.C., *Evening Star*, April 2, 1948.

48. BBC, *Monitoring Service*, April 10, 1942.

49. Best did not reveal his identity over the air until May 21, 1942. E. S. Pisko, "Tuning in on the Traitors," *Christian Science*, vol. 18, (July 18, 1942): 6; Shirer, "The American Radio Traitors," 399–400; "Nazi Best," *Time*, vol. 40, No. 1 (July 8, 1942): 2–3; Joseph M. McLaughlin to Author, February 12, 1980.

50. BBC, *Monitoring Service*, April 17; May 13; June 24, 1942.

51. Z. A. B. Zeman, *Nazi Propaganda* (New York: Oxford University Press, 1964): 172–179; Derrick Sington and Arthur Weidenfeld, *The Goebbels Experiment: A Study of the Nazi Propaganda Machine* (New York: Yale University Press, 1943): 181–190. Field Report, January 5, 1943, Doc. No. 100–103780–44, Robert H. Best Files, FBI; Field Report, July 6, 1945, Doc. No. 100–103780, Robert H. Best Files, FBI.

52. *Editor & Publisher*, April 10, 1948, 76; BBC, *Monitoring Service*, September 16, 1942; Boston *Daily Globe*, April 7, 1948.

53. Boston *Daily Globe*, April 6, 8, 1948.

54. Boston *Herald*, April 7, 1948.

55. New York *Herald Tribune*, April 3, 1948; BBC, *Monitoring Service*, October 21; December 29, 1942; January 20, 21; February 26, 1943.

56. BBC, *Monitoring Service*, January 27, 1943.

57. Ibid., January 22; February 3, 1943.

58. Ibid., June 3, 1943.

59. Ibid., September 24, 1943.

60. Boston *Daily Globe*, April 2, 14, 1948.

61. William Greenough Schofield, *Treason Trail* (New York: Rand McNally and Company, 1964), 120; *Best Deposition*, 266–267. For a concise account of Best's working colleagues, see Boveri, *Treason in the Twentieth Century*, 176–181; Werner Schwipps and Gerhart Goebel, *Wortschlacht Im Äther: Der Deutsche Auslands Rundfunk in Weltkreig* (Berlin: Haude and Spenersche, 1971): 70–71.

62. BBC, *Monitoring Service*, March 5, 1943.

63. Ibid., March 29, 1944.

64. Ibid., May 9, 1943.

65. London *Times*, July 27, 1943; New York *Times*, July 27, 1943.

66. BBC, *Monitoring Service*, June 30; July 27, 28, 1944.

67. Ibid., July 2, 1944.

68. Ibid., October 6, 1944.

69. Ibid., January 17, 1945.

70. *Best Deposition*, 267–268; Schofield, *Treason Trail*, 42.

71. Schofield, *Treason Trail*, 96; Federal Supplement: *Cases Argued and Determined in the District Courts of the United States and the Court of Claims*, vol. 76 (St. Paul: West Publishing Co.): 654–655; Nathaniel Weyl, *Treason: The Story of Disloyalty and Betrayal in American History* (Washington, D.C.: Public Affairs Press, 1950): 366.

72. New York *Times*, February 13; April 3, 6, 1948; Hastings William Sackville Russell, Twelfth Duke of Bedford, was well known in Britain for his pro-German sympathies. He maintained close friendships with members of Sir Oswald Mosley's British Union of Fascists. After the outbreak of war the duke joined the British

Council for Christian Settlement in Europe, whose officers John Beckett and Captain Gordon Canning had been former members of The Link, an organization which had been disbanded as an agency of enemy propaganda. Russell went so far as to initiate a private peace offensive with Germany through its Dublin legation. John, Duke of Bedford, *A Silver-Plated Spoon* (London: Carsell and Co., 1959): 154–164; *Time*, vol. 62, No. 16 (October 19, 1953): 104.

73. Washington, D.C., *Evening Star*, April 2, 1948.

74. New York *Times*, April 15, 1948.

75. Ibid., July 1, 1948; New York *Herald Tribune*, April 17, 1948.

76. R. H. Best to Harry S. Truman, July 10, 1950, Harry S. Truman Library, Independence, Missouri. Xerox copy in possession of Author.

77. New York *Times*, February 27, 1951; December 21, 1952.

CHAPTER 5

1. Records of the U.S. District Court for the District of Massachusetts, Record Group 276, Criminal Case No. 4296, Stenographic Record, vol. I, Federal Archives and Records Center, Waltham, Massachusetts, 126–129. Hereafter cited [Dr. Clarence A.] *Bonner Testimony*; William Greenough Schofield, *Treason Trail* (New York: Rand McNally and Company, 1964); 20–21.

2. New York *Times*, April 1, 1934; Baltimore *Sun*, April 1, 1934; *Handbook of the Best Private Schools of the United States and Canada: An Annual Publication* (Boston: Porter E. Sargent, 1915): 140; *Bonner Testimony*, 129.

3. *Bonner Testimony*, 127.

4. Charles J. Rolo, *Radio Goes to War: The Fourth Front* (New York: G. P. Putnam's Sons, 1940): 103; *Newsweek* (August 11, 1947): 20; *Time* (July 7, 1947): 22; Field Report, December 17, 1942, Doc. No. 100–32785–39, Douglas Chandler Files, FBI, Department of Justice, Washington, D.C.

5. Schofield, *Treason Trail*, 21; *Newsweek* (August 11, 1947): 20. From 1929 to 1931, Chandler was assistant editor of the Baltimore *Sunday American*. "Memorandum," October 16, 1942, Doc. No. 100–32785–16, Douglas Chandler Files, FBI.

6. New York *Times*, June 3; August 27, 1924; January 10, 1929; Nathaniel Weyl, *Treason: The Story of Disloyalty and Betrayal in American History* (Washington, D.C.: Public Affairs Press, 1950): 367–368; *Bonner Testimony*, 132; Records of the U.S. District Court for the District of Massachusetts, Record Group 276, Criminal Case No. 4296, Stenographic Record, vol. II, Federal Archives and Records Center, Waltham, Massachusetts, 601–602. Hereafter cited [J. Eldon] *Dunn Deposition*. For information on Alexander Jay Wurtz see *Who Was Who in America*, vol. 16 (Chicago: A. N. Marquis Company, 1942): 2424; New York *Times*, January 22, 1932; Field Report, February 23, 1943, Doc. No. 100–32785–58, Douglas Chandler Files, FBI.

7. Confidential Source to Author, November 10; November 11, 1987.

8. *Bonner Testimony*, 130–131.

9. *Newsweek* (August 11, 1947): 20; *Dunn Deposition*, 583.

10. *Dunn Deposition*, 584–585.

11. Ibid.

12. Ibid., 586; Schofield, *Treason Trail*, 31.

13. *Dunn Deposition*, 587.

14. Ibid., 588–589.

15. Ibid., 590–591.

16. Confidential Source to Author, November 11, 1987.

17. BBC, *Monitoring Service*, May 27, 1941; *Dunn Deposition*, 591; Schofield, *Treason Trail*, 34.

18. *Dunn Deposition*, 592. Also see Douglas Chandler, "Changing Berlin," *National Geographic*, vol. LXXI, No. 2 (February 1937): 131–177; ibid., "Flying around the Baltic," *National Geographic*, vol. LXXIII, No. 3 (June 1938): 767–806; ibid., "The Transformation of Turkey," *National Geographic*, vol. LXXV, No. 1 (January 1939): 1–50; ibid., "Kaleidoscopic Land of Europe's Youngest King," *National Geographic*, vol. LXXV, No. 4 (June 1939): 691–738.

19. George Seldes, "Geographic Published U.S. Traitor, Pro-Fascist Dope of Reader's Digest Man," *In Fact*, vol. VII, No. 26 (October 4, 1943): 1–2; See, too, ibid., ed., *In Fact*, vol. VIII, No. 23 (March 13, 1944); ibid., ed., *In Fact*, vol. XIV, No. 16 (January 20, 1947); ibid., ed., *In Fact*, vol. XV, No. 13 (June 30, 1947).

20. Roger Burlingame, *Don't Let Them Scare You: The Life and Times of Elmer Davis* (New York: J. B. Lippincott Company, 1961): 294.

21. Chandler, "Changing Berlin," 131–177.

22. Ibid., "Flying around the Baltic," 785.

23. *Dunn Deposition*, 593.

24. Justice D. Doenecke, "A Military Observer in Hitler's Reich," *Reviews in American History*, vol. XII, No. 4 (December 1984): 583–588; Robert Hessen, *Berlin Alert: The Memoirs and Reports of Truman Smith* (Stanford, Calif.: Hoover Institution Press, 1984): VII–XX.

25. J. C. Poggendorff, *Biographisch-Literarisches Handwörterbuch Der Exakten Naturwissenschaften* (Berlin: Akademie-Verlag, 1956): 309; John Turkevich and Ludmilla B. Turkevich, comp., *Prominent Scientists of Continental Europe* (New York: American Elsevier Publishing Company, 1968): 72; *Geologie: Zeitschrift Für Das Gesamtgebiet Der Geologie Und Mineralogie Sourè Der Angewandten Geophysik Mit Beiheften*, January 4, 1955 (Berlin: Akademie-Verlag, 1955): 3, 309; Fred Taylor, ed., *The Goebbels Diaries: 1939–41* (New York: G. P. Putnam's Sons, 1983): 26, 357; J. A. Cole, *Lord Haw-Haw & William Joyce* (New York: Farrar, Strauss & Giroux, 1964): 59, 104–105.

26. *Dunn Deposition*, 594–595.

27. D. Talbot Rice, comp., *The University Portraits* (Edinburgh: Edinburgh University Press, 1957): 227; *Who Was Who, 1951–1960*, vol. V (New York: The MacMillan Company, 1961): 966.

28. *Dunn Deposition*, 596; Field Report, March 15, 1943, Doc. No. 100–32785–62, Douglas Chandler Files, FBI.

29. Richard Griffiths, *Fellow Travellers of the Right: British Enthusiasts for Nazi Germany, 1933–39* (London: Constable, 1980): 179–182, 277, 307–310, 342; Admiral Sir Barry Domville, *From Admiral to Cabin Boy* (London: Boswell Publishing Co., 1947): 54–56.

30. Griffiths, *Fellow Travellers of the Right*, 158–163, 368; John Marlow, *Late Victorian: The Life of Sir Arnold Talbot Wilson* (London: Cresset Press, 1967): 342–384.

31. Chandler, "Kaleidoscopic Land of Europe's Youngest King," 730.

32. *Dunn Deposition*, 597.

33. Records of the U.S. District Court for the District of Massachusetts, Records Group 276, Criminal Case No. 4296, Stenographic Record, vol. III, Federal Archives and Records Center, Waltham, Massachusetts; Douglas Chandler to Killian Family,

August 3, 1940, Defendant's Exhibit B, 1382–1384; Douglas Chandler to Sumner Welles (undated), Government's Exhibit 37, 1375–1380.

34. *Dunn Deposition*, 598; Harold Ettlinger, *The Axis on the Air* (New York: Bobbs-Merrill Company, 1943): 51.

35. Records of the U.S. District Court for the District of Massachusetts, Record Group 276, Criminal Case No. 4296, Stenographic Record, vol. II, Federal Archives and Records Center, Waltham, Massachusetts, 716–717. Hereafter cited *G.O.E. von Lilienfeld Testimony*.

36. Confidential Source to Author, November 11, 1987.

37. *Dunn Deposition*, 599.

38. Ibid., 600–601.

39. Ibid., 602–604.

40. Ibid., 604.

41. Ibid., 605.

42. Ibid., 606–609.

43. BBC, *Monitoring Service*, April 26, 1941.

44. Ibid., May 20, 1941.

45. Ibid., May 26, 1941.

46. Ibid., April 26, 1942; Field Report, March 15, 1943, Doc. No. 100–32785–62, Douglas Chandler Files, FBI.

47. BBC, *Monitoring Service*, March 31, 1944.

48. *Dunn Deposition*, 609–613.

49. Records of the U.S. District Court for the District of Massachusetts, Record Group 276, Criminal Case No. 4296, Stenographic Record, vol. I, Federal Archives and Records Center, Waltham, Massachusetts, 88. Hereafter cited *E. V. Sittler Testimony*.

50. *Dunn Deposition*, 600–602; Records of the U.S. District Court for the District of Massachusetts, Record Group 276, Criminal Case No. 4296, Stenographic Record, vol. II, Federal Archives and Records Center, Waltham, Massachusetts, 822–823. Hereafter cited *Margarette Eggers Testimony*.

51. Records of the U.S. District Court for the District of Massachusetts, Record Group 276, Criminal Case No. 4296, Stenographic Record, vol. III, Federal Archives and Records Center, Waltham, Massachusetts, 982–983. *Lily Margaret Sittler Testimony*, 1119. Hereafter cited as *Gerdt Wagner Testimony*.

52. *E. V. Sittler Testimony*, 90–91; *G.O.E. von Lilienfeld Testimony*, 724; BBC, *Monitoring Service*, April 26, 1942; Schofield, *Treason Trail*, 74.

53. *E. V. Sittler Testimony*, 85, 94–95.

54. Schofield, *Treason Trail*, 72; *E. V. Sittler Testimony*, 89.

55. *E. V. Sittler Testimony*, 81; Schofield, *Treason Trail*, 59.

56. *E. V. Sittler Testimony*, 85–89; Rolo, *Radio Goes to War*, 103.

57. Records of the U.S. District Court for the District of Massachusetts, Record Group 276, Criminal Case No. 4296, Stenographic Record, vol. II, Federal Archives and Records Center, Waltham, Massachusetts, 780–784. Hereafter cited *Anton Winkelnkemper Testimony*.

58. *Gerdt Wagner Testimony*, 1088–1092.

59. Ibid., 1084–1086.

60. *E. V. Sittler Testimony*, 916–919.

61. BBC, *Monitoring Service*, June 7, 1941; Margaret Boveri, *Treason in the Twentieth Century* (London: MacDonald, 1956): 179–180.

62. BBC, *Monitoring Service*, June 16, 17, 1941; April 28; May 24, 26, 1942; January 16, 19, 20, 1944.

63. Ibid., October 2, 1941.

64. Ibid., February 22, 1942.

65. Ibid., March 10, 1942.

66. Ibid., April 16, 1942.

67. Ibid., March 16, 1943.

68. Ibid., February 6, 1944.

69. Ibid., January 11, 1945.

70. Ibid., January 12, 1944.

71. Ibid., February 9, 1943.

72. Ibid., March 9, 11; April 29, 1943.

73. Ibid., May 18, 1943.

74. Ibid., May 14, 1942.

75. Ibid., January 26, 28; February 4, 1943.

76. *E. V. Sittler Testimony*, 92–93, 924–925; Records of the U.S. District Court for the District of Massachusetts, Record Group 276, Criminal Case No. 4296, Stenographic Record, vol. II, Federal Archives and Records Center, Waltham, Massachusetts, 744–745. Hereafter cited *Dietrich Abrens Testimony*.

77. BBC, *Monitoring Service*, June 28, 1942.

78. Ibid., April 21, 1942.

79. Ibid., March 22, 1942.

80. Ibid., September 13, 1942.

81. *E. V. Sittler Testimony*, 77–80; Schofield, *Treason Trail*, 80.

82. *E. V. Sittler Testimony*, 81–82.

83. Ibid., 82–85.

84. *L. M. Sittler Testimony*, 1022–1025.

85. *E. V. Sittler Testimony*, 900–901.

86. Ibid., 908.

87. Ibid., 845–857.

88. *Gerdt Wagner Testimony*, 1081–1082, 1106–1107.

89. Ibid., 1095–1096; *E. V. Sittler Testimony*, 840.

90. *Dunn Deposition*, 615–618; *Gerdt Wagner Testimony*, 1095–1108.

91. *Gerdt Wagner Testimony*, 1100–1104; Schofield, *Treason Trail*, 77–78.

92. Weyl, *Treason*, 370–371.

93. BBC, *Monitoring Service*, June 4, 1942.

94. Ibid., March 1, 1944.

95. Ibid., February 4; July 18, 1944.

96. *Dunn Deposition*, 622.

97. BBC, *Monitoring Service*, July 5, 1942.

98. Ibid., February 20; May 14, 1944.

99. *E. V. Sittler Testimony*, 874–877.

100. New York *Times*, June 10, 1947; Special Interrogation Series, No. 20, July 12, 1945, Doc. No. 100–32785–144, Military Intelligence Service, War Department, Washington, D.C.

101. For an elaboration of these arguments, see *Federal Supplement: Cases Argued*

and Determined in the District Courts of the United States and the Court of Claims, vol. 72 (St. Paul: West Publishing Co.): 230–238.

102. William Schofield to Author, December 20, 1982.

103. Weyl, *Treason*, 371.

104. *Federal Supplement*, vol. 72, 238.

105. Boston *Globe*, August 10, 1963.

106. Andrew F. Oehmann (Exec. Asst. to the Attorney General) to Lee C. White (Asst. Spec. Counsel to the President), January 15, 1962. John Fitzgerald Kennedy Presidential Library, Boston, Massachusetts.

107. Boston *Globe*, September 25, 1963.

108. Sylvia Chandler to President John F. Kennedy, July 11, 1963. John Fitzgerald Kennedy Presidential Library.

109. Walter M. Hanshalter (Rector, Church of St. Luke and the Epiphany, Philadelphia, Penn.) to President John F. Kennedy, July 31, 1963. John Fitzgerald Kennedy Presidential Library.

CHAPTER 6

1. *In Fact*, vol. 5, No. 25 (September 28, 1942).

2. Phillip M. Runkel (Curator, Dorothy Day Collection, Marquette University) to Author, December 30, 1985; *Who's Who in America*, 41st ed., 1980–1981, vol. 1; Charles Moritz, ed., *Current Biography Yearbook* (New York: H. W. Wilson, Co., 1962): 94–96.

3. William D. Miller, *Dorothy Day: A Biography* (San Francisco: Harper & Row Publishers, 1982): 2–7.

4. Ibid., 10.

5. Ibid., 14; William D. Miller, *A Harsh and Dreadful Love: Dorothy Day and the Catholic Worker Movement* (New York: Liveright Publishers, 1973), 37; Dorothy Day, *The Long Loneliness: An Autobiography* (New York: Image Books, 1959): 24.

6. Dorothy Day, *The Eleventh Virgin*, (New York: Albert and Charles Boni, 1924): 37–38.

7. Day, *The Long Loneliness*, 33.

8. Day, *The Eleventh Virgin*, 11; Miller, *Dorothy Day*, 15–16.

9. Day, *The Eleventh Virgin*, 21.

10. Ibid., 30; Miller, *Dorothy Day*, 24.

11. Day, *The Long Loneliness*, p. 35; Mel Piehl, *Breaking Bread: The Catholic Worker and the Origin of Catholic Radicalism in America* (Philadelphia: Temple University Press, 1982): 6; Miller, *A Harsh and Dreadful Love*, 39; Oliver Knight, ed., *I Protest: Selected Disquisitions of E. W. Scripps* (Madison: The University of Wisconsin, 1966): 208–209; Negley D. Cochran, *E. W. Scripps* (New York: Harcourt, Brace and Co., 1933): 130–144; Harry Lewis Golden, *Carl Sandburg* (Cleveland: World Publishing Co., 1961): 191–193; Richard Crowder, *Carl Sandburg* (New York: Twayne Publishers, 1964): 43–48.

12. Donald Day, *Onward Christian Soldiers* (Torrance, Calif.: Noontide Press, 1982): vii; Promotional biography of Donald Day (May 11, 1942), Vertical Files, Chicago *Tribune* Archives.

13. Joseph Gies, *The Colonel of Chicago* (New York: E. P. Dutton, 1979): 108;

George Seldes, *Tell the Truth and Run* (New York: Greenberg Publisher, 1953); 128–129.

14. New York *Times*, October 23, 1948; Robert K. Murray, *Red Scare: A Study in National Hysteria, 1919–1920* (Minneapolis: University of Minnesota Press, 1955): 98–99, 274–275; *Revolutionary Radicalism: Report of the Joint Legislative Committee Investigating Seditious Activities, Filed April 24, 1920, in the Senate of the State of New York*, Part 1, vol. 1 (Albany: J. B. Lyon Company, 1920): 639–657; Field Report, November 3, 1943, Doc. No. 62–71129–6, Donald Day Files, FBI, Department of Justice, Washington, D.C.

15. Promotional biography of Donald Day (May 11, 1942), Chicago *Tribune* Archives; "Who's Who Abroad" (undated), Vertical Files, Chicago *Tribune* Archives.

16. George Seldes to Author, July 23, 1983; January 19, 1985; Arthur U. Pope, *Maxim Litvinoff* (New York: L. B. Fischer, 1943): 172–178.

17. George Seldes, "The Men Who Fake the News," *New Masses*, vol. XXXIV (January 30, 1940): 14–17; Virginia Gardner, *Friend and Lover: The Life of Louise Bryant* (New York: Horizon Press, 1982): 347; Donald Day to Marlen E. Pew, June 8, 16; July 20; August 16, 1921; Donald Day to E. C. Reeves, August 2, 1921, Kurt Von Wiegand Collection, Box 8, Hoover Institution on War, Revolution and Peace, Stanford, California.

18. William L. Shirer to Author, December 4, 1984.

19. *In Fact*, vol. 5, No. 25 (September 28, 1942): 1.

20. Day, *Onward Christian Soldiers*, vii-viii; Walter Trohan to Author, January 27; March 15; May 9, 1985. On March 15, Trohan wrote: "I do . . . ask you to consider anything from either of the Seldes, who were enthused by the Russian experiment, so much so that they were fellow travellers if not more."

21. George Seldes to Author, February 1, 1985; Robert W. Desmond, *Crisis and Conflict: World News Reporting between Two Wars, 1920–1940* (Iowa City: University of Iowa Press, 1982): 40–41. For Seldes' assessment of Colonel Robert McCormick see "My Decade with Col. McCormick," *Lost Generation Journal*, vol. 2, No. 3 (Fall 1974): 24–29.

22. George Seldes, "Donald Day," unpublished biographical sketch in possession of the author; Miller, *Dorothy Day*, 311.

23. Day, *Onward Christian Soldiers*, 43–44.

24. Ibid.

25. Ibid., 3–4.

26. Ibid., 43–45.

27. Ibid., 47–51. Trohan recalled:

Day made it clear he would not tolerate censorship in Russia, which is why he was pilloried. And the Communists did not like his stories from Riga, which came from many discontented [individuals], but offered a picture those based in Moscow could not give or could not get out if they wished.

Trohan to Author, December 17, 1984.

28. Ibid., 133–135; "Who's Who Abroad," Chicago *Tribune* Archives.

29. Day, *Onward Christian Soldiers*, 136–143.

30. Ibid., 155–157.

31. Ibid., 68, 94.

32. Ibid., 78–80.

33. Ibid., 75–77.

34. Beatrice Farnsworth, *William C. Bullitt and the Soviet Union* (Bloomington: Indiana University Press, 1967): 116–119; Maxine Block, ed. *Current Biography: Who's Who and Why, 1940* (New York: H. W. Wilson, Co., 1940): 122–125.

35. Chicago *Tribune*, March 31, 1929; October 23, 1932.

36. Ibid., October 23, 1932.

37. Ibid., August 30, 1933.

38. Jerome E. Edwards, *The Foreign Policy of Col. McCormick's Tribune, 1929–1941* (Reno: University of Nevada Press, 1971): 104–105. Also see Elmer Gertz, "Chicago's Adult Delinquent: 'The Tribune,' " *Public Opinion Quarterly*, vol. 8, No. 3 (Fall 1944): 419–424.

39. Day, *Onward Christian Soldiers*, 120.

40. "From *Tribune* Faker to Nazi Stooge," Chicago *Daily Times*, September 7, 1944; Lloyd Wendt, Chicago Tribune: *The Rise of a Great American Newspaper* (New York: Rand McNally & Co., 1979): 573; George Seldes, *Lords of the Press* (New York: Julian Messner, 1938): 55–56; ibid., *The Facts Are . . . A Guide to Falsehood and Propaganda in the Press and Radio* (New York: In Fact, 1940): 86–87; Chicago *Tribune*, August 9; October 14, 1936.

41. Day, *Onward Christian Soldiers*, 53–55.

42. Ibid., 56–61.

43. Ibid., 186–195.

44. Chicago *Tribune*, December 4, 1939.

45. Ibid., December 8, 12, 1939.

46. Ibid., December 13, 16, 1939.

47. Ibid., February 5, 1940; Day, *Onward Christian Soldiers*, 194–195.

48. Chicago *Tribune*, February 7, 24, 1940.

49. Day, *Onward Christian Soldiers*, 166; Chicago *Tribune*, February 25; March 3, 13, 14, 1940.

50. Chicago *Tribune*, April 16, 20, 1940; Day, *Onward Christian Soldiers*, 171.

51. Chicago *Tribune*, April 26, 30, 1940; Day, *Onward Christian Soldiers*, 176–177.

52. Day, *Onward Christian Soldiers*, 178–179.

53. Chicago *Tribune*, May 7, 8, 9, 1940.

54. Ibid., June 18, 1940; Day, *Onward Christian Soldiers*, 39.

55. Chicago *Tribune*, July 3, 5, 22, 1940.

56. Ibid., July 25, 1940; Day, *Onward Christian Soldiers*, 181; Visvaldis Mangulis, *Latvia in the Wars of the 20th Century* (Princeton Junction, N.J.: Cognition Books, 1983): 87.

57. Chicago *Tribune*, October 18, 20; December 9, 24, 1940; March 24, April 10, 1941.

58. Chicago *Tribune*, April 10, 11, 17; June 14, 15, 20, 1941.

59. Ibid., December 7, 1940; June 1, 21, 1941.

60. Ibid., June 23, 1941. Donald Day to Samuel H. Day, April 24, 1941, Donald Day Folder, Hoover Institution on War, Revolution and Peace, Stanford, California.

61. Chicago *Tribune*, July 7, 8, 1941.

62. Ibid., July 24, 1941; John McCutcheon to Author, June 4, 1985.

63. Chicago *Tribune*, July 25, 26, 1941.

64. Ibid., July 27, 1941. Harold Lavine and James Wechsler, *War Propaganda and the United States* (New Haven, Conn.: Yale University Press, 1940): 312–313.

65. Chicago *Tribune*, June 24, 25; August 28; September 11, 12, 1941.

66. Ibid., September 17, 1941.

67. Ibid., September 21, 1941.

68. Ibid., October 28, 1941.

69. Ibid., November 7, 12, 1941.

70. Ibid., February 3, 10, 1942.

71. Ibid., February 21, 1942.

72. *In Fact*, vol. 5, No. 25 (September 28, 1942): 1–2.

73. Chicago *Tribune*, November 30, 1941; February 21, 22; March 3, 1942.

74. Ibid., March 9, 1942.

75. Elmer Gertz, *The People vs. the Chicago* Tribune (Chicago: Union for Democratic Action, 1942): 28; *P.M.*, March 18, 1942; Elmer Gertz to Author, February 21, 1985.

76. BBC, *Monitoring Service*, September 21, 1944; Chicago *Tribune*, September 15, 1942; Day, *Onward Christian Soldiers*, 1–6. It was reported that Day meant to join one of several groups of foreign volunteers led by an Irishman. New York *Times*, September 15, 19, 1942. For a discussion of the regular and irregular German-Finnish units operating inside Finland, see Kristina Nyman, *Finland's War Years, 1939–1945* (Helsinki: Society of Military History, 1973): IX–XXXII; Roger James Bender and Hugh P. Taylor, *Uniforms, Organization and History of the Waffen-SS* (Mountain View, Calif.: R. J. Bender Publishers, 1971): 148–151; Bruce Quarrie, *Hitler's Samurai: The Waffen-SS in Action* (New York: Arco Publishing, 1983): 30–34; S. J. Drayton to J. Edgar Hoover, October 7, 1943, Doc. No. 62–71129–5, Donald Day Files, FBI.

77. John McCutcheon to Author, June 4, 1985; O. John Rogge, *The Official German Report: Nazi Penetration 1924–1942, Pan-Arabism 1939–Today* (New York: Thomas Yoseloff, 1961): 311–312; Chicago *Sun*, September 14, 1945.

78. Chicago *Sun*, July 9, 1945; New York *Times*, July 8, 1945; J. A. Cole, *Lord Haw-Haw & William Joyce: The Full Story* (New York: Farrar, Straus & Giroux, 1964): 219–220.

79. BBC, *Monitoring Service*, August 31, 1944; Chicago *Sun*, August 31, 1944.

80. BBC, *Monitoring Service*, September 21, 1944.

81. Ibid., October 7, October 19, 1944. By early December 1944, Day's name topped an Allies list of nearly 100 U.S. and British traitors in service to Nazi Germany. *Editor & Publisher*, December 9, 1944, 16.

82. BBC, *Monitoring Service*, February 24, 1945.

83. Ibid., February 17, 1945.

84. Ibid., January 13, 1945.

85. Ibid., March 29, 1945.

86. Chicago *Tribune*, March 30, 1945; Chicago *Sun*, December 24, 1946; New York *Times*, December 24, 1946; Chicago *Tribune*, December 24, 1946.

87. Benedict A. Henderson to Dorothy Day, February 21, 1947, Dorothy Day–Catholic Worker Collection Series D–8, Box 4, Division of Special Collections, Marquette University, Milwaukee, Wisconsin.

88. John McCutcheon to Author, June 14, 1985; Walter Trohan to Author, December 19, 1984; May 31, 1985; Miller, *Dorothy Day*, 509–510; Chicago *Tribune*, October 1, 1966; Donald Day to Kurt Von Wiegand, July 20, 1953, Kurt Von Wiegand Collection, Box 8, Hoover Institution on War, Revolution and Peace, Stanford, California; John Foster Dulles to U.S. Embassy, Helsinki, May 17, 1957, Doc. No. 62–71129–NR5–17–57, Department of State, Washington, D.C.; Donald Day

to Senator Joseph McCarthy, February 26, 1950, Exhibit "A" A/R, File IV, 4116, Department of State.

EPILOGUE

1. Robert E. Park, *Race and Culture* (Glencoe, Ill.: Free Press, 1950): 318, 356; E. V. Stonequist, *The Marginal Man: A Study in Personality and Culture Conflict* (New York: Charles Scribner's Sons, 1937), XV, 139–179; Francis Biddle, *In Brief Authority* (Westport, Conn.: Greenwood Press, 1962): 290–292.

Selected Bibliography

MANUSCRIPT MATERIALS AND PRIMARY CORRESPONDENTS

Robert H. Best Folder/Vertical File, Department of Special Collections, South Carolina Division, University of South Carolina.

Donald Day Folders/Vertical File, Chicago *Tribune* Archives, Chicago, Illinois.

Dorothy Day-Catholic Worker Collection, Division of Special Collections, Marquette University, Milwaukee, Wisconsin.

E. L. Delaney Folders/Vertical File, Division of Special Collections, Glendale Public Library, Glendale California.

John F. Kennedy Papers, John Fitzgerald Kennedy Presidential Library, Boston, Massachusetts.

Max Otto Koischwitz Files, Hunter College Archives, Hunter College, New York City.

Katherine Anne Porter Collection, McKeldin Library, University of Maryland, College Park.

William Howard Taft Papers, Series 3 & 8, Presidential Papers Microfilm.

Dorothy Thompson Collection, The George Arent Research Library, Syracuse University, Syracuse, New York.

Harry S. Truman papers, Truman Library, Independence, Missouri.

H. G. Wells Collection, University Library, University of Illinois, Urbana-Champaign.

Kurt von Wiegand Collection, Hoover Institution on War, Revolution and Peace, Stanford, California.

Woodrow Wilson Papers, Series 3, Presidential Papers Microfilm.

Beverly Place Chance

Francis Cunningham
Elmer Gertz
Joan Givner
Vivian Glaus
Joseph W. Grigg
Louis J. Halle
Joseph C. Harsch
Thomas J. Jeffers
John McCutcheon
Joseph McLaughlin
Frederick Oechsner
William Schofield
George Seldes
William L. Shirer
Walter Trohan
Dame Rebecca West

OFFICIAL RECORDS AND PUBLICATIONS

Jane Anderson Files, Federal Bureau of Investigation, Department of Justice, Washington, D.C.

Jane Anderson Files, Division of Communication and Records, Department of State, Washington, D.C.

Robert H. Best Files, Federal Bureau of Investigation, Department of Justice, Washington, D.C.

Douglas Chandler Files, Federal Bureau of Investigation, Department of Justice, Washington, D.C.

Congressional Record, vol. 95, Part 13, 81st Congress, 1st Session (March 14, 1949– May 10, 1949): A2319.

Congressional Record, vol. 95, Part 15, 81st Congress, 1st Session (July 5, 1949–August 25, 1949): A4551.

Donald Day Files, Federal Bureau of Investigation, Department of Justice, Washington, D.C.

Donald Day Files, Division of Communication and Records, Department of State, Washington, D.C.

E. L. Delaney Files, Federal Bureau of Investigation, Department of Justice, Washington, D.C.

E. L. Delaney Files, Office of the Attorney General, Department of Justice, Washington, D.C.

E. L. Delaney Files, Communications Section, Department of Justice, Washington, D.C.

E. L. Delaney Files, Division of Records, Department of Justice, Washington, D.C.

E. L. Delaney Files, Criminal Internal Security Section, Department of Justice, Washington, D.C.

E. L. Delaney Files, Criminal Division, Department of Justice, Washington, D.C.

E. L. Delaney Files, Department of State, Washington, D.C.

E. L. Delaney Files, Vital Statistics Branch, Department of Health Services, Sacramento, California.

Constance Drexel Files, Federal Bureau of Investigation, Department of Justice, Washington, D.C.

Constance Drexel, *Disarmament, Security and Control: A Draft of Convention for Disarmament, Security and Control Based on the Kellogg Pact*, Senate Document No. 33, 74th Congress, 1st Session, Washington, D.C.: Government Printing Office, 1935.

Federal Reporter, vol. 182F. 2d. St. Paul: West Publishing Co., 1951.

Federal Supplement: Cases Argued and Determined in the District Courts of the United States and the Court of Claims, vol. 72. St. Paul: West Publishing Co.

Federal Supplement: Cases Argued and Determined in the District Courts of the United States and the Court of Claims, vol. 76. St. Paul: West Publishing Co.

Foreign Relations of the United States, Diplomatic Papers (Europe), 1936, vol. II. United States: Government Printing Office, 1934.

Grade Book, N.D.: Wofford College Fitting School, Wofford College Archives, Wofford College, Spartanburg, South Carolina.

Frederick W. Kaltenbach Files, Federal Bureau of Investigation, Department of Justice, Washington, D.C.

Max Otto Koischwitz Files, Federal Bureau of Investigation, Department of Justice, Washington, D.C.

Minutes, Carlisle Literary Society, Wofford College Archives, Wofford College, Spartanburg, South Carolina.

Minutes of the Upper South Carolina Conference of the Methodist Church, 1940. South Carolina Conference, Methodist Church Archives, Wofford College, Spartanburg, South Carolina.

Nazi Conspiracy and Aggression: Office of the U.S. Chief of Counsel for Prosecution of Axis Criminality. Washington, D.C.: Government Printing Office, 1946, I.

Nazi Conspiracy and Aggression. vol. VI. Washington, D.C.: Government Printing Office, 1946.

Nazi Conspiracy and Aggression—Opinion and Judgment. Washington, D.C.: Government Printing Office, 1947.

Records of the U.S. District Court for the District of Massachusetts, Record Group 276, Criminal Case No. 4296, Stenographic Record, vol. I, Federal Archives and Records Center, Waltham, Massachusetts.

Records of the U.S. District Court for the District of Massachusetts, RG 276, Criminal Case No. 4296, Stenographic Record, vol. II, Federal Archives and Records Center, Waltham, Massachusetts.

Records of the U.S. District Court for the District of Massachusetts, RG 276, Criminal Case No. 4296, Stenographic Record, vol. III, Federal Archives and Records Center, Waltham, Massachusetts.

Records of the U.S. District Court for the District of Massachusetts, RG 21, Criminal Case No. 17666, Stenographic Record, vol. X, Federal Archives and Records Center, Waltham, Massachusetts.

Revolutionary Radicalism: Report of the Joint Legislative Committee Investigating Seditious Activities, Filed April 24, 1920, in the Senate of the State of New York, Part I, vol. I. Albany, N.Y.: J. B. Lyon Company, 1920.

Rooms and Waiters. 1912–1916. Wofford College Archives, Wofford College, Spartanburg, South Carolina.

Special Interrogation Series, Military Intelligence Service, War Department, Washington, D.C.

BOOKS AND PAMPHLETS

Austrian Federal Press Department, ed. *The Austrian Year Book*, 1931. Vienna: Manzsche Verlags–Und Universitats–Buchhandlung, 1931.

Baillie, Hugh. *High Tension*. New York: Harper and Brothers Publishers, 1959.

Balfour, Michael. *Propaganda in War, 1939–1945: Organizations, Policies and Publics in Britain and Germany*. London: Routledge & Kegan Paul, 1979.

Bender, Roger James, and Hugh P. Taylor. *Uniforms, Organization and History of the Waffen-SS*. Mountain View, Calif.: R. J. Bender Publishers, 1971.

Betts, Albert Deems. *History of South Carolina Methodism*, Columbia, S.C.: Advocate Press, 1952, M.C.A.

Biddle, Francis. *In Brief Authority*. Westport, Conn.: Greenwood Press, 1962.

Block, Maxine, ed. *Current Biography: Who's Who and Why, 1940*. New York: H. W. Wilson, Co., 1940.

The Bohemian, 1916. [Wofford College Yearbook]

Boughner, Genevieve J. *Women in Journalism*. New York: D. Appleton Century, 1942.

Boveri, Margaret. *Treason in the Twentieth Century*. London: MacDonald, 1956.

Brook, Herbert, ed. *The Blue Book of Awards*. Chicago: Marquis—Who's Who, 1956.

Burlingame, Roger. *Don't Let Them Scare You: The Life and Times of Elmer Davis*. New York: J. B. Lippincott Company, 1961.

Carlson, John Roy. *Under Cover: My Four Years in the Nazi Underworld of America*. New York: E. P. Dutton & Co., 1943.

Childs, Harwood L., and John B. Whiddon, eds. *Propaganda by Short Wave*. Princeton, N.J.: Princeton University Press, 1943.

Childs, Marquis W. *I Write from Washington*. New York: Harper & Brothers Publishers, 1942.

Clark, Elmer T. *The Chiangs of China*. New York: Abingdon-Cokesbury Press, 1943.

Cochran, Negley D. *E. W. Scripps*. New York: Harcourt, Brace and Co., 1933.

Cole, J. A. *Lord Haw-Haw & William Joyce: The Full Story*. New York: Farrar, Straus & Giroux, 1964.

Coon, Horace. *Columbia: Colossus on the Hudson*. New York: E. P. Dutton & Company, 1947.

Crowder, Richard. *Carl Sandburg*. New York: Twayne Publishers, 1964.

Deakin, Motley F. *Rebecca West*. Boston: Twayne Publishers, 1980.

Desmond, Robert W. *Crisis and Conflict: World News Reporting between Two Wars, 1920–1940*. Iowa City: University of Iowa Press, 1982.

Desmond, Robert W. *The Press and World Affairs*. New York: D. Appleton-Century Company, 1937.

Edwards, Jerome E. *The Foreign Policy of Col. McCormick's Tribune, 1929–1941*. Reno: University of Nevada Press, 1971.

Ettlinger, Harold. *The Axis on the Air*. New York: Bobbs-Merrill Co., 1943.

Farnsworth, Beatrice. *William C. Bullitt and the Soviet Union*. Bloomington: Indiana University Press, 1967.

Federal Writers' Project. *New York City Guide*. New York: Octagon Books, 1970.

Foy, David. *For You the War Is Over*. New York: Stein & Day, 1984.

Gardner, Virginia. *Friend and Lover: The Life of Louise Bryant*. New York: Horizon Press, 1982.

Garrett, Franklin M. *Atlanta and Environs: A Chronicle of Its People and Events*, vol. I. Athens: University of Georgia Press, 1954.

Geddes, Gary. *Conrad's Later Novels*. Montreal: McGill-Queen's University Press, 1980.

Geologie: Zeitschrift Für Das Gesamtgebiet Der Geologie Und Mineralogie Sourè Der Angewandten Geophysik Mit Beiheften, January 4, 1955. Berlin: Academie-Verlag, 1955.

Gertz, Elmer. *The People vs. the Chicago* Tribune. Chicago: Union for Democratic Action, 1942.

Gies, Joseph. *The Colonel of Chicago*. New York: E. P. Dutton, 1979.

Givner, Joan. *Katherine Anne Porter: A Life*. New York: Simon and Schuster, 1982.

Golden, Harry Lewis. *Carl Sandburg*. Cleveland: World Publishing Co., 1961.

Gombrich, E. H. *Myth and Reality in German Wartime Broadcasts*. London: Athlone Press, 1970.

Graves, Harold N., Jr. *War on the Short Wave*. New York: Foreign Policy Association, 1941.

Griffiths, Richard. *Fellow Travellers of the Right: British Enthusiasts for Nazi Germany, 1933–39*. London: Constable, 1980.

Gunther, John. *Behind the Curtain*. New York: Harper and Brothers Publishers, 1949.

Gunther, John. *The Lost City*. New York: Harper and Brothers Publishers, 1964.

Hahn, Emily. *The Soon Sisters*. New York: Garden City Publishing Co., 1945.

Hamilton, Thomas J. *Appeasement's Child: The Franco Regime in Spain*. New York: Alfred A. Knopf, 1943.

Handbook of the Best Private Schools of the United States and Canada: An Annual Publication. Boston: Porter E. Sargent, 1915.

Harsch, Joseph C. *Pattern of Conquest*. New York: Doubleday, Doran and Co., 1941.

Hayes, Jess G. *Sheriff Thompson's Day: Turbulence in the Arizona Territory*. Tucson: University of Arizona Press, 1968.

Herzstein, Robert Edwin. *The War That Hitler Won: The Most Infamous Propaganda Campaign in History*. New York: G. P. Putnam's Sons, 1978.

Hohenberg, John. *Foreign Correspondents: The Great Reporters and Their Times*. New York: Columbia University Press, 1964.

Hunter College *Yearbook*, 1938.

John, Duke of Bedford. *A Silver-Plated Spoon*. London: Crasell and Co., 1959.

Kaltenbach, F. W. *Self-Determination 1919: A Study in Frontier-Making between Germany and Poland*. London: Jarrolds Publishers, 1938.

Karl, Frederick R. *Joseph Conrad: The Three Lives, A Biography*. New York: Farrar, Straus & Giroux, 1979.

Kelley, Douglas M. *22 Cells in Nuremberg: A Psychiatrist Examines the Nazi Criminals*. New York: Greenberg Publisher, 1947.

Knight, Oliver, ed. *I Protest: Selected Disquisitions of E. W. Scripps*. Madison: University of Wisconsin, 1966.

Knoblaugh, H. Edward. *Correspondent in Spain*. New York: Sheed & Ward, 1937.

Koischwitz, Max Otto. *O'Neill*. Berlin: Junker and Dünnhaupt, 1938.

Kruglak, Theodore Edward. *The Foreign Correspondents: A Study of the Men and Women*

Reporting for the American Information Media in Western Europe. Geneva: Librairie
    E. Droz, 1955.
Lavine, Harold, and James Wechsler. *War Propaganda and the United States.* New
    Haven, Conn.: Yale University Press, 1940.
Lewis, Ward B. *Eugene O'Neill: The German Reception of America's First Dramatist.* New
    York: Peter Lang Publishers, 1984.
Mangulis, Visvaldis. *Latvia in the Wars of the 20th Century.* Princeton Junction, N.J.:
    Cognition Books, 1983.
Marlow, John. *Late Victorian: The Life of Sir Arnold Talbot Wilson.* London: Cresset
    Press, 1967.
Miale, Florence R., and Michael Selzer. *The Nuremberg Mind: The Psychology of the
    Nazi Leaders.* New York: New York Times Book Co., 1975.
Miller, William D. *Dorothy Day: A Biography.* San Francisco: Harper & Row Pub-
    lishers, 1982.
Miller, William D. *A Harsh and Dreadful Love: Dorothy Day and the Catholic Worker
    Movement.* New York: Liveright Publishers, 1973.
Moritz, Charles, ed. *Current Biography Yearbook.* New York: H. W. Wilson Co., 1962.
Morris, Joe Alex. *Deadline Every Minute: The Story of the United Press.* New York:
    Greenwood Press, 1968.
Murray, Robert K. *Red Scare: A Study in National Hysteria, 1919–1920.* Minneapolis:
    University of Minnesota Press, 1955.
Nyman, Kristina. *Finland's War Years, 1939–1945.* Helsinki: Society of Military His-
    tory, 1973.
*The Official Roster of South Carolina Soldiers, Sailors and Marines in the World War, 1917–
    18,* vol. I. Columbia, S.C.: General Assembly, 1929.
Park, Robert E. *Race and Culture.* Glencoe, Ill.: Free Press, 1950.
Piehl, Mel. *Breaking Bread: The Catholic Worker and the Origin of Catholic Radicalism in
    America.* Philadelphia: Temple University Press, 1982.
Poggendorff, J.C. *Biographisch-Literarisches Handwörterbuch Der Exakten Naturwissen-
    schaften.* Berlin: Akademie-Verlag, 1956.
Pomain, John, ed. *Joseph Retinger: Memoirs of an Eminence Grise.* Sussex, England:
    Sussex University Press, 1972.
Pope, Arthur U. *Maxim Litvinoff.* New York: L. B. Fischer, 1943.
"Propaganda Techniques of German Fascism," in *Modern English Readings,* eds. Roger
    S. Loomis and Donald L. Clark. New York: Rinehart & Company, 1949.
Quarrie, Bruce. *Hitler's Samurai: The Waffen-SS in Action.* New York: Arco Publishing,
    1983.
Randall, Dale B. J. *Joseph Conrad and Warrington Dawson: The Record of a Friendship.*
    Durham, N.C.: Duke University Press, 1968.
Reed, Douglas. *Insanity Fair.* London: Jonathan Cape, 1964.
Retinger, J. H. *Conrad and His Contemporaries.* New York: Roy Publishers, 1943.
Rice, D. Talbot, comp. *The University Portraits.* Edinburgh: Edinburgh University
    Press, 1957.
Rogge, O. John. *The Official German Report: Nazi Penetration 1924–1942, Pan-Arabism
    1939–Today.* New York: Thomas Yoseloff, 1961.
Rolo, Charles J. *Radio Goes to War: The Fourth Front.* New York: G. P. Putnam's
    Sons, 1940.

Ross, Ishbel. *Ladies of the Press: The Story of Women in Journalism by an Insider*. New York: Harper & Brothers Publishers, 1936.

Sampson, Francis L. *Paratroopers Padre*. Washington, D.C.: Catholic Unit of America Press, 1948.

Schofield, William Greenough. *Treason Trail*. New York: Rand McNally and Company, 1964.

Schwipps, Werner, and Gerhart Goebel. *Wortschlacht Im Äther: Der Deutsche Auslands Rundfunk in Weltkreig*. Berlin: Hande and Spenersche, 1971.

Seldes, George. *The Facts Are . . . A Guide to Falsehood and Propaganda in the Press and Radio*. New York: In Fact, 1940.

Seldes, George. *Lords of the Press*. New York: Julian Messner, 1938.

Seldes, George. *Tell the Truth and Run*. New York: Greenberg Publisher, 1953.

Shirer, William L. *Berlin Diary: The Journal of a Foreign Correspondent, 1934–1941*. New York: Alfred A. Knopf, 1942.

Shirer, William L. *Midcentury Journey: The Western World through Its Years of Conflict*. New York: Farrar, Straus and Young, 1952.

Shirer, William L. *The Traitor*. New York: Farrar, Straus and Company, 1950.

Shirer, William L. *20th Century Journey: A Memoir of a Life and the Times*. New York: Simon and Schuster, 1976.

Sinclair, W. A. *The Voice of the Nazi: Being Eight Broadcast Talks Given between December 1939 and May 1940*. London: Collins Publishers, 1940.

Sington, Derrick, and Arthur Weidenfeld. *The Goebbels Experiment: A Study of the Nazi Propaganda Machine*. New Haven, Conn.: Yale University Press, 1943.

Sproat, Iain. *Wodehouse at War*. New Haven: Ticknor & Fields, 1981.

Stonequist, E. V. *The Marginal Man: A Study in Personality and Culture Conflict*. New York: Charles Scribner's Sons, 1937.

Taylor, Fred, ed. *The Goebbels Diaries: 1939–41*. New York: G. P. Putnam's Sons, 1983.

Tennant, Roger. *Joseph Conrad*. New York: Atheneum, 1981.

Thrapp, Dan L. *Al Sieber: Chief of Scouts*. Norman: University of Oklahoma Press, 1964.

Turkevich, John, and Ludmilla B. Turkevich, comp. *Prominent Scientists of Continental Europe*. New York: American Elsevier Publishing Company, 1968.

Watson, E. O. *Builders: Sketches of Methodist Preachers in South Carolina with Historical Data*. Columbia, S.C.: Southern Christian Advocate, 1932, M.C.A.

Wendt, Lloyd. *Chicago Tribune: The Rise of a Great American Newspaper*. New York: Rand McNally & Co., 1979.

Weyl, Nathaniel. *Treason: The Story of Disloyalty and Betrayal in American History*. Washington, D.C.: Public Affairs Press, 1950.

Who Was Who, 1951–1960, vol. V. New York: MacMillan Company, 1961.

Who Was Who in America, vol. 16. Chicago: A. N. Marquis Company, 1942.

Zeman, Z.A.B. *Nazi Propaganda*. New York: Oxford University Press, 1964.

PUBLISHED AND UNPUBLISHED MEMOIRS, PAPERS, SPEECHES, AND LETTERS

Anderson, Jane, and Gordon Bruce. "Looping-the-Loop over London." *Flying, Submarining and Mine Sweeping*. London: Sir Joseph Canston & Sons, 1916.

Conrad, Borys. *My Father: Joseph Conrad*. London: Calder & Boyars, 1970.

Conrad, Jessie. *Joseph Conrad and His Circle*. London: Jarrolds Publishers, 1935.

Conrad, Jessie. *Joseph Conrad's Letters to His Wife*. London: Privately Printed, 1927.

Conrad, John. *Joseph Conrad: Times Remembered*. Cambridge: Cambridge University Press, 1981.

Day, Donald. *Onward Christian Soldiers*. Torrance, Calif.: Noontide Press, 1982.

Day, Dorothy. *The Eleventh Virgin*. New York: Albert and Charles Boni, 1924.

Day, Dorothy. *The Long Loneliness: An Autobiography*. New York: Image Books, 1959.

Delaney, Edward Leopold. *False Freedom*. Los Angeles: Sequoia University Press, 1954.

Delaney, E. L. *Five Decades before Dawn*. Pasadena, Calif.: Deljon Publishers, 1969.

Delaney, E. L. *Freedom's Frontier*. Sacramento, Calif.: H. A. Nickel Co., 1964.

Domville, Admiral Sir Barry. *From Admiral to Cabin Boy*. London: Boswell Publishing Co., 1947.

Douglas, Robin. "My Boyhood with Conrad." *Cornhill Magazine*, vol. 139. London: John Murray, Albemarle Street, 1929.

Flannery, Harry W. *Assignment to Berlin*. New York: Alfred A. Knopf, 1942.

Fredborg, Arvid. *Behind the Steel Wall: A Swedish Journalist in Berlin, 1941–43*. New York: Viking Press, 1944.

Hessen, Robert. *Berlin Alert: The Memoirs and Reports of Truman Smith*. Stanford, Calif.: Hoover Institution Press, 1984.

Koischwitz, Max Otto. *A German-American Interprets Germany*. Milwaukee: Gutenberg Publishing Co., 1935.

Lochner, Louis P. *What About Germany?* New York: Dodd, Mead and Company, 1942.

Porter, Katherine Anne. *The Collected Essays and Occasional Writings of Katherine Anne Porter.* New York: Delacorte Press, 1970.

Scheu, Friedrich. *Der Weg Ins Ungewisse: Osterreichs Schick Salskurve 1929–1938*. Vienna: Verlag Fritz Molden, 1972.

Seldes, George. "Donald Day." Unpublished biographical sketch in possession of the Author.

Seldes, George. "My Decade with Col. McCormick." *Lost Generation Journal*, vol. II, No. 3 (Fall 1974): 24–29.

Seldes, Gilbert. "Geometry." Chapter from an unpublished memoir (New York, 1967): 60–62.

PRIMARY ARTICLES AND PERIODICALS

"Action to Be Taken in the Case of Koischwitz." *The Hour*, No. 13 (September 30, 1939): 3.

Anderson, Jane. "The Burying of Lil." *Harper's Weekly*, August 13, 1910.

Anderson, Jane. "El Valiente." *Harper's Weekly*, June 22, 1912.

Anderson, Jane. "The Gift of the Hills." *Harper's Weekly*, October 21, 1911.

Anderson, Jane. "The Keeper of the Well." *Harper's Weekly*, April 23, 1910.

Anderson, Jane. "The Spur of Courage." *Harper's Weekly*, January 13, 1912.

Anderson de Cienfuegos, Jane. "Horror in Spain." *Catholic Digest* 1 (1937): 69–74.

Arizona *Daily Star* (Tucson), 1951.

Atlanta *Constitution*, 1942.

Atlanta *Journal*, January 20, 1942.

"Back from the Axis." *Time*, vol. 30, No. 24 (June 15, 1942): 69.

Baltimore *Sun*, April 1, 1934.

Best, R. H. "Old World Sees Something New," in *Reconstruction* (June-September 1923), Nos. 47–54.

Best, R. H. "Student Internationalism in Austria," in *Reconstruction* (June-September 1923), Nos. 47–54.

Books Abroad, vol. 13 (Winter, 1938): 58–59.

Boston *Daily Globe*, 1948; 1963.

Boston *Herald*, 1948.

British Broadcasting Corporation (BBC), *Monitoring Service*, 1939–1945.

Burnett, Whit. "Hunting Headlines in the Balkans." *American Mercury*, vol. 30, No. 117 (September 1933): 42–49.

Chandler, Douglas. "Changing Berlin." *National Geographic*, vol. LXXI, No. 2 (February 1937): 131–177.

Chandler, Douglas. "Flying around the Baltic." *National Geographic*, vol. LXXIII, No. 3 (June 1938): 767–806.

Chandler, Douglas. "Kaleidoscopic Land of Europe's Youngest King." *National Geographic*, vol. LXXV, No. 4 (June 1939): 691–738.

Chandler, Douglas. "The Transformation of Turkey." *National Geographic*, vol. LXXV, No. 1 (January 1939): 1–50.

Charleston *News and Courier*, January 12, 1941.

Chicago *Sun*, 1944–1946.

Chicago *Tribune*, 1929–1946.

Columbia (S.C.) *State*, June 8, 1942.

Drexel, Constance. "A Brief Outline of Efforts to Control the Manufacture and Sale of Munitions and Implements of War," in "International Traffic in Arms and Munitions," *Reference Shelf*, vol. 9, No. 9. New York: H. W. Wilson Company, 1934.

Drexel, Constance. "Are We Our Brothers' Keepers? How Our Country Is Fighting the Drug Evil." *Harper's*, vol. 149 (November 1924): 736–43.

Drexel, Constance. "Armament Manufacture and Trade." *International Conciliation*, No. 295. Worcester, Mass.: Carnegie Endowment for International Peace, 1933.

Drexel, Constance. "Bananas across the Sea." *Collier's*, vol. 73, No. 9 (March 1, 1924): 31.

Drexel, Constance. "Feminism More Effective in Europe Than America." *Current History*, vol. 24, No. 2 (May 1926): 211.

Drexel, Constance. "German Women Active in Political Affairs." New York *Times*, August 24, 1924.

Drexel, Constance. "Have Women Failed as Citizens?" *Collier's*, vol. 71 (May 12, 1923): 5–6.

Drexel, Constance. "The Continuing Curse of Opium." *Ladies Home Journal*, vol. 42 (July 1925): 6, 58, 60.

Drexel, Constance. "The Foreign Correspondent." *New Republic*, vol. 37 (January 30, 1924): 252–254.

Drexel, Constance. "The Munitions Traffic." *North American Review*, vol. 236, No. 1 (July 1933): 64–72.

Drexel, Constance. "The New Woman—Power in Europe." *Harper's*, vol. 149 (June 1924): 73–81.

Drexel, Constance. "The Woman behind the Gun." *Delineator*, vol. 87, No. 19 (November 1915): 19.

Drexel, Constance. "The Woman Pays." *Delineator*, vol. 87, No. 1 (July 1915).

Drexel, Constance. "Unpublished Letters of F.D.R. to His French Governess." *Parents' Magazine*, vol. 26, No. 9 (September 1951): 30–31, 80–84.

Editor & Publisher, 1942–1948.

"Facts in Review." *German Library of Information*, vol. 11, No. 27 (July 1940): 291.

"Former Newsman among 8 Indicted for Treason by U.S." *Editor & Publisher* (July 28, 1943).

"From *Tribune* Faker to Nazi Stooge." Chicago *Daily Times*, September 7, 1944.

German Quarterly, vol. 6, No. 4 (November 1933): 185–186.

German Quarterly, vol. 9, No. 1 (January 1936): 32.

German Quarterly, vol. 10, No. 2 (March 1937): 151–152.

Gertz, Elmer. "Chicago's Adult Delinquent: 'The Tribune.' " *Public Opinion Quarterly*, vol. 8, No. 3 (Fall 1944): 419–424.

Glendale (Calif.) *News-Press*, July 3; July 5, 1972.

Graves, Harold N. "Propaganda by Shortwave: Berlin Calling America." *Public Opinion Quarterly* (December 1940): 601–618.

Gunther, John. "Dateline Vienna." *Harper's*, vol. 171 (July 1935): 198–208.

"Merwin K. Hart." *Current Biography*, 1941.

"Hitlerite Teaches German in New York's Hunter College." *The Hour*, No. 9 (August 30, 1939): 9.

In Fact, 1942–1945.

"Koischwitz Broadcasts Nazi Propaganda to America." *The Hour*, No. 54 (July 20, 1940): 3.

Koischwitz, Max Otto. "Der Theaterherold Im Deutschen Schanspiel Des Mittelalters Und Der Reformationzeit Germanische." *Studien*, No. 46. Berlin: E. Eberring, 1926.

Koischwitz, Max Otto. "Echo from Abroad: American Letter." *Literatur* (August 1939): 555–557.

Koischwitz, Max Otto. "German Readers Turn to Foreign Countries." *Books Abroad*, vol. 13 (Winter 1938): 431–434.

Koischwitz, Max Otto. "A New Method of Testing Extensive Reading in Contemporary Literature Classes." *German Quarterly*, vol. 7, No. 1 (January 1934): 9–18.

Koischwitz, Max Otto. "Our Textbooks and Kulturkunde." *German Quarterly*, vol. 1, No. 3 (May 1928): 107–115.

London *Times*, July 27, 1943.

Los Angeles *Times*, 1947–1948.

Lyons, Eugene. "Why Foreign Correspondents Go Home." *Saturday Review*, vol. 16, No. 18 (August 28, 1937): 4, 17.

"Mr. Wisecrack." *Time* (May 20, 1940): 52–54.

Muller, Edwin. "Waging War with Words." *Current History*, vol. L, No. 6 (August 1939): 24–27.

"Nazi Best." *Time*, vol. 40, No. 1 (July 9, 1942): 2–3.

New York American, 1937.

New York *Herald Tribune*, 1948; 1956.

New York *Post*, September 24, 1940.

New York *Times*, 1916–1956.

Newsweek, August 11, 1947.

Old Gold and Black [Wofford College Student Newspaper], Wofford College Archives, Wofford College, Spartanburg, S.C.

"Our Family Album." *Ladies Home Journal*, vol. 43 (January 1926): 26.

Padover, S. K. "How the Nazis Picture America." *Public Opinion Quarterly*, vol. 3, No. 4 (October 1939): 663–669.

Parry, Albert. "Short-Wave Traitors." *Cosmopolitan*, vol. 114, No. 4 (April 1943): 59, 119.

Pisko, E. S. "Tuning in on the Traitors." *Christian Science Monthly Magazine*, vol. 40, No. 1 (July 18, 1942): 6.

P.M., 1941–1942.

Rennie, John O. "Dr. Goebbel's Awkward Squad." *Atlantic Monthly*, vol. 172 (September 1943): 107.

Rocky Mountain News, July 8, 1919.

Rolo, Charles J. "Germany Calling!" *Current History & Forum*, vol. 52, No. 2 (October 22, 1940): 28–31.

Rolo, Charles J. "Radio War on the U.S.A." *American Mercury*, vol. 52, No. 205 (January 1941): 67–74.

Rovere, Richard H. "Letter from Washington." *New Yorker*, vol. 25 (February 26, 1949): 77–82.

Scanlan, Ross. "The Nazi Party Speaker System." *Speech Monographs*, vol. XVI, No. 1 (August 1949): 82–89.

Scanlan, Ross. "The Nazi Party Speaker System." *Speech Monographs*, vol. XVII, No. 2 (June 1950): 134–148.

Scanlan, Ross. "The Nazi Rhetorician." *Quarterly Journal of Speech*, vol. XXXVII, No. 4 (December 1951): 430–440.

Seldes, George. "The Men Who Fake the News." *New Masses*, vol. XXXIV (January 30, 1940): 14–17.

Seldes, George. "The Poisoned Springs of World News." *Harper's*, vol. 169 (November 1934): 719, 731.

Shirer, William L. "The American Radio Traitors." *Harper's*, vol. 187 (October 1943): 397–403.

Shirer, William L. "What the Germans Told the Prisoners." *Harper's*, vol. 189, No. 1134 (November 1944): 537–538.

Skilling, Gordon. "Organising Hatred." *Dalhousie Review*, vol. 23 (April 1943): 11–22.

Smith, Col. Albert. "The Little Brown Hen at Stalag 11-B." *Saturday Evening Post*, vol. 218, No. 10 (September 8, 1945): 34.

Snyder, Louis L., ed. "Radio in the Third Reich." *Encyclopedia of the Third Reich*. New York: McGraw-Hill, 1976.

Spartanburg *Herald*, May 13, 1940.

Sproat, Iain. "Wodehouse's War." *Encounter*, vol. 59 (September-October 1982): 98–100.

Thompson, Dorothy. "Who Goes Nazi?" *Harper's*, vol. 183 (August 1941): 237–242.

Time, 1942, 1947, 1949, 1953.

Tucson (Arizona) *Daily Citizen*, August 2, 1951.
Waldo, Richard Harold, in *The National Cyclopaedia of American Biography*, vol. 32. New York: James T. White & Co., 1945.
Washington, D.C., *Evening Star*, April 2, 1948.
Washington *Post*, 1942–1949.
Waterbury *American*, August 28, 1956.
Waterbury *Republican*, August 29; August 31, 1956.
Whiddon, John B. "War by Radio." *Foreign Affairs*, vol. 19, No. 3 (April 1941): 584–596.
Wilson, Charles H. "Hitler, Goebbels, and the Ministry for Propaganda." *Political Quarterly*, vol. X, No. 1 (January-March 1939): 99.
Wofford College Journal. Wofford College Archives, 1913–1916.

SECONDARY ARTICLES

Doenecke, Justice D. "A Military Observer in Hitler's Reich." *Reviews in American History*, vol. XII, No. 4 (December 1984): 583–588.
Halle, Louis J. "O.K." *Virginia Quarterly Review*, vol. 51, No. 2 (Spring 1975): 214–221.
Valaik, J. David. "Catholics, Neutrality and the Spanish Embargo, 1937–1939." *Journal of American History*, vol. 54, No. 1 (June 1967): 73–85.

Index

ABOUT THE AUTHOR

A historian, JOHN CARVER EDWARDS is on the administrative faculty of the University of Georgia where he is a university archivist. *Berlin Calling* is the result of his lifelong fascination with a fellow native son of Spartanburg, South Carolina, with whom he shared the same alma mater, Wofford College, who broadcast for the Nazis. Research into Robert Best's life served as a springboard into a twelve-year study of Best's U.S.A. Zone colleagues. John Carver Edwards is the author of more than 25 popular and scholarly articles and another book, *Patriots in Pin Stripe: Men of the National Security League.*